How We Got to Coney Island

How We Got
to Coney Island

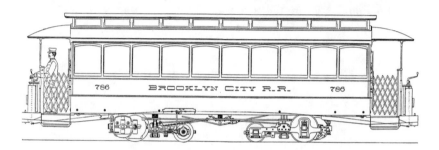

THE DEVELOPMENT
OF MASS TRANSPORTATION
IN BROOKLYN AND KINGS COUNTY

BRIAN J. CUDAHY

Fordham University Press
New York
2002

Library of Congress Cataloging-in-Publication Data

Cudahy, Brian J.
    How we got to Coney Island : the development of mass transportation in Brooklyn and Kings County / Brian J. Cudahy.
      p. cm.
    Includes bibliographical references and index.
    ISBN 0-8232-2208-X (cloth)—ISBN 0-8232-2209-8 (pbk.)
    1. Local transit—New York Metropolitan Area—History.
    2. Transportation—New York Metropolitan Area—History.
    3. Coney Island (New York, N.Y.)—History.   I. Title.
HE4491.N65 C8   2002
388.4′09747′23—dc21   2002009084

Printed in the United States of America
02 03 04 05 06 5 4 3 2 1
First Edition

CONTENTS

FOREWORD

WHAT MENTAL PICTURE ARISES when one thinks of Coney Island? Persons not from the New York area will probably think first of photographs of the beach crowded with thousands of people on a warm summer afternoon. Another image is that of the Steeple-chase amusement park. The images are not incorrect, but they are incomplete. Today, the image of Coney Island from the air is of a residential place, much like the vast expanse of Brooklyn, north to downtown Brooklyn, Prospect Park, and the green of the many cemeteries. Actions have consequences, and transportation actions for the nineteenth and twentieth centuries continue to have consequences in the development of King's County, Brooklyn, and Coney Island.

Certain factors are essential for the location and growth of urban places. Today, one would admit that water, sewers, and transportation are a must if a place is to attract residents and economic activity. In a time before the preservation of foodstuffs by canning, freezing, or modern radiation, salt was a major necessity for food preservation if any number of souls were to dwell permanently in a particular place. Coney Island played a role in the quest for salt. The first permanent European residents of New York, the people of Dutch New Amsterdam, in 1660 granted the right to construct a saltwork on Coney Island; the production of salt in the seventeenth century often involved evaporating seawater to separate the salt from the water, and seawater was and is abundant at Coney Island.

Transportation actions, such as operating steamboats and building a railroad line or highway or streetcar line, make a place accessible and attractive. Such was the case when a handful of entrepreneurs sought to link Coney Island to Brooklyn and King's County and to the entirety of New York City.

The nineteenth century was a time of tremendous urban activity in the United States. The growth of the American railway system led to the founding of new cities in the western United States. Immigrants from abroad came to the United States in large numbers beginning in the 1830s and 1840s. After the Civil War, immigrants from rural areas joined the foreign immigrants in flooding into older urban areas, which pushed the substantial expansion of eastern cities. Indeed, New York, already the largest city in the country, began to expand by developing new neighborhoods. Manhattan pushed northward, and the Bronx, Queens, and Brooklyn pushed outward from the center of activity in Manhattan. Staten Island grew slowly. Eventually, this growth led to an amalgamation of once independent cities. By the end of the nineteenth century, five boroughs—Richmond, the Bronx, Manhattan, Brooklyn, and Queens—had come together to form the greater New York City we know today.

This gigantic urban area was served at first by a large, if often uncoordinated, public transportation operation. New services and new companies typically followed in the pathways blazed by earlier lines. MTA New York City Transit produces excellent maps of its bus and subway services. Today, they show an intense public transportation service, and the area between downtown Brooklyn and Coney Island is served by many subway lines. Indeed, four of these rapid transit services terminate at Stillwell and Surf Avenues in Coney Island.

Maps are highly informative, but often they leave questions unanswered. As an outlander, originally from Philadelphia and a resident of the Midwest for over fifty years, I look at the MTA maps and wonder why several of the subway lines between downtown Brooklyn and Coney Island have names as well as the usual letter designation used in the New York rapid transit system. Why are the lines named West End, Sea Beach, Culver, and Brighton? Why is the F train route along McDonald Avenue dubbed the Culver line?

The answers to these questions are among the great benefits of reading the book you hold in your hands. In short, what exists today is a reflection of the work of nineteenth-century entrepreneurs who aimed at getting people to Coney Island.

The main reason people wanted to reach Coney Island for many years was to bring change to their lives. One of my very favorite college professors told us about what it was like growing up in the

Bronx in modest circumstances. A great day out was a subway ride to Coney Island and its beach to catch a fresh breeze, take a cool dip in the ocean, and enjoy a square yard or two of sand. It was a welcome break from the hot, sweaty Bronx apartment. Hundreds of thousands of New Yorkers had the same experience.

Among the first Europeans to visit Coney Island was Henry Hudson; he and his crew did some modest exploring of the island before sailing up the broad river in search of the Northwest Passage. After a long voyage, it is sad to note, Hudson and his crew were too early to stop at Nathan's to buy and enjoy a great hot dog. By the second quarter of the nineteenth century, regular steamboat service operated between Manhattan and Coney Island. While there were several carriers, the Iron Steamboat Company (great name!) was one of the largest firms and served the route for the longest time.

Brian Cudahy is a gifted historian and an especially gifted writer. It is a pleasure to go along with Brian as the story unfolds and we find out the different ways that people got to Coney Island. Along the way he introduces many interesting people, giving the human touch to the narrative.

The attraction of beach and cool breezes was a powerful reason to go to Coney Island, and entrepreneurs were quick to see economic opportunities. To meet the demand, a number of railroad lines were built between downtown Brooklyn and Coney Island. The risk takers entering the railroad business included "Deacon" Richardson of the Atlantic Avenue Railway Company and other ventures. General Henry Slocum of the Coney Island & Brooklyn Railroad appeared on the scene. W. Fontaine Bruff of the Brooklyn Elevated was one of the players, and readers will discover what happened at the corner of Reid and Lexington Avenues in Brooklyn in 1879.

Destinations are important to success in transportation. Some entrepreneurs, banking on the blandishments of surf and sand, erected hotels, some of them lavish enough to attract the carriage trade for vacations. More mundane hostelries attracted another segment of the vacation market. Of course, the great market for transportation to Coney Island was composed of day-trippers to the beaches and the major amusement parks, such as Steeple-

chase, Luna Park, and Dreamland. Racetracks were an attraction
for a time.

In addition to steamboats and steam railways, there were horsecar lines linking the heart of Brooklyn with Coney Island. The
shortcomings of animal-powered railways stimulated a search for
better means of locomotion. Cable railways were one means cho-
sen. Brian Cudahy tells an interesting anecdote concerning the
Brooklyn Heights Cable Railroad. In order to get the cable from
the powerhouse out to the running line—which was some distance
away—a boy was employed to crawl through the cable tunnel, pulling a cord that was attached to a heavier cord that was attached to
a heavier cord, and so on, until eventually the heavy steel cable
could be pulled through to the running line by a team of strong
men. Then the boy made the trip through the tunnel back to the
powerhouse so that the cable could be spliced together.

Robert Moses had a role in the development of Coney Island
and how to get there by automobile. Not surprising, Mr. Moses
built a road to Coney Island. The power of Mr. Moses is manifested in the fact that New York has not constructed a rapid transit
line since 1940, but many roadways and superhighways have been
built. In an interesting sidelight, Mussolini planned a world's fair
to be held in Italy in 1942. The amusements at the Italian fair were
planned to duplicate those on Coney Island.

The early steam railroad corridors eventually became electric
railroads that were the forerunners of today's rapid transit lines.
For the most part, they initially became lines of the Brooklyn
Rapid Transit or BRT. These include the Brooklyn Heights Railroad, the Brooklyn City Railroad, the Brooklyn, Queens County &
Suburban Railroad, the Brooklyn Union Elevated Railroads, and
the Nassau Electric Railroad.

The Brooklyn, Bath & West End Railroad became part of the
rapid transit system as the West End line. The Culver line, now
the F train, was originally the Prospect Park & Coney Island Railroad that was promoted by a gentleman named Culver. The names
attached to the rapid transit lines in Brooklyn today are the names
given to the early railroads. New Yorkers are reluctant to change
what was a familiar name. Even today, native New Yorkers refer
to the various subways as the IRT (Interboro Rapid Transit), BMT
(Brooklyn Manhattan Transit, successor to the BRT), and IND

(Independent Rapid Transit), even though the several companies were all merged by the city in 1940.

This book is a social and transportation history of a part of New York City. It is important because we learn how transportation helped to develop vital parts of the great Borough of Brooklyn. The amusement parks are gone, as are the fancy hotels and Coney Island racetracks. Residential areas fill the space. The railway lines pioneered in the nineteenth century remain.

A happy note: Brooklyn has been bereft of professional baseball since the Dodgers made the dreadful mistake of moving to Los Angeles. But now there is Keyspan Park, a new minor league baseball park built, fittingly enough, on the site of Steeplechase Park. It houses the minor league Brooklyn Cyclones.

Now largely a residential area, Coney Island is still the people's Riviera on those warm and humid summer afternoons when the residents of New York need a place to find relief from the weather in a place of surf and sand at the end of the subway ride.

George M. Smerk

PREFACE

AN IRREGULAR PROCESSION of offshore islands helps define the eastern seaboard of the United States. Formed in many cases of nothing more substantial than shifting sand, and subject to constant change by the natural forces of wind and tide, these islands evoke pleasant images of rolling surf breaking onto white sandy beaches, leisurely afternoons under the hot sun, pleasant shore dinners, good friends, amusements in near infinite variety, cold drinks, lively music, and romantic evenings. Among these wonderful islands are such familiar names as Key West, Miami Beach, Hilton Head, the Outer Banks, Atlantic City, Fire Island, Nantucket, and Martha's Vineyard.

This is a story about a particular offshore island of relaxation and recreation. It is not a terribly large island—a little less than five miles long, and no more than a half mile wide. And to begin our story on a totally appropriate note of ambiguity, confusion, and linguistic imprecision, the offshore island whose history we are about to explore is not really an island at all—at least not any more.

One hundred and fifty years ago it was a true island. And a hundred years before that, the island that is no longer an island was actually two or three separate islands. This, then, is the story of Coney Island, a wonderful, mystical, sad, happy, sometimes dangerous, often different, and utterly contradictory place whose contribution to the development of a distinctly American culture is as profound as it is underappreciated.

Coney Island—in the borough of Brooklyn, the county of Kings, the city and state of New York. Coney Island—40 degrees, 35 minutes north latitude; 74 degrees, 59 minutes west longitude; postal ZIP code 11224, with a little spillover into 11235. Coney Island—the one, not really the only one any more, but certainly the original. Coney Island—where the hot dog is often said to have been invented, but actually wasn't. Coney Island—where any distinction between illusion and reality is probably in the eye of the beholder. But then again, maybe it isn't.

This tale of Coney Island is not a tale of its beaches and its restaurants, its amusement parks and its hotels, its racetracks and its beer gardens. Or at least it is not primarily such a story. Rather, on the assumption that before one can enjoy Coney Island one must first get there, this is a tale of how the allure and attraction of Coney Island led to the development of a marvelous network of transportation over the years to link the oceanfront sand spit with the rest of Brooklyn and, somewhat less important, with the rest of the world. It is a tale of steamboats and steam trains, of trolley cars and elevated lines, of internal combustion engines and coaches drawn by teams of horses, of subways and highways, of plans and dreams that were realized, and of plans and dreams that were never quite realized. The Cyclone, the Wonder Wheel, the Parachute Jump, and Steeplechase are famous Coney Island institutions. But so are the Brighton Line, the Culver Line, the West End, and the Sea Beach.

Telling the story of how we got to Coney Island necessarily provides a look into how urban and local transportation has evolved in Brooklyn and Kings County from the middle years of the nineteenth century right up to the present. Indeed, this story focuses on Brooklyn to a substantially greater degree than it does on Coney Island. The transportation history of Brooklyn is rich and distinctive, and yet it is all too easily overshadowed by the history of transportation in the larger polity of the City of New York. Such New York institutions as the Third Avenue elevated train, the Interborough Rapid Transit Company (IRT) subway, Penn Station, and the Hudson River Day Line are well known and have provided appropriate subject matter for a shelf full of important books. Far less known, but equally colorful and possibly just as important, are such Brooklyn-oriented transport undertakings as the Prospect Park and Coney Island Railroad, the Iron Steamboat Company, the Fulton Street elevated train, and the Brooklyn City Railroad.

The fact that Brooklyn transportation history has been largely overshadowed by that of New York is understandable but unfortunate. It is understandable because, since the stroke of midnight on January 1, 1898, Brooklyn has been one of five boroughs within an expanded political jurisdiction called the City of New York and its status as an independent city has been relegated to history. It is unfortunate because the social and cultural substance of Brooklyn—and this includes its transportation history—is distinctive and deserves appreciation on its own, regardless of the political relationship between Brooklyn and New York.

Before beginning, it is necessary to mention a few procedural details. They largely involve questions of language and usage, but they also help bring the book's subject matter into sharper focus. Compass headings are not commonly used in Brooklyn. "Go five blocks north, then turn east for two more blocks" would rarely prove helpful to a Brooklyn motorist or pedestrian seeking directions to some local destination. (There are sets of numbered streets in Brooklyn that are prefaced by North, East, South, and West. But unlike in other cities where, for example, East 24th Street becomes West 24th Street when it crosses some central north-south avenue, in Brooklyn such streets do not lead into their compass-opposites. To make matters more confusing, west-series streets are found in the southernmost portion of Brooklyn, including Coney Island.) There are two compass-related terms that do enjoy popular coinage in and around Brooklyn, though—east and south.

If we establish reference to what is commonly called downtown Brooklyn—the business and commercial center that extends about a mile or so inland from the banks of the East River under the Brooklyn Bridge—north and west have little local import. North generally takes one across the East River into the hostile territory of Manhattan, while west extends out over the waters of New York Bay. Most of Brooklyn and Kings County is located in the two remaining directions away from downtown Brooklyn, east and south.

Territory sometimes referred to as Brooklyn's Eastern District lies between downtown and the Queens County line and includes such interesting neighborhoods as Williamsburg, Bushwick, and East New York. In an unexpected instance of linguistic consistency, the neighborhood known as East New York is actually located within Brooklyn's Eastern District.

Proceeding south from downtown Brooklyn leads to an expansive and rather poorly defined area known as South Brooklyn. When our narrative reaches the final years of the nineteenth century and we are introduced to the Brooklyn Rapid Transit Company (BRT), we shall learn that, unlike all of Gaul, the BRT divided all of Brooklyn into two parts, an Eastern Division and a Southern Division. Because travel to and from Coney Island involves the BRT's Southern Division more extensively than its Eastern Division, our story focuses on Southern Division matters to a greater degree than those of the company's Eastern Division.

In the pages that follow, the term *City of New York* is reserved in its application for the amalgamated entity that was created in 1898. *New York City,* on the other hand, refers to the municipal entity that preceded the City of New York. Another distinction of language involves the evolution of surface transportation from streetcars to motor buses. When the Board of Transportation was implementing such conversions in Brooklyn during the 1940s and the 1950s, it referred to streetcar service as *lines,* and motor bus service as *routes.* For example, "Effective March 4, 1951, trolley car service on the Flatbush Avenue Line will be discontinued and replaced by motor bus service that will be known as the B-41, Flatbush Avenue Route." Although there is nothing fundamental about this distinction, and no dictionary that I know of sanctions it, it is observed in the pages that follow.

There is another potentially confusing question of usage that arises when one discusses Coney Island—apart from the fact that Coney Island is no longer an island. During the nineteenth century, the entire island was generally called Coney Island, while sections within it were identified by proper names such as Brighton Beach, Manhattan Beach, West Brighton, and so forth. Today, only a portion of the former island is correctly identified by the name Coney Island. This is discussed more fully in chapter 1, but it is a situation that is confusing, resists any facile explanation, and so merits this preliminary advisory.

In the narrative that follows, chapter 1 provides introductory and background material about Brooklyn and Coney Island, while chapters 2 through 5 contain parallel historical accounts of the development of various kinds of transportation in Kings County— streetcars, steamboats, excursion railways, and elevated lines—in the years prior to 1890. Chapters 2 through 5, then, each cover essentially the same period of time, albeit from the perspective of different styles of transport. In chapter 6, the narrative assumes a more sequential character, examining how various styles of transportation to and from Coney Island evolved into a cohesive system during one critical decade, the 1890s. Sequential treatment continues in subsequent chapters, which carry the story through the twentieth century.

A few portions of this book have appeared previously. Much of the material about the Iron Steamboat Company is an update of chapter 4 from my *Around Manhattan Island and Other Maritime Tales of New York*. The treatment of the Brooklyn, Flatbush and Coney Island Railroad and its successors that is found in chapter 4 previously appeared in chapter 2 of my earlier work, *The Malbone Street Wreck*.[1]

I want to thank my friend, Professor George M. Smerk, of Indiana University, for graciously writing a foreword for this book. I also want to acknowledge the enormous store of primary source material on Coney Island that has recently been made available thanks to the scholarly work of Professor Michael P. Onorato, of Bellingham, Washington. Professor Onorato's father, the late James J. Onorato, was the general manager of Steeplechase Park in Coney Island from 1928 until Steeplechase closed its doors for good at the end of the 1964 summer season. During the summers of 1954, 1955, 1956, and 1959, "Jimmy the Manager," as the senior Onorato was universally known, was my boss. Special thanks must also be paid to my long-time friend, Donald Harold, whose knowledge of Brooklyn transport matters is without equal. A word of thanks is also due to Loomis Mayer, production manager at Fordham University Press.

Beyond these few, many other individuals—far too many to mention—have shared their time and their recollections with me over the years about one aspect of Coney Island or another. They include motormen, historians, lifeguards, city planners, cops and firemen, economists, bus drivers, mass transit executives, and amusement park workers. Perhaps most important, they include just plain folks who fondly remember traveling down to Coney Island on the Brighton Local or the Coney Island Avenue trolley, once or twice a year, and spending the day with a circular Steeplechase pasteboard ticket tied to one of their shirt buttons—a ticket with ten little circles around its perimeter, one of which would be dutifully punched out by a man in a red and green hat each time they went on one of the park's "thirty-six rides and attractions."

(Some even remember earlier days when a Steeplechase ticket included a number for each of the park's rides, and a ticket entitled a patron to ride every one of them.)

The last time I looked, a one-day ticket to the Magic Kingdom at Disneyland, or Walt Disney World, cost in excess of fifty dollars. And that, of course, does not include airfare to Orlando or the West Coast. The tariff at Steeplechase, circa 1954, was any ten rides for a dollar. A pair of subway tokens for a round-trip to Coney Island, though, added another thirty cents to the day's tab.

Burke, Virginia
April 2002

How We Got to Coney Island

1

A Primer on Coney Island and Brooklyn

To ESTABLISH some geographic terms of reference for the largely historical narrative that follows, let us take a brief look at the lay of the land in Coney Island today. And what could possibly be a more appropriate way to explore Coney Island in the early years of the twenty-first century than by taking an imaginary ride in a hot air balloon from the eastern to the western end of the island? Never mind such minor details as whether prevailing winds would cooperate in allowing such an endeavor to happen. We are talking here about Coney Island, a place where mere facts must never interfere with higher realities.

FROM ORIENTAL POINT TO NORTON'S POINT

As our balloon begins its journey and approaches Coney Island from the east, we find ourselves over a body of water called Jamaica Bay. If we look about a mile or so across the bay to the southeast and away from Coney Island, another offshore beach spit called the Rockaway peninsula runs roughly parallel with Coney Island. Beyond Rockaway to the south and east is nothing but the endless expanse of the North Atlantic Ocean, while seven miles due south of Coney Island, a peninsula called Sandy Hook juts into the sea from the New Jersey shore. Ships entering and leaving New York Harbor navigate their way through Ambrose Channel, a deep-water course that runs midway between Coney Island and Sandy Hook.

The Rockaway peninsula and Sandy Hook shelter Coney Island from much of the Atlantic's full fury, but they do not do so completely. They mitigate the force of the surf that breaks onto Coney Island, and while the beach along Coney Island is always, and correctly, referred to as "the ocean," Coney Island is hardly a place where people travel with surfboards in search of the perfect wave. (Many transit buses in Orange County, California, for instance, feature racks so surfers—and their surfboards—can use public transportation en route to the beach. Subway trains bound for Coney Island require no such capability.) The surf here is normally quite gentle, and the virtual absence of undertow was instrumental not only in popularizing Coney Island as a bathing beach, but in popularizing the very notion of ocean bathing as a form of warm weather recreation during the nineteenth century.

The first section of Coney Island that our balloon passes over is called Manhattan Beach. Like all of Coney Island, Manhattan Beach faces the ocean on its southern side. There is a large, sandy public beach scalloped out of the shore in the middle of Manhattan Beach. On its parallel northern side, less than a half-mile from the oceanfront, Manhattan Beach abuts a narrow tidal inlet known as Sheepshead Bay, a small body of water whose shoreline is permanently and geometrically defined by concrete bulkheads. The sheepshead, of Sheepshead Bay, refers to a species of fish that once populated the area but is today almost as uncommon in Coney Island waters as wooly mammoths are along the shore (see map 1).

Sheepshead Bay is home port for many private yachts and party fishing boats, although all of these dock on the mainland side of the bay opposite Manhattan Beach in a community that is called, appropriately enough, Sheepshead Bay. This is where seafood restaurants, fast food stands, bait and tackle shops, and other commercial establishments are found. Among these is a famous restaurant called Lundy's, recently reopened under new ownership after being closed for several decades. Manhattan Beach, on the opposite side of Sheepshead Bay, is practically (but not absolutely) devoid of commercial activity.

The eastern extreme of Manhattan Beach—the portion of Coney Island our balloon drifts over first—is home to the sixty-seven-acre campus of Kingsborough Community College. If anyone aboard out imaginary balloon looks down and suggests that the grounds of the campus have a bit of a military appearance to them, their observation would be reasonable enough. During the Second World War and for some years afterward, the place served

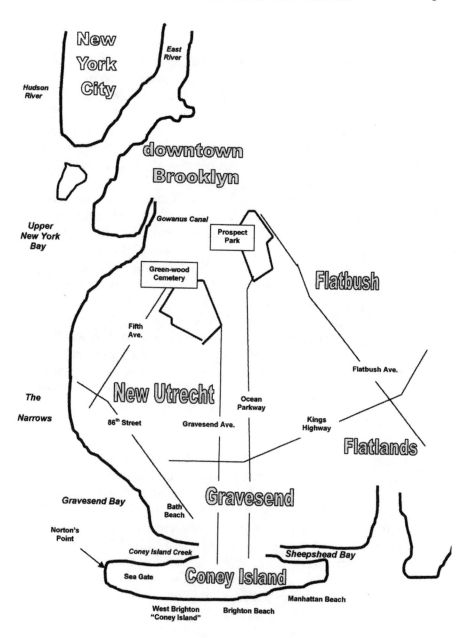

Map 1: A general view of Coney Island and
associated coordinates and landmarks.

as a training facility for both the Army Air Corps and the U.S. Merchant Marine. Precisely why the Air Corps chose to establish a training base at a facility surrounded by water on three sides and with no dimension remotely adequate for any kind of serious runway can only be attributed to the unusual logic that seems to prevail in Coney Island.

The eastern tip of Coney Island has been called Oriental Point and Point Breeze at various times. Neither name enjoys popular usage today, except that the principal east-west avenue in Manhattan Beach is called Oriental Boulevard.

Immediately inland of the campus, Manhattan Beach becomes block after block of conventional, single-family houses situated on pleasant, tree-lined streets. These homes are little different from those in other quiet Brooklyn residential neighborhoods save for the fact that all are within walking distance of the Atlantic Ocean in one direction and Sheepshead Bay in the other, and they exhibit a decidedly upscale style and tone. We shall learn shortly of a time in the nineteenth century when Manhattan Beach was the site of two seasonal resort hotels that were the most stylish in all of Coney Island, and comparable in luxury, according to many with informed opinions on the subject, to any hotels in the world. Today, Manhattan Beach bears little relationship to the luxury seaside resort it once was. In many respects, it is the least exceptional section of Coney Island.

As our balloon continues its westward journey and reaches the headwaters of Sheepshead Bay a trifle more than a mile from the eastern end of Coney Island, we leave Manhattan Beach behind and begin to drift over an extraordinarily colorful Brooklyn neighborhood, a place that is called Brighton Beach. Brighton Beach, the middle section of the Coney Island landmass, occupies that mile or so of the island's length that is attached to the Kings County mainland on its north side. (As noted in the preface, contemporary Coney Island is not an island at all—although it once was—and it is best described as a hammerhead peninsula jutting into the ocean from the southern end of Kings County.)

Unlike Manhattan Beach, where single-family homes predominate, Brighton Beach is block after block of multiple-story apartment houses. Explore any section of the City of New York and this truth emerges as almost absolute: When apartment houses begin to replace single-family homes, it is likely that a subway line is nearby. Brighton Beach is no exception to this rule, and it is here that a four-track, elevated rapid transit line from downtown Brooklyn and Manhattan over which D trains and Q trains normally operate makes its Coney Island landfall from the north. Q trains normally terminate in Brighton Beach, while D trains turn west and continue parallel with the oceanfront to a large subway terminal in the central portion of Coney Island.[1]

In New York, when subway lines emerge from their underground tunnels and operate along elevated structures they are usually called subways. Not all elevated trains are subways, though; some are called elevated trains (Els).[2]

As late as the mid-1990s, there was a large outdoor swim club in Brighton Beach—its site is now a seaside condominium development—which was the last commercial reminder of the days when Brighton Beach was primarily a seaside resort. It is also in Brighton Beach that the 3.5-mile Coney Island Boardwalk has its eastern end. Unlike in Manhattan Beach, where the beach itself includes both public and private sections, the beach at Brighton— and the boardwalk—is protected, in season, by municipal lifeguards and is fully open to the general public for its entire length.

The community of Brighton Beach, however, remains primarily a residential neighborhood, albeit one that happens to be adjacent to the sea. Commercial activity here is geared to support an active residential neighborhood rather than the needs of tourists or beach-goers. One is more likely to find groceries and home appliances rather than t-shirts, sun screen, and souvenirs. In recent decades, Brighton Beach has taken on an interesting new ethnic identity as it has become the home of many Jewish refugees from the former Soviet Union. Bright neon signs in store windows along Brighton Beach Avenue, the east-west thoroughfare over which the elevated (that is, subway) trains run, promote such enterprises as the Odessa Café, in brightly illuminated neon signs rendered in the Cyrillic alphabet. Passengers in our balloon will have to take most of this on faith, though, since the presence of the elevated line precludes any direct observations of Brighton Beach Avenue from above.

Brighton Beach is less than a mile from one end to the other, and if we look to the north when we reach its western end, we see a wide, tree-lined boulevard making a perpendicular approach to the Coney Island beachfront from inland. This is Ocean Parkway, which marks the demarcation between Brighton Beach to the east and, to the west, that limited portion of the overall island that is properly called Coney Island today. During the days when the entire island was commonly called Coney Island, the smaller section that is now known as Coney Island was generally referred to as West Brighton, or the West End.

(Should any of the passengers aboard our balloon happen to have a copy of the *Brooklyn Daily Eagle* of July 2, 1878, we could read the following on page 2: "The tendency of modern years to newly name parts of Coney Island is a good one for three reasons: It gives a definite classification to the Island, it introduces pleasing and effective names—the West End, Brighton Beach and Manhattan Beach—to public use, and it obliterates the objectionable associations which for long years clustered in the mind round the words Coney Island, when it was a place deficient in comforts and not relieved from a reputation for elementary and flagrant immorality.")

Back to Ocean Parkway. It is an old and venerable Kings County thoroughfare, which was laid out in the nineteenth century as part of a strategic approach to Prospect Park. (If the weather is clear as we take our balloon ride, we can probably make out the elevated greensward that is Prospect Park, five miles to the north at the opposite end of Ocean Parkway.) We can observe how Ocean Parkway bends sharply to the west as it approaches the shore and assumes a curving but generally east-west orientation parallel to the oceanfront. Street signs are not visible from the height of our balloon, but once Ocean Parkway turns to the west and runs parallel to the beach it turns into Surf Avenue, the main street of Coney Island.

The elevated rapid transit line that we initially encountered in Brighton Beach and that turns westward there is joined by another, served by the F train, shortly after we reach Coney Island proper. Both lines then continue westward along an unusual double-deck, elevated line to a huge terminal station inland from the intersection of Surf and Stillwell Avenues where no fewer than four important subway lines end their journeys from downtown Brooklyn, Manhattan, the Bronx, and Queens. N trains and B trains, along with D trains and F trains, normally terminate at Still-well Avenue. In subsequent chapters, we shall learn about the ori-gins of these contemporary subway lines, including some older nomenclature that is far more colorful and descriptive than the antiseptic alphabet identity that the trains bear today. We shall also learn how even the letter designations of contemporary trains are subject to change from time to time.

Between Surf Avenue and the Coney Island Boardwalk, one of the first sights to catch our attention is the fourteen-acre grounds of the New York Aquarium, adjacent to an amusement park called Astroland. Astroland is the last remnant of a one-thriving Coney Island amusement industry that we shall hear more about in sub-sequent chapters. Two classic rides from Coney Island's past con-tinue to dominate Astroland, a 150-foot high Ferris wheel called the Wonder Wheel that has been in operation since 1920, and a classic roller coaster that even contemporary roller coaster aficio-nados regard with downright awe, the 1927-built Cyclone. (Two earlier roller coasters occupied this same site, including the Switchback Railroad of 1884 that is generally acknowledged as the world's first roller coaster.)

At this point in our balloon journey, if we look carefully to the north we notice that Coney Island is again separated from the Kings County mainland. A small twisting and brackish waterway called Coney Island Creek—really a tidal inlet, not a true creek—extends inland from the larger expanse of Gravesend Bay, which is further to the west.

More than a century ago, Coney Island Creek and Sheepshead Bay were connected, thus rendering Coney a true island. Artificial concrete bulkheads permanently define the interior limit of Coney Island Creek, as they do for Sheepshead Bay. Just to the mainland side of Coney Island Creek we see the vast expanse of Coney Island Yard, a storage and maintenance facility for city subway trains that is reputed to be the largest such facility in the known universe.

As our balloon continues westward beyond the active amuse-ment area of Astroland, we see remnants of Coney Island's past in the decaying structures of old rides and other attractions. Between Surf Avenue and the boardwalk and roughly parallel to both is a largely abandoned pedestrian walkway called the Bowery that served for many decades as a midway for the entire Coney Island amusement area. Inland of Surf Avenue and the elevated rapid transit line that we have been following since Brighton Beach, we can see acre upon acre of tall apartment buildings that, during the last half of the twentieth century, have turned Coney Island into much more of a year-round residential community than it was in earlier times. Many of these apartment buildings are municipal projects that provide subsidized housing for low-income residents.

For the past century or more, the epicenter of Coney Island has been the intersection of Surf and Stillwell Avenues. Here is where the large subway terminal is located. It is likely the busiest electric railway terminal on the face of the earth, and possibly the busiest of all time. On the south side of Surf Avenue, diagonally across from the terminal, we notice an intensified level of automotive and pedestrian traffic—police officers attempting to dissuade motorists from double parking, lines of waiting people stretching across the sidewalk, and more noise than elsewhere. This is Nathan's, the most famous hot dog emporium in the world. Had we made previous arrangements, perhaps we might have been able to lower a basket and pick up some of Nathan's delicacies for the passengers in our balloon as we drift past. One can find stores and stands with the distinctive Nathan's logo selling Nathan's hot dogs in various parts of the country these days. The establishment at Surf and Stillwell is the original, and many claim that a hot dog tastes much better when enjoyed here than at any other Nathan's.

As our balloon continues westward and we move beyond Nathan's, a new structure looms ahead. On a large plot of land between Surf Avenue and the boardwalk, defined by the alignment of West 16th and West 19th Streets, and adjacent to a 300-foot, red tower that was once a thrill ride known as the Parachute Jump, there is a new professional baseball park whose brilliant green grass and new steel and concrete grandstands contrast sharply with the white sand of the beach and the more-or-less fading hues that characterize the rest of Coney Island. Opened in 2001 and built on the site of Steeplechase (one of three major amusement parks from Coney Island's glory years), Keyspan Park is the home of the Brooklyn Cyclones, a minor league farm team of the New York Mets that plays in the Class A New York–Penn League.

A fishing pier juts out into the ocean from the boardwalk near the new ballpark and close to the base of the Parachute Jump. Still called Steeplechase Pier, the contemporary structure is on the same site as the original pier that was built in 1907 as a landing stage for side-wheel steamboats from Manhattan.

West of the new ballpark our balloon drifts over still more high-rise apartments, and while the boardwalk and the beach continue to define Coney Island's southern exposure, there is very little here to suggest Coney Island's rambunctious past. This is the widest portion of the island. Mermaid Avenue and Neptune Avenue now parallel Surf Avenue to the north, with the territory between the two thoroughfares constituting an important residential community. If we look to the north, we see that Coney Island is more separated from the Kings County mainland on its western end than elsewhere along its length. The body of water that does the separating here is called Gravesend Bay.

From the time our balloon reached the neighborhood that is today called Coney Island, cross streets running inland from the ocean have been numbered in the "west series"—West 5th Street, West 8th Street, West 30th Street, and so forth. With a typically Coney Island disdain for anything as predictable as numerical sequence, however, there is no West 18th, West 26th, or West 34th Street, and no obvious explanation for their absence.[3] Cross streets running inland from the ocean in Brighton Beach are designated Brighton First Street, Brighton Second Street, and so forth, while parallel streets in Manhattan Beach have nonnumeric names such as Falmouth Street and Oxford Street.

Finally, with less than a half-mile of Coney Island remaining to be explored, our balloon drifts over an unexpected enclave, a gated residential community of about 900 single-family houses on tree-lined streets that is called Sea Gate. Well that we are traveling by balloon, since otherwise the corps of police officers who guard Sea Gate might exclude our entry!

The municipal boardwalk and public beach both end, prior to Sea Gate, at West 37th Street. At the very tip of Sea Gate on Coney Island's western extreme, a small but active lighthouse, now administered by the U.S. Coast Guard, helps guide ocean-going ships into New York Harbor from the sea. Built in 1890, it was long said to be the last manned lighthouse in the United States. The western tip of Coney Island is called Norton's Point, named after a nineteenth-century Coney Island legend known as Mike "Thunderbolt" Norton, a man whose unsavory exploits will be discussed presently—and who would surely be denied admission to contemporary Sea Gate if he were foolish enough to seek it.[4]

To travel from Kingsborough Community College at the end of Manhattan Beach to Sea Gate and Norton's Point, our balloon has drifted a distance of about four-and-a-half miles. We have traveled from east to west on a course of roughly 270 degrees. For a little more than a mile of our journey in the area of Brighton Beach, the Coney Island land mass is firmly attached to the Kings County mainland. For the remainder of its length, first Sheepshead Bay, then Coney Island Creek, and finally Gravesend Bay serve as a reminder of the days when Coney was a bona fide island.

As our balloon continues westward beyond Norton's Point, we find ourselves over the waters of Lower New York Bay. To the north we see the Verrazano-Narrows Bridge linking Brooklyn with Staten Island, and between the towers of the bridge in the distance looms the always imposing skyline of lower Manhattan.

From Norton's Point to the Battery at the southern tip of Manhattan, as the crow flies, is a distance of just less than nine miles. How nineteenth-century New Yorkers navigated their way across and around these nine miles, by sea and by land—and in so doing developed an extraordinary urban transportation system in Brooklyn and Kings County—is the subject addressed in the sections and chapters that follow.

EUROPEANS FIRST VISIT CONEY ISLAND

Although what really happened is shrouded in ample quantities of myth, legend, and just plain untruth, the first Europeans thought to have set foot on the land that is today called Coney Island did so in the month of September during the long-ago year of 1609. While popular histories of Coney Island discuss the events of September 1609 with near-dogmatic certitude, the only contemporary account of this visit is less than persuasive that Coney Island was even visited at all.

Europeans surely sailed into New York Harbor that September, though. They were captain and crew, about eighteen strong, of a stout vessel called the *Half Moon* (or *Halve Maen*). Captain Henry Hudson and his men, although British by birth and continued allegiance, were sailing a vessel that flew the flag of Holland with a commission from the Dutch East India Company. They were in search of the all-elusive passage to the spice lands of the Far East.

It was the third voyage of exploration that Hudson is known to have made. In both 1607 and 1608, he sailed north under British colors and explored waters between Greenland and Norway's Spitzbergen Island in the Arctic Ocean, seeking a passage to the east. The reputation Hudson gained from these two earlier voyages into polar waters led to a contract with the Dutch East India Company to continue such exploration. Departing from Amsterdam on March 25, 1609, Hudson found that sea ice beyond the North Cape made further navigation there impossible. So he turned south and west, crossed the North Atlantic Ocean, and decided to seek a passage to the far east along the coast of North America.

After sailing from Labrador and Newfoundland south to the Chesapeake Bay during the summer months of 1609, early autumn winds brought the *Half Moon* into the sheltered confines of what is known today as Lower New York Bay, and perhaps into the more sheltered waters of Gravesend Bay. Natives rowed out to the *Half Moon* in dugout canoes and some trading took place—European knives and trinkets for tobacco and maize.

A day or so later, on September 6, a landing party under the command of the ship's first mate, John Coleman, headed for shore. Whether the real estate where they landed was Coney Island or not is less important than the manner in which fact and legend have since surrounded the event. Because this first visit by individuals of European extraction to the windswept sands of Coney Island—or to a piece of land reasonably close by—proved to be singularly unfortunate. Following contretemps of one sort or another between visitors and natives, Coleman was shot through the throat by an arrow while returning to the *Half Moon,* and he died of his wounds shortly afterward.[5]

Captain Hudson weighed anchor and sailed further inland in the hope that the broad waterway flowing down into the sea from the north would lead to the mysterious spice land of the east that was his ultimate goal. It did not, of course. It led instead to an upriver place that would later be called Fort Orange, after that Albany, and still later it would be celebrated in the fiction of William Kennedy. With a fitting touch of modesty, the captain of the *Half Moon* decided to call the waterway he thought he had discovered the Hudson River.

However, Henry Hudson was not the first European to sail the river. Giovanni da Verrazano arrived eighty-five years earlier in 1524 and sailed some distance upriver, although not nearly as far as the site of Albany. A Portuguese navigator by the name of Esteban Gomez visited the area in the following year, and believed he settled matters once and for all by naming the waterway Rio de San Antonio. Neither Verrazano nor Gomez was foolish enough to let any crew members go ashore and visit Coney Island as they sailed past on their way in and out of the harbor.

BROOKLYN

An important benchmark in any discussion of Brooklyn is the moment when December 31, 1897, became January 1, 1898. At that time, Brooklyn became one of five boroughs within a larger political entity known as the City of New York—arguably the nation's most dynamic and interesting city. Each of New York's five boroughs—Brooklyn, Queens, Manhattan, the Bronx, and Richmond—has its own elected borough president.

Things become a trifle confusing, however—and imprecision, linguistic and otherwise, are a permanent hallmark of the Coney Island story—when one learns that the political subdivisions that are called the boroughs of the City of New York are geographically coextensive with five separate counties. In the United States, it is more common for a major city to be located wholly within the confines of a single county, with the county's territory typically being larger than that of the city. (Chicago and Los Angeles are both examples of such a state of affairs.) Little about New York is typical, though, and the political geography of this most unusual of cities includes five separate counties wholly within its boundaries.

The territory that is the borough of Brooklyn is also Kings County; the borough of Queens is coextensive with Queens County; the borough of Richmond includes the same territory as does Richmond County, although in common parlance both county and borough are called Staten Island; the borough of Manhattan is the same as New York County; while the Bronx is the Bronx, be it borough or county. The only major change to this county-borough arrangement since the amalgamation of Greater New York in 1898 is that, when the unified City of New York was created, New York County included two boroughs, Manhattan and the Bronx; Bronx County was separated from New York County effective January 1, 1914.

While the five boroughs of the City of New York are subdivisions of the city government, the five counties are, in essence, subdivisions of the state government. Each county has a governmental apparatus that includes such functions as a district attorney, sheriff, and courts. This apparatus is separate from whatever municipal apparatus is appropriate to each borough's governance as a subdivision of the City of New York.

Before the establishment of the current territorial limits of the City of New York in 1898, Brooklyn was a separate city unto itself. Indeed, as it was about to surrender its municipal autonomy and become part of a larger political entity that was then commonly called Greater New York, Brooklyn could boast that, with a population of 1.2 million, it was the third largest city in the United States. A public building in downtown Brooklyn at Court and Joralemon Streets that was constructed in 1849 and that is today called Borough Hall, for example, was known as City Hall prior to the 1898 amalgamation. By the late 1890s and with amalgamation looming, the city of Brooklyn had grown to the point where, like today's borough, it was coextensive with the territorial limits of Kings County. However, this was not always so.

To learn a little about the origins of Brooklyn one must return to seventeenth-century New York. In 1683, almost a century before the American Revolution, Kings County was established by authority of the British Crown. On the day it was formed, Kings County included six fledgling towns: Bushwick, Flatbush, New Utrecht, Flatlands, Gravesend, and a place that was then called Breuckelen—and would later be Brooklyn. The town of Breuckelen had been incorporated 37 years earlier in 1646. The limits and borders of the six Kings County towns fluctuated a bit over the years. The town of New Lots, for example, was crafted out of the eastern portion of Flatbush in 1852; the town of Williamsburgh separated from Bushwick in 1827, only to be annexed to Brooklyn in 1886. Brooklyn itself advanced from town to city status in 1834, and the city's boundaries continued to expand throughout the nineteenth century.

The first European settlement in the land that is today known as Kings County dates to the mid-1630s. The Dutch rulers of New Amsterdam issued patents, which gave various groups the right to settle in specified territory, and it was from such patents that many of the early towns emerged. In 1643, in the first recorded act that addresses the land that is today called Coney Island, Dutch rulers issued such a patent to the founders of a town called Gravesend.

THE TOWN OF GRAVESEND

Gravesend was established when Lady Deborah Moody led a small band of Anabaptists south from the Massachusetts Bay Colony where their lately adopted religious beliefs had made them unwelcome. The Dutch governors of New Netherlands were favorably disposed toward these English refugees from Massachusetts and allowed them to establish a settlement in the southern part of what would later become Kings County. The Dutch rulers were not motivated purely by altruism, though, since a formal settlement in the area that Moody and her followers called Gravesend represented a buffer between Dutch-settled territory to the north and the potentially hostile Canarsie Indians. Lady Moody is rightly remembered as the first woman to lead the establishment of a formal European settlement in the New World, and Gravesend was the only town in the territory that would later be called Kings County that was organized by English, and not Dutch, settlers. (The English name, Gravesend, must have fallen awkwardly on ears accustomed to the area's otherwise universal Dutch nomenclature.)[6]

The original Gravesend settlement, and its evolution into the Kings County town of Gravesend in the nineteenth century, is pertinent to our story. The patent that was awarded to Lady Moody in 1643—and confirmed in 1645—extended outward from a central point that was approximately where Gravesend Neck Road and McDonald Avenue intersect today. A walled fortress sixteen acres in size was built at the center of the settlement; settlers retreated inside this stockade each evening after tending their crops in fields beyond the walls. Farming and grazing land outside the fortress walls was divided evenly in pie-shaped slices among the original settlers of Gravesend, and formal title to these divided lands was conveyed to the individual settlers. At first there were forty settlers, but one appears to have dropped by the wayside. Most accounts speak of thirty-nine original settlers, or patentees, of Gravesend.[7]

As Gravesend expanded its activities and additional real estate was needed, it was appropriated from the settlement's unapportioned land. However, the land was always divided into thirty-nine equal parcels and conveyed from public to private hands. Gravesend's jurisdiction, as established in the original patent, extended south to where ocean waves rolled onto grassy, offshore sand spits. But for almost 250 years, citizens of Gravesend saw little practical use for these island dunes at the southern end of their settlement. Some hunting of rabbits may have taken place from time to time, and venturesome souls in search of solitude may have walked quietly along the beach contemplating the ocean. In general, fording the tidal estuaries that separated the offshore sand spits from the rest of Gravesend and the Kings County mainland seemed to be an exercise devoid of practicality. However, at some point the elders of Gravesend followed their usual practice of dividing this land into thirty-nine equal parts and awarding it to the thirty-nine original settlers or their heirs. For unknown reasons, the Gravesend elders did not allocate the entirety of Coney Island. A key section in the very middle of the island remained common land that was owned by the corporate entity of Gravesend. This fact would substantially impact the late-nineteenth-century development of Coney Island.

During the seventeenth and eighteenth centuries, while Coney Island lay barren and more or less unused, dramatic events were taking place close by that would help define and establish a new nation. In the late seventeenth century, the British took over New Amsterdam from the Dutch and renamed it New York; the Battle of Long Island, a key conflict in the Revolutionary War, was waged in 1776. The first U.S. Census in 1790 reported a Kings County population of 4,495; of these souls, 1,603 lived in the town of Brooklyn and considerably fewer resided in Gravesend. In 1814, a steam-powered ferryboat built by Robert Fulton was put in service across the East River between Brooklyn and New York.

It was during the middle of the nineteenth century that attitudes about the barren offshore lands in the town of Gravesend began to change, and some people began to regard the territory known as Coney Island as valuable. In 1823, an initiative that was largely the work of a Gravesend town supervisor by the name of John Terhune established the Coney Island Road and Bridge Company. Its purpose was to build a toll road through the barren southern portions of Gravesend and across the creek and marshes to Coney Island. Six years later in 1829, the project was completed. A thoroughfare called the Shell Road thus opened to traffic, and people could travel to Coney Island without getting their feet wet. On the Coney Island end of the turnpike, the company built a small hotel called the Coney Island House, an establishment whose guests in the years before 1850 included such American notables as Daniel Webster, Henry Clay, Washington Irving, and Walt Whitman.[8] Additional hotels soon followed.

A wonderful mixture of Coney Island fact and legend had its origins in 1830, the year after the Shell Road collected its first tolls. The crew of a stout brig called the *Vineyard* took it upon themselves to dispatch the vessel's captain to his eternal reward and head for shore in two small boats, along with several chests filled with Mexican silver dollars that constituted the ship's cargo. One of the boats was lost at sea, and the other had to toss some of its treasure overboard to lighten the load. The rest of the cargo was supposedly buried on Coney Island, where, for all anyone knows, it may still lie.[9]

In the summer of 1850, a second toll road was built between the Kings County mainland and Coney Island. This one followed a right-of-way that is today's Coney Island Avenue, and it made its landfall on the island in the area that is today called Brighton Beach.

Moving ahead to 1867, the annual town meeting of Gravesend freeholders took a seemingly unimportant action that propelled a scoundrel of rare proportions onto the Coney Island stage. They elected three constables that year, one of whom—a contractor from the Sheepshead Bay section of Gravesend by the name of John Y. McKane—would use his newly acquired office to exercise near total control over Coney Island for the next quarter-century. The historical contingency that gave McKane the leverage he needed to proceed with his nefarious ways was the fact that so much land in the central part of Coney Island had never been conveyed into private hands and remained under the ownership of the town of Gravesend.[10] It was largely under McKane—and all his works and pomp—that Coney Island grew from a random collection of seashore retreats and hotels into a world-renowned center of amusement and recreation.

The Coney Island Experience by Categories

As we explore various kinds of public transport systems that were deployed to serve Coney Island over the years, we shall take passing note of the activities and attractions that made the seaside resort such a popular destination in the first place. The entertainment and recreation options that were available at Coney Island can be categorized under five broad headings: (1) the ocean and the beach; (2) hotels, restaurants, and food stands; (3) rides, amusements, and games of chance; (4) formal entertainment; and (5) professional sporting events. Under one or another of these five categories can probably be placed all of the legal entertainment that drew visitors to Coney Island. To these five, of course, must be added a broad range of less-than-legal activities that also helped popularize—or stigmatize—Coney Island. These included prostitution, gambling, the distribution and sale of opium, the sale of bootleg liquor during Prohibition, murder-for-hire, and probably more.

The Beach

In our own day, "the beach" conjures visions of sunbathing and swimming, activities that are routinely practiced in clothing that can only be called minimal—sometimes less than minimal. A century ago, though, swimming was hardly the popular activity that it is today, nor was there any consensus among health-care professionals about the medical implications of exposing one's skin to the rays of the sun or immersing oneself in the sea. Nineteenth-century physicians, for example, exhorted that people who were intent to frolic in the surf on a hot summer's day should be careful to protect themselves with multiple layers of clothing—woolen clothing—from neck to wrist to ankle. Obviously, medical opinion on this subject would evolve as Coney Island itself helped popularize the concept of ocean bathing.

In fact, as a measure of how things evolved, in later years Coney Island became the scene of extended public policy discussions on the propriety of certain people appearing "topless" on a public beach. Such debates raged with special enthusiasm during the 1930s. The "certain people" whose toplessness had become a cause of such serious public concern were men. (Although the law was not universally enforced, as late as 1936 it was illegal for adult males to appear on a public beach in the City of New York in a bathing suit that lacked a top.)[11]

In any event, one of the perennial appeals of Coney Island is the fact that along its entire length, from Manhattan Beach to Sea Gate, there is a sandy ocean beach with gently rolling waves that beckon visitors to abandon their cares and take a dip.

Hotels and Restaurants

The first public attraction to open for business on Coney Island was undoubtedly the Coney Island House of 1829. Dozens of additional hotels were soon built, although many of them burned to the ground shortly after they were built. Ramshackle wooden construction, fresh sea breezes, plus the absence of any kind of a fire department in the early years all contributed to the fiery toll. However, once insurance was available to compensate such losses, a perennial suspicion in Coney Island is that a well-placed torch was a perfectly ordinary managerial option in the face of less-than-profitable performance.

In the final quarter of the nineteenth century, some genuinely luxurious, resort-style hotels were built on the eastern end of Coney Island in Manhattan Beach and Brighton Beach. In 1927, a large, multistory hotel was built on the boardwalk at West 29th Street—the first step, its builders thought at the time, in creating a new atmosphere in Coney Island that would transform the place into an upscale, all-season resort. Sad to say, the Half Moon Hotel, as the venture was called, was a last step as well as a first step, and the era of grand hotels in Coney Island remains a nineteenth-century phenomenon.

Overnight guests require feeding, of course, and the various hotels typically included dining facilities. But people heading for nothing more than a day at the beach also get hungry, and over the years the range of eateries on Coney Island has included everything from fancy restaurants to midrange beer gardens to stands selling hot dogs, corn on the cob, cotton candy, and salt water taffy.

Rides, Amusements, and Games of Chance

This is a broad category that encompasses everything from multiple-acre amusement parks where, for a single admission fee patrons could spend an entire day, to small stands where people paid money and tried their luck at knocking down targets by throwing baseballs at them and winning a prize for their success.

The formal amusement park was, in fact, "invented" on Coney Island in 1895 when Paul Boyton opened the gates of Sea Lion Park. Coney Island's three subsequent amusement parks—Steeplechase, Luna Park, and Dreamland—were built between 1897 and 1904 and quickly became the most famous of their kind in the world.

There were many rides and attractions in Coney Island that were never part of the island's formal amusement parks. Over the years, fifty or so roller coasters operated at Coney Island, with no more than a dozen-and-a-half of these situated inside the major amusement parks. A similar ratio applies to that most basic of amusement rides, the carousel.

The era of mechanical rides and amusements at Coney Island began in the late 1870s, blossomed in the 1880s and the 1890s, and saw its final spurt in the aftermath of the New York World's Fair of 1939–40.

Formal Entertainment

In the early years of the twentieth century, Coney Island was a place where patrons could sit back and enjoy some of the world's best cabaret-style entertainment—singers, musicians, and various other performers. Coney Island is, certainly, more famous for entertainment that can only be called unusual—side shows, wax museums featuring gruesome recreations of bloody crimes, fat ladies, that sort of thing. But the fact remains that many first-rate entertainers including Jimmy Durante, Eddie Cantor, and Vincent Lopez earned some of their early dollars in one or another of Coney Island's cabarets.[12]

The owners of both Luna Park and Dreamland made efforts to incorporate a certain number of uplifting scientific or educational exhibitions among their attractions. But, as a general matter, Coney Island was a place of release and recreation, not education under the guise of entertainment.[13]

Professional Sporting Events

Coney Island has hosted many world championship prize fights and countless lesser matches, and it has even added a few especially sordid chapters of its own to that sport's checkered history.[14] But the sport that is most associated with the seaside resort and that has substantially impacted its development is thoroughbred horse racing.

In the nineteenth century, no fewer than three racetracks were built at Coney Island or close enough to Coney Island on the Kings County mainland that they are spoken of as part of the Coney Island experience. It is difficult to overestimate the importance of horse racing in bringing visitors to the shore with money in their pockets and a willingness to spend it on food, drink, or entertainment before they called it a day and headed home. A working-class family spending a day at the beach, bringing lunch along in a wicker basket and heading home by trolley car in time for supper, contributed relatively little to the Coney Island economy. People out for a day at the races, though—win, lose, or draw—were a totally different matter. After the last race was run, many repaired to one of the luxury hotels in Brighton Beach or Manhattan Beach for the evening, spent money quite freely, and then headed back to the track the next day to do it all over again. Early in the twentieth century, New York State enacted legislation that made betting on horse racing illegal, and the Coney Island tracks were closed. Betting would be revived some years later, but thoroughbred racing never returned to Coney Island.

In a nutshell, this is what people did once they traveled to Coney Island. Now let us explore how they got there.

Street Railways
(1854–1890)

FEW MUNICIPALITIES in the world ever enjoyed as close an association with street railways as Brooklyn once did. The National League baseball team that currently plays its home games in Los Angeles and whose white uniform shirts have "Dodgers" written across them in blue script letters was so named because the team was once based in Brooklyn, a place whose denizens were forever "dodging" the trolley cars that seemed to run up and down every major Brooklyn thoroughfare.[1] Street railways played an important role in transporting people to Coney Island over the years, although they served wider Brooklyn markets, as well.

THE BROOKLYN CITY RAILROAD COMPANY

The first company to offer horse-drawn street railway service in Brooklyn or Kings County called itself the Brooklyn City Railroad Company (Brooklyn City). Brooklyn was merely the third city in all of America whose citizens were afforded access to street railway services. The first was New York City, whose initial line opened in 1832. The second was New Orleans, where a street railway began operating in 1835.[2] It was another two decades before Brooklyn emulated New York and New Orleans. Brooklyn City was chartered on December 17, 1853, under the authority of state legislation passed in 1850. Once the company was formally established, the Brooklyn Common Council enacted a franchise measure permitting the company to operate cars over city streets. To finance its operations, Brooklyn City was authorized to issue $2 million in capital stock. On February 21, 1854, it began to accept stock subscriptions, and 150 investors quickly came forward and fully bought out the offer.

Brooklyn City inaugurated street railway service in July 1854 over a line that ran inland from Fulton Ferry—long the principal East River crossing between Brooklyn and New York City—and then two miles eastward into the heart of residential Brooklyn along Myrtle Avenue to a terminal at Marcy Avenue. Democrat Franklin Pierce was president of the United States on the day in 1854 when Brooklyn's first streetcar carried its first passenger. Brooklyn's last streetcar would carry its final passenger 102 years later in 1956, during the presidential administration of Republican Dwight Eisenhower.

Brooklyn City conducted a ceremonial trial trip aboard several of its new streetcars on Saturday afternoon, July 1, 1854, for invited stockholders, members of the company's board of directors, and other dignitaries. A half-dozen or so streetcars were hauled down Fulton Street to the ferry by teams of horses smartly decorated with festive plumes. The *Brooklyn Daily Eagle* reported the development with uncritical superlatives that newspapers seem to be unable to avoid when discussing civic developments. "Never was any public improvement inaugurated amid a more universal feeling of favor than these railroads."[3]

Street railway service was opened to the general public the following Monday, July 3, and many Brooklyn residents took their first trip aboard the new streetcars on Tuesday, the Fourth of July. "The company did a thriving business from early morning until a late hour at night," reported the *Eagle*, noting that the only operational difficulty was an occasional tendency of cars to derail when grooves adjacent to the new tracks along Fulton Street and Myrtle Avenue became filled with gravel.[4] Such problems were quickly overcome since several strong men were all that it usually took to push wayward cars back onto their tracks.

Two young boys were injured during the inaugural days of the street railway. On the first day the cars were running, one youngster pushed another off a car's platform causing the latter minor injuries on one of his arms. The next day, July 4, young Patrick Grant demonstrated the dangers associated with a "sport" that would soon become quite popular with Brooklyn youth, hitching a free ride on the outside of a streetcar. As one of the new Myrtle Avenue cars was approaching Graham Street, Grant lost his grip on the window panel that he was perilously clinging to; he fell to

the street and suffered a compound fracture of his right leg. For
the next century, generations of Brooklyn school teachers continually cautioned their students about the dangers associated with
the practice young Grant pioneered in 1854, but to relatively little
avail.

Founders of the Brooklyn City Railroad did not envision that
their company's operations would be restricted to this initial line
along Myrtle Avenue. From the outset, they had plans to construct
an impressive four-line urban transport network that would serve
diverse neighborhoods of Brooklyn. Before 1854 had run its
course, the new company began operating horse-drawn railcars
along Fulton Street (to Brooklyn City Hall initially, to New York
Avenue shortly afterward), Court Street and Third Avenue (to Bay
Ridge), and Flushing Avenue (to Greenpoint). These lines, of
course, were in addition to the initial Myrtle Avenue Line, which
was itself extended eastward from its original terminal at Myrtle
and Marcy to Myrtle and Broadway during that same year.

A separate car barn, or stable as such facilities were generally
called during the horsecar era, was built to serve each of the new
company's four lines. Some of the Brooklyn City services charged
a fare of four cents, others five cents. Because many streetcar lines
operated along streets and avenues that had previously been
served by horse-drawn stagecoaches that connected sections of
Brooklyn and Kings County with the East River ferry slips, the
new company bought out the interests of various stage operators
"so that there will be no clashing from this quarter," in the words
of the *New York Times*.[5] Brooklyn City's original Myrtle Avenue
Line of 1854, for example, only began operating after the railway
company purchased the operating rights of a stage line along the
same thoroughfare that had been operated for many years by Seymour L. Husted.

The style of rolling stock that quickly became a mainstay of the
early street railway industry was a brightly enameled wooden car,
sixteen or eighteen feet in length. At either end of the car there
was a small open platform, protected above by an overhang of the
roof and featuring a waist-high dash that extended upward from
the floor. A driver rode on the front platform and worked the reins
of the horse, or horses, that pulled the car. A second crew mem-

ber, a conductor, typically rode on the rear platform and collected fares from passengers.

Streetcars in the horse-drawn era were typically unheated in winter, with handfuls of straw thrown on the car floor to provide minimal insulation. Passengers usually sat facing one another on benches that ran the length of the car on both sides. Cars could change directions at the end of the line, with driver and horses moving to the opposite end for the return trip. One style of horse-car that could only run in one direction was a slightly smaller vehicle that was designed for service on more lightly traveled lines. Known as a bobtail car, it lacked a rear platform, passengers boarded through a door in the end bulkhead, and it was typically operated with a single on-board crew member and a drawn by a single horse.

Street railway companies owned and stabled three or four times as many horses, or mules, as streetcars. A wooden streetcar could remain in service from early morning until late evening but, during that time, two or three changes of horses were required. When street railways began to unionize in the final years of the nineteenth century, a frequent charge leveled by labor organizers was that, during early horsecar days, street railway companies often showed more concern for the welfare of their horses than for their men.

The next two decades saw steady expansion of streetcar service in Brooklyn. Brooklyn City's original four-line network of 1854 grew into a larger system as the company inaugurated additional lines. In addition, new street railway companies began to offer service. In 1860, with Brooklyn City by then a robust six-year-old operation, the residential population of Kings County stood at 279,000.

During this period of street railway expansion, Brooklyn and its environs experienced a never-ending dynamic of merger and amalgamation among street railway companies. Mergers were not restricted to the street railway companies that were actually operating horse-drawn cars along Brooklyn streets and avenues. Many companies received charters from the state government in Albany, secured operating franchises from Brooklyn municipal officials, perhaps even issued stock to raise capital, but never reached the point of placing streetcars into service. Such companies often

figured prominently in subsequent merger or consolidation transactions because the franchise instruments they held were themselves considerations of value that operating companies were
anxious to acquire and quite willing to pay for.

In 1886, for instance, a formal report issued by the New York
State Board of Railroad Commissioners identified no fewer than
sixty-one railways with Brooklyn, or the name of a Kings County
neighborhood, in their title. Three-quarters or more of these companies, although formally chartered and required to submit annual
reports to the state railroad commission, would never build a foot
of trackage, own a single streetcar, or carry a single passenger.[6]

Many of the major streetcar-building firms whose reputations
would largely be earned during a later era of electric-powered trolley cars—firms like J. G. Brill and the Saint Louis Car Company—
had their beginnings during the days of the horsecar. One
important firm that is primarily associated with the design and
construction of horse-drawn streetcars, though, is that of John Stephenson. From his plant on 27th Street in New York City, Stephenson produced smart and attractive-looking cars for street railways
all over the world, and he is credited with the development of
many design features that became standard in the new industry.
For example, around 1860 Stephenson built a car for a street railway in Brooklyn that was called the Broadway Railroad. The car
pioneered a design feature that many street railways soon emulated—it was an open car that lacked sidewalls of any sort so passengers could be refreshed and cooled by summer breezes. Such
open cars only operated during warm-weather months and, not
surprisingly, they would become especially popular on various
streetcar lines to and from Coney Island. Like the fictional horse-
drawn carriage that would later achieve immortality in the Rod-
gers and Hammerstein musical "Oklahoma!" open streetcars were
equipped with side curtains "that roll right down, in case there's a
change in the weather."[7]

Another company that played an important early role in supplying streetcars to Brooklyn companies was a firm called Lewis and
Fowler. Corporate linkages between Brooklyn-based Lewis and
Fowler and officials of the Brooklyn City Railroad are explored in
chapter 6.

While new street railways like Brooklyn City provided enhanced levels of inexpensive mobility for the citizens of the city they served, such benefits were not achieved without attendant risk and danger. Consider, for example, an incident that occurred on the moonless evening of Wednesday, August 21, 1863, less than a decade after Brooklyn City's first streetcar carried its inaugural passenger. Car no. 199 with a two-horse team was inbound from Greenwood on the Third Avenue Line and was approaching a swing bridge that carried Hamilton Avenue across a famous Brooklyn waterway called Gowanus Canal.[8] The bridge had recently opened to permit a coal-carrying canal barge to pass though. As was uncovered during later investigations, a lantern normally displayed while the bridge was open was not in place this night, and driver John Ferris failed to notice that his car was heading for danger.

The missing lantern was not the only disadvantage that passengers aboard car no. 199 faced that evening. Driver Ferris later admitted to having four glasses of beer during the afternoon and evening, while some witnesses described him as thoroughly intoxicated. In any event, the car continued at full speed toward the open bridge and plunged into the creek. Two passengers were killed in the mishap—a clergyman by the name of William C. Shannon who was returning to his Brooklyn home at 119 Degraw Street after spending the day conducting religious services for U.S. troops stationed at Fort Hamilton, and a young boy whose name was Thomas Stewart. Reverend Shannon was blind, a condition that may well have prevented his escaping from the car after it plunged into the water. Another passenger, as well as driver Ferris and conductor Francis Hunt, all survived the mishap. Car no. 199 was a total loss; one of the two horses survived, but the other did not. A coroner's jury later found that the accident was due to "carelessness and neglect on the part of the driver of the car." The jury also faulted Brooklyn municipal officials "for not providing better signals and protection against the like occurrence" and found that managers of the Brooklyn City Railroad "are censurable for employing parties to drive their cars who are, in the opinion of this jury, incompetent and unfit to discharge their duty."[9]

Such mishaps were the exception, not the rule, and after a quarter-century of growth and expansion, by 1880 the Brooklyn City

Railroad had matured into one of the country's important street railways. Managed from its headquarters at 10 Fulton Street in the heart of Brooklyn, with William H. Hazzard as president and Daniel F. Lewis as treasurer, the company entered the 1880s as a system whose routes encompassed forty-three miles of track.[10] In addition, the company owned 621 passenger cars and stabled 2,400 horses to haul them. The company transported approximately 37 million passengers each year, charging fares that ranged from three cents for children to as much as ten cents on certain through trips for adult passengers. The value of its assets was reported to be slightly in excess of $3 million, an investment that was almost equally divided among three categories: track and rail, land and buildings, and railcars and horses.[11]

In 1881, the Brooklyn City Railroad reported operating and maintenance expenses of $1.7 million against receipts of $2.0 million. Most of the company's receipts, $1.86 million, were derived from fares paid by its passengers. Among miscellaneous receipts, Brooklyn City realized $10,399.90 that year from the sale of the manure that naturally accrued within an enterprise that owned large numbers of horses.[12] In addition to extensions of the four original lines of 1854, important street railway services that were now part of the Brooklyn City system included streetcar lines along Gates Avenue, Flatbush Avenue, Hamilton Avenue, and Graham Avenue. A variety of interlocking services provided through streetcar service over two or more individual lines.

At the end of the company's first quarter-century of operation, the horse-drawn streetcar remained the company's principal mass transit vehicle (as noted, it owned 621 of them). Brooklyn City also included sixteen steam-powered railcars on its roster in 1881. These steam-powered cars did not provide basic service over the company's principal trunk lines. Rather they were largely experimental vehicles that were deployed on outlying lines in an effort to develop a mechanical replacement for the industry's horse-drawn streetcar, a vehicle whose animal power was a widely recognized liability in a society that was becoming more and more mechanized.

Some steam-powered "motors," as they were often called, were themselves passenger-carrying vehicles. Most, however, functioned as diminutive locomotives that were more or less disguised to look like ordinary streetcars and that hauled one or more of the company's conventional horsecars in train-like fashion. Because these steam-powered street railway vehicles were fitted with devices to muffle their exhaust and keep noise to a minimum, they were commonly, albeit insensitively, referred to as "dummies."

Brooklyn City first deployed steam cars in 1877 on a line that ran along Third Avenue from Brooklyn city limits out to Fort Hamilton, one of the fortifications that guarded the entrance to New York. The company's initial order was for five of these vehicles, which were powered by steam engines built by the Baldwin Locomotive Works of Philadelphia. Baldwin also built the body of one of the five cars, while the other four were turned out in New York by the John Stephenson Company. The five-car fleet cost in excess of $15,000, and the cars were described in the *Brooklyn Daily Eagle* as "much like the ordinary street cars with the exception of the engine in the front and the additional length of two feet."[13]

The Broadway Railroad also experimented with steam-powered equipment. It placed such vehicles in service on July 19, 1878, operating along the company's Broadway trunk line, but only between Flushing Avenue, East New York, and Cypress Hills.[14] Horsecars continued as that company's sole vehicles on the more heavily trafficked portion of the Broadway line, between Flushing Avenue and the East River ferry slips. The Bushwick Railroad—a street railway that would be absorbed by Brooklyn City in 1888— was another company that conducted experiments with steam-powered vehicles.

An effective mechanical replacement for animal power on America's street railways was available by the end of the 1880s. But the technology was not based on and did not at all resemble the small fleet of steam-powered motors that Brooklyn City began operating in 1877, and the Broadway Railroad and the Bushwick Railroad put in service in 1878. Rather, it was electricity that enabled the growing street railway industry—in Brooklyn and in the world—to put its horses out to pasture and enter an era of industrial growth that few could have envisioned a few years earlier when the power that hauled America's streetcars stood on four feet and was fed a diet of oats.

GROWTH OF STREET RAILWAYS IN BROOKLYN

By 1890—with the Brooklyn City Railroad Company now a mature and robust thirty-five-year-old company that was substantially larger than it had been even ten years earlier, and with the shift from horse-drawn vehicles to cars powered by electricity beginning to revolutionize the street railway industry—ten separate street railway companies existed in Brooklyn and surrounding areas of Kings County. Brooklyn City was, by far, the largest and most important of these companies. It owned more streetcars, operated over more miles of track, and carried more passengers than the other nine combined, and its dominance would continue during the early years of the new decade. The table on pages 34–35 displays the ten Kings County street railway companies that were in operation in 1890.

With respect to travel to and from Coney Island, few of these early street railways, including Brooklyn City, played any role at all. The Broadway Railroad, for example, which operated the world's first open car, was established in 1860 and largely involved trunk line service to inland points in Brooklyn's Eastern District from East River ferry slips at the foot of Broadway. The Brooklyn, Bushwick and Queens County Railroad—itself a merger of three earlier street railways—offered similar and roughly parallel service, with its routes radiating from the ferry slips at the foot of Broadway, as well as an equally important Greenpoint ferry terminal at the foot of Grand Street.[15]

Even though its cars would never reach Coney Island, the Brooklyn and Jamaica Railway played an important role in the development of Kings County street railways. Brooklyn and Jamaica was a street railway that ran from East New York, then the eastern extreme of the city of Brooklyn, to Jamaica, in Queens County. One of its important claims to fame is that in 1887 it became the first street railway in Kings County to operate cars powered by electricity. This achievement is significant for a number of reasons. One, of course, is the fact that it was the first electric-powered streetcar service in Kings County, even though the company's right-of-way was far from the urban districts of downtown Brooklyn and the railway offered a service that was decidedly suburban, even rural, in nature. Also significant is the fact that this

milestone achievement predates by several months the electrification in February 1888 of a street railway system in Richmond,
Virginia, which is commonly regarded as the first important street
railway electrification in the world to achieve permanent and lasting success.[16]

The technology initially adopted by the Brooklyn and Jamaica
was developed by Charles Van Depoele, one of the pioneers in
street railway electrification. However, the railway soon grew dissatisfied with Van Depoele electrical gear and converted its cars
to Edison equipment. Writing many years later about the early
days of street railway electrification, Frank Sprague, the man who
orchestrated the successful electrification at Richmond in 1888,
made the following observation about the Brooklyn and Jamaica:
"In many places where the line crossed the roads used by the
truckmen, rails were missing and it was necessary to push the car
across. The schedule between Jamaica and East New York was
six miles an hour."[17] Brooklyn and Jamaica's electrification was
important because it was King County's first, not because it was
an outstanding technical success.

The Brooklyn City Railroad deployed its first electric-powered
streetcars on an outlying suburban line in 1892, making it the third
Kings County street railway to begin the replacement of horse-
drawn streetcars with electric vehicles. (More on the second
Kings County street railway to electrify its operations shortly.)
Brooklyn City's line began at the 39th Street Ferry slip in South
Brooklyn, traveled south along Second Avenue, and eventually ter-
minated seven miles away in the Bensonhurst section of Kings
County.

The Brooklyn City Railroad Company purchased the franchise
rights for this service from the South Brooklyn Street Railroad
Company, and it saw the line as an appropriate test bed for real-
time experiments with electrically powered streetcars. Brooklyn
City did not wish to encumber any of its more heavily trafficked
streetcar lines with the uncertainties associated with the introduction of a new technology. An equally salient consideration in the
choice of this Second Avenue Line was the fact that it could be
electrified without securing any approvals from public officials in
the city of Brooklyn, since its route was entirely beyond the city
limits of 1892. A report in the trade press even suggested that

KINGS COUNTY STREET RAILWAYS, 1890

Company	Brooklyn City Railroad[a]	Brooklyn City & Newtown Railroad[b]	Coney Island & Brooklyn Railroad	Van Brunt Street & Erie Basin Railway
Original charter issued	Dec. 17, 1853	May 22, 1860	Dec. 10, 1860	Feb. 15, 1861
Total miles of track	180	21.5	22	3
—Horse	142	21.5	16	3
—Steam	18	—	—	—
—Electric	20	—	6	—
—Cable	—	—	—	—
Total cars owned	1,548	218	115	14
—Closed (horse)	815	113	40	6
—Open (horse)	714	105	61	8
—Steam	29	—	—	—
—Electric	20	—	14	—
—Cable	—	—	—	—
Number of horses	5,500	642	200	27
Annual number of passengers	56,300,000	9,620,369	4,830,645	856,975
Annual operating expenses	$2,141,769	$309,469	$188,169	$20,521

Sources: Compiled from "Brooklyn Street Railways," *Street Railway Journal* (May 1892): 272–276; *Annual Report of the Board of Railroad Commissioners of the State of New York* (Albany, 1891).

[a] By 1890, Brooklyn City Railroad had acquired the following street railways: Bushwick Railroad (chartered in 1867); Brooklyn Crosstown Railroad (1872); Calvary Cemetery, Greenpoint & Brooklyn Railroad (1884); New Williamsburgh & Flatbush Railroad (1873); Greenpoint & Lorimer Railroad (1884); Grand Street & Newtown Railroad (1860).

[b] By 1890, Brooklyn City & Newtown Railroad had acquired the Grand Street, Prospect Park & Franklin Railroad (chartered in 1870).

when Brooklyn City purchased franchise rights to operate along Second Avenue, the company considered using the route for the experimental deployment of cable-powered streetcars.[18]

Brooklyn City made the decision to electrify Second Avenue, and the company set up a temporary power station at Second Avenue near 52nd Street. The fleet of twenty-eight new streetcars that it deployed on its first electrified line were each powered by two fifteen-horsepower Thomson-Houston motors fitted onto Manier trucks. After acquiring operating rights from South Brooklyn

Broadway Railroad[c]	Atlantic Avenue Railroad[d]	Prospect Park & Flatbush Railroad[e]	Brooklyn & Jamaica Railway	Brooklyn, Bushwick & Queens County Railroad	Brooklyn Heights Railroad
Aug. 20, 1868	May 1, 1872	Oct. 30, 1875	N/A	Feb. 7, 1885	Nov. 10, 1886
23	23	3	12.8	11	0.5
23	23	3	—	11	—
—	—	—	—	—	—
—	—	—	—	—	—
—	—	—	—	—	0.5
204	383	4	23	47	23
118	191	3	—	22	—
86	192	1	—	25	—
—	—	—	—	—	—
—	—	—	18 motor; 5 trailers	—	—
—	—	—	—	—	23
635	1,600	14	—	173	—
6,945,801	10,948,327	58,758	598,482	1,527,600	N/A
$292,415	$456,136	$3,487	N/A	$73,251	N/A

[c] By 1890, Broadway Railroad had acquired the Gates Avenue & Flatbush Railroad (chartered in 1881).

[d] By 1890, included "city division" of the Prospect Park & Coney Island Railroad (see chapter 4).

[e] Leased to the Brooklyn City & Newtown via the latter's Grand Street, Prospect Park & Flatbush subsidiary.

Street Railroad, Brooklyn City had an overhead trolley wire in place by early 1891. However, because the rest of the electrification project was not completed for another year or more, the company had to operate a single horse-drawn streetcar over the Second Avenue Line each day to preserve its franchise rights. The first ceremonial electric-powered car operated on May 20, 1892. By May 23, all nonelectrified equipment—horsecars as well as steam-powered motors—had been withdrawn, and the line was entrusted to electric cars exclusively.[19]

Brooklyn City's experimental work in 1891–92 was judged successful, and the company quickly initiated a large-scale electrification program. The first five of its streetcar lines to be converted following the Second Avenue trial were Fort Hamilton, Hamilton Avenue, Court Street, Third Avenue, and Flatbush Avenue. The company replaced its temporary power-generating plant with a permanent facility on New York Bay at the foot of 52nd Street, adjacent to the temporary station. It featured eight 1,000-horse-power E. P. Allis and Company steam engines linked to Thomson-Houston electric generators.

The Coney Island and Brooklyn Railroad

The second Kings County street railway to shift from animal power to electrical power played a very important role in the story of transport to and from the Coney Island beachfront.

The Coney Island and Brooklyn Railroad (CI&B) was chartered on December 10, 1860, to build and operate a horse-powered street railway from the banks of the East River in the city of Brooklyn to the seashore on Coney Island. The new line made its way out of downtown Brooklyn along Smith Street, crossed the Gowanus on Ninth Street, and reached the Brooklyn city line at the southwest extreme of Prospect Park. Southward from the park, the new line headed overland to the Atlantic Ocean along the alignment of the Coney Island Plank Road, a corridor that later would be known as Coney Island Avenue.

By the summer of 1862—with the horrors of Civil War providing a steady diet of dispiriting news—the company had laid tracks over its intended route and was ready to institute service. However, the Coney Island Plank Road Company secured a preliminary injunction restraining the new company from running its cars. The plank road company claimed the railway had no legal right to lay tracks and that "serious, if not irreparable damage would be sustained" if the company were allowed to operate its new railway.[20]

The matter was heard on June 30, 1862, before Judge Lott in New York State Supreme Court. (In keeping with the linguistic imprecision that is so much a part of the Coney Island story, in the state of New York the court that is called "supreme" is actually the very first level of adjudication. Subsequent appeals and final determinations are rendered by higher tribunals that are, in fact, "supreme," although not called such.) The court held that the new company could begin operations. With the injunction discharged and court costs levied against the plaintiff, the CI&B instituted horsecar service to Coney Island on July 4, 1862, eight years and one day after the Brooklyn City Railroad welcomed passengers aboard the city's first street railway. The new line was the first rail service of any kind to reach Coney Island, but the company would enjoy this monopoly for a mere two years.

The company's president, James A. Van Brunt, drew up an announcement and ran it as a paid advertisement in area newspapers to promote the new service. It read, "The public is respectfully informed that the cars of this Company are now running to Coney Island from Fulton and Catherine Ferries."[21] Fulton Ferry was the famous East River crossing operated by the Union Ferry Company of Brooklyn that connected Brooklyn's Fulton Street with Fulton Street in New York. The Catherine Ferry, also operated by Union Ferry, linked the foot of Main Street in Brooklyn with the foot of Catherine Street in New York. Other important Union Ferry routes across the lower East River terminated in Brooklyn at Montague Street, Atlantic Avenue, and Hamilton Avenue.[22]

The new horse-powered railway crossed Coney Island Creek on a small bridge and made its landfall on Coney Island in an area that would later be called Brighton Beach, but was largely undeveloped and nameless beachfront in 1862. The rails then turned westward and ran parallel to Coney Island Creek and the shore for another mile-and-a-half before ending in a section of Coney Island that would soon become known as West Brighton. The new horsecars terminated in Coney Island at a point that would today be slightly east of the West Eighth Street subway station and just north of Surf Avenue. In 1862, the principal commercial activity adjacent to the street railway terminal was Van Sicklen's Hotel. Roller coasters and merry-go-rounds were still in the resort's future by several decades, and the Coney Island of 1862 had yet to experience the formative influence of Gravesend's John Y. McKane, whose ascendancy to a position of control would begin toward the end of the 1860s.

Coney Island–bound passengers, while able to travel all the way from the East River aboard the new company's cars, generally had to change cars at Park Circle. The CI&B charged passengers five cents to travel between the East River and the Brooklyn city line at Park Circle. To continue all the way to Coney Island cost twenty cents. Running time from one end of the line to the other was in excess of an hour-and-a-half, which included changing cars at Park Circle.

On the Brooklyn side of Park Circle, the new line was a typical two-track city street railway with cars operating frequently in both directions. Between Park Circle and Coney Island, however, where cars generally ran on an hourly basis—half-hourly at best—a single track with passing sidings strategically located was more than sufficient to accommodate traffic. The day before the new line opened for business, the *Brooklyn Daily Eagle* noted, "The opening of this road will be a great accommodation to our citizens; for who does not desire to go to the sea shore in hot weather, and now especially that the opportunity is afforded, at so reasonable a price? And now for Coney Island!"[23]

From 1862 through 1864, the CI&B was the only railway offering service from the East River to Coney Island. Its horse-drawn railcars, however, were hardly the last word in speed. As newer and faster steam-powered railways were built on competitive routes parallel to CI&B's horsecar line in the 1870s and the 1880s, the company realized that if it were to survive in the Coney Island trade, it had to improve the caliber of service it offered.

As early as 1876, the company experimented with a steam-powered motor, such as Brooklyn City Railroad and the Broadway Railroad would later deploy. As would be the case with most American street railways, however, fitting a complex steam engine and such associated equipment as a boiler, water tanks, fuel bunkers, and a firebox within the limited dimensions of a twenty-foot-long streetcar did not prove practical. After the 1876 experiment, horsecars once again became the railway's sole motive power.

Before the company was a decade old, management of the CI&B Railroad passed into the hands of Henry Warner Slocum. Slocum graduated from West Point in 1852 and was commissioned a lieutenant in the U.S. Army. He resigned his commission in 1857 and began to practice law in his native Syracuse. Attorney Slocum had a flare for politics and was elected to the New York state legislature in 1858. The outbreak of Civil War saw Slocum return to the Army, where he was seriously wounded in the first Battle of Bull

Run. After a speedy recovery, he returned to active duty and was soon promoted to the rank of brigadier general and then major general. He served under General Joseph Hooker at Chancellorsville and, in July 1863, General Slocum was in command of the Twelfth Corps on the right flank of General George Meade's Army of the Potomac at Gettysburg. Here, on the evening of July 2, he repulsed a Confederate assault on East Cemetery Hill. Later Slocum saw action with General William Sherman in Georgia.

With the cessation of hostilities in 1865, Slocum returned to a civilian life of law, politics, and business—first in Syracuse, and later in Brooklyn. Success followed success, including three terms in the U.S. House of Representatives. When the Democratic Party convened in 1882 to nominate a candidate for governor, two names were put forward—Slocum and Roswell P. Flower. (Flower made an especially important contribution to Brooklyn mass transportation, which is discussed in chapter 6.) When Flower and Slocum each received an equal number of votes from Democratic delegates, the convention turned to a third candidate to break the deadlock. Thus, a relative unknown by the name of Grover Cleveland was put on a path that led first to the New York governor's mansion and eventually to the White House, because of a convention deadlock between two men who would later play important roles in the development of transportation to and from Coney Island.

Henry Slocum served as an early trustee of the New York and Brooklyn Bridge, and soon he added the challenging and developing business of street railways to his other business interests. Following an association with the Brooklyn Crosstown Railroad, Slocum added a lengthy tenure as president of the CI&B to his responsibilities and achievements. Slocum acquired his financial stake in the CI&B from fellow Civil War veteran James Jourdan. Although the press commonly referred to Jourdan as "General Jourdan" during his postwar street railway days, the highest rank that the Irish-born soldier actually achieved during the Civil War was that of colonel. The title of general was a legitimate element of his discharge, and its use was quite proper; however, unlike Slocum, Jourdan never held this rank in the field.

Jourdan grew frustrated when he was unable to upgrade the slow street railway service offered by the CI&B into a faster-paced rapid transit operation, and press accounts claim that he "un-loaded" his interest in the CI&B to Slocum.[24] After severing his connection with the CI&B, Jourdan went on to help create true rapid transit service to and from Coney Island (see chapter 4).

General Slocum had a son, another Henry W. Slocum, who was born in 1862. The younger Slocum graduated from Yale in 1883; after completing legal studies in Washington, D.C., he was admitted to the bar in New York in 1885. Following his father into the street railway industry, Slocum served as president of the Brooklyn Crosstown Railroad Company from 1886 until its acquisition by Brooklyn City Railroad in 1889. Young Slocum then joined his father at the CI&B and, when the latter passed away on April 14, 1894, he succeeded his father as president of the company.

The name General Slocum will forever be linked with a terrible 1904 New York tragedy, although it is a tragedy for which he bears no responsibility. Knickerbocker Steamboat Company's 1890-built side-wheel excursion boat was called *General Slocum* to honor the Civil War hero. The vessel—which operated to and from Coney Island from time to time, although her principal service was between Manhattan and Rockaway Beach—came to grief while heading up the East River on June 16 with a church group on board. The wooden excursion boat caught fire, the captain was unable to beach the vessel as the superstructure became fully involved, and the death toll reached 1,029. This event stood as the deadliest tragedy ever to befall the New York metropolitan area until the destruction of the World Trade Center on September 11, 2001.[25]

Several years before the elder Slocum passed away in 1894, the CI&B made a corporate decision to convert its street railway operations from animal power to electricity. Authorization to convert the Park Circle–Coney Island leg of the route was relatively easy to obtain, as officials in such outlying Kings County jurisdictions as Flatbush and Gravesend welcomed the transport improvements that electrification would bring to their constituents. Slocum correctly anticipated that the company's newly electrified service would carry considerably more passengers than it did during horsecar days, and so the single-track line between Park Circle and Coney Island was expanded to two-track capability at the same time it was electrified. Electric operation south of Park Circle began on April 19, 1890, and passengers heading to Coney Island that summer could travel aboard electric-powered railcars. (Details are a bit sketchy, but Leo Daft, one of the pioneers in the development of electric-powered streetcars, is known to have demonstrated some kind of electric-powered railcar on one of the Coney Island ocean piers during the summer of 1884. This accomplishment could, but probably should not, be cited as Coney Island's first "electric railway."[26])

The company acquired twelve new electric trolley cars from the Brooklyn car-building firm of Lewis and Fowler that were fitted with Thomson-Houston electrical gear. (Two additional cars with Edison equipment soon supplemented the original dozen.) These were single-truck vehicles that could also haul trailer cars—which is to say, some of the company's older horsecars—as traffic might warrant. The company's generating plant was located along its line south of Park Circle and was equipped with a pair of 250-horsepower McIntosh and Seymour steam engines, fed by Babcock and Wilcox boilers, that drove two Thomson-Houston 100-horsepower electric generators.

When Slocum's road to Coney Island was electrified in 1890, its right-of-way was moved a bit here and there, especially at the Coney Island end of the line. One change brought CI&B cars much closer to a large resort hotel that had opened in Brighton Beach in 1878. One of the principals behind this hotel was the same General Jourdan who had earlier sold his own interest in the CI&B to Slocum. Jourdan was less than pleased when the street railway began to offer modern, electrified transportation to and from his hotel because it drew passengers from the steam-powered railroad he had built to serve the resort.[27]

The CI&B Railroad was not content to electrify only the southern portion of its East River-to-Coney Island line. The company's aim was to string electric wires over its entire road from Coney Island all the way to the East River and power all of its cars with the new source of energy. However, the company faced difficulties when it sought approval from Brooklyn city officials for the change. Although the CI&B faced a unique kind of opposition when it tried to electrify north of Park Circle, general opposition to street railway electrification efforts proved to be widespread in Brooklyn. "A general antipathy against introducing the trolley electric system within the city limits has existed in Brooklyn for several years," the trade magazine *Street Railway Journal* noted in 1891.[28]

The *New York Times* also proved to be a serious foe of electrifying Brooklyn streetcar lines, and not merely in the expression of editorial opinion. In news accounts, the paper's reporters routinely used expressions like "the deadly trolley," and "the dangerous trolley system of electric propulsion." The newspaper routinely ridiculed arguments that were put forth by street railway officials at public hearings as they attempted to explain the benefits of their electrification proposals, while contrary opinion proffered by electrification opponents was accorded far more weight and respect.

In order to convert a horsecar line to electricity, a street railway company had to obtain approval from a majority of property owners along the route, with "majority" being determined by the assessed valuation of the property involved. For example, the owner of one parcel with an assessed valuation of $2,000 enjoyed the same voting weight as the owners of two lots with an assessed valuation of $1,000 each. Armed with such approvals, the company then had to seek authorization from the appropriate political jurisdiction through which the line ran. Park Circle to Coney Island, CI&B's initial electrified segment of 1890, largely ran through Flatbush and Gravesend, towns that were not hostile to the idea of electrification. The Park Circle to Fulton Ferry segment, however, involved operation over streets in the city of Brooklyn, where there was severe opposition to overhead electrical wires.

In addition, the CI&B route to Fulton Ferry from Park Circle ran along two important sides of Prospect Park. Thus, the fate of the railroad's electrification proposal fell almost entirely in the hands of the park commissioners, who were adamantly opposed to the idea of stringing electric wires adjacent to their facility. The commissioners pointed out that as many as a hundred carriages entered the park each day through the park's boulevard entrance adjacent to Park Circle. They argued that the presence of overhead electric wires across this entrance would constitute a danger.[29] In a later automotive era, this same entrance to Prospect Park would often see one hundred automobiles enter the park not each day, but each minute!

New York state law provided a way to override municipal officials' opposition to electrification. A company could file an appeal with the Board of Railroad Commissioners, an important state agency that exercised broad regulatory control over intercity, suburban, and street railways. A street railway could even go beyond this board and plead its case before a special state judiciary tribunal, which is how the CI&B eventually broke the logjam and secured necessary approbation to electrify its entire system.

OTHER BROOKLYN STREET RAILWAYS

Although no Kings County street railway other than the CI&B reached the oceanfront before 1890, it is useful to discuss two other Brooklyn railways of this era, the Atlantic Avenue Railroad and the Brooklyn City and Newtown. These companies became involved in later merger and acquisition activities that allowed their cars to play an important role in travel to and from Coney Island.

The Atlantic Avenue Railroad was chartered in May 1872, but the company's roots went back to the early 1830s, two decades before the Brooklyn City Railroad operated the first street railway in Kings County. In 1832, a charter was issued to a company called the Brooklyn and Jamaica Railroad—no corporate kin to the Brooklyn and Jamaica Railway discussed earlier. Its purpose was to build and operate a steam-powered railroad from the foot of Atlantic Street (later called Atlantic Avenue), in what was then the village of Brooklyn, to Jamaica, about ten miles away. Two years later, before the Brooklyn and Jamaica operated its first train, a company called the Long Island Railroad (LIRR) was chartered. Although the LIRR achieved considerable fame in the twentieth century as the largest commuter railroad in the country, its original corporate mission was quite different from its subsequent fate. Investors behind the LIRR planned to lease the still unfinished Brooklyn and Jamaica Railroad and incorporate it into a larger endeavor that would extend rail service to the far eastern end of Long Island. The new LIRR was not seen primarily as a means of local travel between communities on Long Island, but rather as a link in an intercity route between New York City and Boston; passengers would cross Long Island Sound by steamboat from Greenport and then continue on to Boston aboard other trains.

The early LIRR, though, was a free-standing and independent rail-road; it had no formal corporate links with either the cross-sound steamboat services, or rail lines on the opposite side that would be an integral part of the journey between New York and Boston. However, there was common-sense cooperation among the various companies on matters of scheduling and service. The LIRR executed a lease of the Brooklyn and Jamaica Railroad in 1835, and on April 18, 1836, the first train ran between Brooklyn and Jamaica. The new road was completed to Greenport, at the eastern end of Long Island's north fork, in 1844.

Conventional wisdom, in the 1830s and the 1840s, held that the many tidal inlets along the Connecticut shore of Long Island Sound precluded the construction of a more direct New York–Boston railroad there, and so a route to Boston via Long Island seemed eminently sensible. What conventional wisdom failed to anticipate, though, was the emergence of economical processes for refining structural steel—a development that made the construction of railroad bridges across the tidal inlets in Connecticut eminently practical and doomed the LIRR's plan of serving the New York–Boston market. Such a "shoreline" railroad was completed across Connecticut by 1848, and two years later the LIRR was in receivership. To make matters worse, in its haste to reach the steamer connection in Greenport, the company built its line across lightly settled flatlands in the center of Long Island where there were limited sources of local traffic to compensate for the lost Boston business.[30]

Even though its market had been radically altered, the LIRR continued to operate trains to the ferry slip at the foot of Atlantic Avenue in Brooklyn, a facility that was generally known as South Ferry. (This facility should not be confused with the South Ferry across the East River at the southern tip of Manhattan Island.) However, in 1859, municipal officials in what had by then become the city of Brooklyn concluded that steam-powered railroad trains had no place along Atlantic Avenue. Writing in 1898, Elizabeth Hinsdale characterized matters as follows: "It was believed by [Brooklyn] citizens that the operation of a steam railroad through the city down to the water's edge was a detriment to the city and a menace to the lives of its citizens, and they commenced an agitation to have steam power removed from within the city limits."[31] It may be, of course, that the motivation to ban LIRR locomotives from Brooklyn streets was less a popular uprising of the citizenry than a carefully orchestrated effort by the emerging street railway industry to protect its lines from competition by railroads operating steam-powered trains. In any event, the municipal government of Brooklyn enacted a measure that prohibited the operation of steam-powered railroad trains along Brooklyn streets.

Anticipating such an ordinance, the LIRR acquired a new right-of-way between Jamaica and ferry connections to New York City. In 1860, the company began running its trains to Hunter's Point on the East River, a place known today as Long Island City. The original Brooklyn and Jamaica route to the foot of Atlantic Avenue was converted into a branch line, but LIRR trains ran only between Jamaica and East New York, roughly the halfway point. From East New York down to the Atlantic Avenue ferry slip, the line was downgraded into a city street railway that operated horse-drawn cars. This operation was the start of what would later be called the Atlantic Avenue Railroad.

In 1867 William Richardson—who was popularly known as "Deacon" Richardson, although he held no formal office in any ecclesiastical organization—leased the Atlantic Avenue right-of-way from the railroad. Richardson was born in England in 1822, and his family emigrated to the United States when he was a boy of twelve. After serving as an army paymaster during the Civil War, Richardson came to New York. He took an executive position with the Dry Dock, East Broadway and Battery Railroad, a street railway in New York City, before turning his attention to Brooklyn in 1867. In 1872 a mortgage on the LIRR's Atlantic Avenue right-of-way was foreclosed, Richardson acquired the property, and the Atlantic Avenue Railroad was chartered on May 1 of that same year.

In 1877, the LIRR was able to return to Brooklyn along Atlantic Avenue. Its new terminal was established at Flatbush and Atlantic Avenues, rather than South Ferry. The Atlantic Avenue right-of-way eastward from Flatbush Avenue was leased to the LIRR by the Atlantic Avenue Railroad effective June 1, 1877, with the latter reserving the right to operate streetcars on the southern side of the thoroughfare between Flatbush Avenue and Washington Street.[32]

Under Richardson, the Atlantic Avenue Railroad grew into a major force on the Brooklyn street railway scene, although it never rivaled the Brooklyn City Railroad in size or importance. The Atlantic Avenue Railroad focused its operations on the ferry slip at the foot of Atlantic Avenue—South Ferry—and its early streetcar lines funneled from various Brooklyn residential neighborhoods onto Atlantic Avenue as they made their way toward South Ferry. Brooklyn City, for the most part, operated streetcar lines that fanned out into residential and commercial sections from East River ferry slips at the foot of Fulton Street (Fulton Ferry).

By 1890, the Atlantic Avenue Railroad had acquired other Brooklyn street railway properties and was operating 383 cars over 23 miles of track. It carried almost 11 million passengers each year, stabled 1,600 horses, and was drawing up plans to replace its horse-drawn fleet with new, electric-powered cars. In addition to trunk line service down Atlantic Avenue to South Ferry, the company operated streetcars along Fifth Avenue, Park Avenue, Seventh Avenue, and Vanderbilt Avenue, as well as Bergen Street, Butler Street, and 15th Street. The company's offices were located at Third and Atlantic Avenues.

Just as the Slocums, father and son, were active in the management of first the Crosstown Railroad and then the CI&B, two generations of Richardsons put their mark on the Atlantic Avenue Railroad. Both men bore the first name William. The elder Richardson was popularly called "the Deacon." His son, William J., earned a reputation in the street railway industry that extended far beyond the territory served by the Atlantic Avenue Railroad. In December 1882, the U.S. street railway industry convened in Boston and formed a professional trade association. The younger Richardson served for many years as the secretary of what was originally called the American Street Railway Association. Through Richardson, the new organization used the Atlantic Avenue Railroad's Brooklyn headquarters as its formal mailing address and secretariat for many years. William J. Richardson also played an important role in the establishment, in 1883, of a parallel statewide trade association, the Street-Railway Association of the State of New York. He handled much of the business of this state association from the offices of the Atlantic Avenue Railroad.

Early in the 1890s, Deacon Richardson liquidated his holdings in the Atlantic Avenue Railroad as new investors assumed control. Then, in the mid-1890s, the same company merged into a larger entity called the Nassau Electric Railroad, and it begin to play a much larger role with respect to the Coney Island market. These developments are explored in more detail in chapter 6.

Another important Kings County street railway of the late nineteenth century was the Brooklyn City and Newtown Railroad (BC&N). In size of operation and scope of service provided, BC&N was closer to the Atlantic Avenue Railroad than to Brooklyn City. Despite similarity of nomenclature, there was no corporate connection between the Brooklyn City Railroad and the BC&N. BC&N was chartered on May 22, 1860, and opened for business on January 28, 1862. The company's initial line linked the East River waterfront and business district of the city of Brooklyn with suburban Newtown Township in Queens County, nine-and-a-half miles away. The line principally operated along De Kalb Avenue and was parallel to Brooklyn City's original Myrtle Avenue Line, although it proceeded further out into the suburbs than did the Myrtle Avenue Line.

An individual who enjoyed a long association with BC&N and managed the company for many years was, like Henry Slocum, a veteran of the Civil War. John N. Partridge was born in Leicester, Massachusetts, in 1838 and earned the rank of colonel while serving with the Twenty-Fourth Massachusetts Volunteers. As did Slocum, Partridge moved to Brooklyn after the war to pursue a civilian career. In early 1886, he was elected president of BC&N, a post he would hold for more than a decade.

BC&N built a substantial depot and office complex at the corner of De Kalb and Central Avenues. In addition, it effected an important merger with the Grand Street, Prospect Park and Flatbush Railroad, a company whose streetcars intersected BC&N's De Kalb Avenue Line while providing service primarily along Franklin Avenue between the southern end of Prospect Park and East River ferries that operated from the foot of Grand Street, in Williamsburgh.[33] This merger expanded the previously one-line BC&N into an X-shaped street railway system that served an expansive portion of Brooklyn, with each of its two lines feeding passengers to the other. Some years later, the company's Franklin Avenue Line was extended beyond its initial terminal at the southern end of

Prospect Park to a connection with the CI&B Railroad at Park Circle and—in a development that is explored in chapter 6—BC&N merged with CI&B to play an important role in providing streetcar service to and from Coney Island.

The street railways of Brooklyn continued to expand and upgrade their operations: electricity replaced animal power, mergers and acquisitions continually altered corporate structures, and newer (and faster) equipment was acquired. Before discussing these developments and further aspects of streetcar travel to and from Coney Island, we shall explore other Coney Island transportation options.

3

Iron Piers and Iron Steamboats (1845–1918)

THANKS TO THE DISTINCTIVE GEOGRAPHY of western Long Island, the shortest distance between New York City and Coney Island is a water route rather than a land route. Prior to the construction of railway lines across Kings County in the 1860s and afterward, travel by water was also the fastest and the easiest route. In the mid-nineteenth century when Coney Island was becoming an attractive seasonal destination for New Yorkers anxious to escape the heat of the city for a few relaxing hours, steamboats emerged as an obvious and convenient way to reach the oceanfront. Other than private liveries operating along the Shell Road or the Coney Island Plank Road, steamboats were the first true form of public transport to carry passengers to and from Coney Island. Even after the Coney Island and Brooklyn Railroad opened for business in 1862—and excursion railways were constructed in the years following—steamboats remained an attractive option for people whose destination was the beach. The overland journey from downtown Brooklyn to Coney Island involved travel by horsecar out to the Brooklyn city limits and then a ride aboard another railway from there to the shore; the entire trip took more than two hours to complete. On the other hand, one could board a paddle-wheel steamboat in either Brooklyn or New York and, after a pleasant cruise down New York Bay and through the Narrows, step ashore at Coney Island Point less than an hour later.

Some people who took the mid-nineteenth-century voyage to Coney Island might fault the idea of calling the steamboat ride there a "pleasant cruise." The boats were often crowded, and passengers tended to be rowdy. The fact remains, though, that steamboats were a popular way to get to Coney Island. They began carrying people to the oceanfront for fun in the sun a full decade before the Brooklyn City Railroad carried its first passengers, two decades before the Coney Island and Brooklyn dispatched the first railcars to the shore. Steamboats would play an important role in the Coney Island travel picture until just before the Second World War. This chapter discusses steamboat service to and from Coney Island from its mid-nineteenth-century origins through the First World War.

EARLY STEAMBOATS TO CONEY ISLAND

Details about the very first steamboats to reach Coney Island are shrouded in imprecision, but there is reason to believe that steamboat services were running on a more or less regular basis by the early 1850s, and that the first such vessels entered service in the mid-1840s. A lithograph bearing the date July 26, 1845, for example, clearly shows a twin-stack, side-wheel steamboat tied up to a dock at Coney Island Point, with Thomas Bielby identified in a caption beneath the print as the proprietor of the Fort Hamilton and Coney Island Ferry Company.[1]

A vessel known to have been an early visitor to Coney Island bore the name *Naushon*. It cannot be confirmed that *Naushon* was the very first steamboat to offer Coney Island service. However, since she was built in New York in 1845, she is old enough to have been the vessel in the 1845 painting. A crosshead engine powered the 240-gross-ton *Naushon* and, since she was primarily intended for service between Martha's Vineyard and the Cape Cod mainland, her initial port of registry was Edgartown, Massachusetts.[2]

The first vessels that served Coney Island with any kind of regularity were *Union* and *Norwalk,* both owned by Taylor and Wilson. The 303-gross-ton *Norwalk,* powered by a single-cylinder crosshead engine, was built in New York in 1857, while the *Union* that ran to Coney Island was likely a 296-ton paddlewheel steamboat that was built in New York in 1844.[3]

Early steamboats to Coney Island docked at the very western end of the resort, at a place that was then known as Coney Island Point and would later be called Norton's Point. They docked at a pier that had been built on the sheltered side of the island on the shore of Gravesend Bay near the point. A milestone event in Coney Island history was the construction of a pavilion at Coney

Island Point in the mid-1840s, an enterprise that was a joint undertaking of Thomas Bielby, the aforementioned ferry entrepreneur, and Alonzo Reed.[4] The term *pavilion* may be an exaggeration, although it is the term that Bielby and Reed themselves used. The facility was merely a raised platform, which could be used as a dance floor or a bandstand, that was protected from the weather by nothing more substantial than a tent. Food stands, picnic grounds, and other attractions—more ramshackle than not—soon sprouted up adjacent to the pavilion. Eventually, facilities were available for excursionists to rent bathing attire, change their clothes, and immerse themselves in the ocean's waters in an activity that came to be called "bathing."

In the mid-nineteenth century, deliberately placing one's body in the surf was not yet a popular pastime. The health implications of such behavior were largely unknown, and all manner of self-appointed experts broke into print at the beginning of each summer with frenzied advice about the specialized clothing one should don before entering the water. In 1880, a popular guidebook to Coney Island offered this advice. "According to Dr. Packard, the material should always be woolen, and flannel is decidedly the best. Those who do not swim will find it more comfortable to protect the skin of the arms and legs from sunburn by having the sleeves come down to the wrist and the trousers to the ankle."[5]

Given the isolated character of Coney Island Point—walking was the only means of overland access until the last quarter of the nineteenth century—it is not surprising that it quickly became known for its permissiveness. A card swindle called three-card monte quickly became popular, and when Mike "Thunderbolt" Norton emerged as the boss of Coney Island Point after the Civil War, mere permissiveness escalated into utter lawlessness. More serious forms of gambling than three-card monte began to flourish, as did prostitution.

Among the factors that allowed Norton to promote such lawlessness at Coney Island Point was the fact that the area was entirely within the jurisdiction of the town of Gravesend. John Y. McKane had been appointed a Gravesend town commissioner in April 1869, and with his appointment came the additional title of commissioner of common lands. Common lands, in Coney Island, accounted for the central portion that the town had never apportioned among the descendants of the original thirty-nine settlers; title to these lands remained vested in the town of Gravesend itself. McKane's stature quickly grew. In addition to being the final authority in the award of leases for the common lands, McKane was a private contractor who was anxious to earn a dollar or two by constructing whatever it was that leaseholders wanted to build. Although he was neither a law enforcement officer nor the chief executive of Gravesend, McKane's power was unequaled throughout the 1880s and into the 1890s.

As a formula for corruption, it was absolutely perfect. The common lands were more or less coextensive with the West Brighton territory that would become the heart of the Coney Island entertainment and amusement district. McKane quickly developed a reputation for overlooking what was in his own best interest to overlook, and enforcing what assisted his own ends. Norton and McKane were in no sense allies, and each regarded the other with suspicion. However, the style of governance McKane was popularizing in Gravesend rendered him singularly ill-suited to challenge Norton's activities at Coney Island Point.[6] Coney Island Point even became a place of refuge for fugitives from the law—the most notorious of whom was William Marcy Tweed, who escaped from detention in New York City in December 1875 and found refuge at Norton's Coney Island Point. Newspaper accounts reported that Tweed had been seen in Canada, Cuba, and England. However, until he finally did flee the country in May 1876, Tweed was hiding out less than ten miles from lower Manhattan.

Coney Island Point was never entirely a place of iniquity, though. Decent people traveled there by steamboat for such wholesome entertainment as shore dinners; good music; and, of course, ocean bathing.

By the 1870s, steamboat service to Coney Island was thriving to such an extent that vessels larger than *Naushon, Norwalk,* or *Union* were placed into service. A one-time Long Island Sound flyer, the 1,752-gross-ton *Plymouth Rock* that had been built in New York in 1854, entered the Coney Island trade.[7] Not only was *Plymouth Rock* larger than all steamboats that had previously served Coney Island, she outmeasured all vessels that would ever run to Coney Island on a regular basis save one, the 1878-built *Grand*

Republic. And *Grand Republic* exceeded *Plymouth Rock* by a hair-thin margin of only eight gross registered tons.

New York steamboat service in the mid-to-late nineteenth century was not the regularly scheduled service that later became common, with departures and arrivals from specified landings at clearly established times. Vessels were usually owned by individuals, who frequently served as captain and typically lived aboard the vessel, and steamboats plying the excursion trade frequently operated a variety of routes and services from one day to the next. Unlike trains or trolley cars that operate over a fixed route on a regularly scheduled basis, mid-nineteenth-century excursion boats operated services that were more akin to today's taxi cabs or charter buses. They were sensitive to shifting whims of the market and carried passengers to a variety of destinations, even while specializing in service to preferred destinations.

The single fleet of steamboats that would be most associated with Coney Island service over the years flew the house flag of the Iron Steamboat Company. Before discussing the advent of this storied company in the fall of 1881, a brief word is in order about an earlier fleet of New York Harbor steamboats that made a pronounced contribution to the Coney Island scene—in a fashion that can only be called accidental. These were the Sylvan Steamboats, a marvelous fleet of five small side-wheelers that—before the advent of elevated railways in New York City between downtown and a certain uptown neighborhood—were "the quickest way to get to Harlem."[8] Sylvan boats were known to be fast and, when elevated railways came on the scene in the 1870s and rendered the steamboats obsolete on the downtown-to-Harlem run, surviving units in the fleet were available for alternative assignments. Since two of the Coney Island excursion railways discussed in chapter 4—the New York and Manhattan Beach and the New York and Sea Beach—required steamboat connections between their northern railheads and New York City, elements of the displaced Sylvan fleet were a near-perfect match for such assignments. Their speed allowed them to make many sailings during a day's time, and their compact size was perfect for the rapid turnaround service the excursion railways required.

Some, perhaps all, of the Sylvan boats carried passengers all the way to Coney Island from time to time. However, the major role of the fleet in the history of travel to and from Coney Island is the connecting service it provided to and from various rail terminals. The following table displays information about the five steamboats that sailed for Sylvan.

Vessel	Sylvan Shore	Sylvan Grove	Sylvan Stream	Sylvan Glen	Sylvan Dell
Year built	1856	1858	1863	1869	1872
Length (feet)	136	148.5	157	160	185
Disposition	Broken up, 1877	Lost (fire), 1891	Lost (fire), 1903	Dismantled, ca. 1922	Lost (fire), 1919

Source: *Merchant Vessels of the United States, 1790–1868* (Staten Island, N.Y.: Steamship Historical Society of America, 1975, 1978, 1982, 1984).

An important milestone in expanding the opportunity for additional steamboat service to Coney Island was the construction, in time for the 1879 season, of the resort's first ocean pier. The guiding force behind this venture was Coney Island restaurateur Charles Feltman, a man whose principal contribution to a distinctively American cuisine was the invention of the hot dog. He achieved this accomplishment in East New York before shifting his base of operations to Coney Island in 1871. Because the West Brighton section where Feltman opened a restaurant and beer garden in 1871 was inaccessible to passengers arriving at Coney Island Point by steamboat, Feltman formed a company called the Ocean Navigation and Pier Company. The company's mission was to build a pier on the ocean side of Coney Island where steamboats from New York could dock and discharge passengers. However, Feltman's Iron Pier was not simply a landing stage for steamboats; it was an attraction of its own that people paid an admission charge to enter so they could relax and enjoy the cool ocean breezes and perhaps take in a concert. The Iron Pier was 1,400 feet in length, included a 1,000-foot grand promenade, and could accommodate 30,000 patrons. A gala celebration was held to mark the opening of Feltman's Iron Pier on the Fourth of July in 1879 that included concerts throughout the day by Grafulla's Seventh Regimental Band, a famous musical aggregation of the day. Various steamboats were scheduled to make fourteen trips to the new pier that day, and a steamboat ticket included free admission to the magnificent new pier. A one-way fare from New York was thirty-five cents, a round trip went for half-a-dollar.

The steamboats that called at the Iron Pier on that Fourth of July included *J. B. Schuyler, Minnie Cornell, Eliza Hancox, Americus,* and *Grand Republic.* Meanwhile, *Rosedale, Idlewild, Chrystenah, Riverdale,* and *Sylvan Dell* provided frequent service that year between various landings in New York City and Coney Island Point, with several trips each day linking Coney Island Point with nearby cities in New Jersey such as Bayonne and Newark. (Steamboats made the run to Coney Island Point during this era from cities even further away, but not with the same frequency. For example, the New Haven Steamboat Company specialized in overnight service between New York City and New Haven, Connecticut. Its 1855-built *Elm City* continued on to Coney Island Point several times a week after unloading passengers and cargo in New York.)

The following summer, 1880, *John Sylvester, Eliza Hancox, Nelly White, Stockton,* and *Kill Von Kull* operated between the Iron Pier on Coney Island and three Hudson River landings—Pier 8, the foot of Leroy Street, and the foot of West 22nd Street. During that same summer, the steamers *Idlewild* and *Josephine* provided connecting service from four Hudson River piers and the Bay Ridge terminal of the New York and Sea Beach Railroad. *Sylvan Grove* was used in ferry service across the East River between the foot of East 23rd Street and the Greenpoint terminal of the New York and Manhattan Beach Railroad, while *D. R. Martin* ran for the same railroad between the foot of Whitehall Street in lower Manhattan and the company's Bay Ridge depot. Thus, by the start of the 1880s, numerous steamboats were running to and from Coney Island.[9]

The Iron Steamboat Company

The Iron Steamboat Company had its formal beginnings on Tuesday, September 28, 1880, at the Monmouth County Courthouse in Freehold, New Jersey. Papers filed that day named thirteen distinguished citizens as incorporators of a new company whose purpose was "the building, furnishing, fitting, purchasing, chartering,

managing, navigating and owning of steam-boats and other vessels, to be used and employed for carrying and transporting passengers and freight on the Hudson River, New-York Bay, Long
Island Sound and other waters."[10] More specifically, the company
planned to operate seasonal excursion boats at frequent intervals
between Manhattan and Coney Island. In addition, the new company would link New York and Long Branch, New Jersey, and it
had plans for an even more extensive steamboat network. A
world's fair was being planned for New York in 1883—former U.S.
President Ulysses S. Grant was serving as head of the commission
that attempted to organize the exposition—and the opportunities
for expanded water transportation throughout New York Harbor
seemed limitless.

A fleet of eight or nine new steamboats was to be designed and
built in time for the 1881 excursion season, and a total of thirty
such vessels were slated to be in service by the summer of 1883.
Of $10 million in capital stock the new company was prepared to
offer, a serious sum of money for the day, $800,000, was said to
have already been pledged at the time of incorporation. But plans
are just plans, and the Iron Steamboat Company's fleet never remotely approached thirty vessels in size. (The world's fair of 1883
never happened, either.) Even the first order of vessels, announced as eight or nine boats on the day the firm was founded,
turned out to be only seven. With the exception of a pair of second-
hand vessels acquired for short-term use early in the twentieth
century, these seven steamboats proved to be the backbone and
full extent of the company's fleet for each of the fifty-two summers
it remained in business.

The company quickly placed orders for the new vessels with
two famous Delaware River shipyards, each of which had a family
member among the new company's incorporators. William Cramp
and Sons of Philadelphia turned out four boats; the other three
were built downriver in Chester, Pennsylvania, by John Roache
and Son. Although the seven boats looked like typical excursion
steamboats of the era—which is to say built of wood—they had
iron hulls that were divided into twelve separate watertight compartments, the decks were made of iron, and the cabin work was
iron-plated. In the words of the *New York Times,* "It would be impossible for a fire to make any serious headway even if one should

originate."[11] A promotional slogan the company often used to describe its iron steamboats was "They Cannot Burn! They Cannot Sink!" Another example of the company's self-promotion was, "The boats of this company are iron, palatial, first-class sea-going steamers, fitted with every convenience for safety and comfort of passengers, and officered by competent and experienced men."[12]

Twelve watertight compartments in a steamboat slightly more than 200 feet long was unusual—three or four would have been normal. The design was dictated by the fact that the company's vessels would not be restricted to the calm waters of inland rivers and bays. To reach Coney Island, they would sail around Coney Island Point and dock at the Iron Pier on the ocean side of the resort; to reach Long Branch, they would sail outside Sandy Hook into the even less sheltered waters of the North Atlantic Ocean. Furthermore, the company envisioned sending its fleet south when the New York excursion season ended each fall, and the watertight compartments would provide additional protection during the exposed ocean voyage back and forth to winter service in Savannah, Jacksonville, or along the Gulf Coast.

Although company officials originally talked of using modern, multiple-cylinder compound engines, the new vessels were powered by single-cylinder, vertical-beam steam engines—fairly standard engines of the era. Undoubtedly, the need to build the boats quickly was a factor in the choice of engines. Some of the fleet had engines fabricated by W. & A. Fletcher, others were powered by engines from Cramp and Sons; all turned paddlewheels equipped with radial-style buckets. Like the Sylvan Steamboats, the Iron Steamboat Company's seven-boat fleet proved to be quite fast, easily maintaining speeds of twenty miles per hour or better.

The first of the seven three-deck excursion boats, the Roach-built *Cygnus,* arrived in New York in early May 1881; she bore a price tag of about $200,000. On Monday, May 23, the new steamboat took a shakedown cruise around the harbor from the foot of East 8th Street and the East River where final fitting out had been done. Company officials and the press were effusive in their praise of the new steamboat, harbor craft greeted the newcomer with lusty whistle salutes, and everyone looked forward to the inauguration of regular steamboat service to Coney Island on the following Saturday.

Two days later, on May 25, *Cygnus* took members of the press and various dignitaries on another preinaugural sail, this one a champagne cruise all the way to Coney Island. On May 26, the company's second vessel, *Cetus,* left Cramp's Delaware River yard, although only after some frantic telegraphing back and forth between Philadelphia and Washington, D.C., to secure the issuance of an "official number" by the federal government, a requirement for formally enrolling the vessel as a documented U.S. merchant vessel. The steamboat *Cetus,* official number 125903, reached New York on the morning of Friday, May 27. As she had been completely fitted out and tested before steaming north, she was ready to help *Cygnus* inaugurate the new company's service the next day. The first revenue trip from Manhattan to Coney Island on Saturday, May 28, 1881, carried 52 paying customers—52 people aboard a steamboat built to carry 2,000. Remaining units of the seven-boat fleet were completed and sent north during June and early July.

As to the names of the boats, this exchange on opening day says it all. "Where did you get those queer names for your boats?" a passenger asked the first mate on one of the afternoon trips. "I see there the *Cygnus,* and we are on the *Cetus.* What does it all mean?" Instead of answering himself, the officer felt it would be better to demonstrate for his passenger how the new company's policies were infused throughout the ranks. So he called over a uniformed deckhand and said, "Tell this gentleman where we got those names, *Cygnus* and *Cetus.*" The deckhand replied promptly, "From astronomy, sir: the constellation of the heavens. Cygnus means a swan. Cetus a whale. We are now on a whale, sir," the deckhand concluded, and tipping his cap he returned to his regular duties.[13] Perhaps more interesting than the names themselves is the way they were downplayed in the style of decoration the company selected for its new vessels. Sidewheel steamboats of the era almost universally featured a vessel's name rendered in bold and unmistakable letters across the paddleboxes. On these seven boats, what stood out in large letters across the paddleboxes was not the name of the individual vessel, but rather the name of the firm, "Iron Steamboat Co." Each vessel's name was also rendered on its paddleboxes, but in lettering completely overshadowed by the name of the organization.

Clearly, the goal was to call public attention less to one boat or another, and more to the overall steamboat service. One might even suggest that the choice of vessel names—*Cetus, Cepheus, Cygnus,* and *Perseus* and *Pegasus*—were so like sounding as to blur further the identity of individual boats and emphasize the total operation. The remaining two constellations in the new iron firmament were *Sirius* and *Taurus.* The following table displays relevant information about the seven-boat fleet of the Iron Steamboat Company.

Official Number	Vessel	Dimensions (Feet)	Gross Tonnage	Builder
125903	*Cetus*	213 × 32 × 10	847	Cramp & Sons
125904	*Cepheus*	213 × 32 × 11	882	Roache & Son
125900	*Cygnus*	212 × 31 × 11	857	Roache & Son
150214	*Pegasus*	211 × 32 × 10	847	Cramp & Sons
150213	*Perseus*	211 × 32 × 10	847	Cramp & Sons
115774	*Sirius*	229 × 32 × 11	993	Roache & Son
145253	*Taurus*	226 × 32 × 11	916	Cramp & Son

Source: Vessel documentation certificates on file at the National Archives, Washington, D.C.

During that first season of 1881, Iron Steamboat Company service ran between Manhattan and Feltman's Iron Pier in Coney Island. That year, the new company was not alone in serving the Iron Pier from Manhattan. Two steamboats of White's Regular Line, *Columbia* and *Grand Republic,* called at the facility en route to and from Rockaway, and the same company used *Americus, Adelphi,* and *Twilight* on the Coney Island run exclusively. Because of the competition, patronage levels on the new service never developed to a point that would justify the investment the company had made. During its first year, the Iron Steamboat Company was not terribly successful. Officials even complained that free daily orchestra concerts they sponsored on Pier 1 in Manhattan, nominally to attract customers to the company's steamboats, were frequented more by the patrons of its competitors.

Over the winter of 1881–82, the Iron Steamboat Company took steps to better its position. First, it negotiated a contract with Feltman's Ocean Navigation and Pier Company to be the exclusive steamboat line serving the facility from Manhattan. Iron Steamboat then executed a similar agreement with the owners of a second Coney Island iron pier that was ready to open for the 1882 season. This second ocean pier had been built amid much controversy and litigation by the Brighton Navigation and Pier Company, a subsidiary of the Prospect Park and Coney Island Railroad—a firm whose excursion railway trains first reached Coney Island in 1875 (see chapter 4). Finally that winter, Iron Steamboat negotiated a third exclusive landing contract, this one with the Ocean Pier Company, owners of an iron pier in Long Branch, New Jersey.

Thus, armed with agreements that shut out a good deal of competition from important steamboat landings, Iron Steamboat approached its second season with more confidence. Service to Coney Island was doubled over what the company provided in 1881. Departures were scheduled to leave Manhattan every thirty minutes during the summer. On odd days, boats leaving lower Manhattan on the hour operated to the older iron pier, while boats leaving on the half-hour operated to the newer pier; on even days, the pattern was reversed.

With these arrangements in place, and with a man by the name of C. H. Longstreet serving as superintendent, the company called itself "the only line having exclusive control of all the docks and piers at which it lands passengers, thus preventing annoying changes from boats to cars, laying out in a stream waiting to land, and other vexatious delays."[14] The company also tightened up its policy with respect to concerts on Pier 1. Unless one could show a ticket to ride the company's vessels, attending the concerts cost fifteen cents in 1882. Finally, Iron Steamboat and the Prospect Park and Coney Island Railroad worked out a joint arrangement to allow passengers to travel in one direction by land, the other by sea.

Manhattan-to-Coney Island service would always be the meat and potatoes of the Iron Steamboat Company's business. The great bulk of the company's scheduled departures were over this route, with fifteen to twenty round trips a day during high summer, sometimes more. But the company also offered scheduled service to other places from time to time. In 1883, the company established a service between Coney Island and Long Branch, permitting patrons to combine a (rather short) visit to Coney Island and Long Branch into a single day's outing. In 1884, the company added a direct Manhattan–Long Branch route with as many as four daily round-trips, and it discontinued the Coney Island–Long Branch service. In 1906, after some earlier experimentation, the company established regular service between Manhattan and Rockaway Beach; two or three round-trips per day were typical for this route. Once the company began Manhattan–Long Branch service in 1884, it continued such service through the summer of 1891. It was then offered sporadically until the end of the 1901 season, when it was permanently dropped. The company continued to serve Rockaway Beach until 1931, its next-to-last season.

The company's service to Rockaway and Long Branch never came close to rivaling its service to Coney Island in terms of frequency, but each service was run for many years. The company also ran other operations for a single season, like the Coney Island–Long Branch service of 1883.

During the company's first year, 1881, it supplemented its regular New York–Coney Island operation with a ferry-like service between lower Manhattan and Bay Ridge, where passengers could continue on to Coney Island aboard trains of the New York and Sea Beach Railroad. In 1892, with Long Branch service temporarily discontinued, the company established a route linking lower Manhattan and downtown Brooklyn with Belden Point, a resort on Long Island Sound.

The Iron Steamboat Company's Manhattan landing sites changed over the years. There was always service from the southern tip of Manhattan Island—North River Pier 1, almost exclusively—but at one time or another Iron Steamboat vessels called at West 23rd Street, West 41st Street, West 129th Street, and East 31st Street; even Yonkers saw scheduled Iron Steamboat service from time to time.

The dual pier arrangement at Coney Island continued for a number of years, although with less complexity than the odd-days/even-days arrangement of 1882. However, by the mid-1890s, the company's boats landed only at the New Iron Pier in Coney Island. At times during the early years, some boats en route to the iron piers in Coney Island also paused at Coney Island Point—the only steamboat landing at Coney Island before the first Iron Pier was built in 1879.

Sunday, June 30, 1901, was an exceptionally hot day in New

York, and many city residents sought relief at Coney Island. The next morning's *New York Herald* contained this critique of the Iron Steamboat Company's role in the exodus: "All (boats) went down the bay crowded to suffocation, loaded to the guards, and some of them careening so heavily toward the shady side that the opposite paddle wheel barely caught the water, while its fellow was churning deep in the brine." The paper went on to say, "When the *Sirius* started down the bay, a little after four o'clock, she was densely packed, and so listed to one side that her funnel leaned like a tree in a gale, at an angle of 8 or 10 degrees."[15]

Steamboat competition between Manhattan and Coney Island emerged from time to time when Iron Steamboat was unable to maintain exclusive landing rights at the resort. In 1895, with Iron Steamboat running only to the New Iron Pier, a competitor came on the scene and used the Old Iron Pier. In 1904, as another example, the steamboats *Dreamland, St. John, City of Lawrence,* and *Rosedale,* running as the "Dreamland Line of Fast Steamers," jointly operated eleven daily round trips opposite the Iron Steamboat Company. They were off the run by 1905, though, as few steamboat operators had the resources to match the frequent service Iron Steamboat normally operated to Coney Island.

On the company's Rockaway route—where only two, three, or at very most four trips a day were the rule—smaller companies could give the larger firm a run for its money, and competition was more common. In the summer of 1913, Iron Steamboat took out an ad in the newspapers because it believed that agents of another company were misleading potential Rockaway-bound passengers. It read, "Special Notice. Strs. Rosedale and Sylvester are NOT operated by this Co. Patrons at W.129th St. Dock are cautioned to buy tickets only at Iron Steamboat Co.'s Box Office."[16]

Over the years, two older and larger boats—with hulls made of wood—joined the original seven "iron steamboats" to give the company added carrying capacity. *Columbia,* a hog-frame side-wheeler built in 1877, was purchased from the Baltimore & Ohio Railroad at the start of the 1900 season and ran for two years before the company sold it to Delaware River interests. Primarily used on the restored Manhattan–Long Branch route, often with *Taurus* as her running mate, she was about forty feet longer (and 700 gross tons larger) than the seven sister ships. The second vessel to join the fleet was *Grand Republic,* built at the John Englis yard in Brooklyn in 1878. She was seventy feet longer (and 1,000 gross tons larger) than the iron steamboats. *Grand Republic*'s normal assignment with Iron Steamboat was the route from Manhattan to Rockaway Beach. Wooden hulled, she became an "honorary iron steamboat" in 1906 and stayed with the fleet until 1917 when she was sold to the McAllister organization's Highlands Navigation Company. Neither the *Columbia* nor the *Grand Republic* was technically owned by the Iron Steamboat Company; they were owned by a subsidiary, the New Jersey Navigation Company.

Before joining the Iron Steamboat fleet, *Columbia* and *Grand Republic* had run together for a time between Manhattan and Rockaway Beach under the house flag of White's Regular Line and later the Knickerbocker Steamboat Company. After *Columbia* joined the Iron Steamboat Company in 1900, *Grand Republic* ran to Rockaway for a few seasons in tandem with *General Slocum,* an excursion boat named after General Henry W. Slocum (see chapter 2).

Columbia and *Grand Republic,* while both running for White's Regular Line in 1881, were among the vessels that competed with the Iron Steamboat Company between New York and Coney Island during the company's first season, pausing at the Iron Pier en route to Rockaway.

The Iron Steamboat Company underwent management changes after about two decades of service. In the late 1890s the company's finances had grown shaky, and in 1902 a reorganization saw a change in the company's formal name. Gone was the Iron Steamboat Company of Long Branch, Incorporated, the firm founded in 1880; in its place was the Iron Steamboat Company of New Jersey, a name that would remain until the end. With this change, a forty-one-year-old Brooklyn native by the name of Frederick Bishop took over operation of the line, eventually advancing to the position of president. Bishop remained in that post until the company was liquidated in 1933.

Bishop was an ardent fisherman, and his interest resulted in an unusual venture for Iron Steamboat. In 1904 he took the steamboat *Taurus* off the Coney Island excursion run and operated her every day as an offshore fishing boat to give city residents an opportunity to experience the pleasures of Bishop's favorite sport out on the ocean fishing banks. In 1915, new federal safety legislation passed in the aftermath of disasters to the *Titanic,* the *Empress of Ireland,* and the *Lusitania* specified the number and kind of life-boats and the number of able-bodied seamen required aboard ocean-going merchant vessels. The U.S. Steamboat Inspection Service decided that when *Taurus* headed out to the fishing banks, she was to be regarded as "a merchant vessel carrying passengers in coastwise trade," and therefore Bishop had to observe a host of new rules and regulations.

Bishop was livid; he threatened to discontinue the fishing trips entirely and spoke of assurances he believed he had received from federal officials that *Taurus* would not be treated as if she were a trans-Atlantic mail boat. But the federal regulation of, and intrusion into, all sorts of commercial activities was the wave of the future, not just a one-time occurrence. When Bishop realized what he was up against, he gave in; and when *Taurus* headed out to the fishing banks in 1916, her capacity had been reduced to 500 people, Captain Henry Beebe conducted mandatory lifeboat drills each day, and two able-bodied seamen and three boat handlers were aboard for each lifeboat, all of which had federally mandated stores of biscuits stashed away to forestall starvation by survivors of any mishap at sea.

A year later, during the wartime summer of 1917, offshore fishing trips aboard *Taurus* took on a new dimension. Posted at the pier from which she sailed each morning was this stern warning: "No alien can go aboard without a passport from his consulate, which must be shown at the gangway and all naturalized Americans must show their citizenship papers, which will be examined by a government official at the pier. No alien enemy can go aboard the TAURUS at all."[17]

With respect to Bishop's impact on the company's regular excursion services, in 1905 he developed a working relationship with one of the three principal amusement parks that had by then come to dominate the Coney Island scene. As a result, a round-trip ticket aboard his company's vessels gave the holder free admission to Dreamland Park. When Dreamland burned to the ground at the start of the 1911 season, Bishop quickly negotiated a new arrangement with George C. Tilyou, the driving force behind rival Steeplechase Park. On the day after the fire, with ashes still smoldering on the site where Dreamland once stood, Bishop's boats deposited

Coney Island–bound patrons at Tilyou's Steeplechase Pier, the third and last major ocean pier to be built at Coney Island. An Iron Steamboat ticket to Coney Island now included free admission to Steeplechase. (For more about Coney Island's amusement parks, see chapter 6.)

The original Iron Pier of 1879 and the second one that was built in 1882 by a subsidiary of the Prospect Park and Coney Island Railroad were effectively destroyed in the Dreamland fire, and their usefulness was negated. Tilyou built Steeplechase Pier in 1907 and, after a fashion, it is still standing at the dawn of the twenty-first century. The pier was deeded over to the City of New York when the Coney Island municipal boardwalk was built in the mid-1920s. Thanks to fire and weather damage over the years—not to mention routine maintenance and modernization—Steeplechase Pier in 2002 is a completely different structure from the one that, in 1911, became the final Coney Island landing spot for the Iron Steamboat Company.

During the early years of the Iron Steamboat Company, many members of its fleet were sent south once the New York excursion season was over to earn money in warm waters rather than sit idle through the northern winter. This was a common practice with many New York steamboat operators, at least through the turn of the century. However, it seems to have been more common among the operators of smaller vessels, like Iron Steamboat, than companies whose fleets consisted of larger steamboats such as the Hudson River Day Line. ("Smaller," in this case means 200 feet or so in length, "larger" means closer to 300 feet.) While the full story of when and where Iron Steamboat vessels worked through the winter remains to be told, it is known that *Cygnus* ran in the Jacksonville area over the winter of 1883–84, with Captain Charles Foster in command.[18] However, as railroads expanded throughout Florida in the early years of the twentieth century, the basic inland and coastal transportation services provided by wintering New York excursion boats grew less important, and the annual trek south became less attractive from an economic perspective. The common cycle for such vessels soon became one of steaming in excursion service during a short summer season in New York, and then going into a prolonged period of inactivity called "winter quarters" until the days grew long again.

From the economic perspective of an excursion boat operator, though, the summer season was always a big risk. As a case in point, on Sunday, September 19, 1915, a week after the Coney Island service had shut down for the season, president Bishop welcomed the Iron Steamboat Company's employees aboard *Grand Republic* for the firm's annual outing. The two-stack, hog-frame side-wheeler pulled away from North River Pier 1 early that morning for a sail up the Hudson to Newburgh. While the outing was largely a day of relaxation and entertainment, it also gave Bishop a chance to talk to his workers about the state of the firm, its finances, and the recently concluded excursion season. His report this day was anything but upbeat. In fact, he was certain that 1915 was the worst business year the company had ever experienced since it ran its first steamboat in 1881. "Reports show that rain fell on ten Sundays out of thirteen during June, July and August; there were eight rainy Saturdays, and it rained on fifty-three days in ninety-two," the president pointed out.[19]

Of course, any commercial venture seeking to turn a profit on the basis of a short summer season at Coney Island—then, now, or ever—is necessarily vulnerable to the weather. At the beginning of the 1915 season, Iron Steamboat had planned to operate 3,556 summer trips between Manhattan and Coney Island. By the end of the season, only 2,732 trips had actually been run. Given the frequency of its service, if a particular sailing had but a few passengers aboard, it was smart business to cancel the trip entirely and hold passengers over for the next boat, often less than an hour away.

As the company's employees headed back down the Hudson that Sunday in September 1915 aboard *Grand Republic,* listening to the steady syncopated slap of the steamer's paddlewheels, they could only look ahead to 1916 and hope the weather would be more auspicious to the excursion boat business than it had been in the season just concluded.[20]

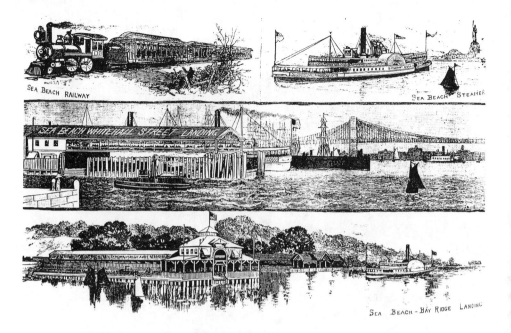

SEA BEACH RAILWAY

SEA BEACH STEAMER

SEA BEACH WHITEHALL STREET LANDING

SEA BEACH - BAY RIDGE LANDING

Excursion Railway Panorama. In July 1885, *Frank Leslie's Illustrated Newspaper* sponsored an all-day excursion to Coney Island over the New York and Sea Beach Railway. Travel from lower Manhattan to the rail head in Bay Ridge was aboard the side-wheel steamboat *Sylvan Dell*. Once passengers arrived at the seashore aboard a NY&SB train, they could visit such attractions as the Balloon Carousel and a hotel built in the form of an elephant *(All photos: Author's collection)*.

Saturday, July 25, 1885.

New York & Sea Beach
RAILWAY CO.

1

BAY RIDGE
—TO—
Coney Island
On above date only.

W. H. Bidgood

G. P. A.

COMPLIMENTARY

The Person using this Pass assumes all risk of Travel.

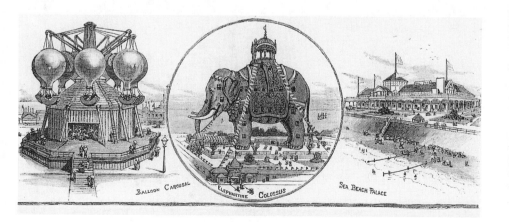

BALLOON CAROUSAL

ELEPHANTINE COLOSSUS

SEA BEACH PALACE

The view looking westward from the top of the Shoot the Chutes ride in Dreamland. Buildings in the foreground are part of the Old Iron Pier, built by Charles Feltman in 1879, where steamboats from New York docked. Off in the distance, the new Pavilion of Fun can be seen at Steeplechase Park. The pavilion at Steeplechase was built in 1908 and Dreamland burned to the ground in 1911, thus bracketing the time when this photo was taken. Inset (left) shows the night lights of Luna Park. (*Both photos: Library of Congress*).

The year is 1910 and bathers are enjoying themselves in the surf. The building looming in the background is Austin Corbin's exclusive Oriental Hotel (*Library of Congress*).

The New Iron Pier.

Published and Copyrighted 1879, by WM. B. HOLMES, New York.   No. 10. EXTERIOR VIEW.

Charles Feltman's Iron Pier, which opened in 1879, was more than simply a place for steamboats to dock; it was a venue that charged an admission fee and featured music and other entertainment *(Library of Congress)*. Side-wheelers of the Iron Steamboat Company were frequent visitors to the Iron Pier *(Author's collection)*. At right: a 1901 newspaper ad for Iron Steamboat services *(Author's collection)*.

Iron Steamboat's *Perseus* approaches North River Pier 1 in lower Manhattan on a run to Coney Island *(Author's collection)*. Below: Among the popular attractions at Dreamland was a miniature railway with real steam engines that hauled patrons around the park *(Library of Congress)*.

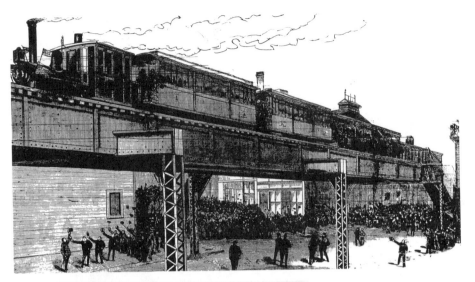

Two drawings depict the inauguration of steam-powered elevated railway service in Brooklyn in 1885. Top rendition, from *Frank Leslie's Illustrated Newspaper,* is a ground-level view, while *Harper's Weekly* sent its artist up on the platform to record the important event *(Both drawings: Author's collection).*

The two drawings depict public transportation during the horsecar era. Drivers worked on an open platform that afforded little protection from the elements. With the advent of electric-powered streetcars in the 1890s, motormen continued to work out-of-doors. In the photo of car no. 2998, the motorman has his left hand on the controller, while his right hand is holding a manual brake handle that had to be cranked vigorously to bring the car to a halt *(Author's collection)*.

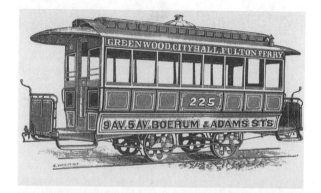

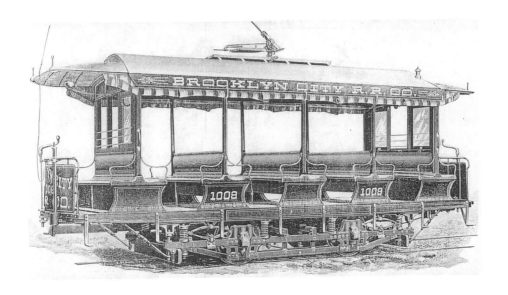

The two drawings show the difference between an open car (top) and a closed car (bottom). Open car no. 1008 is shown without the running board that passengers would later use to board the car. Both of these Brooklyn City streetcars are of "single truck" design, with a fixed frame, two axles, and four wheels *(Author's collection)*.

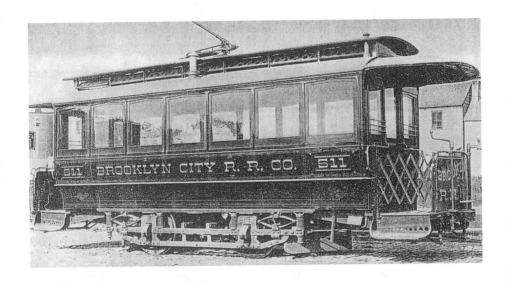

A latter-day view of a Brooklyn elevated train shows a Park Row–bound train on the Fulton Street Line leaving the Franklin Avenue station *(Donald W. Harold)*. Below: Brooklyn Rapid Transit had a large trolley terminal at Brighton Beach to handle the crowds that flocked to the seashore on warm summer days *(Author's collection)*.

An artist's rendition of the Brooklyn Bridge cable railway, including deck-roof cable car, a stationary steam engine that drove the endless cable, and one of the small steam locomotives used to shift cars around the terminals *(Library of Congress)*.

To give the bridge railway greater flexibility for shifting trains at the Manhattan end of the famous span, the elevated appendage in the top photo was built beyond the terminal and out into City Hall Park. Entrance kiosks to the 1904-built Interborough subway are visible below the structure. Lower photo shows the potential for congestion that developed when electric-powered streetcars began to cross the Brooklyn Bridge in 1898 *(Author's collection)*.

Remembrance of times past. A manhole cover outside an electrical substation on the Brighton Line
(top left) bears the initials of the Brooklyn Heights
Railroad, while Brooklyn City is memorialized in
granite atop a building that was once that railroad's 52nd Street Depot in Bay Ridge. At right, a
likeness of General Henry W. Slocum permanently surveys a battlefield at Gettysburg where
he won fame before turning to such peaceful pur-
suits as managing the Coney Island and Brooklyn
Railroad, and a short street in contemporary Manhattan Beach (below left) memorializes Austin
Corbin. A sign that displayed mass transit options
for passengers entering the Stillwell Avenue Station (lower right) has recently earned retirement,
but outmoded nomenclature from the BMT era
was used long after such terminology had fallen
into official disfavor *(All photos: Author's collection)*.

Excursion Railways
(1864–1890)

As CONEY ISLAND GREW in popularity as a seasonal seaside resort, five steam railways were constructed in Kings County in the 1860s and the 1870s to carry passengers there from the southern limits of the city of Brooklyn or from steamboat and ferry connections with Manhattan. The rights-of-way used by four of the five excursion railways remain in operation in the twenty-first century as elements of the subway network of New York City Transit; the fifth was abandoned in the early decades of the twentieth century. In addition to the five excursion railways that provided service to and from Coney Island, several kinds of intra-island railways were constructed to link sections of Coney Island with one another, and the area saw a variety of other short-lived steam railroad ventures. By every measure, the excursion railways constituted the largest and most distinctive early transport system to and from Coney Island.

THE BROOKLYN, BATH AND CONEY ISLAND RAILROAD

Each of the five steam-powered excursion railways enjoys unique characteristics. An operation that began during the Civil War as the Brooklyn, Bath and Coney Island Railroad (BB&CI) was the first of the breed. However, when it carried its initial passengers in the summer of 1864, it was not a steam-powered excursion railroad, but a horse-drawn railway not that much different in operation from typical city streetcars or from the service provided by the Coney Island and Brooklyn Railroad.

More important than the new road's initial source of power, though, was the nature of the service it provided. While many of the other Coney Island excursion railways saw their mission as speeding across the lightly settled flatlands in southern Kings County so passengers from the city of Brooklyn could reach the oceanfront at Coney Island in the least time and with the least bother, the BB&CI had an important intermediate market it wished to serve along the way.

Bath Beach, named after the famous spa city of Bath, England, was both a seasonal resort on the shore of Gravesend Bay in the town of New Utrecht, and a community with a year-round residential population. As an early seashore resort, Bath Beach was never the equal of Coney Island in scope or size, although it did boast such attractions as mechanical amusements, a bathing beach, and a steamboat landing at one time or other. Bath Beach was a sufficiently important source of passenger traffic that the BB&CI was laid out so it would reach Coney Island via Bath Beach and link the city of Brooklyn with both.

Construction of the new railway began in 1862, the same year the Coney Island and Brooklyn Railroad inaugurated horsecar service to the shore. The company's northern terminal was an off-street depot in Brooklyn on Fifth Avenue between 26th and 27th Streets and opposite Green-wood Cemetery, which passengers could reach from downtown Brooklyn aboard horse-drawn streetcars. To this day, the cemetery preserves the older and hyphenated rendition of its name, unlike Greenwood, the neighborhood adjacent to the cemetery (see map 2).

Railway service was inaugurated between the 27th Street terminal and Bath Beach on June 4, 1864, and it was this initial service that used horse-drawn railcars. The company's right-of-way was largely along such thoroughfares as Fifth Avenue and New Utrecht Avenue.

In 1867, three years after service was inaugurated between Greenwood and Bath Beach, the road was extended to Coney Island. It was also during the late 1860s that steam-powered trains at first supplemented and eventually replaced the company's original horse-drawn equipment. Documentation about precisely when the company shifted from animal-powered cars to trains hauled by steam locomotives is scanty, but it seems that by the time the BB&CI reached Coney Island in 1867, the company had begun to use mechanical motive power.

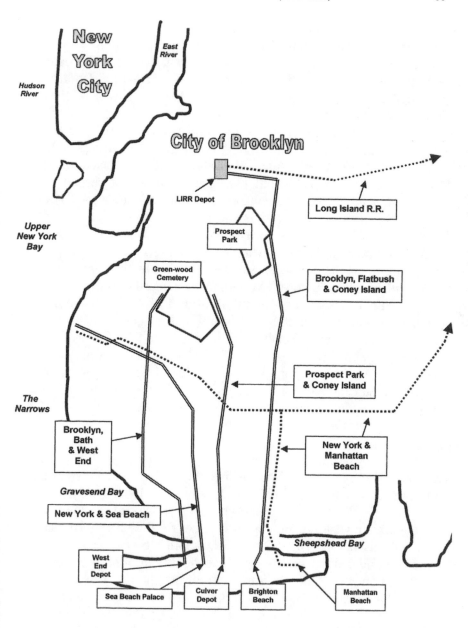

Map 2: Relative orientation of the five major
Coney Island excursion railroads.

The BB&CI underwent a series of corporate realignments in the years between its founding and 1890. The first change came on September 18, 1868, when the company was sold under foreclosure proceedings and control passed into the hands of C. Godfrey Gunther, a wealthy merchant who had served as mayor of New York City between 1864 and 1866.[1] In keeping with a fairly common convention in nineteenth-century railroading, the BB&CI was frequently identified by the name of its principal and so was commonly called "Gunther's Road." By 1882, Gunther's Road owned and operated six steam locomotives and twenty-eight passenger cars, and it carried almost 400,000 passengers each year.[2] The company's terminal on Coney Island occupied roughly the same site that today's massive subway station does, which is to say it was on the mainland side of what is now Surf Avenue just east of the point where it intersects Stillwell Avenue. In the mid-to-late nineteenth century, before anyone had ever heard of Surf or Stillwell Avenues, passengers alighting from BB&CI trains found themselves in a section of Coney Island that included hotels, restaurants, and pavilions. For most of its days, the BB&CI terminal in Coney Island was called West End Depot. The railroad later built a storage yard and maintenance facility for its rolling stock at a place called Unionville on the inland side of Coney Island Creek, close to where Cropsey and 26th Avenues intersect today.

Godfrey Gunther's control of the BB&CI would not endure. Long plagued by inadequate earnings, and not at all helped by an economic downturn that the entire county suffered in 1883, the company was reorganized as the Brooklyn, Bath and West End Railroad Company (BB&WE) on December 5, 1885. Ownership of Gunther's Road was now largely in the hands of a group of Philadelphia investors. A few years afterward, the line's northern terminal was shifted from 27th Street to 36th Street where Coney Island–bound trains could be fed passengers not only by surface horsecars operating along Fifth Avenue from the heart of Brooklyn—as had been the case at 27th Street—but also, after 1890, by new steam-powered, elevated trains operating along a new line built over Fifth Avenue by the Brooklyn Elevated Railroad Company. Why duplicate and parallel the newer and faster elevated service, the company's executives reasoned, if most connections would take place at 36th Street anyway?

The year before the new elevated line was extended out Fifth Avenue to 36th Street, the BB&WE joined forces with another of the Coney Island excursion railways, the Prospect Park and Coney Island, to construct a joint facility called Union Depot at 36th Street and Fifth Avenue. Here passengers heading for the seashore could conveniently change from elevated trains out of downtown Brooklyn to whichever of the excursion railways suited their recreational purposes. To avoid senseless competition between the two roads, both agreed to charge Coney Island–bound passengers boarding trains at Union Depot the same fare. In addition, the two companies agreed to pool and split evenly all ticket revenue generated at the new depot. (More on the Prospect Park and Coney Island shortly; more on Brooklyn elevated railways in chapter 5.)

The BB&WE had its eye on another source of Coney Island–bound passengers—the waterfront area to the west of Union Depot, where the New York and South Brooklyn Ferry and Transportation Company had instituted ferry service in 1887 between the foot of 39th Street in Brooklyn and Whitehall Street at the southern tip of Manhattan Island. The ferry company's Whitehall Street slip was adjacent to the South Ferry terminal of various elevated railways that were being built in Manhattan in the late 1870s. Gaining access to the foot of 39th Street in Brooklyn became an important strategic objective of the railway, since the ferry line represented a link with the new elevated railways in Manhattan and the Coney Island–bound traffic they could be expected to originate. "The effort of the Brooklyn, Bath and West End railroad has been continuous to reach the water front, for on that is believed to rest its future," said the *Brooklyn Daily Eagle*.[3]

Reaching the Brooklyn waterfront was not easy. The business of railway franchise rights and leases was complex, and it was not until 1892 that the BB&WE was able to negotiate with the South Brooklyn Railway and Terminal Company and secure trackage rights through a railroad cut the latter company had built parallel to 39th Street between Ninth and Third Avenues. Since local property owners were adamantly opposed to the idea of steam-powered railroad trains operating over city streets in this area, the South Brooklyn company's cut was the only way that trains could reach the ferry slip. Building the cut required the excavation of 700,000 cubic yards of material and the construction of eight bridges to carry thoroughfares across the right-of-way. The *New York Times* described the South Brooklyn Railway and Terminal Company as "one of the most costly in the country." While this was surely hyperbole, it does suggest that the railway cut was not an incidental transportation investment.[4]

Negotiations between the two railroads could not be concluded rapidly, and the South Brooklyn cut was largely unused for several years while discussions continued between its owner and the BB& WE. By the summer of 1892, the two companies reached an agreement. While Union Depot at 36th Street and Fifth Avenue remained the BB&WE's principal northern terminal, certain trains to and from Coney Island began operating through the cut and down to the ferry slip in mid-July of that year.

"South Brooklyn" is a recurring title in the nineteenth-century Kings County railways. Brooklyn City acquired franchise rights from a street railway that was called the South Brooklyn Street Railroad Company, for instance, and we have just learned of the New York and South Brooklyn Ferry and Transportation Company. The South Brooklyn Railway and Terminal Company, whose tracks the BB&WE used to reach the ferry slip at the foot of 39th Street in 1892 is yet another company that identified itself with the words "South Brooklyn."

The South Brooklyn Railway and Terminal Company did not envision itself as an operating railway. From the outset, its corporate purpose was to build the cut and earn revenue from trackage rights agreements executed with other railroads. The company also built an impressive passenger station close to the 39th Street ferry slips, an eight-track facility whose platforms were protected from the weather by a roof that was 600 feet long and 150 feet wide.[5] While the company hoped to earn money by leasing this facility to other railroads, the terminal was never used for its intended purpose, and it remained empty until converted into a repair facility for Brooklyn elevated trains at the turn of the twentieth century.

Some years later, in 1896, the South Brooklyn Railway and Terminal Company was reported as interested in turning itself into an operating railroad by building an electrified line eastward from the end of the cut all the way to Jamaica in direct competition with the

Long Island Railroad. The *Eagle* reported, "This road, if built, will pass through property to be acquired by condemnation proceedings and is to cross most of the streets below grade. In connection with this enterprise the Terminal company has planned enormous improvements to its water front property including slips, which, it is said, will give five miles of dock room."[6]

Between 1862 and early 1892, the first of the Coney Island excursion railways advanced from a horse-powered railway linking Brooklyn and Bath Beach into a steam-powered service to and from Coney Island with dual northern terminals. By 1891, before the connecting link to the 39th Street ferry was in operation, the BB&WE owned seven steam locomotives and forty-seven passenger cars; during 1890 the company transported 922,102 passengers.[7] Important developments that affected the BB&WE after it began running trains down to the waterfront in 1892 are discussed in chapter 6.

The first of the Coney Island excursion railways—the BB&WE, nee the BB&CI—was never an outstanding success as a commercial enterprise. What may seem imponderable is that, during the very years when its economic performance was least impressive, other investors were motivated to finance and build four additional excursion railways to Coney Island.

THE PROSPECT PARK AND CONEY ISLAND RAILROAD

The second nineteenth-century steam railroad to reach Coney Island did so during the summer of 1875, eight years after the BB& CI extended its service to the shore and thirteen years after horsecars of the Coney Island and Brooklyn Railroad made their initial landfall on the island. The company called itself the Prospect Park and Coney Island Railroad (PP&CI), and its initial service involved two distinct modes of travel. It operated conventional city streetcars from points in the city of Brooklyn as far away as the East River ferry landings. These carried passengers southward toward the Prospect Park area primarily by way of Park and Vanderbilt Avenues. Just beyond Prospect Park on the eastern side of Greenwood Cemetery at Ninth Avenue and 20th Street—a point roughly halfway between Fulton Ferry and Coney Island—passengers disembarked from their horse-drawn city streetcars and boarded steam-powered trains for the final six-mile trip to the oceanfront.

The PP&CI enterprise, which was organized on September 3, 1874, and awarded a state charter on October 9 of that same year, was spearheaded by Andrew N. Culver. Culver was born in Northport, Long Island, in 1831 but lived most of his life in Brooklyn. As a young man he studied law, and shortly after the Civil War he was elected to the New York state legislature. Politics, though, did not prove to be Culver's forte, and he soon turned to the challenges represented by the newly emerging street railway industry. He was one of the promoters of Brooklyn's Crosstown Railroad, a company that was chartered in April 1872, linked Erie Basin and Long Island City, and was eventually absorbed by the larger Brooklyn City Railroad. (As mentioned in chapter 2, it was the Crosstown Railroad that also provided the Slocums, both father and son, with their earliest street railway experience.) Culver also became interested in the development of tourist and amusement attractions at Coney Island, an activity that helps explain his interest in building a new railway to bring customers to the seashore. His PP&CI Railroad began service in June 1875.

The right-of-way of Culver's excursion railway largely followed the alignment of an old and important Kings County thoroughfare, Gravesend Avenue. The new railway crossed Coney Island Creek close by the point where the Shell Road of 1829 reached Coney Island. Culver's new railway sought to develop an important customer base among seasonal travelers to and from the shore. However, because Gravesend Avenue passed through the very heart of the nineteenth-century Kings County town of Gravesend on its way to Coney Island, the railway's location ensured a source of steady, year-round passenger traffic.

As construction of the new railroad to Coney Island was entering its final phases in the spring of 1875, Culver still hoped to put the entire line into operation by mid-June. But the outer end of the line, the final mile or so across Coney Island Creek to West Brighton, was not quite ready. Thus, the *Brooklyn Daily Eagle* was forced to report on June 19, 1875, "The announcement in the EAGLE of last evening that [the PP&CI] would be open for public travel to Coney Island on and after to-morrow (Sunday), was premature. It appears that a local train for the accommodation of the residents of Gravesend and Parkville is run hourly from Green-wood to Gravesend, and that the company will not run trains through to Coney Island until Friday of next week."⁸ The *Eagle's* prediction proved accurate, and PP&CI trains reached Coney Island on June 27, 1875.

Culver's PP&CI Railroad underwent a variety of corporate adjustments over the years. In 1878, a mere three years after the line opened, fifty-six-year-old Andrew Culver announced that he planned to divest himself of all his railway holdings and retire from active business, citing both the state of his own health and what he felt were endless frustrations in dealing with public officials over railway matters as the reasons for his action. "Mr. Culver said last evening that when he advertised the sale of his stock, he did so with the intention of disposing of his business and retiring from active life. He said he had been beset by Brooklyn politicians on all sides, but that he did not propose to 'bleed like a martyr,'" reported the *Eagle*.⁹

Culver owned 3,739 of the 5,000 shares that the PP&CI had issued—the rest were held by friends of Culver. However, on June 26, 1878, when Culver's shares were put up for bid, no offers were received. The holdings were "bid in" by a representative of Culver himself, and any plans for retirement were put off for another day—a day that would not dawn for several decades.

In 1886, the PP&CI divested itself of its street railway operations on the Brooklyn end of the line and conveyed this service to "Deacon" William Richardson's Atlantic Avenue Railroad. Following his stint on the Brooklyn Crosstown Railroad, Culver had associated himself with a company called the Park and Vanderbilt Avenue Horse Railroad, and it was this enterprise that he later combined with his new PP&CI to create a transport link from the East River to the Atlantic Ocean. Between 1875 and 1886, the street railway and the excursion road were jointly managed. In 1881, for instance, a formal report that Culver submitted to New York state officials spoke of a "Brooklyn Division" of the PP&CI as well as a "West Brighton Beach Division."¹⁰ The former was made up of the horse-drawn streetcars that operated over Park and Vanderbilt Avenues, while the latter consisted of the steam-powered excursion trains that ran between Greenwood and Coney Island.

The 1886 transaction between Culver and Richardson was a

lease, which was converted into an out-and-out purchase the following year. Andrew Culver informed the Street Railway Association of the State of New York of this change in status, by letter, on January 14, 1886. *"Dear Sir*—I have to inform you officially that the Prospect Park and Coney Island Railroad Company has disposed of, by lease, to the Atlantic Avenue Railroad Company, of Brooklyn, all its horsecar railroad franchises and property in the city of Brooklyn, for the full term of its corporate existence, and that hereafter the same will be represented in your Association by that Company." Culver then went on to say that since the PP&CI would no longer be operating streetcars, membership in a street railway trade association was no longer appropriate.[11]

Divesting himself of his street railway division in 1886 did not mean that Culver intended to be less active in the railway business. Instead, Culver and his railway would concentrate on what was thought to be an important core business, year-round suburban service between Greenwood and Gravesend, plus seasonal service beyond to Coney Island. Culver also hoped to devote more time and attention to his many Coney Island entertainment investments, which would be consistent with his decision to reduce his railway holdings to the line that brought excursionists to the seashore.

In 1879, Culver chartered a new company, a subsidiary of the PP&CI, whose purpose was to build a two-and-a-half mile westward extension beyond the PP&CI's depot in West Brighton to the steamboat landing on Gravesend Bay at Coney Island Point. This was an important expansion that had a major impact on the development of the amusement areas in West Brighton since it allowed steamboat passengers arriving at Coney Island Point to travel to West Brighton quickly and easily and spend an enjoyable day there. By this time, Coney Island Point had earned a reputation for tawdriness; although many excursionists traveled there by steamboat for respectable activities like ocean bathing and enjoying a shore dinner, its bawdiness, and even lawlessness, were said to be manifest and unavoidable. However, the ability to catch a train immediately after coming ashore at Coney Island Point allowed steamboat passengers to bypass this unsavory underbelly of Coney Island and continue on to West Brighton for a more respectable day's enjoyment.

This subsidiary company was called the New York and Coney Island Railroad, and its first train ran on June 9, 1879. Later that summer, the New York and Coney Island was formally acquired by the PP&CI under the terms of a ninety-five-year lease. The extension was internally identified as the "Coney Island Beach Division" within Culver's overall railway enterprise.

In 1881 the PP&CI Railroad sought and—after a bit of controversy and opposition—eventually received authorization to build an ocean pier at Coney Island. The company planned to build a facility that would bring steamboats from New York to a spot in West Brighton that was directly across from the terminal where PP&CI trains boarded passengers. Eventually, joint fares were established between the PP&CI and the Iron Steamboat Company, tariffs that enabled passengers headed for a day at Coney Island to travel one way by sea, the other by rail. Culver's iron pier—the New Iron Pier, as it was popularly called—which was built and managed by yet another subsidiary company, the Brighton Navigation and Pier Company, opened in 1882.

Operating headquarters for Andrew Culver's excursion railway were located in the company's in-town terminal at Ninth Avenue and 20th Street, adjacent to Green-Wood Cemetery. Here most maintenance was carried out on the railway's rolling stock, and here the line's administrative offices were located. The company's executive offices, though, were in downtown Brooklyn at 16 Court Street.

Culver and the PP&CI also developed a working alliance with the Long Island Railroad (LIRR), a relationship that would grow from modest cooperation into something considerably more formal and extensive in the 1890s. By the late 1880s, one of the seven seats on the PP&CI board of directors was held by Austin Corbin, who was chief officer of the LIRR. The PP&CI–LIRR cooperative efforts are discussed more fully in chapter 6.

The first PP&CI–LIRR agreement gave Culver's railroad trackage rights over the LIRR between Parkville and Bay Ridge along an east-west LIRR line that bisected Kings County while connecting Bay Ridge with East New York and, ultimately, other points on the LIRR. This agreement meant that, in addition to boarding Coney Island–bound passengers at the line's original Greenwood terminal at Ninth Avenue and 20th Street, PP&CI trains made connections with steamboats to and from Manhattan in Bay Ridge on the shore of Upper New York Bay.

As mentioned earlier, Culver became a partner in 1889 in the construction of the new Union Depot for Coney Island–bound trains on the western edge of Green-wood Cemetery at Ninth Avenue and 36th Street. Culver realized that once Brooklyn Elevated's new Fifth Avenue line was in operation from downtown Brooklyn to 36th Street, it would provide a far better connecting service for his Coney Island–bound trains than did the horse-drawn street-cars his passengers had to ride to reach Ninth Avenue and 20th Street. However, for its trains to enter Union Depot, the PP&CI had to execute a trackage rights agreement with the BB&WE, a lease that gave the PP&CI access to 0.22 miles of the older company's right-of-way. In addition, to get from its own right-of-way along Gravesend Avenue to BB&WE trackage at the outer limits of the new Union Depot, PP&CI had to build a mile-and-a-half of new right-of-way from Kensington Junction on Gravesend Avenue to Union Depot. Another subsidiary company, this one called the Prospect Park and South Brooklyn Railroad, was created for this purpose. Once the new connection was finished, the Prospect Park and South Brooklyn was leased to the PP&CI.

Before extending the PP&CI to Fifth Avenue and 36th Street, where Coney Island passengers could change to the new elevated railway along Fifth Avenue, Culver had explored the possibility of constructing an elevated railway between the Brooklyn end of the new East River Bridge and the Ninth Avenue and 20th Street terminal of his Coney Island excursion railway. In the early 1880s, Culver was instrumental in establishing a company called the East River Bridge and Coney Island Steam Transit Company, which attempted to secure authorization from Brooklyn's political establishment to build a line that would have largely followed the same route Brooklyn Elevated's Fifth Avenue Line eventually did— Hudson Avenue to Flatbush Avenue to Fifth Avenue—except it would have angled southward to an outer terminal at Ninth Avenue and 20th Street rather than continue directly over Fifth Avenue to 36th Street.

Rival Brooklyn Elevated eventually secured municipal authorization to build a line in this corridor. However, before all plans were complete, Brooklyn Elevated proposed a branch line that would have left the Fifth Avenue Line at Prospect Avenue and reached the northern terminal of the PP&CI through a subway tunnel. Such a branch was never incorporated into the Fifth Avenue Line and, instead, Culver rerouted his excursion railway into the new Union Depot at 36th Street and Fifth Avenue. The important point, though, is that Culver realized the importance of linking the PP&CI with whatever new elevated railway line might be constructed outward from downtown Brooklyn. And well that he did, for it was the construction of elevated rapid transit lines in Brooklyn—and the connections they established with the older Kings County excursion railways to and from Coney Island—that permanently altered the very nature of the excursion railways and began their permanent transformation into something very different.

With the shift of its northern terminal to 36th Street and Fifth Avenue in 1889, PP&CI service between the line's original terminal at Ninth Avenue and 20th Street and the point where the line now veered westward to reach Union Depot was reduced to a shuttle operation. By 1890, Culver's PP&CI Railroad owned eleven steam locomotives and fifty-six passenger cars and carried 1.2 million passengers each year.[12]

During the rambunctious decade of the 1890s, the PP&CI Railroad became involved in further corporate developments before it became the Culver Line of New York City Transit in even later years. These developments are treated in subsequent chapters.

THE NEW YORK AND MANHATTAN BEACH RAILROAD

A company that began operations in 1877 as the New York and Manhattan Beach Railroad (NY&MB) was, without question, the most unusual of the five nineteenth-century Coney Island excursion railways. Unlike the other four, all of which remain in operation today as rapid transit branches of the New York City subway system, the NY&MB was largely abandoned in 1924. The line's final and most important leg southward across Kings County to the Manhattan Beach section of Coney Island operated its last passenger train less than a decade after the end of the First World War. And yet, because the railroad was so unusual and was more than a single-purpose excursion railway to and from the seashore, a portion of the right-of-way its trains once traveled still remains in freight railway service in the early years of the twenty-first century.

The NY&MB would eventually become part of the LIRR, a fact that substantially impacted its subsequent development. But this is to get too far ahead of the story too quickly. Let us begin, instead, in the summer of 1873. A wealthy New York banker, financier, and sometime railroad executive by the name of Austin Corbin was told by physicians that his child suffered an illness that should be treated with a quiet summer's stay at a comfortable seashore retreat. There the youngster could relax, be refreshed by gentle ocean breezes, and breathe clean and fresh sea air. This was a commonly recommended course of medical therapy at a time when physicians did not have recourse to the broad range of medications that became available in a later era.

Corbin clearly had the financial resources to take his child anywhere—Bar Harbor, Fire Island, or the south of France. However, because business interests demanded his presence in New York City, Corbin and his family selected a small but fashionable hotel in Coney Island for their child's summer of therapy. Corbin traveled back and forth between office and oceanfront in a private, horse-drawn carriage over the Shell Road.

Corbin's child responded well to the ocean climate. The summer at the shore also had an impact on Austin Corbin himself, although the effect was neither medical nor restorative. Corbin was impressed by the potential that the largely undeveloped eastern end of Coney Island represented as a location for a high-quality resort hotel that would cater to a far more upscale clientele than did the less-refined establishments then characteristic of the West Brighton area adjacent to the terminal of Andrew Culver's PP&CI Railroad. Needless to say, Corbin held in total disdain the even coarser atmosphere and clientele that could be found further west at Mike Norton's Coney Island Point.

Corbin quickly put together a group of financiers. Most were supposedly from Boston, which should come as no surprise since Corbin himself was a New Englander whose business career began in his native Newport, New Hampshire. In the summer of 1878, five years after Corbin's first visit to Coney Island, his new Manhattan Beach Hotel opened for business. It would be followed two years later by a second and equally palatial oceanfront resort, the Oriental Hotel, located to the east of the original facility.

Designing and building a large, seaside hotel was one thing. Arranging an easy way for customers to reach the oceanfront was quite another. The summer that he spent traveling between Coney Island and New York City by horse-drawn carriage was more than enough to convince Corbin that a better alternative was needed if his new hotels were to succeed.

And so, parallel with the development of the resort properties, Corbin's syndicate constructed the NY&MB, a new railway line that would bring guests from New York City to the beach. Among the characteristics that distinguished the new railroad from, say, Andrew Culver's PP&CI or Godfrey Gunther's BB&CI was its emphasis on a market composed primarily of people who lived in Manhattan, not Brooklyn. Although Culver and Gunther might have been content to see their primary customers as folks who were willing to ride a Brooklyn streetcar to the northern terminal of an excursion railway before heading overland to West Brighton, Corbin had something very different in mind. Austin Corbin wanted to provide the most direct travel possible between Manhattan Beach and upscale neighborhoods of New York City. Indeed, calling his newly developed area Manhattan Beach was not accidental. It was part of a very carefully crafted marketing strategy designed to identify the customers Corbin wished to lure to the new resort.

Linking New York City with Coney Island in the 1870s necessarily demanded a combined rail-water route. The NY&MB Railroad approached this challenge by acquiring control of a new east-west railroad whose initial leg had opened in 1876 and whose intended purpose was to run from the shore of Upper New York Bay in the Bay Ridge section of Kings County to Jamaica, in neighboring Queens County. This was the New York, Bay Ridge and Jamaica Railroad, a company that had taken over earlier rights that had been secured by the New York and Hempstead Railroad, a company whose route would have extended even further eastward than Jamaica. On its own, the New York, Bay Ridge and Jamaica never managed to get anything in operation beyond a modest, two-mile shuttle service linking the Bay Ridge waterfront—and a steamboat connection to New York—with a station on the BB&CI

Railroad at an inland point called Bath Junction. Here passengers were able to transfer to Coney Island–bound trains of the BB&CI. (To find the site of Bath Junction on a contemporary map of Brooklyn, go to the point where New Utrecht Avenue intersects 62nd Street and New York City Transit's N train crosses the route of the B train.)

Corbin and his associates acquired a controlling interest in the New York, Bay Ridge and Jamaica and leased it to the NY&MB. The New York, Bay Ridge and Jamaica line was extended eastward using a franchise the company already held over a right-of-way it already owned to a point in Flatbush close to the intersection of today's East 15th Street and Avenue H, a location the railway identified as Manhattan Beach Junction. Here trains made a ninety-degree turn to the south and continued along newly constructed NY&MB trackage for the final leg of the trip from Bay Ridge to the east end of Coney Island, the place Corbin called Manhattan Beach.

The first ceremonial train over the new line operated on July 19, 1877. Corbin and a party of dignitaries boarded the steamboat *Norwalk* at the foot of Whitehall Street in Manhattan and proceeded to the railhead in Bay Ridge. There they boarded a ten-car train hauled by a locomotive that bore the name *Manhattan*. While Grafulla's Seventh Regimental Band delivered a spirited rendition of "Hail Columbia," the train moved off. It proceeded first to East New York, where more dignitaries were taken aboard, and then it backtracked to Manhattan Beach Junction for the final leg of the trip southward to the seashore. The Manhattan Beach Hotel was still a year away from completion, although construction was sufficiently well along so the guests could enjoy a dinner of "excellent clam chowder, salmon, salads in chicken and lobster, roast and boiled meats, tongues and chicken, for the earlier courses, with jellies, russes, creams, etc., for the later, made more palatable by unstinted allowance of champagne (the latter said to have been of the best quality by those who indulged) the whole concluding with delicious *café et noir*."[13] Manhattan Beach, it would seem safe to say, would not be a travel destination for those whose idea of an appropriate Coney Island meal was a hot dog with sauerkraut and mustard.

Because the Manhattan Beach Hotel was not ready for paying

guests in 1877, the new railway during its first year of operation was largely used to haul construction materials and construction workers to and from Manhattan Beach—instead of upscale passengers from New York heading for an equally upscale resort hotel.

Corbin never regarded the Bay Ridge steamboat connection as the perfect way to tap the New York City markets he intended as the core of his new resort hotel's business. His syndicate's acquisition of the New York, Bay Ridge and Jamaica Railroad included a right-of-way that extended eastward from the connection with the NY&MB to East New York. In a complex series of deals—combinations of purchases and leases—Corbin was able to piece together a right-of-way beyond East New York to the banks of the East River in Greenpoint, where a short ferry ride across the river would link his trains to and from Manhattan Beach with fashionable residential districts on the east side of Manhattan. Trains began operating between this new Greenpoint terminal and Manhattan Beach on May 15, 1878, the same day that Corbin's Manhattan Beach Hotel opened its doors for business.[14]

The new railway that Corbin put together through construction, acquisition, and lease was essentially a T-shaped operation. Manhattan Beach and the Atlantic Ocean were at the base of the T, and from here trains headed north until they reached the cross member at Manhattan Beach Junction. If they turned west at the intersection, they eventually reached the steamboat connection in Bay Ridge; if they turned east and followed a somewhat longer course—the T analogy gets a little strained at this point—they wound up in Greenpoint, where passengers could make connections to New York by ferryboat. (In later years, Long Island City would became a substitute East River terminal for trains to and from Manhattan Beach.)

Another unusual feature of the NY&MB Railroad is that it was built as a "narrow-gauge" railroad. Conventional railways are said to be "standard gauge" if their rails are spiked down four feet, eight-and-a-half inches apart. The PP&CI, the BB&CI, and even typical urban street railways such as the Brooklyn City Railroad were all standard gauge. Corbin, however, selected a narrow-gauge specification for his new line; it was built with its rails three feet apart. Cars and locomotives could thus be somewhat

smaller—and less expensive—than standard-gauge equivalents.
Corbin believed that, given the largely seasonal nature of the business, narrow-gauge track was a perfect choice for his new enterprise.[15]

While the NY&MB itself was narrow gauge from the outset,
Corbin's track crews had to regauge the New York, Bay Ridge
and Jamaica from its original standard gauge. Corbin was able to
acquire a narrow-gauge locomotive and a train of luxury passenger
cars that had operated in Philadelphia during the 1876 Centennial
Exposition. (It was this train that was used for the special inaugural trip in July 1877.) Additional cars and locomotives were acquired as traffic grew during the new railway's early years of
service. By 1878, the year that both the Greenpoint extension and
the Manhattan Beach Hotel opened for business, the company
owned thirteen locomotives and almost a hundred passenger cars,
a substantial fleet for a Coney Island excursion railway. While the
company made some early efforts to run trains until the onset of
winter each year, the NY&MB soon established itself as a high-
summer operation whose first train each year operated in mid-to-
late May, and whose final train of the season ran in late September
or early October.

One unexpected dividend that the NY&MB Railroad quickly delivered was that it convinced its principal, Austin Corbin, that the
New York railway industry represented an appropriate and challenging venue for his own continued involvement.[16] In 1881, Corbin managed to have himself appointed receiver of what was then
a bankrupt Long Island Railroad. With his skillful hand on the
throttle, the receivership was discharged less than a year later,
control of the company was returned to its board of directors, and
Corbin was promptly named president of the company (a post he
would hold until his sudden death in 1896).

Corbin's tenure as president of the LIRR would affect the story
of mass transportation in Kings County in a variety of ways. For
the NY&MB, a benchmark development was the leasing of the
NY&MB by the LIRR in 1883, when both companies were under
the control of Austin Corbin. In his definitive treatment of U.S.
narrow-gauge railways, transportation historian George W. Hilton
has suggested that the NY&MB "was successful enough that the
railroad might have survived for some years as an isolated narrow

gauge [railway]."[17] But once the NY&MB was acquired by LIRR, its narrow-gauge lines were incompatible with an otherwise standard-gauge rail network. Before the onset of summer service to Manhattan Beach in 1883, crews were put to work and the line was regauged as standard.

The effective merger of the NY&MB and the LIRR allowed some Manhattan Beach–bound trains to originate at the LIRR's Brooklyn terminal at Flatbush and Atlantic Avenues and connect with the NY&MB in East New York, even though this was anything but a direct route. Manhattan Beach–bound trains of the NY&MB primarily started their trips from the LIRR's principal western terminal in Long Island City, where passengers could cross to and from Manhattan by ferry. With this shift to Long Island City, the NY&MB's original Greenpoint terminal was served by shuttle trains for several seasons, but abandoned outright in 1886.

A fascinating side issue involving the NY&MB Railroad involves a short-lived railway enterprise that was an effort by Corbin to tap Brooklyn markets that he was otherwise content to shun. It was a steam-powered line that was less than four miles long, which began at the southern end of Prospect Park near the intersection of Flatbush Avenue and Malbone Street. Here streetcar connections were available from a variety of points in Brooklyn, and the new line proceeded in a generally southerly direction to a connection with the NY&MB at a place called Kings County Central Junction. (Using contemporary landmarks as coordinates, Kings County Central Junction was close to the point where Bedford Avenue crosses the Brooklyn College campus today.)

The narrow-gauge Kings County Central did not proceed directly from the southern end of Prospect Park to the right-of-way of the NY&MB, though. It veered eastward in an effort to serve such important institutions—and sources of passenger traffic—as Kings County Penitentiary, Kings County Hospital, and Holy Cross Cemetery before reaching the NY&MB right-of-way at Kings County Central Junction.[18]

The Kings County Central, which was organized in September 1876 by E. B. Litchfield, saw its mission as providing seasonal service between Prospect Park and Manhattan Beach, while providing year-round service to the cemetery and hospital complex.

Under Litchfield, construction work on the line was begun, but it was quickly interrupted by litigation. It was only after Corbin entered the picture and Kings County Central was reconfigured into a feeder line of the NY&MB that an operational segment was completed, with NY&MB equipment and personnel handling all operations over the Kings County Central.

Because the Brooklyn, Flatbush and Coney Island Railroad—a more direct excursion railway that also originated at Flatbush Avenue and Malbone Street—was only days away from completion when service was inaugurated over the Kings County Central Railroad on June 29, 1878, the Litchfield-initiated venture survived for only one summer season. Kings County Central declared bankruptcy in early 1879, and its tracks were pulled up shortly afterward.[19] The Kings County Central Railroad represents but a minor footnote to the story of the NY&MB, and it is virtually a forgotten part of the history of nineteenth-century Coney Island excursion railways.

More about Austin Corbin and his transport ideas is presented in chapter 6. Before concluding this introduction to the NY&MB Railroad, it is necessary to mention that Corbin was infected with a virulent strain of anti-Semitism.

Simply put, Corbin did not welcome Jews at his Manhattan Beach hotels. "We don't want Jewish patronage, and we won't have it if we can help it," Corbin told a reporter in 1879.[20] As might be expected, Corbin insisted that this was merely a business decision and in no sense was he "influenced in this matter by any prejudice against the Jewish religion or even against the race."[21] Other directors of Corbin's Manhattan Beach Improvement Company—the subsidiary company that owned and operated the hotel properties—made an effort to distance themselves from his views, but generally they refused to be quoted directly. A statement issued by the Union of American Hebrew Congregations decried Corbin's policies and concluded, "It is beneath our dignity to take any further notice of so despicable an assailant; we may safely leave our defense to the intelligent and advanced public sentiment of our fellow-citizens, irrespective of creed or race."[22]

Manhattan Beach presents a rich and interesting chapter in the story of Coney Island, and the NY&MB Railroad adds variety to the transportation history of Kings County. It is unfortunate that the individual most responsible for the development of Manhattan Beach, and the railway that served it, perpetuated a disease whose evil dimensions would reach such terrible proportions several decades later.[23] In Manhattan Beach today, Austin Corbin is all but forgotten, although his name is memorialized by a street name—Corbin Place.

THE BROOKLYN, FLATBUSH, AND CONEY ISLAND RAILROAD

The first train to operate over the Brooklyn, Flatbush and Coney Island (BF&CI) Railroad did so on Tuesday afternoon, July 2, 1878, three days after the Kings County Central inaugurated service along a somewhat parallel route. The inaugural train was hauled by a steam locomotive named *John A. Lott,* in honor of a Kings County judge who was the company's first and by this time former president, and it was appropriately decorated with flags and bunting for the ceremonial occasion. It left a station at the southern end of Prospect Park close by the intersection of Flatbush Avenue and Malbone Street at 5:00 P.M. and reached Brighton Beach less than fourteen minutes later. "The big engine . . . puffed and snorted at the station . . . as if impatient to start away on the wings of the wind," reported the *Brooklyn Daily Eagle.*[24] The initial portion of the trip was through tunnels and cuts "50 feet deep that nothing but the sky was visible."[25] Then the train emerged into open country dotted with neat farmhouses that featured blooming kitchen gardens surrounded by fertile potato and melon patches. The fast-stepping inaugural special overtook and passed a two-car, narrow-gauge train of the parallel NY&MB Railroad. Once the trip was concluded, and after a second ceremonial train from Prospect Park had steamed into Brighton Beach several minutes behind the first one, a festive supper of cold meats was served at the Brighton Beach Hotel to more than 1,000 invited guests. Judge Lott addressed the guests, as did his successor as president of the new railway, James N. Smith.

The corporate mission of the new company was to link built-up sections of Kings County with a fashionable seaside resort hotel that faced the ocean at Brighton Beach. In fact, railway and seaside hotel were a joint venture, the latter owned by the former.

"The great resort . . . in the immediate future bids fair to outstrip in popularity its rivals on both sides of the Atlantic," claimed the *Brooklyn Daily Eagle* on the day the railway and resort opened for business.[26]

The exuberance of the hometown newspaper for the new enterprise is certainly understandable. The benefit of hindsight, however, would suggest that the *Eagle*'s superlatives were only correct if one were willing to overlook the considerably more palatial Manhattan Beach Hotel that had opened a month-and-a-half earlier just a mile or so east of the Brighton Beach Hotel.

(There has been some confusion about Brighton Beach and its hotels. The man who pioneered Brighton's first major hotel, the Ocean Hotel of 1873, was William A. Engeman. Engeman was also the principal force behind the Brighton Beach Race Track, which opened in 1879. Engeman had no association, however, with the Brighton Beach Hotel that was built by the BF&CI Railroad and that opened in 1878.)

When the BF&CI Railroad was organized in 1877, it represented a consolidation of two earlier railway ventures that had been incorporated in 1876 with the intention of building parallel and competitive excursion railways between Brooklyn and Coney Island. One was called the Flatbush and Coney Island Park and Concourse Railroad Company, the other the Coney Island and East River Railroad. The two were consolidated as the Brooklyn, Flatbush and Coney Island in 1877.

When the new company inaugurated service at the start of the 1878 summer season, it ran from an in-town terminal at the southeast corner of Prospect Park, known as the Willink Entrance to the park. (It is still the Willink Entrance today, but the name is not commonly used. A Willink family once owned a fashionable home on Ocean Avenue opposite Prospect Park and adjacent to where the BF&CI Railroad would build its Prospect Park station. The building later became the Hotel Melrose and catered to passengers heading for Brighton Beach aboard the new company's trains.)

Investors behind the BF&CI Railroad believed that they had a way of getting their trains closer to the heart of commercial and residential Brooklyn than any of the other excursion railways. Even as the railroad was inaugurating service on that July day, workers were completing a further incursion that would bring the new company's trains closer to the source of its traffic. Any alignment directly through, or even adjacent to, the greensward of Prospect Park was totally out of the question. Prospect Park had been completed in 1874 as a refuge and retreat from precisely the kind of fast-paced industrialism that the new railway represented. So, instead, the line bore slightly to the east and away from a straight-line route into downtown Brooklyn, and made its way up and over Crown Heights. There, the right-of-way crossed the city limits that separated what was then the town of Flatbush on the south from the city of Brooklyn on the north, a political boundary that ran on an east-west course in the vicinity of today's Montgomery Street. Cresting Crown Heights and tunneling under the magnificent boulevard called Eastern Parkway that Frederick Law Olmsted and Calvert Vaux had designed as part of their strategic plan for access to Prospect Park, the new railway found itself making a perpendicular approach to Atlantic Avenue, a major east-west artery. Trains of the LIRR operated on a fenced-in right-of-way in the middle of Atlantic Avenue en route from Jamaica, and points east, to the Brooklyn terminal at Flatbush and Atlantic Avenues.

Contractual arrangements had been made between the BF&CI and the LIRR to allow the new excursion railway's trains to enter the older railroad's trackage at this point and terminate its trains in the latter's Brooklyn depot. Flatbush Avenue itself would have been a shorter and straight-line route between the Willink Entrance to Prospect Park and the LIRR depot. The roundabout course over Crown Heights and down to Atlantic Avenue, though, was an effective substitute, even though at 2.3 miles it was slightly longer than the 1.7-mile direct route.

On August 19, 1878, a month-and-a-half after the railway opened, the final link was ready and the BF&CI began running its trains from Brighton Beach over Crown Heights, onto Atlantic Avenue, and into the LIRR depot at Flatbush and Atlantic, by far the most advantageous Brooklyn terminal any of the Kings County excursion railways would ever enjoy. "The opening of the completed road to the corner of Flatbush and Atlantic avenues considerably increased the traffic over that route, and long into the evening the trains of five and six cars were filled," noted the *Brooklyn Daily Eagle*. "Passengers were delighted with the trip over the new road

and poured blessings on the heads of the projectors of the enterprise, which brought Coney Island almost to their very doors,"
the newspaper continued.[27] LIRR agents sold tickets to Brighton
Beach–bound passengers at Flatbush and Atlantic Avenues, and
the host railroad retained 20 percent of the proceeds for the use
of its facilities.

By September 30, 1879, when the BF&CI had been in operation
for a little more than a year, its fleet consisted of seven steam
locomotives, forty-four passenger cars, and eight freight or express cars. In the twelve-month period prior to that September 30,
the new railroad had carried 873,960 passengers.[28]

Most of its cars were typical railroad-style passenger equipment
of the day. Some cars, however, were adapted to the needs of a
railway whose principal clientele were seasonal travelers headed
for the beachfront. These cars were similar to the open streetcar
that John Stevenson built for the Broadway Railroad. Passengers
sat on wooden benches that ran from one side of the car to the
other; the cars lacked sidewalls and were fully open to the summer
breezes. With the arrival of autumn each year, the open cars were
put in storage until nice weather returned the following spring.

Because BF&CI steam locomotives were commonly turned
around after every trip, the company installed turntables at strategic locations. There was one at Brighton Beach, another at Prospect Park, and a third at Bedford Terminal at Franklin and Atlantic
Avenues—the end of the railway's own right-of-way and the point
where BF&CI trains connected with the LIRR. The BF&CI was
able to use the LIRR's engine facilities—including its turntable—at
the latter's Flatbush and Atlantic terminal in downtown Brooklyn.
The BF&CI Railroad hauled a small amount of freight and express
but, for all of its days, its principal business was moving passengers.

The corporate relationship between the BF&CI and the LIRR
that was so important in providing the excursion railway with an
in-town terminal at Flatbush and Atlantic Avenues proved to be
fragile. The LIRR has a complex history of mergers, takeovers,
and subsidiary companies—which is to say it is cut from the same
cloth as virtually all major U.S. railroads. In 1883, under Austin
Corbin, the NY&MB that closely paralleled the BF&CI became a
subsidiary of the LIRR. The LIRR thus found itself in the awkward

position of providing a direct competitor, the BF&CI, with an advantageous Brooklyn terminal that could adversely impact patronage on its own NY&MB.

On December 14, 1883—supposedly at Austin Corbin's personal direction—the LIRR evicted the BF&CI from its Brooklyn depot after five seasons of service between Brighton Beach and Flatbush and Atlantic Avenues and canceled the contract that permitted BF&CI trains to use LIRR trackage. The excursion railroad found itself cut back to Bedford Terminal at Atlantic and Franklin Avenues, the limit of its own tracks and the point where it had previously joined up with the LIRR. This was too far from the heart of Brooklyn to generate enough passenger traffic to sustain the excursion railway enterprise. Absent the all-important connection with the LIRR and the patronage that was generated at Flatbush and Atlantic Avenues, the expense of building the BF&CI up and over Crown Heights was nothing short of a business folly.

The BF&CI Railroad would eventually prevail over the LIRR in court on this matter, but the case was not settled until 1889. While the case was in progress, the excursion railway was unable to use LIRR trackage. By the time the litigation had run its course, transportation matters had evolved in Brooklyn so as to make the former arrangement unnecessary and irrelevant.

With competition from the NY&MB Railroad and such other excursion railways as Andrew Culver's PP&CI, the BF&CI had little chance of profitability in its truncated form. The company entered receivership on January 16, 1884, a month after the LIRR's action. "Over capitalization" was cited as the technical reason for the move; in simple terms, the railway had no possibility of taking in enough money over its shortened route to pay its bills and service the debt it had incurred.

Two important developments would follow. In 1887, the 1884 receivership was discharged when the company was sold to a group of second-mortgage bond holders of the original company under what was described as an "auction under friendly foreclosure proceedings."[29] Once reorganized, the company was renamed the Brooklyn and Brighton Beach Railroad. Fresh capital became available to restore the line's physical plant, the care and maintenance of which had been somewhat neglected during the years the former company was in receivership. The railway-owned

Brighton Beach Hotel was also in need of work, since the ocean was slowly encroaching on the land where the building stood. The hotel was jacked up, and twenty-four railroad tracks were installed under the 550-by-120-foot wooden structure. With 112 freight cars put in position to bear the weight of the four-story building, the hotel was lowered onto the cars. On April 3, 1888, it was hauled 595 feet inland to a new location by six of the company's locomotives. There it would remain, reasonably high and more or less dry, for the next thirty-five years.

In addition to dragging the company-owned Brighton Beach Hotel back from the brink of destruction, the company made other improvements to the Brighton Beach Line after the reorganization of 1887. Track was realigned and replaced, as necessary; the below-grade cut south of Prospect Park was rebuilt with stone retaining walls; and a new terminal station was constructed at Brighton Beach.

The person who emerged as president of the reorganized railway was James J. Jourdan, a Brooklyn man who had been a member of the board of directors of the BF&CI Railroad and who had played a role in the early development of the Coney Island and Brooklyn. Jourdan was also active in the development of elevated railways in Brooklyn, and his interest in such elevated lines would profoundly change the character of the Brooklyn and Brighton Beach Railroad in the final years of the nineteenth century. As of June 30, 1890, the company owned eight steam locomotives and forty-two passenger cars; its right-of-way between Bedford Terminal and Brighton Beach included twelve bridges or trestles and thirteen grade crossings.[30]

THE NEW YORK AND SEA BEACH RAILROAD

The New York and Sea Beach (NY&SB) Railroad operated its first train to Coney Island on July 18, 1877, a year before the BF&CI inaugurated service. A variety of circumstances, however, kept the new company from being built over the entirety of its intended route until 1879, and the line did not operate at all in 1878. If one regards 1879 as the year the line opened—and ignores the odd bit of service that was provided in 1877—the NY&SB can be called the the newest of the five Coney Island excursion railways.

New York investors behind the NY&SB Railroad had in mind an excursion line that would begin on the shores of Upper New York Bay in Bay Ridge and proceed on a direct route all the way to Coney Island. One minor difficulty the new company quickly ran into was the fact that the chief officer of the potentially competitive BB&CI Railroad, Godfrey Gunther, was unwilling to allow the new line to cross his road at grade at Bath Junction in the town of New Utrecht. Officials from the NY&SB eventually reached an agreement with Gunther, but that was not the only problem the new road faced. Still to be reckoned with was the fact that the New York, Bay Ridge and Jamaica Railroad, which the NY&SB had hoped to use to reach the waterfront from Bath Junction under a trackage rights arrangement, was converted to narrow gauge in 1877 after it had been absorbed by the NY&MB. Standard-gauge trains could—and often did—operate jointly with narrow-gauge ones, but it required the installation of an additional "third rail" to accommodate the larger stock. (Such a third rail bears no relationship to the more common usage of the term in the context of electrified railways.) The New York, Bay Ridge and Jamaica Railroad, however, was unwilling to have its narrow-gauge right-of-way so equipped, and the NY&SB was once again thwarted in its effort to reach tidewater and a steamboat connection that investors believed would generate the bulk of the line's business. "The managers of the Manhattan Beach Road did all in their power to prevent the Sea Beach Road from running to Bay Ridge," reported the *Brooklyn Daily Eagle*.[31]

During 1877, the company's initial season of service, NY&SB trains only operated between Bath Junction and Coney Island. Because many of the new road's customers had to travel aboard BB&CI trains to reach Bath Junction, the new company did not generate a healthy level of business during that inaugural summer. Furthermore, lacking any steamboat connection to and from New York, the new road found itself catering largely to Brooklyn residents who already enjoyed a variety of options for traveling to Coney Island, rather than the New Yorkers the company's investors had planned to serve.

The NY&SB had its own terminal in Coney Island. Called Sea

Beach Palace, it was a magnificent facility that was located midway between the Coney Island terminals of Culver's PP&CI and Gunther's BB&CI. The Sea Beach Palace had originally been constructed on the grounds of the 1876 Centennial Exposition in Philadelphia, where it served as the United States Pavilion. Dismantled and shipped to Coney Island by barge over the winter of 1876–77, it was one of several structures from the exposition that were later moved to Coney Island and helped create the amusement area's distinctive profile in the final years of the nineteenth century. The main building of Sea Beach Palace was a domed structure 375 feet long and 60 feet deep, with spacious wings on either side. The facility included a dining room that could seat 3,000 guests, and the railway terminal was to the rear of the structure.[32]

After operating over this four-and-a-half-mile route between Bath Junction and Coney Island in 1877—service was inaugurated the day before the NY&MB opened for business, incidentally—the NY&SB shut down at the end of the Coney Island season and did not reopen until the summer of 1879. During this interval of inactivity, additional investment resources were secured. After exploring a number of options, company officials decided to extend the line beyond Bath Junction to Upper New York over the company's own newly built right-of-way where direct steamboat connections would be available to New York. This was essentially the same route that had originally been intended when it was assumed NY&SB trains would reach tidewater over trackage rights on the New York, Bay Ridge and Jamaica. Instead, the NY&SB had its own exclusive right-of-way close by and parallel to the older road, and the NY&SB built a waterside terminal just to the north of the older New York, Bay Ridge and Jamaica terminal, which was being used by narrow-gauge trains of Corbin's NY&MB Railroad.

The first train to operate over the full NY&SB Railroad—from Bay Ridge to Sea Beach Palace—did so on July 17, 1879, and this is usually cited as the day that NY&SB service was inaugurated. The fifth and final Coney Island excursion railway was now complete and in full service.

Once it began running between Coney Island and the steamer connection in Bay Ridge, the NY&SB engaged in a series of rate wars, particularly with the NY&MB. Thanks to the Bay Ridge connection and swift steamboats to and from New York, the NY&SB quickly promoted itself as the fastest route to Coney Island. In addition, because the steamboats docked in New York, the NY& SB saw the primary market for its Coney Island service as residents of New York, a market that Corbin had long felt should be his alone.

None of the Coney Island destinations one could reach aboard NY&SB trains came close to rivaling Corbin's Manhattan Beach Hotel for luxury. Sea Beach Palace was in the middle of West Brighton. While West Brighton was a world removed from the tawdry atmosphere that prevailed at Coney Island Point, its appeal was considerably more universal than the exclusive tone Corbin sought to maintain at his resort properties.

However, Austin Corbin soon came to realize that mass market patrons headed for a day's fun at Coney Island represented a far larger travel market than the upscale guests Corbin continued to believe would always be the exclusive patrons of his two Manhattan Beach resorts. He was more than happy to have conductors aboard his railroad trains collect fares from passengers he would continually seek to exclude from the grounds of his resort hotels.

Despite aggressive pricing, the NY&SB never became a solid performer from a business perspective. The line entered receivership in the early 1880s, and this led to at least two ownership changes. In early 1882, the company was reorganized as the New York and Sea Beach Railway, but business success still proved elusive. New York Supreme Court Justice William J. Gaynor appointed another receiver in early 1896 in response to a suit that charged "the corporation's business is good for so small a portion of the year, the income runs far behind the receipts."[33]

After it inaugurated full service in 1879, the NY&SB effected modest changes to its operating patterns. During the early years, the line was a seasonal operation only, shutting down at the end of each Coney Island summer and reopening the following spring. By the mid-1880s, the NY&SB was operating year-round. The territory through which it operated was starting to become Kings County residential territory, and the NY&SB recognized the importance of altering its identity from a strictly summer excursion railway to more of a basic mass transportation service.[34]

In 1889, the NY&SB built a single-track spur off its Bay Ridge–

Sea Beach Palace route. Just over a half-mile in length, it left the main line south of Kings Highway and continued eastward to Gravesend Avenue. The purpose of this extension was to allow the NY&SB to operate special trains to a racetrack operated by the Brooklyn Jockey Club that was located at Gravesend Avenue just to the south of Kings Highway. The racetrack was primarily served by the PP&CI Railroad, whose trackage along Gravesend Avenue paralleled the home stretch just behind the grandstand. Trains on Culver's PP&CI even included extra-fare parlor cars, in season, for racetrack patrons.[35]

The NY&SB believed that the Brooklyn Jockey Club was an important enough destination that it warranted additional service. However, improvers of the breed were unimpressed by the new NY&SB operation to the track, and they continued to patronize Culver's PP&CI. The NY&SB extension was discontinued after but a single season of service.

In 1880, with the five major excursion railways a permanent feature of the Coney Island transport scene, the population of Kings County stood at 599,000.

Intra-Island Transportation on Coney Island

During the years of Coney Island's post–Civil War growth, it was often easier to get from New York City to Manhattan Beach, or from downtown Brooklyn to West Brighton, than it was to travel between West Brighton and Manhattan Beach. Intra-island transport was not a strong suit in nineteenth-century Coney Island.

The horse-drawn railcars of the Coney Island and Brooklyn Railroad offered a measure of east-west transportation when they reached Coney Island in 1862. However, Andrew Culver's extension of his PP&CI Railroad to Coney Island Point in 1879 was the first major rail project whose primary purpose was to carry people from one part of Coney Island to another. Yet another important development in intra-island mobility was the construction shortly before 1880 of an east-west roadway known as the Concourse—an asphalt, half-mile thoroughfare that ran between Brighton Beach and West Brighton along a right-of-way that would later become part of Surf Avenue.

Austin Corbin, despite his outspoken views about the exclusivity he wished to maintain at his Manhattan Beach hotels, built a railway whose purpose was to provide transport between Manhattan Beach and other points on Coney Island. In 1878, a short rail extension was constructed from Manhattan Beach proper to a place that was then called Point Breeze at the eastern end of Coney Island. The extension, which was called the Marine Railway, linked the Manhattan Beach Hotel with a pavilion Corbin had built at Point Breeze—an establishment he saw as appealing to a broader cross-section of customers than the exclusive Manhattan Beach Hotel. Shortly afterward, Corbin extended the Marine Railway westward to Brighton Beach. The full length of the line—Point Breeze to Brighton Beach—was less than a mile, with a short stretch in the middle operating over trackage of the NY& MB proper. Transport professionals often said that the Marine Railway earned more money in proportion to its length than any other railroad in the country.[36]

Like the NY&MB, the Marine Railway was built as narrow gauge and later converted to standard gauge, and for all of its days it used NY&MB equipment and was operated by NY&MB personnel. The Marine Railway survived until 1896, when ocean encroachment had so deteriorated its right-of-way that further service was no longer possible. In addition, problems developed between the Marine Railway and hotel operators in Brighton Beach who built a barricade that prevented the railway's passengers from entering their property. To compensate for the loss of the Marine Railway's intra-Coney Island service, the LIRR instituted a roundabout service so passengers could travel between West Brighton and Manhattan Beach. Leaving Manhattan Beach, the train headed inland along the NY&MB line, turned west at Manhattan Beach Junction, and then headed south at Parkville and continued to West Brighton along the PP&CI line. Such a journey took thirty-five minutes to complete.[37]

The Sea View Railroad can perhaps be called the first elevated railway in Kings County, although this claim that requires qualification. As discussed in chapter 5, a company called the Brooklyn Elevated Railroad inaugurated service along the first bona fide elevated railway in Kings County in 1885.

The Sea View Railroad was a Coney Island phenomenon that

operated along a mile-long elevated trestle between Brighton Beach and West Brighton. Most of its elevated structure was built of wood, although structural steel was used for a truss bridge that vaulted across Ocean Parkway. Because the Sea View Railroad opened in 1881—four years before Brooklyn Elevated's first line entered service—the company can make a tenuous claim to being the first "elevated railway" in Kings County.

The Sea View name actually dates to an 1886 foreclosure and reorganization. The company that built the line and inaugurated service in 1881 was called the Coney Island Elevated Railway. Among the directors of the post-1886 company were "Deacon" William Richardson of the Atlantic Avenue Railroad and James Jourdan of Kings County Elevated.

The line's eastern terminal was on the west side of the Brighton Beach Hotel, while its opposite terminal was just to the west of Culver Depot. Coney Island Elevated faced opposition when the company sought to cross Ocean Parkway, and completion of the line was delayed a year or more as a result. To address the complaint that the new elevated line would deface the beauty of Ocean Parkway, company officials declared that "in crossing the Boulevard they will use a handsome bridge which will not cost less than $15,000."[38] Although, at one time Coney Island Elevated considered using cable power for its mile-long intra-Coney Island railroad, the line actually featured small, seven-and-a-half-ton steam locomotives each hauling a single passenger car.[39] In 1887, the railway's roster included seven locomotives and seven passenger coaches, and it seems fair to assume that typical operations called for single-car trains with the locomotive remaining on one end, irrespective of the direction of travel. The line operated from 1881 until roughly the turn of the century.

Then there was the famous Boynton Bicycle Railroad. E. Moody Boynton was an investor and an inventor, who developed a unique idea for building a railroad. Somewhat in imitation of a conventional bicycle, it was a monorail-like concept that featured tall, narrow, lightweight locomotives with but one driving wheel, and rolling stock running on a single rail. Cars and locomotives were held upright by an overhead support structure.

In the early days of railroading, new and unusual technical concepts and schemes were forever being advanced and promoted. It

was an extraordinary degree of standardization, though, that became one of the principal strengths of the railroad industry. Most
novel concepts, whatever their individual merit, failed to make inroads against standardized designs and practices.

Although most novel railway concepts never advanced beyond
the talking stage, Boynton managed to develop several prototype
engines and cars. In September 1888, a short stretch of "bicycle
railroad" between Gravesend Avenue and Brighton Beach, a distance of a mile-and-three-quarters, was ready for its first trial trips.

Boynton's first locomotive, "cycle no. 1" as it was designated,
proved to be a bit too heavy for the short Coney Island line. (Built
to Boynton's specifications in Portland, Maine, it weighed twenty-
three tons, and its single eight-foot driving wheel was turned by a
pair of twelve-by-fourteen-inch cylinders.) A line that was less than
two miles long was hardly a proper place to demonstrate the 100-
miles-per-hour (and higher) speeds Boynton believed would be a
characteristic of his bicycle railroad. Cycle no. 2 was a smaller and
lighter locomotive—nine tons with a six-foot driving wheel—and
it was placed in service on August 16, 1890.

Its demise is not well documented, but there is little reason to
believe that the Boynton Bicycle Railroad operated for more than
two or three seasons. Needless to say, Boynton's concept never
became a serious alternative to conventional railway technology of
the era. A short Brooklyn street near the intersection of today's
McDonald Avenue and Avenue X—the western terminal of the bicycle railroad—is called Boynton Place.[40]

The Boynton Bicycle Railroad of 1888–90 was actually built
along a portion of the right-of-way of an earlier Coney Island venture that represents another little-known effort at intra-island rail
transport. In fact, the New York and Brighton Beach Railroad, as
the venture was initially called, was a bit more than an "intra-island" link. It could almost be regarded as a separate excursion
railway to and from Coney Island, although one that did not
achieve any significant measure of success.

The New York and Brighton Beach was chartered in 1878, during the heyday of enthusiasm for building Coney Island–bound
excursion railways. Its proposed route was to begin at a steamer
landing on Gravesend Bay in a place called Locust Grove, roughly
the foot of today's 18th Avenue. The new railway would then head

in a generally southeasterly direction to Brighton Beach. Because its railroad right-of-way was less than three miles in length, the New York and Brighton Beach clearly intended to maximize the use of steamboats and minimize the use of trains for travel to and from Coney Island.

The company's original plan to run its trains down the middle of 86th Street was thwarted by local property owners, and the company was forced to build a more expensive, parallel right-of-way through adjacent marshlands. Other Coney Island excursion railways objected to the notion of grade crossings, so the New York and Brighton Beach was forced to build a series of expensive bridges to cross the routes of its competitors. The line eventually opened for business in 1880, but a serious fire the following year was more than enough to do in the struggling line.[41] While the company was in operation, the steamboats *Kill Von Kull, Magenta,* and *H. P. Wilson* provided connecting service between New York and Locust Grove for New York and Brighton Beach passengers.

With service abandoned, the right-of-way sat idle for five years. Then, in 1886, the NY&SB leased a portion of the former New York and Brighton Beach—its eastern end between Brighton Beach and the point where it crossed the NY&SB—with plans to operate it as a branch of its own line. (The entity that the NY&SB leased was formally called the Sea Beach and Brighton Railroad, to add yet another piece of nomenclature to the Coney Island railway story.) The NY&SB achieved little success with its new addition, and there is some dispute as to whether any NY&SB trains ever operated over the newly acquired line. (If they did, it was only for a season or two.)

Several other intra–Coney Island railroads were formally chartered and issued capital stock, but never reached operational status. One was headed by William A. Engeman, a major figure in the development of resort properties in Brighton Beach. His venture, the Sea Breeze Avenue Railroad, would have linked Engeman's hotel in Brighton Beach with the Coney Island and Brooklyn's terminal in West Brighton, a mile away, along a route that was practically identical to the one the Sea View Railroad eventually served. Two similar ventures that were chartered but never built bore the unassuming corporate names Brighton No. 1 and Brighton No. 2.

Another intra–Coney Island railway venture about which little is
known other than that it did reach operational status, was the
Coney Island, Sheepshead Bay and Ocean Avenue Railway. Chartered in 1880, it was very likely a horse-powered street railway,
and it may well have operated primarily or even entirely over the
rails of other companies. There is also reason to suspect that its
operations were restricted to those days the Sheepshead Bay racetrack was in operation. In 1886, the line carried 26,440 passengers
and generated $1,322 in receipts. One of the directors of this com-
pany was William J. Gaynor, a Brooklynite who would become
mayor of the City of New York early in the twentieth century and
who, as a judge during the 1890s, would issue many rulings that
impacted Brooklyn's street and elevated railways.[42]

Finally, when discussing excursion railways to and from Coney
Island—and how four principal ones later evolved into elements of
New York City Transit's subway system—it is important to mention another Kings County excursion railway whose original right-
of-way is transited, at least in part, by contemporary subway trains.
This railway did not afford access to Coney Island, though. It ran
from various elevated, streetcar, and railroad connections in East
New York to the shore of Jamaica Bay in Canarsie, a nineteenth-
century amusement area in its own right and also a steamboat
landing for connections to and from Rockaway Beach across the
bay. The Brooklyn, Canarsie and Rockaway Beach opened in 1865,
and much of its route is today the right-of-way of subway trains
operating on New York City Transit's L train.

Summary

The decade of the 1890s would see substantial change to the various Coney Island excursion railways. Through service would be
inaugurated over excursion railways and the elevated lines of central Brooklyn, steam engines would be replaced by electric-powered equipment, and four of the five companies would come under
the unified management of an agency called the Brooklyn Rapid
Transit Company. The following table displays data and information about the Kings County excursion railways during their days
of independent operation.

The Five Major Coney Island Excursion Railways, 1862–1890

Company	Brooklyn, Bath and Coney Island Railroad[a]	Prospect Park and Coney Island Railroad	New York and Manhattan Beach Railroad[b]	Brooklyn, Flatbush and Coney Island Railroad	New York and Sea Beach Railroad[c]
Service inaugurated	1862	1874	1877	1878	1879[c]
Subsequent name(s)	Brooklyn, Bath and West End	None	Long Island Railroad[b]	Brooklyn and Brighton Beach Railroad	New York and Sea Beach Railway
Northern terminal(s)	• Fifth Ave. & 27th Street • Union Depot (Fifth Ave. & 36th Street) • 39th Street Ferry	• Ninth Ave. & 20th Street • Union Depot (Fifth Ave. & 36th Street)	• Bay Ridge (foot of 66th Street) • Greenpoint • Long Island City	• Long Island Railroad Depot	• Bay Ridge (foot of 66th Street)
One-way mainline miles	6.64	13.51	20.4	7.5	6.6
Southern terminal	West End Depot	Culver Depot	Manhattan Beach	Brighton Beach Hotel	Sea Beach Palace
Passenger cars owned (1890)	47	56	89	42	41
Locomotives owned (1890)	7	11	19	8	6
Operating expenses (1890)	$77,244.91	$112,927.92	N/A	$69,956.00	$52,647.74
Patronage (1890)	922,102	1,195,901	N/A [b]	738,041	301,563
Status (2002)	New York City Transit's M line and W line	New York City Transit's F line		New York City Transit's Q line	New York City Transit's N line

a Service instituted between Fifth Avenue & 27th Street and Bath Beach in 1862; extended to Coney Island in 1867.

b Built as narrow gauge, this railway was leased to the Long Island Railroad and converted to standard gauge in 1883. The section between Manhattan Beach Junction and Manhattan Beach was abandoned outright in 1924. Trackage between Bay Ridge and Long Island City remains in freight service in 2002. New York and Manhattan Beach Railroad was combined with the New York, Bay Ridge and Jamaica Railroad and the Long Island City and Manhattan Beach Railroad to form the New York, Brooklyn and Manhattan Beach Railway in 1885.

c Partial service was instituted in 1877, but no service operated during 1878; full service was instituted in 1879.

OTHER CONEY ISLAND EXCURSION RAILWAYS

Company	Marine Railway[a]	New York and Coney Island Railroad[b]	Kings County Central Railroad[a]	Sea View Railroad[c]	New York & Brighton Beach Railroad	Boynton Bicycle Railroad[d]
Service inaugurated	1878	1879	1878	1881	1880	1888
Corporate affiliation(s)	New York & Manhattan Beach Railroad	Prospect Park & Coney Island Railroad	New York & Manhattan Beach Railroad	None	New York & Sea Beach	None
Northern (or western) terminal	Point Breeze	Coney Island Point	Malbone St. & Flatbush Ave.	Brighton Beach	Locust Grove	Avenue W at New York & Sea Beach right-of-way
Southern (or eastern) terminal	Brighton Beach	Culver Depot	Kings County Junction	West Brighton	Brighton Beach	Ocean Parkway north of Surf Avenue
One-way mainline miles	0.7	2.5	3.5	1	2.7	1
Service discontinued	1896	[b]	1878	ca. 1900	1887	ca. 1892
Current status	Abandoned	Abandoned	Abandoned	Abandoned	Abandoned	Abandoned

Sources: Compiled from information in various annual editions of *Poor's Manual of the Railroads of the United States* and *Annual Report of the Board of Railroad Commissioners of the State of New York.*

[a] Operated as part of the New York & Manhattan Beach, with New York and Manhattan Beach equipment and crews.

[b] Absorbed by parent Prospect Park and Coney Island in 1879. Although currently abandoned, this line saw service for some years as an adjunct of the Brooklyn Rapid Transit Company and Brooklyn-Manhattan Transit Corporation elevated system, and later as an electrified trolley line.

[c] Some elements of current New York City Transit lines operate over a portion of the right-of-way used by this excursion railway, but it would be misleading to suggest that it remains in service in the same way that the major excursion railways are said to remain in service as current transit lines and services.

[d] Operated over a portion of the abandoned right-of-way of the New York and Brighton Beach Railroad.

Elevated Railways
(1880–1890)

ELEVATED RAILWAYS operating along structures built over busy urban thoroughfares played an important role in the development of local transport in Brooklyn and Kings County during the final two decades of the nineteenth century. Two Brooklyn elevated lines of the 1880s were eventually linked with excursion railways that had provided transportation to and from Coney Island since the 1860s, and the elevated railway companies played a prominent role when various passenger railway operations in Kings County merged into the Brooklyn Rapid Transit Company at the turn of the twentieth century. From an economic perspective, however, elevated railways in Brooklyn were not nearly as successful as were those across the East River in New York City. In 1896, the *Street Railway Journal* noted, "Following the great success of the Manhattan Elevated Railway in New York, the experiment of building elevated lines in Brooklyn was made, with results more or less disastrous to security holders."[1]

EARLY PLANS AND PROPOSALS

Political leaders in Brooklyn were reluctant to authorize street railway companies to string trolley wires over city streets in the face of popular opposition. One can only imagine the additional level of public furor that was triggered when a company sought to erect, not a tiny wire that was less than a half-inch in diameter, but a massive railroad right-of-way built of iron and steel that extended from curb to curb, induced perpetual twilight on the streets below, and was transited by trains hauled by soot-spewing steam locomotives. As late as 1878, with proposals for elevated railways moving forward, Brooklyn Mayor James Howell announced with no equivocation that he would veto any resolution passed by the Brooklyn Common Council that authorized the construction of an elevated railway over either Myrtle Avenue or Fulton Street, long thought to be principal Brooklyn arteries over which such railways should be built.[2]

Public meetings were continually held to rally opposition against elevated railway proposals. On July 18, 1878, a group of Myrtle Avenue property owners met in Granada Hall and were whipped into near-frenzy by former Brooklyn mayor Samuel Booth, who assured the assembled throng that Mayor Howell "stands ready with every official power, with every power that God has given him, to oppose this encroachment on our rights."[3] One of the distinguished citizens who was appointed to an ad hoc task force that would oppose any Myrtle Avenue elevated line was Seymour L. Husted, the one-time stagecoach operator who had sold his rights to carry passengers along Myrtle Avenue to the Brooklyn City Railroad a quarter-century earlier.[4]

However, Mayor Howell was not an out-and-out opponent of all elevated railways. He was, despite Booth's rather overheated rhetoric, a conscientious public official who attempted to evaluate the merits of competing and conflicting proposals. In 1880, for instance, Howell sent a formal communication to the Common Council that underscored the extent of his concern. "The question of what is right to do, and what is expedient to undertake with reference to the construction of an elevated railway in our city, I find exceedingly difficult of solution."[5]

Proposals and plans for elevated railways in Brooklyn were never wanting, and there was never much dispute about the thoroughfares that represented likely corridors for such lines. Myrtle Avenue and Fulton Street, despite Mayor Howell's veto threat in 1878, were clearly places where additional transport capacity was needed. Other obvious candidates for an elevated railway were the major thoroughfares that ran toward South Brooklyn, Bay Ridge, and Fort Hamilton from downtown Brooklyn—either Third, Fourth, or Fifth Avenues. A line over Atlantic Avenue down to South Ferry made sense to many people, while in Brooklyn's Eastern District, an elevated railway linking East River ferry slips at the foot of Broadway in Williamsburgh with East New York also seemed like a good bet.

One early Brooklyn proposal is interesting on several counts. On June 2, 1871, an entity called the Brooklyn Steam Transit Company was chartered and authorized to issue $3 million in capital stock. Among the company's incorporators were "Deacon" William Richardson of the Atlantic Avenue Railroad and General Henry Slocum of the Coney Island and Brooklyn (CI&B) Railroad. The new railway was planned to run from Fulton Ferry "to any part of Kings County as may be decided by directors."[6]

The precise route and the style of service proposed for Brooklyn Steam Transit tended to vary from year to year, and the company would never operate a single train or carry a single passenger. At one point in the early 1870s, the company seriously planned to build an underground subway from Fulton Ferry to Flatbush. The line would then separate into two surface-level branches—one to Bay Ridge and Coney Island, the other to East New York, where it would connect with various railroads that served Long Island. The company planned to use steam engines for motive power. Although North America's first subway was an electric-powered line that did not open until 1897, London had pioneered the idea of a steam-powered, underground urban railway in 1862. Brooklyn Steam Transit actually broke ground along Atlantic Avenue in the late 1870s to build foundations for support columns that an elevated railway—but not a subway—would require.[7] Richardson, despite earlier affiliation with the venture, was unpleased by this action. Several hours after the ceremonial groundbreaking, he sent his own men to the site to fill in the holes and cover them over with lengths of streetcar rail.

There is a dispute about what was the first elevated railway to carry passengers in Kings County. The basic facts are not at issue, but there is a question about their interpretation. A small, mile-long shuttle railway opened in Coney Island in 1879, which was called the Sea View Railroad (see chapter 4). Because this line operated along an elevated structure from Brighton Beach to West Brighton—and, more importantly, because it predated by six years the opening of Brooklyn's first urban elevated railway—it can lay a passable claim to being the first "elevated railway" in Kings County.

One could also contend that a cable-powered line that began running trains across the Brooklyn Bridge in 1883 was the first "elevated railway" to serve Brooklyn. However, this service was so exceptional that it is generally not regarded as a conventional El, even if its trains clearly operated on an elevated structure (the Brooklyn Bridge) above the streets of Brooklyn and the streets of New York City. (For more about this Brooklyn Bridge cable railway, see chapter 6.)

THE BROOKLYN ELEVATED RAILROAD

Putting aside these two exceptional operations—the Sea View Railroad and the Brooklyn Bridge cable road—Brooklyn's first elevated railway was one that opened for revenue service on May 14, 1885. Its initial downtown terminal was at the intersection of Washington and York Streets in the shadow, literally, of the two-year-old Brooklyn Bridge. Curiously, although close to the Brooklyn Bridge itself, the elevated station at Washington and York was not situated so passengers could conveniently transfer to and from the transbridge cable railway. (An elevated walkway was built between the two railways, but the El station was three blocks away from the Brooklyn terminal of the bridge cable road.) From an in-town terminal under the Brooklyn Bridge, the new elevated railway headed away from downtown Brooklyn in a generally eastward direction on a course that included a number of ninety-degree curves as the line turned from one thoroughfare onto another: York Street to Hudson Avenue, Hudson to Park Avenue, Park to Grand Avenue, Grand to Lexington Avenue, Lexington to Broadway, and Broadway to Gates Avenue where the line terminated. The railway's termination at Gates Avenue was only temporary, though; a month later, service on Brooklyn's first El was extended out Broadway to the East New York area. Then, in November 1885, a short extension on the in-town end of the six-month-old line gave passengers better access to the Union Ferry Company's river crossing that linked the foot of Fulton Street in Brooklyn with Fulton Street in New York. The new elevated railway still did not provide an especially convenient connection to and from the Brooklyn Bridge cable railway, although many of its passengers walked the three blocks and made the transfer anyway.

And so steam-powered trains inaugurated elevated railway ser-

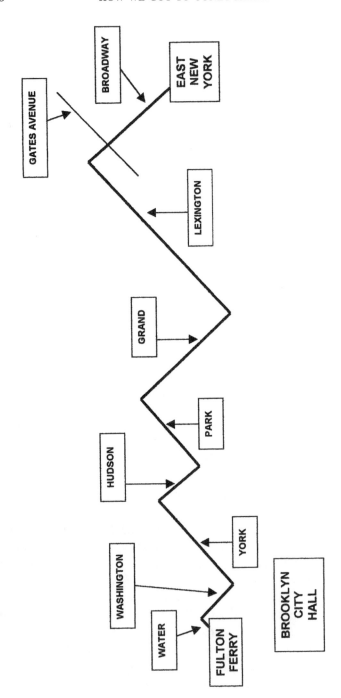

Map 3: Configuration of the original 1885 line of the Brooklyn Elevated Railroad.

vice in Brooklyn in May 1885; the operating company was called the Brooklyn Elevated Railroad. Originally chartered as the Brooklyn Elevated Silent Safety Railway Company on May 26, 1874, the company was renamed the Brooklyn Elevated Railway Company in 1875. In 1884, a year before service was inaugurated, the property was sold under foreclosure proceedings and emerged as the Brooklyn Elevated Railroad.[8]

Between its incorporation in 1874 and the inauguration of railway service eleven years later, Brooklyn Elevated experienced a bewildering sequence of false starts, operational frustrations, economic downturns, and political machinations that have a comic character to them. On May 24, 1876, with a flurry of platform rhetoric from various railway executives and public officials, the company broke ground for its project at Lexington and Reid Avenues in Brooklyn. Workers dug holes at each of the intersection's four corners and "bottomed them with concrete and placed in each a huge foundation stone." But following this one-day groundbreaking ceremony in 1876, "never a stroke of actual work was done" on the project for several more years.[9]

In May 1879, the newly appointed president of Brooklyn Elevated, W. Fontaine Bruff, announced that he was ready to resume construction of the railway. Bruff—English by birth and an engineer by profession—believed that a state charter the company had earlier been awarded was itself all the legal authority that was required for his crews to start digging up Brooklyn streets to build foundations for the railway's support columns. The Brooklyn Common Council took a decidedly different view and passed a resolution directing the city's police commissioner to prevent Bruff's crew from digging along Brooklyn streets.

On the afternoon of May 12, 1879, at the corner of Lexington and Reid Avenues—the same intersection where ground had been broken three years earlier—Bruff arrived by carriage and addressed a group of workers who had been instructed to assemble there. He mounted a makeshift podium—almost losing his balance in the process—and told the group that if any of them were to be arrested for following his orders and initiating construction, he would stand their bail and ensure permanent employment on the railway afterward. The men were then told to take picks and shovels in hand and begin to excavate the street so construction of the railway could resume. Once they did, a Brooklyn police captain from the Ninth Precinct by the name of Dunn stepped forward and arrested fourteen of the workers, as well as Bruff himself. Bruff promptly asked Captain Dunn, "Where is your warrant, Sir?" and the captain replied that he did not have one. Bruff then addressed the crowd, "Then I protest against this . . . gentlemen, workmen, you see that I am arrested without a warrant." There are undoubtedly important social implications associated with the fact that Bruff chose to draw a distinction between "gentlemen" and "workmen" but, whatever they might be, they shall not be pursued. To ensure that his arrest was conducted with a proper tone of civility, not to say high comedy, Bruff then turned to Captain Dunn and asked, "By the way captain, won't you have a cigar?"[10]

Bruff was freed from jail a few hours later. The following day he returned to Reid and Lexington and repeated the events of the previous day. He ordered crews to begin construction, and Bruff and his workers were again arrested by Brooklyn police. In May 1879, it would certainly seem safe to conclude, the city of Brooklyn was not yet ready for its first elevated railway.

Frequently, the major cause of litigation before an elevated railway could be constructed in Brooklyn was not the question of legal authority to permit such construction—although this was the basis of Bruff's dual arrests—but rather the issue of how much and what kind of indemnification property owners along the route should be paid as a result of construction. This was a complex question, as the *New York Times* noted. "If the effect of [elevated railway] construction in front of a piece of property was to render it less available, or less valuable for use or occupation as a dwelling, yet if at the same time it rendered it more available and equally valuable for purposes of business, there was no injury to property of which courts could take notice."[11] On another occasion, the *New York Times* made the following observation about proposed elevated railways in Brooklyn: "The opposition is not to rapid transit, which most people are in favor of, but to the proposed confiscation of private property."[12]

W. Fontaine Bruff—some newspapers identified him as William F. Bruff—eventually settled his problems with the city of Brooklyn and, by the summer of 1879, crews were at work laying foundations along the proposed route of the Brooklyn Elevated Railroad.

When the line opened in 1875, there were exactly 1,700 support columns in place, each resting on a below-ground foundation crafted from a five-ton block of Maine granite. (One may wonder, a century-and-a-quarter after their installation, if any of these blocks of granite still rest below Brooklyn streets.)

Work proceeded very slowly. At one point, Henry Slocum's CI& B Railroad secured an injunction against continued construction of Bruff's Road, as it was often called, claiming the latter's construction crews were interfering with the operation of CI&B streetcars. CI&B was not against construction of the railway per se, it simply wanted to ensure that its operations were not subjected to delays as Bruff's project went forward.

Brooklyn Elevated Railroad persevered. It became the first Brooklyn elevated train to reach operational status, even though it was forced into multiple receiverships and reorganizations while it was still under construction and Bruff was no longer the company's president when its trains began to run. His management of the construction project was anything but frugal. "That he collected and used the funds at his disposal with a recklessness hardly to be commended in honest men cannot be denied," reported the *Brooklyn Daily Eagle*. But the newspaper balanced this assessment by noting that Bruff, despite his shortcomings, "started the Brooklyn Elevated on its successful way."[13]

Revenue passenger service on the Brooklyn Elevated Railroad began early in the morning of Thursday, May 14, 1885. The previous afternoon, ceremonial trains had been operated for 500 invited guests of the company; the day before that, the new railway had run full schedules to help train crews and test equipment. Many of the personnel Brooklyn Elevated hired to operate its trains had previously worked for elevated railways across the river in New York City.

For the ceremonial inaugural on May 13, two special trains left the downtown terminal and ran nonstop to Gates Avenue, a trip that took sixteen minutes. "The engines were burnished brightly and bedecked with flags," reported the *Eagle,* and the first train was under the charge of conductor H. L. Brooks, with engineer Floyd E. Tutbill at the throttle.[14] Guests were invited to disembark and inspect the Gates Avenue station at the end of the line as trains were prepared for the return trip. Each station house along the new line was slate-roofed, and sunlight streaming in was filtered by several panes of stained glass. When the ceremonial trains returned downtown, a lavish reception was held at the elevated company's executive offices, 49 and 51 Fulton Street, that featured "long tables laden with a substantial collation to which the guests did full justice."[15]

Among ten Brooklyn clergymen who were aboard the city's first ceremonial elevated train were the Reverend Henry Ward Beecher, the famed pastor of Brooklyn's Plymouth Church, and the Most Reverend John Loughlin, the first bishop of the Roman Catholic Diocese of Brooklyn. Another guest was the coroner of Kings County. Because riding on an elevated train high above city streets was a novel experience that was approached with a measure of fear, the coroner insisted that he was not participating in the Brooklyn Elevated gala with any anticipation that his professional services would be required.

Despite the fact that Brooklyn Elevated experienced an almost continuous sequence of financial problems during its years of construction and had yet to demonstrate that elevated urban railways in Brooklyn were a sound investment, there was no shortage of other transport companies anxious to invest money and build such railways. In August 1881, the Committee on Railroads of the Brooklyn Board of Aldermen recommended denying petitions submitted by five companies, all of which hoped to build elevated railways in Brooklyn. The five companies were the East River Bridge and Coney Island Steam Transit Company, the Brooklyn Underground Railway Company, the Brooklyn and Long Island City Railway Company, the New-York and Brooklyn Elevated Railway Company, and Brooklyn Elevated Railway Company Number Two.[16]

Of the five, the East River Bridge and Coney Island Steam Transit Company was perhaps the most interesting. One of its backers was Andrew Culver, and the company was proposing to build an elevated railway from the Brooklyn end of the Brooklyn Bridge to a connection with Culver's Prospect Park and Coney Island Railroad at 20th Street and Ninth Avenue in the Greenwood section of Brooklyn.

A few months later, Brooklyn Elevated went into receivership, and construction was halted on its initial line. Still, the company managed to become involved in political and judicial dramatics that rivaled Bruff's exploits at Reid and Lexington Avenues two years earlier. Brooklyn aldermen had voted to give the struggling company authority to expand its unfinished line into a genuine elevated railway system that would operate over a number of other Brooklyn thoroughfares. The company's receivers had believed that such authorization would itself be sufficient to let them go to the market and raise the additional capital the bankrupt company desperately needed. "Aldermen were well paid for the privilege accorded by them to the company," the *New York Times* noted as if this were uncontested fact.[17] However, Brooklyn Mayor James Howell vetoed the measure. When the aldermen announced their intention to override the veto, property owners who were against elevated railway construction adjacent to their homes quietly secured an injunction from Judge Moore restraining the aldermen from taking any such action. When the aldermen entered their chamber on December 27, 1881, to consider the override, each found a copy of the injunction issued by the state's supreme court sitting on his desk.[18] Deterred not at all, the aldermen defied the injunction and overrode the mayor's veto. State Supreme Court Justice Gilbert was not amused, and the fifteen aldermen were each fined $250 and sentenced to ten to thirty days of imprisonment in Brooklyn's Raymond Street Jail.

Protracted judicial proceedings that extended through most of 1882 eventually reduced the jail terms to four days and determined that the correct number of offending aldermen was ten, not fifteen. But the ten were eventually required to serve four days in jail and, when they were subsequently released, the *New York Times* reported that "a madder, more disgusted set of men never saw jail doors close behind them." Upset over their temporary loss of liberty and the ignominy of "doing time," the aldermen were equally angered by the fact that, during their days in Raymond Street Jail, "they had suffered pecuniary losses at a game called poker, which they had been permitted to play undisturbed by their kind jailers."[19]

Humorous as these political actions may seem in retrospect, the fact remains that the franchise awards granted to Brooklyn Elevated over Mayor Howell's veto in December 1882 were perfectly legal actions. On their strength, the company would raise additional capital to finish construction of its first elevated line and then supplement its initial line with a network of complementary routes that served a variety of Brooklyn neighborhoods.

MOTIVE POWER AND ROLLING STOCK

When the Brooklyn Elevated Railroad finally inaugurated service in 1885, the company's trains were hauled by diminutive steam locomotives, engines that were similar in design to those used by elevated railways across the East River in New York City.[20] Unlike conventional locomotives on intercity railroads, elevated motive power did not carry fuel and water in a separate car called a tender. Instead, water tanks and coal bunkers were built into the locomotive itself. Although this design limited carrying capacity, the short-haul nature of urban elevated railways allowed refueling at frequent intervals throughout the day so a separate tender was not necessary. Steam locomotives designed for service on urban elevated railways operated equally well in either direction and did not require complex turntables to reverse direction at the end of the line. Locomotives had to be uncoupled from one end of the train and shifted to the opposite end at each terminal, but the locomotive itself did not have to be turned around. Actually, in common practice, a relay arrangement was employed and locomotives did not typically haul the same train in both directions. After a lead locomotive was uncoupled at the end of the line, a different engine from a previous train was normally attached to the opposite end for the return trip.

The unusual motive power demands of urban elevated railways resulted in the adoption of a locomotive design that proved to be tailor-made for such service. A concept that was patented in 1866 by Matthias Nace Forney—a one-time editor of the trade journal *Railroad Gazette*—later became the de facto standard for elevated railway service. When Brooklyn Elevated inaugurated service in 1885, it had twenty-two Forney-type locomotives from the Rhode Island Locomotive Works, of Providence. Eight more were on order and, in subsequent years, 140 similar engines were put to work hauling elevated trains in Kings County by Brooklyn Elevated and its competition. Brooklyn Elevated's first Forney-style locomotives rode on four forty-two-inch driving wheels, had four additional wheels under their cab, weighed twenty-two tons, and had cylinders with an eleven-inch bore and a sixteen-inch stroke.[21]

Brooklyn Elevated's coaling station, which had a capacity to store 800 tons of fuel, was at Waverly and Park Avenues; a watering station was located at Broadway and Gates Avenue. The company eventually built a maintenance and storage facility for its rolling stock in East New York, a location that remains an important subway car facility in the twenty-first century. The *Brooklyn Daily Eagle* noted, "A further feature of the site is that while within the city limits it is within the reach of cheap houses, where the road's employees may dwell with much more comfort than in crowded city tenements."[22]

Passenger-carrying rolling stock on Brooklyn's first elevated railway was a scaled-down version of conventional railroad passenger cars of the era. Brooklyn Elevated was a standard-gauge railway, but its passenger coaches were about fifty feet long, instead of the eighty-foot coaches found on a typical intercity railroad. Elevated passenger cars were also slightly narrower than conventional railroad stock. The latter were typically ten feet across, while elevated cars were closer to nine. A car had an open platform at each of its two ends, which was typical of conventional railways of the day, and passengers boarded trains by way of these open platforms. Stations along the elevated lines were built at the same height as the floors of the cars, so passengers could pass easily from station to car without having to climb into the car from track level. (This design was not simply for passengers' convenience; it also speeded up service.) The initial rolling stock that inaugurated steam-powered passenger service on the Brooklyn Elevated in May 1885 was a fleet of forty-five wooden cars built by the Pullman Palace Car Company; forty-five additional cars were on order.

BROOKLYN UNION ELEVATED RAILWAY

On the strength of the franchise awards that it received in December 1881, the Brooklyn Elevated Railroad was expanded from a single line into a genuine system. Most of this expansion was under the banner of a parallel company called Union Elevated that was backed by the same investors and run by the same managers as Brooklyn Elevated. On May 13, 1887, Union Elevated was leased, in its entirety, by Brooklyn Elevated. In 1890, the lease was converted into a formal consolidation, and the unified company adopted the unsurprising name Brooklyn Union Elevated Railway. (As a matter of stylistic convenience, we shall use the Brooklyn Union designation to refer to the combined Brooklyn Elevated/ Union Elevated network, even when discussing events that happened before the formal creation of Brooklyn Union in 1890.)

An elevated line was opened along Broadway between East New York and the East River ferry slips in September 1888. A portion of this route—from Broadway and Lexington Avenue to East New York—had been in service since 1885 as part of the company's original line. Closer to downtown Brooklyn, the Old Main Line (as the company's first route came to be called), which served Fulton Ferry over a line beset with ninety-degree curves, was replaced, in stages, by a more efficient, straight east-west trunk line that ran along Myrtle Avenue.[23]

In addition to its straighter route, the Myrtle Avenue El corrected another shortcoming of the original Brooklyn Elevated— the fact that passengers could not transfer directly or easily to and from the bridge cable road. The Myrtle Avenue Line, upon reaching Myrtle Avenue and Adams Street in downtown Brooklyn, turned north onto Adams and terminated at Sands Street, directly over the Brooklyn terminal of the bridge railway. It proved to be a wise decision. Indeed, Manhattan-bound passengers so preferred the convenience of the bridge cable railway for crossing the East River that, by 1890, the original leg of the Old Main Line that terminated at Fulton Ferry was abandoned and torn down.

On November 5, 1888, the first element of an important line that would serve South Brooklyn and Bay Ridge along Fifth Avenue opened for service. It was built as an extension of the Old Main Line and included an at-grade crossing of the company's new Myrtle Avenue Line at Myrtle and Hudson Avenues. On November 6, the second day this new Hudson Avenue route was in service, there was an unfortunate collision at this crossing. "What had been prognosticated by scores of observant citizens happened last night on the Brooklyn Elevated Railroad at the Hudson Avenue crossing of the Flatbush and Myrtle avenue branches," reported the *Brooklyn Daily Eagle*.[24]

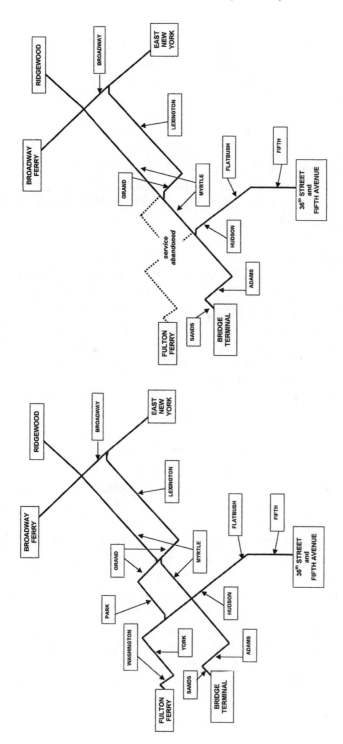

Maps 4 and 5: Schematic rendition of the joint system built by Brooklyn Elevated and Union Elevated and the subsequent rationalization of the system.

At a few minutes after seven o'clock in the evening, a downtown-bound train on the Myrtle Avenue Line left the Navy Street station and was approaching the Myrtle-Hudson crossing. The three-car train was hauled by locomotive no. 58, with engineer William Williams at the throttle. Williams later claimed that he had been given a clear signal by a man assigned to protect the new crossing. When Williams's train was about twenty-five feet from the crossing, another three-car train traveling along the new Hudson Avenue El suddenly came into view. It was hauled by locomotive no. 70, operating backwards, with engineer Ambrose Goodyear at the controls. Goodyear later claimed that he, too, had been given a clear signal to enter the crossover.

Seeing that a collision was inevitable, Engineer Williams threw his engine into reverse and, along with his fireman, quickly jumped out onto a catwalk next to the track. Neither Goodyear nor his fireman had time to jump. They both stayed aboard as their engine slammed squarely into the side of no. 58. Both engines derailed. Although some passengers were shaken up, particularly those aboard the Myrtle Avenue train, there were no fatalities from the accident. The closest call may have been to Matthew O'Connor, who was later watching the rescue effort from street level when a fireman's ax fell from the elevated structure and missed his head by a few inches.[25]

(One New Yorker whose head was, figuratively speaking, squarely hit by a falling ax on Tuesday, November 6, 1888, the day of the Brooklyn Elevated accident, was President Grover Cleveland. It was Election Day and President Cleveland was defeated in his bid for reelection by Republican Benjamin Harrison, even though Cleveland received more popular votes than Harrison.[26])

In the aftermath of the Myrtle-Hudson accident, the new elevated line was promptly closed down for more than seven months and rebuilt as a branch of the Myrtle Avenue Line, not the Old Main Line. As a result of this improvement, trains from one line no longer had to cross over the route of the other.[27] In December 1889, the Fifth Avenue Line reached Fifth Avenue and 36th Street—site of the Union Depot where excursion trains of the Prospect Park and Coney Island and the Brooklyn, Bath and West End terminated. By this time, Andrew Culver had given up on his efforts to have a separate elevated line built that would serve his railroad's in-town terminal at Ninth Avenue and 20th Street.

By the end of 1890, Brooklyn Union Elevated had a full system in operation. Its Broadway Line ran from the East River ferry slips to East New York. The Myrtle Avenue Line connected the Brooklyn end of the Brooklyn Bridge with Ridgewood and also served as a trunk line into downtown Brooklyn for trains of the Lexington Avenue and Fifth Avenue Lines. Meanwhile the curve-plagued elements of the Old Main Line, and its terminal adjacent to Fulton Ferry, had been abandoned.

Brooklyn Union Elevated would see three extensions added to its system during the 1890s. One extended the Broadway Line out Fulton Street from East New York to Cyprus Hills. Another extended the Fifth Avenue Line from 36th Street to 65th Street, although the line turned off Fifth Avenue at 38th Street and then continued south to the new terminal along Third Avenue. The entire line was still called the Fifth Avenue El, though. The third extension involved a modest expansion of terminal facilities at the Brooklyn end of the bridge.

Brooklyn Union created a new subsidiary company to build these extensions, thus adding yet another name to the growing roster of Kings County mass transit providers. Although the corporate name was hardly descriptive of the services provided over the new extensions, all three were built under the auspices of a company called the Seaside and Brooklyn Bridge Railroad Company.

KINGS COUNTY ELEVATED RAILWAY COMPANY

If the joint Brooklyn Elevated/Union Elevated operation is regarded as a single railway system—and it essentially was one from the very start—an enterprise that was incorporated on January 6, 1879, as the Kings County Elevated Railway Company must be seen as a separate and even competitive endeavor.[28] As was the case with Brooklyn Elevated, a disquietingly long interval passed between the company's incorporation and the operation of its first train in 1889. Although not with the company from its outset, a man who became identified with Kings County Elevated onward from 1881 was James J. Jourdan, the Civil War veteran who had earlier headed the CI&B and who played an important role in the reorganization of the Brooklyn, Flatbush and Coney Island Railroad.

Building the Kings County Elevated involved as many delays and frustrations as had plagued Brooklyn Elevated, although the Kings County company managed to avoid the colorful episodes that characterized Brooklyn Elevated. As far as can be determined, for instance, none of its directors or corporate officers were ever arrested—at least not for matters associated with elevated railway business. At several points during the late 1870s and the early 1880s, it even appeared that the Kings County company would be awarded franchise rights to build elevated railways over many of the streets where Brooklyn Union eventually built such lines.[29] In the end, though, Kings County built and operated only a single line, an elevated railway that began at Fulton Ferry on the banks of the East River and proceeded out Fulton Street to the Brooklyn city limits. The Kings County Elevated Railway passed close to the Brooklyn terminal of the bridge railway, and shortly after it was opened an important transfer station was built here so elevated train passengers could use the cable railway en route to Manhattan. Interestingly, such a transfer station was not in place from the outset.

That the Kings County El was built at all is rather remarkable in that its Fulton Street right-of-way closely paralleled the Long Island Railroad (LIRR), which had returned to Atlantic Avenue in 1877. There was general consensus that the LIRR's at-grade line would eventually be converted to elevated construction, thus raising a question as to the need for a separate elevated line along nearby Fulton Street. "Fulton-Street and Atlantic-avenue run so closely parallel that it is hardly conceivable that both should become profitable routes of rapid transit roads," noted the *New York Times* in late 1886.[30]

Like the trains of Brooklyn Elevated, Kings County trains were hauled by Forney-type steam locomotives. The company purchased these locomotives from both the Rhode Island Locomotive Works and the Grant Locomotive Works. Passenger-carrying rolling stock was also similar to that of Brooklyn Elevated; the company's initial cars were built by the Pullman Palace Car Company, and these were supplemented in the early 1890s with cars turned out by Harlan and Hollingsworth of Wilmington, Delaware.

The Kings County company inaugurated service between Fulton Ferry and the intersection of Fulton Street and Nostrand Avenue, a distance of three miles, on April 24, 1888. The *Brooklyn Daily Eagle* greeted the new company's arrival warmly. "The beginning of the era of rapid transit over the vertebral thoroughfare of this city was auspiciously heralded to-day when fair skies and cheery sunshine greeted the pioneer regular trains of the Kings County road."[31] The company operated trains up to four cars in length. However, because the grade between Fulton Ferry and Sands Street was so steep, four-car trains usually required helper engines to help push eastbound departures away from Fulton Ferry.

Fulton Ferry to Nostrand Avenue was not the intended extent of the new railway, and construction continued further westward even as the line was welcoming passengers aboard its first trains. Service was extended to Sumner Avenue at the end of May 1888; to Utica Avenue in August of the same year; and to Sackman Street in East New York, the limit of the original authorization, in November 1889. Sackman Street was sufficiently close to what was then the Brooklyn city line that Kings County trains were usually said to operate between Fulton Ferry and City Line. During the 1890s, the territorial limits of Brooklyn were expanded to be coextensive with Kings County, and so when the Fulton Street El was expanded further eastward to Grant Avenue in 1893, this terminal was commonly referred to as City Line, as well.[32]

However, Kings County's extension in 1893 could not continue along Fulton Street. Brooklyn Union owned the rights to build along Fulton Street beyond East New York, and the company did so in 1893. The Kings County El had to turn off Fulton Street at Snediker Avenue and proceed south for four blocks before turning and continuing east along Pitkin Avenue to Grant Avenue. In any event, when one hears a reference about a Kings County elevated train operating to a terminal station called City Line, it is perfectly reasonable to ask, "Which City Line?"

From the outset, Jourdan had his eye on a possible connection between his Kings County El and one of the Coney Island excursion railways, the Brooklyn, Flatbush and Coney Island. The latter had been denied the use of the LIRR's Brooklyn terminal in 1883, and its trains were forced to terminate at Bedford Terminal, adjacent to the intersection of Atlantic and Franklin Avenues.

The east-west route of Jourdan's Kings County El was two short blocks north of Bedford Terminal, and linking the two railways seemed like an obvious possibility—a possibility that was foreseen when Jourdan led a group of investors who acquired the Brooklyn, Flatbush and Coney Island after it fell into receivership in 1884 and reorganized it as the Brooklyn and Brighton Beach railroad in 1887. Building that two-block link proved to be a taxing endeavor. For one thing, there was the LIRR's Atlantic Avenue right-of-way that had to be crossed. LIRR President Austin Corbin was dead set against the idea of through service over the Fulton Street El and Brooklyn and Brighton Beach railroad that would compete with his own New York and Manhattan Beach operation. (It would take litigation before the LIRR allowed its right-of-way to be crossed.) In addition, property owners in the vicinity of Franklin, Fulton, and Atlantic were opposed to any elevated extensions or connections at all—although they did not vigorously object to the Fulton Street El itself. They were able to have legislation enacted in Albany that prohibited the construction of an elevated railway over certain public streets in the area—the very streets Jourdan would have to use to connect the Fulton Street El with the Brooklyn and Brighton Beach.

The principal motivation behind Jourdan's desire to link the two railroads underscores an important change that was happening in Kings County. Jourdan realized that the potato and melon patches through which Brooklyn, Flatbush and Coney Island locomotives quickly sped en route to the seashore in 1878 were on the verge of becoming prime Kings County residential real estate, and thus a source of passenger traffic bound for downtown Brooklyn the year around.

This is to get ahead of our story, though. The through-routing of trains between the Fulton Street El and the Brooklyn and Brighton Beach Railroad would be an achievement of the 1890s, a decade when public transport in Brooklyn was totally transformed.

The following table displays statistics about the two Brooklyn elevated railways at the start of the 1890s.

When compared with equivalent companies across the East River in New York City, the elevated railways of Brooklyn never

BROOKLYN ELEVATED RAILWAY COMPANIES: COMPARATIVE STATISTICS
FOR 1890

Characteristic	Brooklyn Union Elevated Railroad	Kings County Elevated Railway
Route miles	17.93	6.89
Passengers carried	30,889,535	14,117,875
Train miles	2,750,617	1,155,236
Number of locomotives	76	42
Number of passenger cars	210	130
Operating expenses	$925,580.41	$556,735.92
President	Henry W. Putnam	James Jourdan
Office	31 Sands Street, Brooklyn	346 Fulton Street, Brooklyn

Source: Poor's Manual of the Railroads of the United States (New York, 1891).

became economically sound enterprises. "[Brooklyn] is not well adapted to an elevated railroad service, because it spreads out over too large an area, so that the lines of traffic are not condensed as in New York City, but are free to take whatever course the freaks of residence building and business locations may determine," the *Street Railway Journal* noted.[33] Both Brooklyn elevated railway companies fell into receivership, Brooklyn Union on more than one occasion, and it would not be until the two companies were united under the aegis of the Brooklyn Rapid Transit Company at the dawn of the twentieth century that they would realize their operational promise. No sooner did that come to pass, though, than the very concept of elevated railways in Brooklyn was superceded by a newer form of urban rail rapid transit—subway trains.

6

Merger, Consolidation, and the Emergence of the BRT (1890–1900)

IN THE HISTORY of public transportation in Brooklyn and Kings County, from Colonial times to the present day, no decade was as transformational or as important as the 1890s. When the 1890s began, Brooklyn was served by a number of independent street railway companies whose principal motive power was the horse; elevated railways with trains hauled by steam locomotives were struggling with financing that was anything but sound; and travel to and from Coney Island was dominated by independent excursion railways operating from the periphery of Brooklyn to the shore. By decade's end, the street railways, the elevated lines, and the excursion railways were operating or on the verge of operating electric-powered equipment, and all were under the unified management of a single entity, the Brooklyn Rapid Transit Company (BRT). In addition, by the turn of the twentieth century, the city of Brooklyn had surrendered its municipal autonomy and become one of five boroughs in an expanded City of New York, an event that had a profound impact on subsequent transportation developments. The population of Kings County grew by almost 40 percent during the 1890s—from 839,000 to 1,167,000. And the 1890s also saw the dawn of a new era in American popular entertainment with the opening, on Coney Island, of the very first amusement parks on the face of the earth.

There would be later developments—and important changes—to public transport in Brooklyn, including the construction of a network of subway lines in the early years of the twentieth century, the wholesale shift of mass transportation itself from the corporate world to the public sector some years later, and the emergence of the private automobile as the vehicle of choice for most urban travel. None of these eras, though, can rival the 1890s as a period of fundamental change.

THE BROOKLYN HEIGHTS RAILROAD

When a new Brooklyn street railway that called itself the Brooklyn Heights Railroad operated its first streetcar in the summer of 1891, the company was seen more for the novelty of its equipment than anything else. Rather than using horses that were then powering the majority of American street railways, or even the new electric-powered trolley cars that were beginning to replace older, horse-powered vehicles, the Brooklyn Heights Railroad was a street railway whose cars were propelled by attaching themselves to an endless cable that moved through a vault beneath the pavement.

Cable-powered street railways saw limited deployment in Brooklyn. The original shuttle trains that began to transverse the new Brooklyn Bridge in the fall of 1883 were cable powered—and remained so into the early years of the twentieth century. Because these trains crossed the bridge along a private right-of-way, the cable to which they were attached for traction was not encased in a vault beneath the city's streets but was, rather, a free-running device at track level. (More on the Brooklyn Bridge cable railway later in this chapter.)

The bridge railway aside, there were only two genuine cable street railways that operated in Brooklyn. The Brooklyn Cable Company, which intended to run from Fulton Ferry to East New York, used an experimental form of cable technology. Had the company's plans been successful, Brooklyn Cable would have become part of "Deacon" William Richardson's Atlantic Avenue Railroad. However, for a variety of reasons the company was anything but a success, and a mile-and-a-half deployment along Park Avenue between Broadway and Grand Avenue was the only portion of the route to be equipped for cable operation and to inaugurate service. It carried its first passengers on March 6, 1887, but was shut down, never to reopen, on July 15 of the same year.

The Brooklyn Heights Railroad, on the other hand, was a successful cable road from both a business and an operational perspective. It ran the length of Montague Street from Court Street, adjacent to Brooklyn City Hall, to the Brooklyn slip of the Union Ferry Company's Wall Street Ferry at the foot of Montague Street, a half-mile away. Since a glacial leftover called Brooklyn Heights stood between City Hall and the ferry slip, a double-tracked railway up and down the relatively steep grades of Montague Street proved to be a near-perfect deployment of cable technology, even if the route over which the cars ran was relatively short in length.[1] The inauguration of cable service over the new railway in July 1891 drew considerable attention. Because the new company was unable to acquire real estate for a powerhouse along the route of its railway, it was forced to build this important facility at State Street and Willow Place—almost as far away from Montague Street as the railway itself was long—and the cable reached Montague Street from the powerhouse through an underground vault. At the powerhouse, the cable was powered by a 250-horsepower, tandem compound condensing steam engine that was built in Mount Vernon, Ohio, by the C. and G. Cooper Company.

One feature of the line's final construction that attracted considerable public attention was the manner in which the company installed the cable to which cars would attach themselves as they moved up and down the line. The Brooklyn Heights Railroad hired a young boy to crawl through the newly built underground vault between the powerhouse and Montague Street, hauling an ordinary hemp rope behind him as he crawled along. His progress was checked as he passed under various street-level openings in the vault, and whenever the weight of the rope became too much for the boy to pull, men above would come to his assistance at the various openings and free up additional slack in the line. When the youngster reached Montague Street he emerged from the below-street vault, his task successfully completed. The rope he had pulled was then securely attached to a steel cable back at the powerhouse, and a gang of strong men hauled the cable to the new railway's right-of-way at Hicks and Montague Streets in a kind of one-way tug-of-war. Then the cable was fed into the vault beneath the tracks, cable car no. 1 of the new company was securely attached to the cable, and with a team of horses doing the hauling, the car—and with it the cable—was drawn up Montague Street to Court Street, then down to the ferry, and finally back to Hicks

Street. Company technicians were on hand to ensure that the cable properly engaged various pulleys and other devices in the vault under Montague Street.

The next day the services of the agile young man were again retained. Using the same crawl-through-the-vault-with-a-rope technique, he hauled the cable back to the powerhouse where it was spliced into an endless loop and connected with the big steam engine that would power the new railway. At two o'clock in the afternoon on Wednesday, July 15, 1891, the inaugural trip was made over the new street railway.

The *Brooklyn Daily Eagle* noted the technological advance that the line represented with a backhanded compliment that was more a complaint that a street railway had not been deployed along Montague Street much sooner. "The cart of enterprise has been put before the horse of progress in this case."[2] Rolling stock used to inaugurate service over the new cable railway consisted of a fleet of eight enclosed cable cars—no. 1 through no. 8—that were built in Brooklyn by the firm of Lewis and Fowler. No expense was spared, and the press reported that the cars "cost more than any other cars used for the same purpose."[3] The new cable cars were eighteen feet long; they were framed in solid mahogany, and their interiors were finished with inlaid woods of the highest quality. Three additional cable cars were delivered by Lewis and Fowler shortly afterward—no. 14 through no. 16—but these were open cars to be used only during warm-weather months. When traffic on the line increased later in the decade, Brooklyn Heights Railroad acquired four second-hand horsecars from the Brooklyn City Railroad; these cars were converted for cable operation, and identified as no. 17 through no. 20.

The Montague Street Line remained cable-powered until 1909, an eighteen-year tenure that made it a relatively long-lived example of this unusual technology. The line was converted to electric power in 1909. However, after Union Ferry abandoned service on the Wall Street–Montague Street East River crossing in 1912, the former cable line lost its principal source of customers and the Montague Street trolley line was abandoned outright in 1924.

As a corporation, the Brooklyn Heights Railroad would become a force in Kings County transportation matters far beyond the limited confines of the Montague Street corridor and the unique applications that were appropriate for cable-powered technology. On July 15, 1891, when the first cable car made its celebratory inaugural trip from Court Street down to the ferry, it paused on Montague Street in front of a building that housed the People's Trust Company; here, a group of company officials and civic dignitaries boarded the car. They were led by the new company's president, Daniel F. Lewis. Lewis was also an official with People's Trust, but it was as president of the Brooklyn Heights Railroad that he dutifully rang up the five-cent fares happily paid by each of the invited guests. Actual operation of the car was in the hands of one of the company's uniformed gripmen, a man by the name of Thomas Halliday, who skillfully manipulated the various controls to fasten the car to the moving cable, and then let go and braked to a halt. For a day's work, gripman Halliday was paid a salary of two dollars.[4]

Presidency of the Brooklyn Heights Railroad was not the only corporate office that Daniel Lewis held in 1891. In addition to being an official with People's Trust, Lewis was the president of the Brooklyn City Railroad Company—one of the largest street railways in the country and by far the largest in Brooklyn and Kings County.[5] One newspaper suggested that it was a mere coincidence that businessman Lewis held positions with the two street railways—not to mention a bank and a streetcar-building company—and that nothing should be inferred from these multiple roles.[6] Except it was no coincidence at all, and the corporate relationship between Brooklyn Heights and Brooklyn City was a principal factor in the transformation of Kings County public transportation during the 1890s.

On February 14, 1893, a little more than a year after Brooklyn Heights inaugurated cable service along Montague Street, the Brooklyn Heights Railroad leased the entire Brooklyn City Railroad. Under the terms of the lease, Brooklyn Heights promised to pay a 10 percent dividend each year to holders of Brooklyn City stock, which would be calculated based on Brooklyn City's market quote on the day of the lease. The very next day, Brooklyn City shareholders met and, with a vote well in excess of the necessary two-thirds majority, ratified the lease. As a result, one of the largest street railways in the United States—a company that owned and operated more than 1,500 streetcars, provided service along almost 175 miles of street trackage, and was capitalized at $12 million—was now controlled by a small, cable-powered railway that was a half-mile long and was capitalized at $200,000. Daniel F. Lewis continued to direct the fortunes of both companies, and the lease of Brooklyn City by Brooklyn Heights in 1893 was just the beginning of fundamental corporate change at Brooklyn street railways.

ENTER NASSAU ELECTRIC RAILROAD

Before exploring how the Brooklyn Heights–Brooklyn City relationship impacted mass transport in Kings County, it is helpful to present a few details about another Kings County street railway consortium that developed during the 1890s, the Nassau Electric Railroad. Although Nassau Electric brought several important pre-1890 street railway lines under its corporate wing—the largest being Deacon Richardson's Atlantic Avenue operation, although Richardson was no longer associated with the company at the time of the merger—the company's principal corporate aim was the construction of electric-powered street railways to serve rapidly growing sections of Brooklyn and Kings County not yet served by street railways.

Rather than maturing into a company that achieved any kind of permanence or stability, Nassau Electric was a short-term phenomenon that was a function of the rapidly changing transport scene in Kings County during the 1890s. When the decade began, Nassau Electric did not exist. Yet when the decade had run its course and a new century was at hand, Nassau Electric had already faded into history.

The name Nassau Electric requires some explanation, since in the context of a later era one might assume that the company's streetcars served suburban Nassau County. Nassau Electric was a Brooklyn-based enterprise that saw its primary service market as Kings County. The name is not a reference to the suburban political jurisdiction called Nassau County, but rather to an older designation for the entire body of land that is today called Long Island, but was once known as Nassau Island. (The first steam-powered ferryboat to cross the East River to Brooklyn in 1814 on a route that would later be called the Fulton Ferry bore the name *Nassau*.)

Nassau Electric was chartered on March 13, 1893, and for its initial years the chief factotum behind the company was Patrick H. Flynn. As a result, Nassau Electric was often referred to as "Flynn's Road," although by the 1890s the personification of railway properties was no longer as common as it had been a decade or so earlier.

Prior to the formal creation of Nassau Electric in 1893, Flynn and his financial associates had begun to acquire authorizations to build new electric trolley lines under a variety of companies that would eventually become part of Nassau Electric. For example, in January 1893, a Flynn-controlled enterprise called Kings County Traction secured approval from officials in the town of Flatbush to build a new electric street railway along Ocean Avenue, a corridor that Brooklyn City long felt confident it would serve.

In covering these developments, a reporter for the *Brooklyn Daily Eagle* asked Flatbush town clerk John S. Schenck why he voted for the Flynn proposal over that put forward by Brooklyn City. Schenck cited reasonable enough factors such as improved streetcar service for his Flatbush constituents, but eventually got around to the heart of the matter. "I own 125 acres of land which is on the proposed route of the Kings County Electric Railroad Company and is not so near to the Brooklyn City road," Schenck unashamedly said.[7]

Once completed, the new streetcar line ran out Ocean Avenue to Sheepshead Bay and quickly became an important electric street railway link between central Brooklyn, Flatbush, and areas adjacent to Coney Island that are commonly regarded as part of the oceanfront recreation area. "Improvers of the breed" heading for a day of excitement at the Coney Island Jockey Club's Sheepshead Bay Race Track, for instance, often traveled aboard Nassau Electric's new Ocean Avenue Line. (There were three thoroughbred tracks that are commonly referred to as "Coney Island" racetracks—the Sheepshead Bay that opened in 1880, the Brooklyn Jockey Club's Gravesend track of 1886, and William Engeman's Brighton Beach track that held its first races in 1879. That the three tracks were instrumental in generating additional popularity for Coney Island as a destination goes without saying. However, only one of the three racetracks, Brighton Beach, was located on Coney Island itself. The other two were on the Kings County mainland.)[8]

So if Nassau Electric's Ocean Avenue Line is regarded as providing service to and from Coney Island—and whether it is or is not is as much a matter of semantics as geography—it can be called the second street railway to carry passengers to the seashore aboard electric-powered cars (the first was Henry Slocum's Coney Island and Brooklyn). Flynn's Ocean Avenue Line later connected in Sheepshead Bay with a separately incorporated street railway that was operated by Nassau Electric under the terms of a long-term lease. Formerly called the Coney Island and Gravesend Railroad—in later years it would be known as the Sea Gate Line—it allowed passengers getting off an Ocean Avenue car in Sheepshead Bay to continue on to amusement areas along Surf Avenue in West Brighton.

Flynn's involvement in the street railway business began as an adjunct to earlier interests in real estate development. Frustrated when he was unable to convince existing companies to extend street railway service into Kings County neighborhoods that he was attempting to develop, he decided to build such lines himself. For instance, Flynn owned considerable property along Fifth Avenue—beyond the point where horsecars of the Atlantic Avenue Railroad then terminated—and Deacon Richardson was unwilling to extend his line into the new market Flynn was about to create.[9]

In 1893, Flynn sought authorization from officials in the town of New Utrecht to build an electric trolley line along 86th Street through Bath Beach and to construct the western portion of a new streetcar line that would begin at the 39th Street ferry slip on Upper New York Bay, head east on 39th Street, and then proceed across Kings County and through Flatbush along Church Avenue.[10] Also on the list of projects Flynn planned to build was a new electric streetcar line along Hamburg Avenue that would link East River ferry slips at the foot of Broadway in Williamsburgh with Evergreen Cemetery in East New York.

As Flynn went about the task of creating the Nassau Electric Railroad, his would become a frequent and familiar face in various courtrooms and judicial chambers throughout Brooklyn and New York. His transportation proposals and business arrangements often required litigation—sometimes extended, usually spirited, and frequently acrimonious—before they could be carried forward. For example, after Nassau Electric had completed the Church Avenue Line and the Hamburg Avenue Line and was ready to put both lines in service in 1895, their operation was enjoined by Judge Walter Lloyd Smith in response to a petition filed by the Union Street Railroad. Union believed that earlier action by the city of Brooklyn in awarding the franchise to Nassau Electric for the portion of these two lines within its jurisdiction was improper, and the company sought relief. On July 25, 1895, the state supreme court affirmed the legitimacy of the franchise awards, and Flynn was able to begin service on the two lines.[11]

Flynn also had to retain attorneys and spend a good deal of time in court when he proposed laying rails for Nassau Electric's new Church Avenue Line that would cross Ocean Parkway at grade. A hastily organized citizens group called the Good Government Club of Brooklyn went to court to force Flynn to build a tunnel under Ocean Parkway for his Church Avenue cars, an expense that Flynn wanted to avoid.[12] Flynn lost on this matter, and a short tunnel under Ocean Parkway remains the only place in all of Brooklyn where streetcars operated below ground. (Brooklyn streetcars would descend beneath the surface of the earth at one other location, but it was not in Brooklyn. It was an underground terminal at Delancey Street at the Manhattan end of the Williamsburg Bridge, where a number of Brooklyn trolley lines terminated for many years.)

Flynn also sent his attorneys into court in efforts to affect the outcome of proceedings where Nassau Electric was not itself a party, but Brooklyn Heights or Brooklyn City was. Flynn owned shares in both companies and thus had standing to file suit, even though his true motivation was not the protection of his rights as a stockholder but the economic interests of Nassau Electric.

In spite of these frequent court appearances, Nassau Electric quickly built a reputation as a "customer-friendly" street railway. The company charged a five-cent fare, irrespective of distance traveled. This policy quickly forced other Kings County companies, who generally added an extra fare for trips that extended beyond the limits of the city of Brooklyn, to adopt similar fare policies. Although the Coney Island and Brooklyn Railroad (CI&B)

initially refused to be swayed and continued to charge a double-fare between downtown Brooklyn and Coney Island, it eventually gave in—at least for a few seasons. Even the excursion railways found they had to lower their fares in the face of competition from Flynn's Road. Nassau Electric also offered passengers unlimited free transfer privileges among its various lines, a policy the other roads quickly adopted in response to Nassau's initiative.

Nassau Electric built a large, state-of-the-art electric-generating plant on the shore of Upper New York Bay at the foot of 39th Street, adjacent to the ferry terminal, to provide power for its new electric streetcar lines. To distribute current from this powerhouse to a Nassau Electric system that eventually grew to more than 100 miles of trackage along Brooklyn streets, a 500-ton network of copper cable was required.[13]

The sudden emergence of Nassau Electric took the American street railway industry by surprise. A wire story out of Boston in March 1894, for instance, identified a Bostonian by the name of William A. Boland as one of the investors behind the new undertaking, a venture that was said to involve $12 million in new construction and that would result in "an electric road of about 100 miles in length." Given the Boston origin of this report, it is understandable that the previously unknown Brooklyn street railway was confused with the name of a New England city not far from Boston. The $12 million enterprise in which Boland was said to be involved was called the Nashua Electric Railroad Company.[14]

While Nassau Electric's forte would be the construction of new electric-powered streetcar lines that were intended to develop new Kings County transit markets, Flynn and his associates were not inactive in taking over older systems and companies. In 1896, Nassau Electric acquired the Atlantic Avenue Railroad and, through it, the Brooklyn, Bath and West End Railroad that the Atlantic Avenue company had acquired in 1893. With this transaction, Nassau Electric not only secured entry into downtown Brooklyn over the Atlantic Avenue company's lines, it also enhanced its position with respect to seasonal traffic to and from Coney Island.

Deacon Richardson had divested himself of his interest in the Atlantic Avenue Railroad in 1892, prior to the company's acquisition by Nassau Electric. Press estimates at the time suggested that Richardson realized as much as $3 million in the transaction when a syndicate composed of Philadelphia and New York City interests acquired Richardson's stake in the road.[15] To purchase the property, the new owners were willing to buy stock in the company at 250 percent of par, an offer that Richardson negotiated not only for himself but also for all of his fellow investors.[16] There were rumors that Richardson would continue to run the company after selling his stock, but he quickly put these rumors to rest. "I shall not be President of the new company. My days are not long on this earth, and those remaining I propose to spend in peace and quiet."[17] Richardson did consent to assist the new owners of the Atlantic Avenue Railroad by serving as a paid consultant for a short period of time, but after 1892 he no longer owned a major stake in the company.

Another rumor surrounding this transaction suggested that the Long Island Railroad (LIRR) was behind the acquisition of the Atlantic Avenue property. However, the syndicate that acquired the Atlantic Avenue Railroad was not associated with Corbin and the LIRR; the principal investor was a New Yorker by the name of Isaac Seligman. A possible explanation for this rumor is the fact that the new owners of the Atlantic Avenue Railroad retained as president a man who had previously been an executive with the LIRR, Benjamin Norton. Norton's background with the LIRR was not incidental to his selection as president. The Atlantic Avenue Railroad owned the critical Atlantic Avenue right-of-way leased by the LIRR to reach Brooklyn, and there was some suspicion that over the years the LIRR had not properly fulfilled the terms of this lease agreement. As a former LIRR insider, Norton was thought to be someone who could help rectify these irregularities. In addition, when Seligman and his group bought out Richardson in 1892, Corbin and the LIRR were actively talking about converting the Atlantic Avenue right-of-way into an elevated line, a development that would have affected the street railway's earning power.[18] (As president of the Atlantic Avenue Railroad, Norton quickly made a cosmetic decision that hearkened back to his LIRR days, though. As new electric-powered streetcars were delivered to the company, Norton decided to change their principal exterior from "Portland amber," Richardson's color of choice, to "the color known as Tuscan red, which is the same as that used on the Long Island railroad cars.")[19]

The new investors behind the Atlantic Avenue Railroad had their eye on more improvements than converting the company's streetcar lines from horses to electricity. They were also anxious to explore merger and consolidation possibilities with other Brooklyn street railways. Early in 1893, they acquired the Brooklyn, Bath and West End.[20] As a result of this important acquisition, Atlantic Avenue's financial and technical resources were available to electrify the West End property and make it, in late 1893, the first of the Coney Island excursion railways to operate electric-powered equipment.

In 1892, the year before it was acquired by Atlantic Avenue, the Brooklyn, Bath and West End had upgraded its operations by extending service down to the 39th Street Ferry over trackage of the South Brooklyn Railway and Terminal Company (see chapter 4). Now, a year later, the West End route was offering electrified service from the foot of Atlantic Avenue in Brooklyn all the way to Coney Island. By the summer of 1894, passengers heading for a day at the shore could board a trolley car coming up from South Ferry at, say, Atlantic Avenue and Nevins Street; Nassau Electric would take them all the way to West End Depot, a block from the ocean in Coney Island, with electricity supplying all the traction power.

For electrified service between the 39th Street ferry slip and Coney Island, the Atlantic Avenue Railroad acquired three electric motor cars that had been part of a larger fleet that provided transport around the grounds of the World's Colombian Exposition in Chicago in 1893. (The one-summer Chicago service was called the Intramural Railroad.) There has been some confusion over these cars because, when they were placed into service on the West End Line, they looked totally different from the cars that had run in Chicago. The original car bodies from Chicago—with arched roofs and open sides—were discarded when the trio reached Brooklyn and were replaced with more conventional bodies built in Massachusetts by the Wason Car Company. Only the trucks and electrical equipment ran in both Chicago and Brooklyn; the visible parts of the cars were quite different in each city.[21]

In addition to electrifying its line to the seashore, the Atlantic Avenue Railroad took further steps in 1894 to improve its market share in the Coney Island trade. The company lowered its fare on the Brooklyn, Bath and West End from fifteen cents to ten cents for a one-way ticket, an action that sent officials of the Prospect Park and Coney Island Railroad (PP&CI) rushing into court to enjoin what they regarded as reckless behavior. Citing the contract the two companies had executed when they agreed to terminate their trains in the same Union Depot at Fifth Avenue and 36th Street and to charge identical fares, PP&CI secured judicial relief. With the busy July 4 holiday approaching, and reports circulating that not all ticket agents of the Atlantic Avenue Railroad were observing the court order, PP&CI went back to court on July 3 and prevailed on Justice William J. Gaynor to issue a restraining order in support of the earlier injunction.

An important reason why Richardson was able to liquidate his holdings in the Atlantic Avenue Railroad for such a high price in 1892 is the fact that, in his final years with the railway, Richardson himself had secured municipal authorization to convert the road from animal power to electric traction and to begin the process of building a generating station and acquiring new electric-powered streetcars. The *Brooklyn Daily Eagle* noted, "By this feat, which could not have been accomplished by outside men, not intimately acquainted with Brooklyn methods, he has increased the value of the Atlantic Avenue franchise fully two fold. It is now in just such shape as would be attractive to outside investors, and being in that shape, it is not strange that its sale should have been early made."[22] The *Eagle's* estimate that the property had increased "two fold" was made the day before details of the transaction were announced. In fact, the increase was closer to two-and-a-half fold.

Under Richardson, the Atlantic Avenue Railroad had purchased a piece of property on Third Avenue between First and Second Streets that backed onto Gowanus Canal, and here the company built an electric-generating station. "There is hardly a site in the city better suited to our needs," Richardson proudly boasted.[23] The brick and concrete structure was 234 feet long and 68 feet deep; it was equipped with eight Babcock and Wilcox boilers and four tandem compound steam engines with a combined horsepower of 2,500 that were built by C. and G. Cooper. Each engine drove a Westinghouse electric generator, and the powerhouse included sufficient room so the railway could later double its generating capacity, if demand warranted. The facility represented an investment of $350,000 by the railroad.[24]

The company's first electric-powered trolleys were a fleet of 100 cars turned out by the Saint Louis Car Company, each fitted with two thirty-horsepower Westinghouse motors.[25] Although the precise date when the Atlantic Avenue Railroad operated its first electric-powered streetcar is not known—it was after Richardson had sold the property, though—by mid-March of 1893 a token number of electric cars were in service, and more were being added daily.[26]

Unfortunately, Deacon Richardson did not long survive after selling the Atlantic Avenue Railroad. He passed away at his Brooklyn home, 125 South Oxford Street, on December 31, 1893, at the age of 71.[27] His son, William J. Richardson, while selling off his own equity interest in the company to the new owners in 1892, remained with the railway as corporate secretary and retained a seat on the board of directors. But the younger Richardson ran afoul of the new owners of the Atlantic Avenue Railroad during a bitter Brooklyn trolley car strike in early 1895. Feeling that Richardson had taken sides with the company's workers during the work stoppage, the company relieved him of his post shortly afterward.

Within weeks of his dismissal by the Atlantic Avenue Railroad, the younger Richardson died from meningitis in Brooklyn on April 26, 1895. His death at the age of 46 cut short a career of service to the street railway industry of Brooklyn and the United States. In reporting his passing to the members of the Street-Railway Association of the State of New York, the organization's executive committee said, "He at all times had the welfare of the Association at heart, and never faulted in the discharge of any duty that would enhance its interest."[28] On April 29, 1895, William J. Richardson was laid to rest next to his father in Brooklyn's Green-wood Cemetery. On a quiet day at the Richardson gravesite, one could hear the distant rumble of electric cars of the Atlantic Avenue Railroad, now on their way to Coney Island over the former Brooklyn, Bath and West End Railroad.

As street railway matters in Brooklyn evolved in the wake of the 1895 strike, it became clear to Isaac Seligman and his associates that the acquisition of the Atlantic Avenue property by a larger railway would be in their best interest. So when Nassau Electric emerged as a potential lessor of the property, the owners of the Atlantic Avenue Railroad retained a street railway executive with impeccable coast-to-coast credentials to serve as their road's president and ensure that the pending transaction with Nassau Electric was consummated. The new president, H. M. Littell, managed the Atlantic Avenue company for just a few months before moving on to an important managerial position with the Metropolitan Street Railway Company in New York. Littell executed his mandate ably and, several months after he took office, the Atlantic Avenue Railroad was conveyed to Nassau Electric under the terms of a long-term lease.[29]

Nassau Electric itself proved to be a transitional entity in Kings County. Although Patrick Flynn remained a shareholder in the company for all of its days, by 1899 he was no longer the dominant figure that he had been a few years earlier. Control of Nassau Electric was now largely in the hands of a syndicate that included former Ohio congressman Tom L. Johnson, who later served as the company's president.

Johnson is an especially interesting figure. Although he was an owner and a manager of several street railways, he was an outspoken opponent of private ownership of public transit companies and believed that such services should be provided by the public sector. His initial run for public office was equally contradictory; when drafted for what proved to be an unsuccessful run for Congress in 1888, the man enjoyed the distinction of being so indifferent to politics that he had never before bothered to vote.[30]

In mid-January of 1899 a stock transfer took place, and Johnson and his associates passed control of Nassau Electric to investors who were associated with the new BRT.[31] The next step in the process was for Nassau Electric to be leased to the Brooklyn Heights Railroad, itself then a wholly owned subsidiary of the BRT. The original lease was for but one year, but it was extended to 999 years shortly afterward. A new group of directors, friendly to the BRT, were now controlling the fortunes of what was once known as Flynn's Road. However, one minority shareholder of Nassau Electric opposed the leasing of Nassau Electric to Brooklyn Heights, and he went to court and sought judicial intervention to preserve his rights and prevent the lease from moving forward.

The press referred to this aggressive plaintiff as the "Nassau tiger." He was, of course, Patrick H. Flynn, once the guiding force behind Nassau Electric, but now a minor gadfly within a corporation of much larger scope. Flynn's suit proved ineffectual, the lease went forward, and the Nassau Electric Railroad was wholly absorbed into the broad transport system that was controlled by the Brooklyn Heights Railroad. Flynn, for his part, rode off into the sunset (the sunset, in this case, being eastward from Brooklyn, not westward). Later in the spring of 1899, the *Brooklyn Daily Eagle* reported that Flynn was hired as a contractor by a consortium of Long Island interests who planned to build a series of electric railways between points in Queens County and towns further out on Long Island.[32]

While it was undoubtedly the most significant, Nassau Electric was not the only Kings County street railway consortium created during the 1890s that failed to see the dawn of the twentieth century. In late 1893, Philadelphia interests led by the investment banking house of Drexel, Morgan established a corporation called the Brooklyn, Queens County and Suburban Railroad (BQC&S). Drexel, Morgan then moved quickly and merged three other Kings County street railways it had earlier acquired into BQC&S. These were the Broadway Railroad, which ran between the East River and East New York and included branch lines along such important thoroughfares as Reid Avenue, Sumner Avenue, and Ralph Avenue; the Brooklyn and Jamaica, King's County's first electrified street railway; and a company whose principal service was from East River ferry slips in Williamsburgh out into Queens County along the important Metropolitan Avenue corridor. Street railway service on Metropolitan Avenue operated under a variety of corporate names over the years—Metropolitan Railroad Company; Brooklyn, Bushwick and Queens County Railroad; and Broadway Ferry and Metropolitan Avenue Railroad.[33]

Within months of establishing the BQC&S, Drexel, Morgan realized that its newly established street railway in Brooklyn's Eastern District was not finding ready buyers for its securities. Among the reasons for potential investors' hesitation was the fact that in 1893 the entire country was suffering from what most would call a full-fledged depression. Drexel, Morgan thus began to transfer the property into the ever-expanding orbit of Brooklyn City–Brooklyn Heights. BQC&S retained its identity for a few years, and electrification was advanced on the subsidiary railways under its jurisdiction. By the end of the decade, BQC&S had repeated the Nassau Electric paradigm; it had been created during the turbulent 1890s but was fully absorbed by the BRT before the decade was over.

One reasonably important Kings County street railway managed to survive into the new century without being absorbed by the BRT. It was something of a multiple-company system that included both the CI&B and the Brooklyn City and Newtown (BC&N). CI&B had acquired the mile-and-a-half-long Prospect Park and Flatbush Railroad in 1891, thus establishing a connection along the southern rim of Prospect Park between its Coney Island Avenue Line and BC&N's Franklin Avenue Line. Once CI&B and BC&N were united in late 1897, through streetcar service could be operated to Coney Island from points as far away as Ridgewood. The merger was almost derailed, though, when a minority stockholder of the CI&B obtained a temporary injunction to interdict the arrangement. His name was Patrick H. Flynn.

HORSES GIVE WAY TO ELECTRIC MOTORS

From a technical perspective, an important characteristic of the Kings County street railway scene in the 1890s was a wholesale shift from animal power to electric traction. Although some companies had experimented using electric-powered streetcars in Brooklyn in the late 1880s, the transformation became complete during the early 1890s.

In the summer of 1890, the *Brooklyn Daily Eagle* reported that three important Brooklyn street railways had developed plans "to adopt as a motive power the overhead system of electric wires."[34] The three were identified as the Brooklyn City Railroad, the Atlantic Avenue Railroad, and the CI&B. Daniel Lewis, then the president of Brooklyn City, described his company's plans. "We shall have a trolley wire over each track carrying 500 volts, and there will be an elaborate system of connections with a large underground supply wire, which will be laid under the curbstones. Iron posts on each side of the street will support the trolley wire, and parallel with it will run the wire carrying the current and getting its supply at frequent intervals from the underground supply wire." After describing technical aspects of his company's proposed shift to electric traction, Lewis turned to the political side of things and voiced optimism. "The consents from property owners are coming in very rapidly, and as yet no opposition is manifested to the change."[35]

Approval from property owners was not the only hurdle a street railway had to clear in Brooklyn before it could electrify a horse-powered line. Armed with signed consents, a company then had to secure authorization from the elected aldermen who sat on the Brooklyn Common Council. The *Eagle* viewed this last step, perhaps cynically, as a mere formality. "Money will surmount any difficulties to be met with in that body."[36] But the newspaper correctly predicted that the street railways would face a good deal more opposition from local property owners than President Lewis's optimistic pronouncement suggested. "Public opinion . . . seems to be against any overhead wire system, and whether this prejudice can be overcome is a problem which the officers of the Brooklyn City Company are said to be worrying about."[37]

The debate raged during the winter of 1890–91. In the face of inaction or negative action by the Brooklyn Common Council, a company was legally entitled to appeal to the Board of Railroad Commissioners, a powerful state agency that enjoyed broad regulatory authority in railway matters. Failing at this level, the law gave railways the right to seek judicial review by requesting the appointment of a three-member commission to render a final verdict.

Reaching no accommodation with Brooklyn aldermen, the street railways appealed to the Board of Railway Commissioners, who held a number of public hearings where acrimony was in no short supply. During one such hearing in May 1891, Deacon William Richardson of the Atlantic Avenue Railroad was referred to as a "white-headed old thief" by a disgruntled property owner along the Seventh Avenue Line, one of those proposed for electrification.[38] Citizens charged that the street railways secured consent signatures under fraudulent circumstances, and a steady supply of seemingly anti-electrification technical testimony was provided by engineers who represented street railway electrification systems other than the one that a particular Brooklyn road planned to deploy.[39]

The street railways did not receive favorable treatment from the Board of Railway Commissioners, so the next level of appeal was to a three-member judicial panel. On September 16, 1891, General Henry W. Slocum of the CI&B Railroad filed such an appeal on behalf of his road's petition to electrify the Brooklyn end of its line from Park Circle to the East River. (The CI&B had electrified its line from Park Circle to Coney Island in 1890.) The panel reported unanimously in favor of the railroad's petition. What made this decision so important was the fact that it was rendered even though the railway had failed to secure approval signatures from a majority of property owners along the line. A major property owner Slocum had to contend with, though, was the city of Brooklyn, since his cars traveled along the periphery of Prospect Park on their way into town.[40]

With the success achieved by the CI&B at judicial review as a compelling precedent, Brooklyn politicians decided to end the protracted debate over street railway electrification and allow the process to move forward without further judicial intervention. As long as the courts were going to permit electrification anyway, why not get on the winning side and see what benefits might accrue? And so by vote of the Board of Aldermen on December 21, 1891, "All the main lines of surface railroads were authorized to substitute the overhead electric wires as a motive power to succeed the horses now in use."[41] The *New York Times,* long opposed to the electrification of Brooklyn street railways, continued to press its views. It reported that previously wavering aldermen "had been fully convinced by some specious arguments that the trolley was what they wanted."[42] But specious arguments or otherwise, the long debate was over and the street railways of Brooklyn turned to the task of investing $12 million in the electrification of their properties. This was a massive sum of money, and it was the issuance of requisite securities to raise this capital that helped trigger further corporate changes in the ownership and management of Brooklyn street railways before the decade was over.

Observers would continue to speculate that, in authorizing the electrification of horsecar lines, Brooklyn aldermen were motivated by less-than-honorable intentions. The *Brooklyn Daily Eagle,* for instance, thought it smelled something rotten in late 1892 when John W. Fowler sold his stock in two separate Brooklyn companies that he had founded several years earlier, the Lewis and Fowler Manufacturing Company and the Lewis and Fowler Girder Rail Company. The former built streetcars and owned a number of patents for streetcar parts and accessories. The latter specialized in the high-quality steel rail that was used to replace older iron rail when a streetcar company converted its operations to electric trolleys. (Higher-quality rail was needed because electric streetcars were heavier than their horse-drawn predecessors, and because running rails served as a "return" for the electric circuit that powered the car.) Both of Fowler's companies figured to prosper from the electrification projects that Brooklyn street railways were about to launch.

Fowler's stock was purchased by Frank Barnaby on behalf of an unknown syndicate. However, the Brooklyn City Railroad was another major owner of Lewis and Fowler stock. Daniel Lewis, the president of both Brooklyn City and Brooklyn Heights, was the "Lewis" of Lewis and Fowler as well as the company's president, and it would not be incorrect to call Lewis and Fowler the car-building arm of Brooklyn City and Brooklyn Heights. The *Eagle* wondered if the shares Barnaby acquired would actually wind up in the hands of those Brooklyn aldermen who had voted to allow the electrification of Brooklyn street railways. The paper quoted an anonymous source who was "in a position to know." "Certain members of the common council who voted to give the Brooklyn City railroad company its franchise and a state senator from this city and several other politicians who are interested in electric railroads . . . are the real purchasers of this stock in the Lewis & Fowler companies."[43]

Whether Brooklyn aldermen were given preference in the purchase of Lewis and Fowler stock or not, the company did not long survive as an independent streetcar manufacturer; there is no evidence of its supplying streetcars for any major U.S. properties after 1892. John W. Fowler, on the other hand, did return to the business after selling his stock. In early 1893 he established the J. W. Fowler Car Company in Elizabethport, New Jersey. If the new firm can be said to have had a specialty, it was the design and manufacture of special-purpose streetcars such as snowplows and sweepers. The J. W. Fowler Car Company would not long survive, either. By 1901 Fowler was the president of yet another company, the Fowler and Roberts Manufacturing Company, a Brooklyn firm whose specialty was the manufacture not of streetcars, but of specialty items for the industry such as fare registers and similar equipment.

As noted in chapter 2, the first Brooklyn City streetcar line to be run with electric-powered cars did so, after considerable delay, in May 1892. The project was begun prior to the formal authorization voted by the aldermen in December 1891; however, since the line operated beyond the city limits of Brooklyn, such approval was not required. It began at the 39th Street ferry in South Brooklyn and ran, largely via Second Avenue, to the Bensonhurst section in the town of New Utrecht. Electric current was generated in a temporary company power station located on Second Avenue near 52nd Street. Looking ahead to more widespread use of electric-powered streetcars, Brooklyn City designed and built a permanent electric-generating station adjacent to this temporary facility, a site that permitted easy delivery of coal by barge. This powerhouse was equipped with eight 1,000-horsepower steam engines built by E. P. Allis and Company that were linked to electric generators built by the Thomson-Houston Electric Company.[44]

By late 1882, a mere twelve months after Brooklyn aldermen voted to permit electrification, the Brooklyn City Railroad had strung wires along forty-five miles of trackage and was operating 150 electric cars, each of which could haul a nonmotorized trailer. The first electric cars to run down Fulton Street to Fulton Ferry— where Brooklyn City's first horse-powered streetcars had begun service in 1854—did so on November 7, 1892. But while Brooklyn City's inaugural cars of 1854 turned off Fulton Street and headed east on Myrtle Avenue, the first Brooklyn City electric cars to serve Fulton Ferry in 1891 continued out Fulton Street to Flatbush Avenue, then turned off Flatbush onto Third Avenue, and terminated at 25th Street in South Brooklyn.

One ancillary benefit that Brooklyn street railways were able to achieve in stringing trolley wires along streets where elevated railways existed was the right to hang such wires from the elevated railway structures. Appropriate insulation was required so that electric current would not "stray" into the conductive metal of the structure. But street railways were happy to take advantage of the elevated railways that were otherwise their competitors and use elevated railway structures to help support trolley wires along Brooklyn thoroughfares such as Fulton Street, Myrtle Avenue, and Broadway. (When street railways across the East River in Manhattan began to electrify their operations, no similar benefit was possible. Ordinances there prohibited the use of overhead trolley wires, and companies had to construct more expensive underground conduits to electrify their streetcar lines.)

Brooklyn City quickly expanded its capability to generate electric current for its system and built two additional power plants, one on Kent Avenue and Division Street, adjacent to the Navy yard, and a smaller facility in Ridgewood. The Atlantic Avenue Railroad had built its power plant on the banks of Gowanus Canal between Second and Third Streets, while the CI&B satisfied its requirements for additional electric current by building a new generating station at Smith and Ninth Streets, also adjacent to Gowanus Canal. The original power plant the company built to generate current for its initial electrified segment—from Park Circle to Coney Island—was a small facility along Coney Island Avenue south of Park Circle. Nassau Electric's powerhouse was adjacent to the 39th Street Ferry. Thus, by the early 1890s, four important Kings County street railways owned and operated six permanent electric-generating plants, facilities with a combined output in excess of 25,000 kilowatts. So many electric-generating facilities were needed because the companies operated independently. Once the Brooklyn Rapid Transit Company emerged at the end of the decade and acquired three of the four railways, this abundance of generating capability allowed the company to electrify the elevated railways without constructing additional powerhouses.

THE ELEVATED COMPANIES IN THE 1890s

During the 1890s, continual efforts were made to combine Brooklyn's two elevated railways, Brooklyn Union Elevated and Kings County Elevated, into a single company. Brooklyn Union Elevated, of course, was the product of a merger of Brooklyn Elevated and Union Elevated. But these two companies had been financed and promoted from the outset by interests with considerable overlap, and their union was in no sense a merger of rival or competitive corporate cultures. Bringing Brooklyn Union and Kings County together, though, was an entirely different matter.

By 1892, factions within Brooklyn Union held opposing views on the desirability of a merger with Kings County. Henry Putnam, long the company's president, sided with many of the company's original investors, and they stood foursquare against any merger with Kings County. Frederick Uhlmann, who would eventually become chairman of the combined company, was associated with some of the road's newer stockholders who believed that unification with Kings County was the way the company should proceed. Although the difference between Brooklyn Elevated and Union Elevated was paper-thin, Putnam was a product of the former company, Uhlmann the latter.

Among the stockholders with whom Uhlmann was associated were a number of individuals with strong Brooklyn political connections. Putnam and his allies charged that many of these people had been given shares in the company in exchange for favorable votes in various legislative bodies over the years, and that they were not genuine investors who had the company's long-term interest at heart. Uhlmann's faction would eventually prevail over Putnam's, but Brooklyn Union's dire financial straits prevented any merger with Kings County from going forward and any victory Uhlmann achieved was more symbolic than real. The company entered receivership once again in the 1890s, and it was Uhlmann who was appointed receiver for the bankrupt railway. Despite their opposing views on the important question of merger with Kings County, Uhlmann and Putnam were able to work cooperatively in other matters associated with Brooklyn Union.

On the other side of the merger issue, Kings County's James Jourdan was an active proponent of combining the two Brooklyn elevated companies—or at least that is what he publicly maintained. In early 1892, Jourdan said, "I have no hesitation in saying that I am strongly in favor of consolidation."[45] But when Uhlmann and Brooklyn Union submitted a formal merger proposal to Kings County in March 1892, Jourdan promptly rejected it.[46] His reason was, in a word, money.

Brooklyn Union believed that because its system was much larger than King County's and its capital plant represented a substantially greater investment, its stake in a merged elevated system should be larger. Not that Kings County was any paradigm of financial stability, but Jourdan hoped to capitalize on Brooklyn Union's even shakier financial position and was holding out for a fifty-fifty merger. The result was no merger at all. However, later in 1892, Edward Lauterbach, a director of Brooklyn Elevated and an ally of Uhlmann said, "That some sort of union will be effected I have no doubt, but just when it will come about and just what will be the terms I cannot venture to predict."[47]

Meanwhile the two Brooklyn elevated railways expanded modestly during the 1890s, even if their merger did not come to pass. King County's Fulton Street Line was extended out Pitkin Avenue to Grant Avenue in 1893. Brooklyn Union's Fifth Avenue Line was extended to Third Avenue and 65th Street in Bay Ridge, also in 1893, and both the Lexington Avenue and Broadway Lines of Brooklyn Union were extended over a common line to Cypress Hills in the same year. As noted earlier, a separate corporation was formed to handle these Brooklyn Union extensions, the Seaside and Brooklyn Bridge Railroad. This company even held title to fifty-some passenger coaches that were used to expand the company's fleet to serve the new lines. In practice, though, the Seaside and Brooklyn Bridge name enjoyed an identity that extended no further than the investment community where the company's securities were sold and traded. As far as Brooklyn passengers were concerned, the new extensions were part of the Brooklyn Union elevated railway system and, in practical terms, that is exactly what they were. The expansion of the Kings County elevated line to Grant Avenue also involved the creation of a new and separate "paper" corporation, the Fulton Elevated Railroad Company.

Despite its less-than-robust financial condition, Brooklyn Union was able to finance various improvements to its property. One that drew considerable attention from the engineering community was a project to ease the running grade along the Myrtle Avenue Line between Bridge Street and Grand Avenue where the company's Forney locomotives frequently stalled while hauling heavy trains. A 1,700-foot grade of 2.06 percent between Navy Street and Carleton Avenue was especially troublesome, and its elimination became necessary so the company could run longer trains to accommodate steadily increasing patronage. Many of these new patrons were bound for the Sands Street terminal at the end of the line, where they transferred to the cable railway that crossed the Brooklyn Bridge to New York City.

Without disrupting elevated traffic along the line, the company cut support columns after temporary supporting structures had been placed around them; using a set of hydraulic jacks, workers lowered the entire elevated structure—the differential varied from five feet to a fraction of an inch—to reduce the grade. Part of the project included altering two stations, Washington Avenue and Vanderbilt Avenue, that had originally been built with separate platforms on the outside of each track into a configuration that featured a single platform between the tracks. This configuration allowed the company to realize considerable labor savings by reducing the need for station personnel.[48]

Also in the air during the 1890s was the prospect of converting the two elevated lines from steam power to electricity. In July 1892, Jourdan said that Kings County Elevated was ready to move forward with such a project. However, nothing important was accomplished in this regard until the two elevated companies were later absorbed by the BRT.[49]

One important improvement that Jourdan was able to orchestrate was linking the Fulton Street El with the Brooklyn and Brighton Beach Railroad. A ramp was built that began to the south of the Brooklyn and Brighton Beach's Bedford Terminal and crossed over Atlantic Avenue—and the LIRR, as well. A short elevated line then continued, largely over private property, to Fulton Street where a junction was built with the Kings County Elevated. The cost of the connection was estimated at between $200,000 and $300,000. Jourdan was forced to acquire private property for this link because homeowners had earlier secured passage of state legislation prohibiting elevated construction over public streets in the area.

The company considered various service options as part of this important link. One would have seen conventional Kings County Elevated trains proceeding out the Brighton Line as far as Church Avenue, and the line between Fulton Street and Church Avenue would be converted into part of the Kings County Railroad. Elevated trains from downtown Brooklyn would terminate at Church

Avenue, and connecting service would be provided beyond this point in central Flatbush to Brighton Beach and the seashore, perhaps by electric trolley cars. However, what was actually built was a simple connection between the two lines, and through service was operated over both roads by Kings County locomotives and rolling stock.

Locomotives that formerly ran on the Brooklyn and Brighton Beach—most of which were originally acquired by the Brooklyn, Flatbush and Coney Island—were too heavy for service on the Fulton Street elevated line. Forney-style locomotives of the Kings County Railroad provided the motive power along the Brighton Line for through trains. The first such service operated on August 15, 1896, with trains leaving Sands Street for Brighton Beach every twenty minutes and charging a fare of but ten cents. The *New York Times* reported, "This new route offers New-Yorkers the cheapest, most convenient, and quickest way to Coney Island, thirty-five minutes being the running time."[50]

The Kings County Railroad and the Brooklyn and Brighton Beach remained separate corporations, although James Jourdan continued to serve as president of both companies. Several months earlier, in February 1896, stockholders of the Brooklyn and Brighton Beach authorized that company's directors to lease their road to Kings County. Once the lease was executed and the ramp constructed, joint service over both roads was simple enough to arrange.

During the 1890s, both elevated railway companies made a steady effort to extend service across the Brooklyn Bridge into Manhattan over the right-of-way of the bridge cable railway. This development is discussed below.

Long Island Traction

Because the Kings County transport scene was so dynamic during the 1890s, it can sometimes be misleading to discuss topics in serial fashion. So many things were happening simultaneously, and developments influenced one another in so many ways, that any narrative sequence can easily overlook important relational implications. For instance, during the same years that Patrick

Flynn was directing the early fortunes of a new and expanding Nassau Electric Railroad, Nassau Electric was absorbing other Kings County railways, and the elevated railways were talking merger, a company known as Long Island Traction emerged on the scene and began to exert an altogether different impact on Kings County railway properties.

In late 1892, several months before the Brooklyn City Railroad was leased by Brooklyn Heights in February 1893, rumors began to circulate through the Brooklyn financial district on Montague Street that something big was about to happen to the city's street railways. The *Brooklyn Daily Eagle* reported authoritatively in December 1892 that three separate syndicates were aggressively competing for control of the Brooklyn City Railroad as a first step in the creation of a much wider and broader street railway system.[51] The *Eagle* was as confident as it possibly could be that its reporters had successfully identified the three contending syndicates. One was based in Cincinnati and was associated with former Ohio Congressman Tom L. Johnson, a man who had earlier public transit experience in Cleveland and who would soon become an important figure with Nassau Electric; the second syndicate was from Pittsburgh and had grown out of financial interests in that city; the third syndicate was closer to home and was part of the Metropolitan Street Railway that played so important a role across the East River in New York City. *Eagle* reporters traveled to Pittsburgh and Cincinnati, as well as New York, in search of follow-up stories.[52]

In the end—save for Johnson's association with Nassau Electric—none of these syndicates was successful in securing control of Brooklyn street railways, and there is scant evidence that any of them actively sought to gain control of Brooklyn City Railroad. The consortium that did emerge and begin the process of street railway amalgamation in Brooklyn was called Long Island Traction. The *Eagle* took note of the new consortium's arrival, "The Long Island Traction Company, heretofore unheard of but composed of well known men, will secure control of the Brooklyn City road."[53] However, the men behind Long Island Traction were more than "well known"—they were many of the same individuals who were the principal investors behind Brooklyn City. Long Island Traction was not a case of outside business interests investing fresh capital to expand Brooklyn transport endeavors. It was, rather, financial maneuvering by a group of insiders to increase the return on money that had already been invested in Brooklyn street railways.

From its beginnings in 1892 and for all of its days, Long Island Traction was a holding company that acquired interests in other transport endeavors by sale and lease and that provided its own stockholders and investors with revenue generated by such transactions. Shortly after Brooklyn City was leased to Brooklyn Heights—a transaction that increased the worth of the Brooklyn Heights Railroad without the investment of a single dime—Long Island Traction took over the Brooklyn Heights road and assumed responsibility for the 10 percent dividend that had been guaranteed to Brooklyn City stockholders.

Two subsequent events would doom Long Island Traction—a devastating downturn in the nation's economy that began in 1893 and an almost equally devastating trolley strike that hit Brooklyn street railways in early 1895. The delicately balanced financing scheme that was at the heart of Long Island Traction was unable to weather these dual storms, and the company was forced to reorganize in late 1895. The reorganization was orchestrated by new investors who could also be described as "well-known men," but they were not the same individuals who were originally behind Long Island Traction.

A characteristic of Long Island Traction that was not central to its woes, but that was cited time and time again by its detractors as evidence of some fundamental flaw, was the fact that the company was not incorporated in New York, where its subsidiary companies ran streetcars and carried passengers. Long Island Traction was a Virginia corporation, with formal headquarters in Richmond. (Long Island Traction has been referred to as a West Virginia corporation, but this is incorrect. Certain litigation associated with Long Island Traction took place in federal circuit courts that were located in West Virginia, since such tribunals exercised appellate jurisdiction over matters that initially were heard in Virginia, and this is likely the source of the confusion.)

The goal of transit unification was a sound one, and an agency called the Brooklyn Rapid Transit Company would succeed where Long Island Traction had failed. Before addressing the emergence of the BRT, though, let us briefly explore a few other themes that are part of the Brooklyn mass transit landscape of the 1890s.

THE BROOKLYN TROLLEY STRIKE OF 1895

A strike on a number of Brooklyn street railways in early 1895 stands as an important benchmark in the development of labor-management relations in the mass transit industry. The strike was thought to be the first in the country to involve street railway properties that largely operated electric-powered cars.[54] In addition, it was in the aftermath of the 1895 strike—and in many ways because of the strike—that even further corporate changes would come to pass at various Brooklyn street railway properties.

To understand the background of the Brooklyn trolley strike of 1895, it is helpful to look back to 1889, when another streetcar labor dispute erupted. The 1889 strike began on Brooklyn's Atlantic Avenue Railroad. Because "Deacon" Richardson was known to be an investor in certain street railways across the East River in New York City, the strike quickly spread there and brought streetcar paralysis to both Brooklyn and New York. In all, 7,000 workers walked off the job at more than twenty Brooklyn and New York street railway properties, and three people lost their lives during a turbulent week of bloodshed and rioting. The 1889 strike can be traced to a piece of presumably "pro-labor" legislation that New York State had earlier enacted, which reduced the maximum number of hours an employee could work without receiving premium pay from twelve to ten hours. In redrafting streetcar schedules and work assignments to observe the provisions of the new law, Richardson also reduced a basic day's wages for his workers from $2 to $1.70. Less work should mean less pay, he reasoned. However, a circular that was given to employees at the Atlantic Avenue Railroad when the new schedules went into effect on January 24, 1889, sounded as if work hours were being reduced with no reduction in take-home pay.

The ensuing strike in 1889, then, was more of a wildcat walkout than the product of any long-range or strategic planning. It was an immediate reaction to a sudden and unexpected grievance. Gangs of strikers and their supporters took to the streets in front of various railway stables in an effort to prevent streetcars from heading out on their runs and to prevent nonstriking employees from reporting to work. One concession that strikers were willing to make in 1889 was to allow fellow workers to enter the stables and tend to the horses so the animals would not become unwitting victims of the dispute. A major point on which neither the Atlantic Avenue Railroad nor any of the other properties would make any concession, though, was formal or tacit recognition of labor unions that were then forming, and in which many of the workers held membership.

By 1895, labor organizations such as the Knights of Labor and the Amalgamated Association of Street Railway Employees of America had begun to make inroads, and rudimentary kinds of collective bargaining were starting to take place. Management still believed that on such fundamental matters as the setting of wage rates it enjoyed a unilateral authority akin to the divine right of kings. But because workers and their organizations were able to cause such mischief if they were dissatisfied, some kind of conversations with labor organizations—unofficial, nonbinding, and merely advisory—seemed like a practical course of action for street railway officials to take.

Unlike the wildcat walkout of 1889, the 1895 strike involved a classic labor-management standoff over three basic issues—wage rates, the ratio of lower-paid apprentices a street railway could hire in proportion to fully paid senior workers, and the amount of streetcar service a company provided with full-time workers as opposed to part-timers. The companies responded negatively to labor's demands in all three areas.

Interestingly, the CI&B was able to reach an accommodation with its workers on these matters, and its cars continued to run normally while the other companies' workers were on strike. CI&B was a rather uncomplicated system, and its schedules and assignments were straightforward. But management at four major Brooklyn street railways—Brooklyn City, Atlantic Avenue, Brooklyn City and Newtown, and the Broadway Railroad—refused to budge on any of these issues. On the morning of January 14, 1895, the people of Brooklyn awoke "to find themselves entangled by the greatest surface railroad strike in the history of the city."[55] As many as 5,000 workers, members of twenty-five separate locals, had walked off the job.

At first, none of the affected companies operated anything remotely resembling normal service, although all attempted to put some cars in service. "Upon all of the two hundred miles of track that the Brooklyn Heights railroad operates there are to-day being run only seventeen cars, where usually there are in the busy times of the day about nine hundred," reported the *Brooklyn Daily Eagle.*[56]

Brooklyn City concentrated its available workers on Court Street, and this line operated a reasonably normal number of cars. The rest of the company's lines were either totally devoid of service, or served only by such token operations as a mail car making one or two trips a day. Strikers respected the important role of mail cars and often allowed such specialized streetcars to operate during the strike. Problems developed, though, when companies like Brooklyn City put blue U.S. Government mail flags on ordinary streetcars and tried to fool the strikers by operating conventional passenger service under the guise of delivering the mail.[57]

With the exception of Brooklyn City and Newton, which was able to reach an agreement with its workers early in the strike through the efforts of a board of arbitration, the companies adopted a simple strategy in the face of the 1895 strike, not unlike the strategy they successfully used in 1889—make no concessions whatsoever, hire as many replacement workers as possible, and restore service despite the walkout. Brooklyn City, for example, sent recruiters to Worcester, Massachusetts, and Paterson, New Jersey, in an effort to find experienced street railway workers who were willing to relocate to Brooklyn. As the strike continued, efforts by management to operate cars with newly hired workers began to produce results. More cars were operated each day, and the ultimate outcome of the strike soon became apparent. Management was wearing down the strikers and would eventually prevail.

Almost from the outset, the strike was marred by violence. On January 15, the strike's second day, Brooklyn City car no. 1137 was attempting to make an inbound run toward downtown Brooklyn on the Flatbush Avenue Line. A policeman from the 23rd Precinct was aboard the car for protection, when a mob of strikers who had gathered near the reservoir opposite Prospect Park attacked the car, throwing large stones through the windows. The motorman, fearful for his life, brought the car to a stop, and strikers boarded the car and quickly disabled it by removing the control handles. The lone policeman was unable to offer any protection against the mob.

Minutes later, car no. 1103 came into view. Having finished with no. 1137, the strikers turned their attention to the second car. "Stop that car, you scab" a striker shouted. "Get out or we'll tear you out."[58] When the car stopped, strikers proceeded to beat the motorman and conductor who were operating the car, but their real goal was to disable this car by stealing its control handles. A squad of police officers soon arrived and, after several minutes of struggle, nine of the strikers were arrested.

Despite sporadic arrests, Brooklyn police were generally unable or unwilling to maintain order during the 1895 strike, a situation the *Street Railway Journal* viewed with alarm. "It must be held at this point that the city authorities were, for the first week, seriously remiss in their duties—that the police force openly sympathized with the strikers and refused to do their duty in defending the property of the companies."[59] As incidents of violence increased day after day, Brooklyn's Mayor Schieren was forced to ask for assistance from the National Guard. Troops were dispatched to Brooklyn and, on January 23, a private with the Thirteenth Regiment of the New York National Guard shot a man dead—a man who had no connection with the strike.

National Guard troops were escorting a Hicks Street car of the Atlantic Avenue Railroad. As the car turned from Atlantic onto Hicks, soldiers told residents along the way to get back from their upper-story windows. A man by the name of Thomas Carney was applying hot tar on a roof along Hicks Street as the escorted streetcar approached, and he leaned over to watch the oncoming procession. Accounts differ—Carney was properly warned; he was not warned at all—but the fact remains that one of the guardsmen felt uneasy seeing Carney in a potentially threatening position atop a building. He raised his rifle, took aim, and shot Carney through the thigh, a wound that led to the man's death the next day.

Another troop of mounted National Guardsmen attempted to disperse a group of 300 strikers at Third Avenue and 55th Street.

When the strikers refused, the lieutenant leading the troop ordered his men to draw their swords and he gave the command, "Charge!" "Right into the thick of the mob rode the troopers, striking right and left with the flats of their sabers," reported the *New York Times*. When strikers attempted to gather themselves back together for more agitation, the lieutenant gave another order, "Sheath swords and draw pistols."[60] This time the strikers dispersed. Meanwhile, at the Brooklyn Navy Yard, Commander Thomas Perry, skipper of the gunboat U.S.S. *Castine,* was ordered to drill his crew in street riot formation and stand ready to provide any assistance that might be required.[61]

During the course of the 1895 strike, Justice William J. Gaynor delivered several rulings that were decidedly "pro-labor" in their impact. In response to a petition filed by a Fulton Street furniture dealer, Judge Gaynor issued a *mandamus* order compelling the Brooklyn City Railroad to operate the street railway service it was franchised to operate. Brooklyn City responded with evidence that it was attempting to operate full schedules, which it was. On another occasion, a group of 200 strikers were conducting a meeting in the back room of a saloon in Ridgewood that served as the headquarters of their local. A regiment of National Guard troops surrounded the building and refused to let the strikers leave. This time, modern technology came to the rescue. The strikers placed a telephone call to one of the union leaders explaining what was happening. He, in turn, dispatched a lawyer to see Judge Gaynor. The judge issued a writ of *habeas corpus* requiring the 200 strikers to appear in his court forthwith; the National Guard would be in contempt of court if it continued to prevent the strikers from leaving the building. (When the troops were ordered to stand down, they found that the strikers had earlier managed to sneak out of the building despite their presence.)

From a worker's perspective, the 1895 Brooklyn trolley strike was not a success. It came to an end not with labor and management reaching any kind of mutually satisfactory agreement. It ended, rather, when the companies had hired enough replacement personnel to resume service despite the strike. Meanwhile, the companies made no concessions whatsoever to the striker's demands. Some strikers drifted back to work as the strike wore on. Workers hired during the strike were given permanent senior-ity over workers who had participated in the work stoppage and rejoined the ranks afterward—if they were rehired at all.

President Norton, of the Atlantic Avenue Railroad, announced a new policy after the strike that provides insight into labor-management relations at Brooklyn street railways in the 1890s. Every time a new worker hired during the strike was harassed by any of the railway's rehired strikers, five rehired workers (to be determined by lottery) would be summarily dismissed.[62]

It can be said that unionized street railway workers "lost" the strike of 1895. However, street railway management—not to mention street railway investors—may have been hurt by the strike in an even more fundamental way. One lesson the strike clearly drove home is that the economic stability and earning power of street railways was not guaranteed, and that delicately balanced investment structures—such as Brooklyn Heights' lease of Brooklyn City, Long Island Traction's ownership of Brooklyn Heights, and the expectation that all three companies would pay annual dividends to their shareholders—might not be as stable as they were once assumed to be.

The Knights of Labor declared that the 1895 strike was over in mid-February, but that declaration was little more than a formality. National Guard troops began to return to their home armories toward the end of January, and street railway service was reasonably close to normal less than a week after the strike began. The *Street Railway Journal* commented on the Brooklyn streetcar strike of 1895, "The strikers are defeated at every point and are being re-engaged by the companies as individuals. This has become of late the almost universal ending of most contests between capital and labor, and it is surprising that labor leaders are continually given such enormous powers to delude their followers, and to throw out of employment thousands of men, many of whom will leave work with a sinking heart and an unwilling spirit."[63] The journal's management predilections are certainly understandable, but the question of who were the true winners and losers of the strike of 1895 may not admit of such a simple assessment.

The Brooklyn Bridge Cable Railway

One of the most interesting and unusual urban railways of all time provided service across the Brooklyn Bridge between Brooklyn and New York City. The bridge itself—formally, the New York and Brooklyn Bridge—opened for vehicular and pedestrian traffic on May 24, 1883.[64] The bridge railway carried its first passengers four months later on September 24, and from that September until the first subway tunnel was built under the East River in 1908, this railway across the Brooklyn Bridge was the only rail rapid transit service linking Brooklyn and Manhattan.

One of the characteristics that makes the Brooklyn Bridge railway distinctive is the fact that its trains were cable-powered. Washington Roebling, the chief engineer on the project who took over when his father, John A. Roebling, passed away in 1869, proposed cable traction to the bridge trustees in 1876. It had been used successfully to move heavy railcars up (and down) steep grades such as the 3.75 percent grade that would characterize the new bridge. However, unlike cable street railways, whose cars rarely exceeded eighteen or twenty feet in length, the Brooklyn Bridge railway used much larger rolling stock. The first rolling stock, a fleet of twenty-four cars that inaugurated service in 1883, were thirty-six feet long; subsequent equipment measured almost fifty feet from end to end.[65] Looking much like the rolling stock on a typical city elevated railway, with wooden bodies and open platforms at each end, passenger cars used by the Brooklyn Bridge railway were about a foot wider than typical elevated stock. They were initially boarded by way of end-of-the-car open platforms such as those used on typical elevated or railroad cars of the era. To help speed boarding and alighting during periods of heavy traffic—especially on the Manhattan side—bridge trustees eventually switched to rolling stock with center doors in the body of the car that were operated, not by the train's on-board crew, but by personnel permanently stationed along terminal platforms.

Each car of a multicar train engaged the cable independently. A uniformed gripman was assigned to each car to operate the controls, which were located on one of the car's end platforms. Gripmen on the Brooklyn Bridge cable railway thus worked out-of-doors, much as did the drivers of horse-drawn streetcars. The cable moved at a uniform ten miles per hour. Driving machinery was located under and adjacent to the Brooklyn end of the bridge, near the intersection of Prospect and Washington Streets.

Initially, service was provided by cars operating independently.

Then, as traffic increased, two-car trains were run. Over the years, the railway increased this to three cars and eventually to four. When the line opened in 1883, the one-way fare was five cents. In 1885 it was reduced to three cents, with frequent riders offered an even better bargain—ten rides for twenty-five cents.

The trains of the Brooklyn Bridge cable railway did not engage the cable until after they left their respective terminals. Thus, the railway had to deploy a fleet of small steam locomotives to shift trains from track to track in the terminals; move them in and out of storage areas; and, with passengers aboard, push trains away from the terminal station to the point on the main line where sheaves were located and gripmen aboard the trains picked up the cable and continued across the bridge.[66] Trains disengaged the cable before reaching the opposite terminal and coasted the rest of the way until they were braked to a halt adjacent to the platform. At first, bridge trains were equipped with hand-operated brakes. Toward the end of the 1880s, the fleet was fitted with more efficient and powerful vacuum brakes. Cable power remained the bridge railway's basic source of traction; however, during late night hours, when traffic was light and the cable was shut down for inspection, steam locomotives maintained service by moving single cars across the bridge.

The bridge railway's dependence on dual motive power—cable traction for crossing the bridge and steam engines for terminal shifting—proved to be expensive, and officials of the bridge railway noted that more than 50 percent of their operating costs were attributed to the steam engines.[67] In addition, coupling and uncoupling steam shifters from in-service trains was time consuming, and sending trains across the bridge on the shortest possible headway was a never-ending imperative for improving service. So, once electric traction emerged as a source of traction power for urban railways, the bridge line began to explore its potential.

In early 1896—well into the electric railway era—bridge trustees decided to conduct a test. They invited two suppliers of electric railway equipment, Westinghouse and General Electric, to equip a conventional, passenger-carrying bridge car with electric motors so the car could replace steam locomotives for terminal shifting and late-night transit across the bridge. It was not the intention of the trustees to substitute electricity for the cable traction that was used to haul trains across the bridge, but simply to eliminate the need for the expensive, supplementary steam engines.

General Electric accepted the invitation, Westinghouse did not, and on February 6, 1898, bridge car no. 76, with a fifty-horsepower electric motor fitted to each of its four axles, began a month-long test and evaluation. It was judged a success and, in late March, the trustees decided to acquire a fleet of ten similar cars. The cars, which were built by the Pullman Palace Car Company, featured electrical gear manufactured by General Electric, including a pair of K-14 controllers that, like the controls for cable-attaching apparatus, were located on the outside end platforms of the cars. The bridge railway's new electric cars were not equipped with cable grips; a single electric car powered the train in and around the terminals, while the trailer cars provided traction, via the cable, hauling the electric motor across the bridge.

Each of the car's four motors was rated at 100 horsepower, not 50 as on the test car. By the end of November 1896, all trains crossing the bridge included one of the new electric cars. "The absence of the usual noise that had been made by the ringing of bells and puffing of the little engines was one noticeable relief," commented the *New York Times*.[68] Quickly, the bridge railway trustees increased the order with Pullman to twenty electric-powered bridge cars, and electricity replaced steam for terminal shifting but not for basic service across the bridge. The *Street Railway Journal* reported, "While electricity has been adopted for certain service . . . the Trustees of the bridge property are confident that it will never replace the cable for the work of heavy through transportation."[69] The interiors of the new bridge motor cars were attractively decorated with mahogany, other inlaid woods in various colors, and ceilings ornamented in gold.

As was the case during steam days, when shifter locomotives hauled trains across the bridge when the cable was shut down for maintenance, the electric motor cars provided service from one end of the bridge to the other when necessary. Another important benefit the railway achieved with its new electric cars was the ability to shift to electric traction quickly in the middle of the bridge if problems developed with the cable. During steam days, a shifter locomotive had to be dispatched from one of the terminals to rescue a stranded train, thus causing serious delays in schedules and service. In addition, the onset of electric power for terminal shifting allowed the bridge railway to eliminate steam locomotive engineers from its payroll, since the crew that worked a train across the bridge could also handle terminal movements. And so, with the use of electric traction for terminal shifting, coupled with improved terminal facilities and other improvements, the bridge railway reduced its minimum headway from ninety seconds to seventy-five, then sixty, and eventually forty-five. As many as fourteen four-car trains could be in service at the same time.

A third rail was installed along the bridge railway's right-of-way in 1896. It was made from older running rails that had been replaced with new track but, oddly enough, it was not the first instance of electrification on the transbridge railway. Two years earlier, a 500-volt trolley wire had been strung over the right-of-way from Brooklyn to Manhattan. However, the purpose of this installation was to provide current for car lighting, not propulsion. The trolley wire supplied traction power for the month-long test of car no. 76 in early 1896, and the third rail was only installed in mid-1896 after the bridge trustees decided to equip all their trains with electric motors. Electric current was generated at the nearby Kent Avenue powerhouse of the Brooklyn Heights Railroad and sold to the bridge railway.

With the installation of the third rail in 1896, the bridge right-of-way featured cable power for basic traction, a third rail for supplementary electric traction and terminal shifting, and an overhead trolley wire for car lighting. The trolley wire along the bridge right-of-way wire was taken down shortly after the third rail was installed, but it was restored in 1944 when the right-of-way was converted to streetcar operation.

Expanding capacity and ameliorating overcrowding were the principal issues the bridge railway faced for all of the years that it was the sole means of mass transit crossing of the East River. As early as 1890, former Brooklyn Mayor James Howell, who was then the president of the bridge trustees, said, "It is not only inconvenient, it is dangerous to cross the bridge from New-York to Brooklyn during the busy hours of the evening, and the inconvenience and danger and the necessity and demand for better terminal facilities increase every day."[70] However, progress was painfully slow. Two years later, the *Street Railway Journal* reported, "The plans for improving the terminal facilities and increasing the capacity of the cable railway have not yet been put in practical shape."[71] The *Street Railway Journal* took a special interest in the bridge railway since its New York offices on Park Row overlooked the line's Manhattan terminal and gave the magazine's writers firsthand experience with the line's trials and tribulations.

Various schemes were explored for building larger terminals so trains could load and unload passengers more quickly, and thus more trains could be operated. The original terminals of 1883 each featured two-track design; trains had to load and unload passengers on the same tracks they used to cross the bridge, and the shortest headway the line could operate was about ninety seconds. But this was something of a theoretical calculation that required everything to work flawlessly. Even the slightest delay in a train's loading or unloading impacted the performance of the entire railway.

In the early 1890s, both terminals were extensively rebuilt and expanded to four tracks to facilitate loading and unloading. The Brooklyn terminal was actually moved further inland. On the Manhattan side, an elevated extension was built out across Park Row for the shifting of trains from inbound to outbound tracks. In early 1897, a gauntlet track (separate sets of running rails that overlap each other along a common right-of-way) was installed across the bridge in both directions so trains would not have to negotiate switches entering and leaving the terminals. This improvement reduced the potential for delay even further. For operational purposes, one gauntlet track was called the red track, the other the white track; trains carried colored markers to indicate, from a distance, which track they were using. Dual cables driven by independent engines were installed along with the gauntlets, so trains on each overlapping track were powered by a separate cable. Coupled with expanded terminal platforms on both sides of all tracks, this effectively resulted in "two distinct railroads at the same time on the bridge, each with its own tracks, its own power, and its own platforms."[72] The cumulative effect of these enhancements was that the railway was able to operate trains, during peak periods, on headways as short as forty-five seconds. In order for trains using either of the gauntlet tracks to maintain contact with the same third rail, an oversize third-rail shoe was developed for bridge cars.

Plans and concepts that would allow even more trains to use the bridge railway were continually advanced. A perennial suggestion called for a series of circular, elevated loops at each end of the line so trains would not have to reverse direction, thus reducing headway to as little as twenty-five seconds. The land-taking that would have been necessary to build such loops at the Manhattan end of the bridge rendered this idea impractical, and it was never pursued.

In the years when the Brooklyn Bridge was the sole alternative to ferryboats for crossing the East River, the cable railway was the principal means of crossing the bridge. Both Brooklyn Union and Kings County elevated lines had transfer stations with the trans-bridge railway in Brooklyn; the Manhattan Railway—operator of the elevated lines in New York City—built a branch of its Third Avenue El that terminated on Park Row next to the bridge line's Manhattan terminal.[73]

A serial statistic the bridge railway often used to document the growth of its passenger traffic was one-way passengers per hour, measured at the time of maximum patronage. The following table displays the railway's performance from its opening in 1883 through 1890.

Traffic growth during the late 1880s reflects the fact that Brooklyn elevated railways were opened during this decade and began

Year	Maximum Number of One-Way Passengers per Hour
1883	1,540
1884	4,620
1885	4,725
1886	7,870
1887	10,068
1888	11,413
1889	13,355
1890	13,687

Source: Street Railway Journal (February 1891): 60.

to funnel large volumes of passengers onto the bridge cable road. The bridge railway carried almost 20 million annual riders in 1884; by 1888, this had grown by 50 percent to just shy of 31 million. During the rush hours each morning and evening, the number of passengers increased by 150 percent during this same four-year interval.

There was continual talk during the 1890s about providing through service to Manhattan from various Brooklyn neighborhoods by running trains of both Brooklyn elevated railway companies—Brooklyn Union and Kings County—across the bridge on the cable railway's tracks. Indeed, the prospect of operating elevated trains across the bridge quickly led to suggestions that through service could then be operated over Brooklyn and Manhattan elevated railways, and some began to discuss the possibility of traveling from the Bronx to Coney Island without changing trains. Some even believed that the only real solution to the steady crowding on the bridge cable road was to build additional elevated structures in lower Manhattan and allow bridge trains to carry their passengers beyond Park Row to various inland points.[74]

It took considerable negotiating skill, helped along by judicial intervention and the transfer of authority for bridge matters from quasi-independent trustees to the city government with the amalgamation of Greater New York in 1898, before any Brooklyn elevated railway could operate its trains across the bridge to Park Row. Although no through service with Manhattan elevated lines would ever come to pass, first Brooklyn Union and then Kings County did build track connections at the Brooklyn end of the bridge between their own lines and the bridge cable railway so through service could be operated. The first through train from Park Row—a ceremonial inaugural that took railway and civic officials all the way to Manhattan Beach—operated on May 18, 1898.

Brooklyn Union acquired a fleet of twelve electric elevated cars to move its trains into and out of the bridge terminals. The cars were built by Pullman Palace, rode on McGuire trucks, and were powered by four eighty-horsepower Walker motors. The motors were specially designed for heavy-duty applications by S. H. Short of the Walker Company, one of the many pioneers in railway electrification. The new cars, which Brooklyn Union identified as its 400-series equipment, featured center doors to speed loading and unloading at Park Row and included the Sprague multiple-unit control system. The Sprague system was not something the cars would need while serving as transbridge motors. However, Brooklyn Union would soon be converting from steam to electrical power, and the multiple-unit controls would be needed to run multicar trains of electric-powered cars.[75] Electrification of the Brooklyn elevated railways was a year or more away when Brooklyn Union acquired its first electric-powered cars. The new cars were initially assigned to replace steam locomotive so elevated trains could continue into Manhattan across the Brooklyn Bridge. The Kings County Railroad operated its first trains across the Brooklyn Bridge on November 1, 1898, after taking delivery of its own fleet of electric motor cars.

Brooklyn Union trains reached the bridge over a newly constructed elevated link that left the company's line along Adams Street between Concord and Tillary and headed west to connect with the bridge railway south of the Sands Street Terminal. Kings County trains branched off that company's main line at Fulton and Tillary Streets and linked up with the bridge railway a short distance away.

Electric bridge motors were not the only new equipment that had to be acquired before Brooklyn elevated trains could cross the bridge. Elevated cars used in transbridge service also had to be equipped with cable grips, since the twin moving cables remained the primary source of traction on the Brooklyn Bridge.

The shift of authority from bridge trustees to the City of New York's Department of Bridges in 1898 eliminated the bridge railway as a separate entity. In its place, the Department of Bridges contracted with Brooklyn Union Elevated to handle all aspects of transbridge railway service, including its own through elevated trains as well as the specialized cable railway. If one regards the employees of the bridge trustees as public employees, this shift to Brooklyn Union likely represents the first instance in which a publicly operated U.S. urban railway service was privatized. With the change, almost 400 bridge railway workers were dismissed, although most were promptly rehired by Brooklyn Union.

The years when service across the Brooklyn Bridge was provided by both bridge cable trains and through elevated trains never developed a comfortable operational rhythm, perhaps be-

cause traffic levels continued to increase. Changes were continually made in an effort to achieve balance. Because the bridge
railway could not tolerate delays or uncertainties associated with
changing motive power from steam to electricity during peak rush
hours—when it had to dispatch trains across the bridge on a forty-
five-second headway—no through elevated trains crossed the
bridge during rush hours, and peak-hour service was provided
exclusively by cable-powered bridge railway trains. In addition,
Brooklyn-bound platforms at Park Row could become so thoroughly congested during evening rush hours that the prospect of
passengers headed for Brooklyn waiting on the platform for a train
bound for a particular destination was a little terrifying. Better to
have everyone board the first available train at Park Row and
change to the Lexington Avenue Line or the Fulton Street Line on
the Brooklyn side of the bridge.

The operation of Brooklyn elevated trains across the bridge was
greatly facilitated—and their frequency increased—once steam locomotives were retired and all elevated trains became electrically
powered. This improvement did not occur until after the two original elevated railways were absorbed into the BRT at the end of the
century.

One of the technical issues associated with this full-scale conversion is worth noting. The first electric-powered elevated trains
to operate across the Brooklyn Bridge were equipped with the
same style of extra-wide, third-rail shoes as were bridge railway
cars so they might maintain contact with the third rail from either
the "red" track or the "white" track. As additional elevated lines
began to operate across the bridge, though, clearance problems
on some of the BRT's outlying elevated lines precluded the use
of extra-wide, third-rail shoes. The BRT developed an ingenious
solution.

Conventional rails used by U.S. railroads are wider on the bottom than on the top, a simple but crucial engineering feature that
enables rails to carry the heavy weight of moving trains. Because
third rails do not have to bear substantial weight, but merely maintain contact with a moving train for electrical purposes, the BRT
was able to invert the third rail across the Brooklyn Bridge. This
permitted several extra inches of contact surface and allowed con-

ventional third-rail shoes on the elevated trains to maintain contact with the third rail from either of the bridge's gauntlet tracks.[76]

Three factors were instrumental in the phasing out of trans-bridge cable service in early 1908 and the conversion of the railway into an East River crossing that would be used exclusively by Brooklyn elevated trains. One was the opening of the first subway tunnel under the East River on January 8, 1908. (More on the first subway in chapter 7.) Second, starting on January 22, 1898, the cable railway was no longer the sole rail passenger service across the Brooklyn Bridge. On that day, electric-powered streetcars also began to cross the bridge, using tracks installed in the span's conventional vehicular roadways and a terminal on the Manhattan side that was constructed directly under the elevated station of the bridge cable railway. Streetcars of three Brooklyn companies used the new trackage—Brooklyn City, Coney Island and Brooklyn, and Nassau Electric. When a contract was executed with bridge trustees in August 1897 to operate trolley cars across the bridge, Brooklyn City and Newton was a fourth street railway signatory to the agreement. However, by the time service was inaugurated, BC&N had been absorbed by CI&B.

The first trolley car to cross the bridge, tower car no. 1000 of Nassau Electric, did so late in the evening on New Year's Eve in 1897. A crew of men aboard the car made final adjustments to the new overhead trolley wire. After car no. 1000 returned to Brooklyn, two special parlor-style trolley cars—*Amphion* and *Columbia,* both owned by Brooklyn City—left Brooklyn and carried a delegation of dignitaries across the river. They reached the New York side just before midnight. Moments later, with the ringing in of the New Year of 1898, the city of Brooklyn lost its status as an independent municipality and became the Borough of Brooklyn in an expanded City of New York. When the two parlor cars later made their way back across the bridge, the city of Brooklyn from which they had earlier departed no longer existed.

Street railway service across the Brooklyn Bridge was formally inaugurated some weeks later on Saturday, January 22, 1898. Three special trolley cars—one each from Coney Island and Brooklyn, Nassau Electric, and Brooklyn City—left Borough Hall in Brooklyn at ten-thirty in the morning and proceeded in procession to Park Row on the other side of the bridge, where speechify-ing took place. Several days later, limited revenue service was begun as Brooklyn City's Graham Avenue Line became the first streetcar service to carry fare-paying passengers across the Brook-lyn Bridge.

More complete streetcar service began on February 16, 1898, when three Brooklyn City lines—Fulton Street, Myrtle Avenue, and Graham Avenue—joined CI&B's De Kalb Avenue Line and Nassau Electric's Fifth Avenue Line in terminating at Park Row. There was a good deal of confusion at the Manhattan end of the Brooklyn Bridge that day, since passengers heading to and from the terminal of the bridge cable railway had to walk through and across the new trolley terminal, where streetcars were loading and unloading passengers. The only real mishap occurred late in the evening when car no. 297 of Nassau Electric's Fifth Avenue Line became disabled near the Manhattan anchorage of the bridge on a trip to Park Row. After a delay of fifteen minutes, a following Nassau Electric car—no. 278—pushed the disabled trolley into Park Row and then back to Brooklyn.

A third factor that contributed to the decision to phase out cable-powered railway service across the Brooklyn Bridge was that, with the onset of electric-powered equipment on Brooklyn elevated lines, such trains could operate across the bridge solely on electric power without assistance from the cable. Consequently, the Brooklyn Bridge cable railway was phased out as a separate ser-vice on January 27, 1908.

With the elimination of cable operations across the Brooklyn Bridge, the wider rolling stock used by the bridge railway could not be absorbed into the Brooklyn elevated system, which relied on narrower cars. Passengers alighting from slightly narrower ele-vated cars at Park Row during the years of joint operation were, of course, continually admonished with some local version of London Transport's famous dictum, "Mind the gap!"

The disposition of all of the bridge railway's rolling stock—the full fleet totaled eighty-eight passenger cars—remains something of a mystery. The twenty Pullman-built cars of 1896 that were equipped with electric motors represented valuable equipment in a world where electric railways were a growth industry. They were put up for sale, and several enjoyed lengthy careers on electric railway lines far from the East River they were designed to cross. One eventually wound up as car no. 19 of the Mason City and Clear Lake Railroad in Iowa, but something of an unsolved electric railway mystery surrounds this car. In later years, an inspection card issued by the New York, New Haven and Hartford Railroad was found secreted away aboard this car.[77]

THE BRT

The idea behind the creation of Long Island Traction—the unification of mass transport in and around Kings County—would not be realized by that company. Instead, it would be a new entity, backed by a new group of investors, that would achieve the goal.

Roswell Pettibone Flower was born in Jefferson County in upstate New York in 1835. After trying his hand at both business and education, Flower turned to the enticing world of politics; here, Flower's association with Samuel J. Tilden led to two terms in the U.S. House of Representatives and then, in 1891, election as governor of the state of New York. In 1892, a group of followers started an active canvass on Governor Flower's behalf that might have led to the Democratic nomination for president that year. Instead, fellow New Yorker Grover Cleveland received the party's nod, went on to defeat Republican James K. Blaine, and eventually became the only U.S. president elected to nonconsecutive terms.[78]

Flower served a then-typical three-year term in Albany. After leaving office in early 1895—mere days before the start of the Brooklyn trolley strike—he turned his attention to Wall Street. There, he became an extremely successful investor, specializing in railroad and public utility investments such as Chicago, Rock Island and Pacific; New York Air Brake; and Peoples' Gas of Chicago. The press frequently suggested that some of the investors associated with the former governor were "Standard oil interests." Flower played a strong role in restoring confidence in American investments at a time of economic uncertainty following the explosion and destruction of the battleship U.S.S. *Maine* in Havana Harbor in February 1898.

In regard to the development of unified mass transportation in Brooklyn, the action with which Flower is most notably associated is the creation of the Brooklyn Rapid Transit Company. The BRT can date its founding to January 18, 1896, a year after Flower stepped down as governor. On that date, papers were filed with the New York secretary of state by Timothy S. Williams, a former journalist who had served as Governor Flower's secretary in Albany and who would later become president of the BRT. As set forth in the documents Williams submitted, the purpose of the new corporation was "to construct, repair, improve, equip, and furnish the motive power for railroads and other works."[79] Thirteen distinguished citizens—six from Brooklyn, seven from New York City—were identified as the directors of the new company. While Roswell Flower's brother, Frederick, was one of the thirteen, the former governor was not. Flower would play neither a major nor an active role in the subsequent management and growth of the BRT. In fact, he died in May 1899 at the age of sixty-four, long before the BRT became the dominant force it eventually would become. But it was Roswell Flower who put together the group of investors who capitalized the BRT and succeeded where Long Island Traction had failed. Due in large measure to Flower's association with the new venture, publicly traded BRT securities quickly rose in value from $20 to $140, indicative of a strong measure of confidence that the Wall Street investment community had in the new venture.

Flower's associates began to acquire stock in both Brooklyn City and Long Island Traction shortly after the 1895 trolley strike, and their holdings soon gave them de facto control of these companies. In March 1895, the *Street Railway Journal* reported, "Soon after the recent strike, ex-Governor Flower began to purchase stock in the company [Brooklyn City], and he and his associate capitalists are now believed to hold a controlling interest in its affairs, as well as in those of the Long Island Traction Company, which is to be completely reorganized."[80] The reorganization was needed because Long Island Traction was a financially troubled enterprise. Flower and his people believed that it was broken too badly to warrant repair, and so they effected its merciful demise.

By the summer of 1895, with recollections of the strike still fresh in everyone's mind, control of the Brooklyn Heights–Brooklyn City enterprise had passed into the hands of people associated with Roswell Flower. They believed that a change in the chief officer who was directing both companies was appropriate. Thus did forty-six-year-old Daniel F. Lewis, a man who had been president of Brooklyn City since 1886 and whose career with the company began as a ticket agent, announce his retirement. In his place, Flower and his associates selected Clinton L. Rossiter, an experienced railroad executive whose most recent position had been superintendent of the Buffalo Division of the New York Central Railroad.

Like Long Island Traction, the BRT was envisioned as a holding company that would acquire other properties but would not own or operate streetcars or elevated trains. And although BRT retained the status of a holding company for all of its days, it soon became identified in the mind of Brooklyn residents as the borough's basic provider of mass transit services. The BRT name was prominently displayed on Brooklyn rolling stock, trolley and elevated lines were commonly referred to as BRT services, and maps and brochures unashamedly displayed the BRT logo.

Before the decade was over, the BRT expanded its holdings beyond Brooklyn City–Brooklyn Heights and acquired virtually all the important street, elevated, and excursion railways in Brooklyn. The LIRR would remain independent of Flower's consortium, as would, for several more years, the CI&B. A mile-and-half-long Brooklyn street railway called the Van Brunt Street and Erie Basin Railroad also remained outside the BRT orbit. It was abandoned outright in 1927.

Between its founding in 1896 and early 1899, the BRT directed primary attention to stabilizing its base—the combined Brooklyn City–Brooklyn Heights street railway enterprise. This was important because, in the expansion that would shortly follow, the financial stability of the BRT was critical to raising additional capital. But BRT officials were conducting conversations and negotiations with all interested parties and, in early 1899, everything began to fall into place.

In mid-January of 1899, a massive stock transfer passed control of Nassau Electric into the hands of people associated with the BRT. On February 12, BRT stockholders voted to increase the company's capital stock from $20 million to $45 million, investment resources that were needed to convert January's stock transfer into a formal acquisition. The elevated companies would come next.

Before the BRT could acquire Brooklyn Union, that company's receivership had to be discharged. On the elevated railway's own petition, Justice Maddox of the New York State Supreme Court terminated the receivership on March 25, 1899. The property was conveyed to the BRT several days afterward. A new board of directors was constituted for Brooklyn Union that included BRT officials Timothy S. Williams, Clinton Rossiter, and F. S. Flower. Frederick Uhlmann was retained on the new board to provide needed continuity between the old order and the new. One of the BRT's first priorities for its new elevated subsidiary was the replacement of steam locomotives with electric-powered equipment. Even before the actual acquisition, the *New York Times* quoted an anonymous BRT director, "No power stations will be needed as the energy necessary for the elevated will be furnished by the power stations of the surface roads."[81] The unnamed director went on to speculate that because of this fortunate state of affairs, the elevated lines would be converted to electric power a year earlier than would otherwise have been possible.[82] (The instrumentality by which BRT acquired Brooklyn Union was a 999-year lease. It remains disconcerting to read accounts of the transaction in the trade press that casually speak of the lease expiring on June 30, 2898.)

The early months of 1899 continued to be busy with respect to further BRT acquisitions. In late March, the Brooklyn and Brighton Beach Railroad was sold under foreclosure proceedings and "bid in" by William F. Sheehan, who had been lieutenant governor under Roswell Flower. "I acted on behalf of A. R. Flower, a member of the same banking firm as ex-Governor Roswell P. Flower, whose sympathy with the management of the Brooklyn Rapid Transit is well known. It is to be presumed that Brooklyn Rapid Transit will acquire the property," Sheehan said.[83] Two days later, the *New York Times* reported that the BRT's newly acquired Brighton Line would soon be electrified. Then, in mid-April, came the announcement that the BRT had acquired Kings County Elevated, a transaction Wall Street interests called "the best purchase which the company has made so far."[84] Roswell Flower said that the acquisition of the Kings County company "secures for the Brooklyn

Rapid Transit system all the elevated roads in Brooklyn, and all the traction companies except one."[85]

BRT—by purchases, leases, and other transactions—put together a transport system that the public regarded as a single entity but was actually a bewildering assortment of subsidiary companies. Some years later in 1915, the Public Service Commission of the First District of New York—successor, in 1907, of the earlier State Board of Railroad Commissioners—issued a 1,500-page volume that outlined the corporate and franchise histories of various local streetcar and mass transit companies in Greater New York. With respect to BRT, "No fewer than eighty-three companies are represented. Of these, sixty-seven have lost their identity through absorption. Of the remaining sixteen companies, nine are operated under lease or agreement, so that there are actually seven operating companies in the system, all of which are subject to stock control through the Brooklyn Rapid Transit Company, which is a business corporation and not a transportation company."[86]

For passengers though, it was just the BRT, as they transferred efficiently and smoothly from one line to another and traveled from one end of Brooklyn to the other. For example, a passenger who boarded an Ocean Avenue car in Flatbush, paid a nickel fare, and asked the conductor for a free transfer to the Flatbush Avenue Line likely felt that he or she was taking a single trip aboard a unified BRT mass transport system—and, in practical terms, that is exactly what it was. But if the passenger were to look carefully at the paper transfer he or she had been handed, the letters "N.E.R.R.Co." could be read just below the date. That is because the Ocean Avenue Line was originally a Nassau Electric property and was formally still part of that BRT subsidiary. It would all happen under common BRT auspices. Sooner or later there would be a reconciliation of a few pennies between the books of Nassau Electric and the Brooklyn Heights Railroad, since the Flatbush Avenue Line the passenger transferred to was a Brooklyn City property, under lease to Brooklyn Heights, and that company was entitled to a portion of the original nickel fare that had been collected by Nassau Electric.

In the long run, the BRT was only marginally more successful than was Long Island Traction. On December 31, 1918, the BRT would enter receivership, to be reorganized as the Brooklyn-Manhattan Transit Corporation (BMT) five years later in 1923. The BMT itself would pass from the private sector entirely in 1940 and become the BMT Division of the New York City Board of Transportation, developments that are explored in subsequent chapters. One can argue that the demise of both the BRT and the BMT were largely the result of factors that were unknown in the 1890s, but the fact remains that the financial and operational structure created by ex-governor Roswell P. Flower during the final years of the nineteenth century achieved neither permanence nor longevity.

Perhaps, though, permanence and longevity are inappropriate standards for evaluating Flower's contribution to Kings County mass transport. He put together a corporation that enabled mass transportation in and around Brooklyn to evolve from a collection of independent and uncoordinated railways into a single and unified system, as technically up to date as any in the United States. Permanence and longevity aside, that was hardly a minor accomplishment.

The following table displays the major components of the BRT as the nineteenth century became the twentieth.

EXCURSION RAILWAYS AND THE LONG ISLAND RAILROAD

As Kings County street, excursion, and elevated railways were subjected to the buffeting winds of corporate change in the 1890s—actual change, as well as more extensive change that existed only in the nether world of rumor and speculation—a gray eminence whose actions behind the scenes were always regarded with suspicion and a wary eye was the Long Island Railroad. Many observers believed that, when all the corporate reshuffling had run its course, Austin Corbin and his LIRR would emerge as the single most dominant factor in Kings County transport matters.

That the LIRR was interested in expanding its influence in Kings County transportation is demonstrated by something that happened during the summer of 1891. That was when Corbin and the LIRR acquired the Prospect Park and Coney Island Railroad from Andrew Culver and his investment associates. At the time, the

BRT Subsidiary	Total Track Miles
Brooklyn Heights Railroad	1.26
Brooklyn City Railroad[a]	207.22
Brooklyn, Queens County and Suburban Railroad[b]	45.87
Brooklyn Union Elevated Railroad[c]	45.62
Nassau Electric Railroad[d]	129.81
Coney Island and Gravesend Railroad[e]	6.32
Prospect Park and Coney Island Railroad	24.97
Sea Beach Railway[f]	12.27
Sea View Railway[g]	19.91
Kings County Elevated Railroad[h]	21.72
Total	514.97

Sources: Brooklyn Rapid Transit Corporation, *President's First Annual Report to Stockholders* (Brooklyn, 1899); *Poor's Manual of the Railroads of the United States* (New York, 1900).

(Dates shown below in parenthesis for various predecessor and subsidiary street railways are dates of their incorporation, not the date service was inaugurated.)

[a] Principal street railways absorbed by Brooklyn City over the years are Bushwick Railroad (1867); Brooklyn Crosstown Railroad (1872); Calvary Cemetery, Greenpoint and Brooklyn Railroad (1884); New Williamsburgh and Flatbush Railroad (1873); Greenpoint and Lorimer Railroad (1884); Grand Street and Newtown Railroad (1860).

[b] Includes three subsidiary companies: Broadway Railroad (1858), which itself includes the Gates Avenue and Flatbush Railroad (1881); Broadway Ferry and Metropolitan Avenue Railroad (1892); Brooklyn and Jamaica Railway (1860).

[c] Includes Brooklyn Elevated Railroad (1874); Union Elevated Railroad (1886); Seaside and Brooklyn Bridge Elevated Railroad (1890).

[d] Includes Atlantic Avenue Railroad (1872), which itself includes the Brooklyn, Bath and West End Railroad (1862) and the city division of the Prospect Park and Coney Island Railroad (1864); Kings County Electric (1892); Coney Island, Fort Hamilton and Brooklyn Railroad (1894).

[e] Listed independently for business purposes. Prior to acquisition by BRT, this was operated, under lease, by Nassau Electric.

[f] Predecessor companies include New York and Sea Beach Railroad (ca. 1876) and New York and Sea Beach Railway (1883).

[g] Sea View Railway was a short elevated line in Coney Island that was acquired by BRT in 1897. The Sea View corporate structure was later used by the BRT to purchase the assets of Brooklyn and Brighton Beach Railroad (1887).

[h] Includes Fulton Elevated Railroad (1895).

LIRR was exploring a variety of ways to expand its own markets and was considering instituting ferry service across Long Island Sound from Oyster Bay and establishing some kind of through service to Boston. Culver, for his part, saw two of his principal excursion railway competitors developing linkages with larger systems—Brooklyn, Bath and West End with Nassau Electric and the one-time Brooklyn, Flatbush and Coney Island with Kings County Elevated. Because massive infusions of new capital would soon be necessary to electrify his own railroad if it were to remain competitive, Culver felt that this was an appropriate time to liquidate his holdings.

Corbin was able to secure approval from his stockholders to acquire the PP&CI "with consummate ease" because the acquisition of Culver's road "is manifestly a move designed to provide increased dividends."[87] Among the assets transferred from the PP&CI to the LIRR were eleven locomotives, fifty-six passenger cars, eighty freight and baggage cars, and a dock on Coney Island Creek near the Van Siclen station.

Newspapers speculated that Corbin's acquisition of Culver's road, in conjunction with the new Oyster Bay extension and cross-sound ferry, would soon lead to direct service between Coney Island and Boston. While that never came to pass, Corbin's purchase of the PP&CI from Culver was sufficient to fuel rumors in Brooklyn financial circles that the LIRR was planning to expand its presence in Kings County.

A speculation that quickly made the rounds after the August 1891 announcement of LIRR's acquisition of the PP&CI was that a deal would soon be forthcoming whereby Corbin would acquire the Atlantic Avenue Railroad, and possibly the Brooklyn Union, too. With respect to Atlantic Avenue, Deacon William Richardson issued a swift denial. "I never heard a word about any such arrangement," he said.[88] And, indeed, nothing like it would ever come to pass.

One possibility involving an expanded LIRR presence in Kings County in which Richardson did play a role was a long-standing proposal by the LIRR to convert its at-grade line into Brooklyn into an elevated railway. The LIRR had returned to Brooklyn in 1877 after its earlier banishment, and the company ran its steam-powered trains on a right-of-way down the middle of Atlantic Avenue.

Not only did Corbin want to shift this at-grade line onto a new elevated structure, he wanted to extend any elevated structure that might be built beyond the line's terminal at Flatbush and Atlantic Avenues and continue to South Ferry at the foot of Atlantic Avenue, the site of the road's original Brooklyn terminal back in 1837.

An Atlantic Avenue Rapid Transit Commission was established to help coordinate this effort. Although public officials in Brooklyn welcomed the general idea of an expanded LIRR presence, their preference was to build the new route below grade as a subway. However, Corbin and the LIRR were unwilling to build anything except a less costly elevated line.[89] The dealings were exceedingly complex, and the general consensus is that in the end Richardson's opposition killed the deal. George Wingate, the LIRR's retained counsel for the negotiations on the Atlantic Avenue matter, put it this way: "But for [Richardson], this elevated road would now be in the course of construction. He alone stands in the way, and unless he modifies his unreasonable demands rapid transit will be at a standstill." In reporting on the matter, the *New York Times* pointed out, "Wingate was inclined to grow excited while referring to Mr. Richardson's obstinacy."[90]

Eventually, in the first decade of the twentieth century, the LIRR would remove its surface-level trackage from Atlantic Avenue. Some of the route would be placed on an elevated structure, but much of it would run through a new underground subway tunnel. By this time, the city of Brooklyn had become part of an expanded Greater New York and municipal funds were available to underwrite half the cost of this important railway improvement. Even so, complex litigation was necessary to substantiate the right of the city government and the railroad to undertake the project, including a suit filed by the BRT claiming that the terms of the lease executed between the LIRR and the Atlantic Avenue Railroad stipulated that the Long Island must operate only as a surface road. The courts held otherwise.[91]

If a LIRR "Atlantic Avenue El" did not come to pass in the 1890s, Corbin's acquisition of the PP&CI in 1891 did allow for expanded service to and from Coney Island over both the PP&CI and the LIRR. Even before acquiring Culver's property, the LIRR had enhanced the scope of its services by running trains from the Bay

Ridge steamer landing to Culver Depot in West Brighton under a trackage rights arrangement. Such trains followed the same route away from Bay Ridge as did the New York and Manhattan Beach, but they turned south onto PP&CI tracks at a junction called Parkville where the New York and Manhattan Beach crossed Culver's road—thus giving LIRR passengers access to amusement and entertainment activities of West Brighton, not merely the more constrained recreation available in Manhattan Beach.

Corbin and the LIRR were not pleased when, in 1879, the New York and Sea Beach began to operate service to Coney Island from essentially the same Bay Ridge steamer landing as was used by the New York and Manhattan Beach. Corbin and the LIRR were even less pleased when the New York and Sea Beach began to promote its services with vigorous reductions in fare. A New York and Sea Beach official, speaking to a reporter on the condition of anonymity, articulated his road's displeasure with the LIRR. "Let me premise by saying that Mr. Corbin dislikes to share a good thing with anybody," he began. The man, who felt that his own company was "a thorn in Mr. Corbin's side," summarized the expansionist policies of the LIRR as follows: "Corbin and Corbin's schemes to control all Coney Island transportation are like the poor, ever with us."[92]

Given such feelings, it is not surprising that, as consolidation rumors began to spread through Brooklyn and New York in advance of the creation of the BRT in 1896, the LIRR was rumored to be a major factor in whatever was going to happen. Even after the creation of the BRT and its initial combining of various Kings County street railway properties, rumors that the LIRR still had designs on expanding its presence in Kings County continued to circulate.

But the LIRR did not expand its Brooklyn operations, nor did it acquire other Kings County properties. Instead, in April 1899, it reached a business accommodation with the BRT that served the interests of both companies. In simple terms, each would stay out of the other's territory, Brooklyn being identified as BRT turf and the LIRR being associated with Queens and all territory to the east. The LIRR would continue to run its trains into Brooklyn along Atlantic Avenue, and the BRT would retain existing trolley car and elevated railway incursions into Queens. But neither company would seek to build new lines in the other's territory, and neither would acquire existing railway properties there for consolidation into their respective systems. Also part of the deal was an agreement for the BRT to lease the Prospect Park and Coney Island from the LIRR so it could become part of the BRT's expanding network. (This lease was converted into a formal purchase some years later.) The agreement also allowed BRT trains operating over the Brighton Line to switch onto the New York and Manhattan Beach at Sheepshead Bay and provide BRT service to Manhattan Beach.[93]

The 1899 agreement let stand a joint service arrangement negotiated between the BRT and the LIRR in April 1898 that sanctioned two intraline operations. One was placed in service in July 1898, while the second did not see its first trains until May 1899, the month after the more comprehensive agreement was signed. Essentially, two ramps were built between the LIRR's at-grade Atlantic Avenue Line and the BRT elevated system. The first of the two was at Chestnut Street near the Brooklyn-Queens line; it established a connection to and from the Cypress Hills extension of the one-time Brooklyn Union elevated that allowed through service between Broadway Ferry and Rockaway Park over a unique trestle the LIRR had constructed across Jamaica Bay. This service would remain in operation until 1913. Indeed, when the Broadway elevated was later extended across the Williamsburg Bridge into Manhattan, so was the joint service.

The second of the two connecting services saw a ramp constructed between the Fifth Avenue El at Flatbush and Atlantic Avenues and the LIRR just to the east of its Flatbush Avenue Terminal to permit through service from the Brooklyn end of the Brooklyn Bridge and LIRR points. Through service via this ramp was inaugurated in the spring of 1899, but it was discontinued shortly after it began.[94]

OTHER RAILROAD POSSIBILITIES

When the BRT and the LIRR negotiated their agreement in 1899, Austin Corbin was no longer on the scene. The man had been killed in an unfortunate carriage accident in his native New Hampshire on June 4, 1896—just before his sixty-ninth birthday—and the deal with the BRT was negotiated by LIRR's new president, William H. Baldwin. One can only speculate, of course, whether the LIRR would have been willing to reach such an accommodation with the BRT had Corbin still been directing the railroad's fortunes.

Corbin had never been without extraordinary plans for the LIRR's expansion. One such proposal was to build a deep-water seaport on the eastern end of Long Island at Montauk—to be served, of course, by the LIRR—which, in conjunction with a parallel harbor at Milford Haven in Wales, would shorten travel time between New York and London by a full day by using railroad trains for the first and last leg of the trans-Atlantic crossing. Vessels navigating between Montauk and Milford Haven would eschew two time-consuming uncertainties. One was the constant delay associated with the approach to New York Harbor in the days before Ambrose Channel was opened in 1907, while the other was passage around Land's End and Cornwall and the trip up the English Channel to Southampton. Corbin never tired in the promotion of his trans-Atlantic idea, but it proved to be just another fascinating transport concept that was never actualized.[95]

Austin Corbin's idea of using the LIRR as the first link on a route between New York and London can be seen in conjunction with another unrealized railroad dream of the 1890s, a proposal to make Brooklyn a major eastern terminal for intercity railroads. A letter to the editor of the *Brooklyn Daily Eagle* in 1892 when the matter was under discussion began with a rhetorical question. "If we except Brooklyn, is there another maritime city on earth containing a million inhabitants that would consent to sit quietly down on an island within sight of the mainland and make no effort to reach it by any more direct means than is furnished by ferries, by floats and by bridges to another island almost equally isolated from the main lines of communication?"[96]

Proponents of the proposal made compelling arguments on Brooklyn's behalf. For example, downtown Brooklyn was closer to Philadelphia, by a few miles, than was midtown Manhattan. Before intercity railroad trains could reach Brooklyn, of course, it was necessary to build a rail tunnel under the Narrows between Brooklyn and Staten Island. Although such a project would have represented a challenge in both engineering and construction, it was not regarded as totally unfeasible. An outspoken advocate for a Brooklyn–Staten Island rail tunnel was Canadian-born Erastus Wiman. Wiman was a Staten Island businessman who played a singular role in developing an intra-island enterprise called the Staten Island Rapid Transit Railroad Company, which he believed would play a central role in the expanded rail system that a tunnel to Brooklyn would help create. Wiman was also in active negotiations with the president of the Baltimore and Ohio Railroad (B&O), Robert Garrett. Had Wiman's dream of a railroad tunnel under the Narrows been realized, it is likely that Garrett's B&O would have been the principal intercity company that would have operated its trains into Brooklyn.

Garrett's tenure as president of the B&O ended in 1887, and Wiman's financial empire collapsed during the financial panic of 1893. Staten Island Rapid Transit became a subsidiary of the B&O and was later electrified, and there continued to be talk during the early twentieth century of linking Staten Island Rapid Transit with rapid transit lines in Brooklyn via a tunnel under the Narrows.

Wiman's more grandiose ideas would have made Brooklyn a major terminal for intercity rail services that would have reached Brooklyn via Staten Island. Like Corbin's dream of turning Montauk into a trans-Atlantic seaport, turning Brooklyn into a terminal for intercity freight and passenger railroads was a nineteenth-century transport dream that was never achieved.[97]

The New York, New Haven and Hartford Railroad would operate freight trains through Brooklyn to and from a terminal in Bay Ridge where freight cars were transported across the harbor by barge for interchange with other railroads, but otherwise the LIRR (and its various predecessors and subsidiaries) was the only "Class One" railroad to operate trains on Brooklyn soil. There were a variety of terminal railroads along the Brooklyn waterfront over the years, moving freight cars, usually along city streets, from one industry to another, as well as on and off barges for interchange with other roads. One of these, the Brooklyn Eastern District Terminal Railroad, would achieve fame in the late 1950s as the final railroad in the New York metropolitan area to haul its trains with a fleet of steam locomotives.

THE CONEY ISLAND AND BROOKLYN RAILROAD . . . AGAIN

Brooklyn Rapid Transit achieved its goal of unifying public transit in Brooklyn rather quickly, all things considered. From the day the BRT was chartered in 1896, it took only five years to unify the diverse operations of Brooklyn Union Elevated, Kings County Elevated, Nassau Electric, Brooklyn Heights, Brooklyn City, Prospect Park and Coney Island, New York and Sea Beach, Brooklyn and Brighton Beach, and a number of lesser properties. Add to this impressive merger the new railway's successful negotiation of a service agreement with the LIRR that forestalled any possible competition from that quarter, and the BRT's first five years of work must be regarded as downright impressive.

One old Brooklyn street railway managed to retain its independence throughout all this maneuvering, the Coney Island and Brooklyn Railroad. It was the last major holdout against the expansionism of the BRT. By virtue of its acquisition of the Brooklyn City and Newton Railroad in 1897, CI&B had become a system of significance, even though it was a small fraction of the size of a company like Brooklyn City. CI&B's original line ran from Coney Island all the way to Fulton Ferry; BC&N's De Kalb Avenue Line gave the company an important trunk line from downtown Brooklyn to Ridgewood; and its Franklin Avenue Line gave the company a cross-town link between its two major lines.

In 1900, the combined system controlled by CI&B operated along 47 miles of track and owned 546 electric-powered streetcars. By contrast BRT-controlled street railways included 384 miles of track and more than 3,000 streetcars.

Looking beyond the decade of the 1890s, it is appropriate to consider several CI&B developments. In 1912, CI&B would invest $95,000 to build the final Coney Island rail terminal that was not a product of the BRT or its successors. Located on Surf Avenue and West Fifth Street, it was a new seven-track trolley terminal where the company's streetcars could discharge and board passengers.

The new terminal was designed to provide amenities that would enhance CI&B's competitiveness. A large roofed area gave trolley passengers an opportunity to duck in out of the rain when inclement weather brought an early end to a day at the beach, and the company's shop forces built an impressive carousel that was installed inside the terminal and was said to be the largest carousel in all of Coney Island in 1912. The new terminal included a small restaurant on its second floor. However, officials of the railway rejected any idea for including a hotel in the new trolley terminal; in the early years of the century hotels in West Brighton were regarded as dens of iniquity, and the presence of one in the street-car terminal might have deterred family groups from using the company's streetcars. The terminal project included a car barn to the north of the passenger loading area, where open streetcars could be stored during the long months they were out of service. By an interesting turn of fate, the terminal that the CI&B Railroad built in 1912 would survive as an active street railway facility until October 31, 1956, the day the last trolley car carried revenue passengers in Brooklyn.[98]

Beginning in 1908, a Virginia-born street railway executive by the name of Slaughter W. Huff served as president of the CI&B. Huff's career began with the Union Railway in Richmond, Virginia, in the days when Frank Sprague made that property the world's first successful electrified street railway. He had wide experience on southern and western systems before taking over the CI&B and supervising the design and construction of the new West Fifth Street terminal in Coney Island.[99]

The CI&B was acquired by the BRT in 1912, shortly after the company's new Coney Island terminal was placed in service, and Huff enjoyed a short tenure with the BRT. Then, in 1918, he was named president of the Third Avenue Railway System. Over the next quarter of a century, he would leave a positive and indelible mark on that important New York property. Indeed, the final series of lightweight trolley cars acquired by Third Avenue in the late 1930s were popularly known as "Huffliners" in recognition of the role the company's president played in their development.

FROM COUNTIES TO BOROUGHS

During the final decade of the nineteenth century, at the same time that Brooklyn and Kings County transportation saw unprecedented levels of merger and consolidation, an even larger consolidation took place in the political realm. Indeed, one could argue that the amalgamation of jurisdictions across five separate New York counties into a unified City of New York on January 1, 1898, was more determinative of twentieth-century transportation developments in Brooklyn than purely corporate issues involving the likes of Brooklyn City Railroad and the BRT.

Before amalgamation, New York City was seen as a political entity that was totally under the control of Democrats whose principal allegiance to the Democratic Party was through the political organization known as Tammany Hall. A natural coalition in support of amalgamation was thus formed among non-Tammany Democrats—including many in Brooklyn—and Republicans who saw amalgamation as a way of breaking Tammany control, and possibly Democratic control, of New York City politics.

Following earlier action by the state legislature, the question of amalgamation was placed on the ballot in 1894 as a popular referendum across all the territory that was proposed for inclusion in what was commonly called, at the time, Greater New York. Amalgamation carried, but by a very close margin. In the wards of New York City, the tally in favor of forming a new metropolis was 63,641 to 62,240—a mere 1,401 votes. In Brooklyn it was just as close, but the drama was higher because it took longer to count the votes. Results were in from all the other jurisdictions and amalgamation had carried in all of them; but as late as Thursday, November 8, newspapers were reporting that the outcome was very much in doubt. Unanimity was required among all the jurisdictions, and negative ballots seemed to be outnumbering affirmative ones in Brooklyn. When all the votes were finally counted, though, Brooklyn had joined the others in saying "yes," and Greater New York began the final lap on its journey to actuality.

It was necessary to draft a charter for the new municipality, and the task fell to a large commission with numerous committees and subcommittees. Hearings were held, options explored, drafts prepared, revisions made. Eventually a product was ready for submission to the state legislature for final ratification. It passed the general assembly, New York State's lower house, on March 23, 1897, by a vote of 118 to 28; two days later, it cleared the state senate by a vote of 39 to 9. At nine o'clock in the morning on Wednesday, May 5, 1897, Governor Frank S. Black signed the measure into law.

On November 2, 1897, voters within the boundaries of the soon-to-be-created new city elected their first mayor. He was Robert Van Wyck, a Tammany Hall democrat. (Amalgamation would eventually see the election of a number of non-Tammany mayors, but not right away.) Van Wyck defeated Seth Low, who ran under the banner not of a national political party but of something called Citizens Union. Low, a major force behind amalgamation and a former mayor of the city of Brooklyn, was a Republican. As would often prove necessary in the new New York with an overwhelmingly Democratic electorate, Low ran on a "fusion" ticket, an ad hoc coalition put together across party lines to challenge the more entrenched Democrats. (Low would persevere, and four years later in 1901, his fusion candidacy for mayor was successful.)

So with a charter approved and a mayor elected it was time to launch the new ship—and celebrate, too. At the first stroke of midnight, the mayor of San Francisco pushed a button and sent a telegraph signal eastward that flipped a relay and started an electric motor that hoisted the new flag of the new city to the top of a mast in City Hall Plaza, the New York National Guard fired a 100-gun salute from the grounds of the post office at Park Row and Broadway, searchlights swept the night sky from the tops of downtown buildings, and a choir of 3,000 members added a gallant touch to the midnight extravaganza—despite a cold and steady rain. The U.S. Army was unwilling to fire its cannons in the middle of the night because of a long-standing policy of not wanting to alarm a sleeping citizenry to nonexistent perils, but at first light on New Year's Day, another 100-gun salute was sounded on Governor's Island.

Across the river in Brooklyn, the onset of the new order was celebrated in rather more restrained fashion. The last official act of the chief executive of the city of Brooklyn, Mayor Strong, was to affix his signature to a resolution earlier passed by the Board of Aldermen permitting a property owner on Elm Street to erect a stairway in front of his building—hardly a memorable piece of statecraft. On their final day in office, December 31, 1897, the Brooklyn aldermen were served an injunction that prevented their issuing certain bonds that would have constituted a financial obligation of the new City of New York.

A poet by the name of Will Carleton composed some verse to

commemorate the passing of the city of Brooklyn, and it was read at the conclusion of a low-key ceremony that was held in Brooklyn City Hall on New Year's Eve. As far as poems go, it may safely be described as exquisitely awful.

> We are grieved that a maiden of sweetness,
> Full of life's vigor and joy and completeness,
> With the rich charms of young womanhood laden,
> We are aggrieved that this fair, comely maiden
> At midnight must die.[100]

AMUSEMENT PARKS IN CONEY ISLAND

Something new came on the scene in the mid-1890s—Coney Island's first amusement park, which was also the first amusement park in the world.

Until Paul Boyton opened an establishment called Sea Lion Park in Coney Island in the summer of 1895, the various amusements that drew people to the seashore were largely independent of one another. There were certain useful combinations here and there—a beer garden and a carousel, for example—under common ownership and management. But as the hotels, restaurants, bathing pavilions, and dance halls that were the hallmark of Coney Island's West End in the 1880s began to be supplemented by mechanical amusements of various kinds in the 1890s, the rides and amusements tended to be stand-alone enterprises.

Boyton had a colorful background. A veteran of naval service as a youngster during the Civil War, he later dug for diamonds in South Africa and, in 1873, headed the first lifesaving service in Atlantic City, New Jersey. It was an association between Boyton and a Pittsburgh inventor who had developed an inflatable rubber suit—which the inventor claimed could save the lives of survivors of steamship disasters at sea—that turned Boyton into a true celebrity. Stowing away aboard an ocean liner bound for Europe in 1874, Boyton donned a prototype of the rubber suit 200 miles out of New York and attempted to jump overboard and paddle back to shore. The ship's captain prevented his doing so; days later, off the coast of Ireland, the voluble Boyton had convinced the captain of the soundness of his plan, and over the side Boyton went. Several hours later, despite some truly awful weather along the way, Paul Boyton walked ashore in Skibbereen, and fame was his forever.[101]

Over the winter of 1894–95, Boyton acquired a plot of land in Coney Island adjacent to Sea Beach Palace and behind as unusual an attraction as Coney Island has ever seen, a hotel built in the form of an elephant.[102] It was here in the summer of 1895 that Boyton opened Sea Lion Park, the world's first true amusement park. Boyton himself was a major attraction at the park, as were the forty trained sea lions that gave the establishment its name. There was also a major ride in the new park called Shoot-the-Chutes, a toboggan-like affair that called for patrons to board a flat-bottom boat that was then hauled up a long incline by winch. When it reached the top, the boat was let go, and it slid back down the chute and into a watery lagoon with a mighty splash.

By 1895, new mechanical rides were a commonplace in Coney Island. The feature of Sea Lion Park that would influence the U.S. amusement industry in subsequent decades was the fact that it was enclosed by a fence and patrons paid an admission fee for access to the grounds. Sea Lion Park itself would not long survive, but the concept of a self-contained amusement park was an idea whose time had come.

Another Coney Island entrepreneur of the 1890s was George C. Tilyou, who was born in New York City in 1862. When Tilyou was but a lad of three, his parents leased an oceanfront lot on Coney Island and opened a small resort hotel they called the Surf House. This was in 1865, three years after the CI&B inaugurated street railway service to the shore. As the child became a boy and the boy became a man, much of George Tilyou's world was defined by Coney Island. At the age of fourteen, Tilyou visited the 1876 Centennial Exposition in Philadelphia, seeking ideas for amusement and entertainment schemes that might work on Coney Island. Tilyou was every inch the showman. Although he dabbled in Coney Island real estate over the years, it was the development of eye-catching amusements that proved to be his true calling. In the 1880s, Tilyou ran afoul of the iron rule of Gravesend boss John Y. McKane, which put a temporary crimp in his career and his plans. But McKane's power was on the wane. The state legislature voted to annex Gravesend to the city of Brooklyn in 1894, as an effort to end the free-wheeling days of the McKane era. More important, in December 1893 McKane was indicted on eleven separate counts that included conspiracy, assault, contempt of court, and election law violations. When his case went to trial, rumors circulated that jurors had been bribed and that McKane would never be convicted. But he was and, on February 19, 1894, he was sentenced to six years of hard labor.[103]

Tilyou was fully prepared to move into the breach and put his own mark on Coney Island. In 1893 he married Mary O'Donnell, and for a honeymoon Tilyou and his bride traveled to Chicago where they took in the World's Colombian Exposition. Tilyou was fascinated by a huge Ferris wheel at the Chicago fair that was a massive 250 feet in diameter and that featured thirty-six passenger-carrying cars. The Chicago Ferris wheel had been promised to the promoters of a fair that was scheduled for Saint Louis in 1904, so Tilyou, despite his best efforts, was unable to acquire it.[104] Instead, he borrowed some money and ordered a more modest Ferris wheel, one that was 125 feet in diameter and included twelve cars. Before he had it installed in Coney Island on land he had leased between the ocean and Surf Avenue, Tilyou put up a sign proclaiming that this was to be the site of the world's largest Ferris wheel. Tilyou would become a master of this style of exaggeration, which would never grow old in Coney Island.

When it opened in 1894, Tilyou's Ferris wheel was just another attraction, one that passersby could purchase a ticket and ride if they were so inclined. But Tilyou quickly grasped the importance of Boyton's achievement when Sea Lion Park opened in 1895. Over the next several months, he quietly acquired a fifteen-acre parcel of land surrounding his new Ferris wheel. When the summer season of 1897 dawned over Coney Island, George C. Tilyou's Steeplechase Park, the island's second amusement park, was ready for business.

Steeplechase was located between Surf Avenue and the beach from West 16th to West 19th Streets. Tilyou quickly realized that whatever success Boyton's Sea Lion Park was achieving each summer was due, in no small measure, to the fact the park boasted a single, dominant ride that became its principal identification. At Sea Lion Park it was the Shoot-the-Chutes. Steeplechase quickly became identified by a mechanical horse ride that surrounded the grounds and gave the park its name. The Steeplechase horses were a roller-coaster-like ride with several mechanical horses moving along parallel tracks with two patrons riding each horse. The horses were hauled to the top of a starting hill; once they were let go, they rolled downhill along the tracks of a rambling course around the grounds of the park in horserace-like fashion. (More often than not, the inside horse won the "race," since it had a shorter course to travel. The weight of patrons, as well as wind resistance, could alter the results. But then, the Steeplechase horses were a ride, not a race.)[105]

Steeplechase would be followed in the early years of the twentieth century by two more Coney Island amusement parks, and the beachfront resort was about to experience the busiest seasons in its entire history. Luna Park opened in 1903, largely on the site of Boyton's Sea Lion Park—which closed in failure at the end of the 1902 season. In 1904, a marvelous venue called Dreamland Park opened for business across from Culver Depot. In addition, the Steeplechase Park of 1897 would be destroyed by fire in 1907, and Tilyou would build a new Steeplechase on its ruins. The new amusement park included a large, indoor pavilion so patrons could enjoy themselves and go on rides irrespective of the vagaries of the Coney Island weather. Steeplechase, Luna, and Dreamland are discussed in more detail in subsequent chapters.

7

Subways and the Nickel Empire (1900–1940)

THE AMALGAMATION of a variety of Kings County transport properties under the aegis of a unified Brooklyn Rapid Transit Company
(BRT) as the nineteenth century became the twentieth brought
measured improvement in travel to and from Coney Island. Now
electrified rapid transit service was available to the seashore from
downtown Brooklyn—even from Manhattan—thanks to through
service over excursion railways and elevated lines. After taking
over the elevated and excursion railways at the turn of the twentieth century, the BRT continued to make improvements in its system, including the completion of electrification efforts, the design
and acquisition of new and improved rolling stock, the rebuilding
of Coney Island's Culver Depot to handle summer crowds more
conveniently, and a grand-scale upgrading of the Brighton Line
that expanded portions of the one-time Brooklyn, Flatbush and
Coney Island Railroad into a four-track railway that could operate
both local and express services. The BRT also improved its newly
unified streetcar system by designing some of the most modern
trolley cars the world had ever seen—although not right away (see
map 6).

EARLY DAYS ON THE BRT

By the summer of 1903, all of the Coney Island excursion railways
save the New York and Manhattan Beach had been electrified and
connected with the BRT elevated railway system. The New York
and Manhattan Beach remained unelectrified and part of the Long
Island Railroad (LIRR) and, unlike the other excursion roads, it
never evolved into a twentieth-century rapid transit service. It was
abandoned outright in the 1920s. Another Kings County excursion

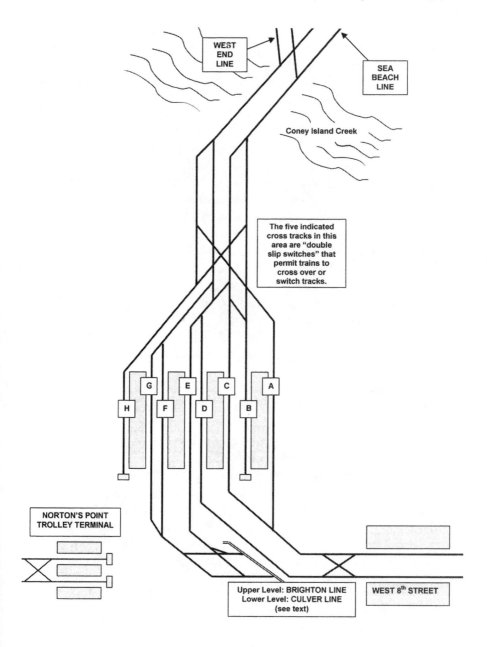

Map 6: The full extent of the BRT elevated railway system in the years prior to the construction of the Dual Contracts subway system.

line, the Brooklyn, Canarsie and Rockaway Beach Railroad that linked East New York with a steamer landing and small amusement area on Jamaica Bay in Canarsie, was absorbed into the BRT network and electrified in 1906. Like the Coney Island roads, it, too, was operated as an extension of the BRT elevated system.

East New York was also a spot where the BRT built a track connection between the Broadway elevated, once a Brooklyn Union property, and the one-time Kings County company's Fulton Street Line. Known as Manhattan Junction, it could well be regarded as the heart of the BRT's Eastern Division.

On the other end of the elevated system, the Southern Division, BRT lines that were formerly the Brooklyn, Bath and West End and the Prospect Park and Coney Island—hereafter known as the West End Line and the Culver Line—featured street running for much of the trip to Coney Island. Both lines connected with the Fifth Avenue El at 36th Street and Fifth Avenue, adjacent to the former Union Depot where the two once terminated. (The BRT converted Union Depot into a maintenance facility for its expanding fleet of elevated cars.)[1]

Passenger cars equipped with both trolley poles and third-rail shoes were able to operate over elevated lines where electric current was distributed by third rail, as well as over surface railways where overhead trolley wire was used to transmit current. Cars also had to be fitted out with traps and steps so passengers could board trains at ground-level stations along the surface portion of the lines, as well as at high-level platforms on the elevated system.

As excursion railways, both the former New York and Sea Beach and the Brooklyn and Brighton Beach included substantial portions of private right-of-way for their trains, not street running. Because both were largely at-grade and featured numerous street crossings, for safety's sake the BRT also elected to use overhead trolley wire for their electrification rather than ground-level third rail. Expectedly enough, under BRT auspices the New York and Sea Beach became the Sea Beach Line, while the Brooklyn and Brighton Beach was called the Brighton Line.

The Sea Beach was actually the first of the former excursion railways to come under BRT control. The transaction occurred in late 1897, prior to the massive acquisitions of early 1899 and just after the property had been reorganized as the Sea Beach Railway

Company. Leased by the BRT to the Brooklyn Heights Railroad for operation, the line was electrified in time for the 1898 summer, but it would be served during its early electric years by trolley cars, not elevated trains. In fact, the Sea Beach Line was used as a conduit to Coney Island by streetcars from a variety of other BRT lines, most of which joined the Sea Beach at Third Avenue and 65th Street. Through operation of trains from the Fifth Avenue El over the Sea Beach Line began in 1903, and for several seasons elevated trains and trolley cars shared the railway. This proved unworkable; beginning in 1907 Sea Beach service to Coney Island was provided by elevated trains exclusively, with the Sea Beach operated largely as a branch of the West End Line.[2] Passengers bound for points along the Sea Beach typically boarded a West End train at a point on the elevated system as far away as Park Row, and then transferred to a Sea Beach train at Bath Junction or rode in the rear-most cars on certain West End trains, which were uncoupled at Bath Junction and continued on to Coney Island over the Sea Beach Line. This was the routine service pattern between September and May each year. During summer, the BRT operated through express trains from downtown Brooklyn and Manhattan that left the West End at Bath Junction and proceeded nonstop from there to Coney Island over the private right-of-way of the Sea Beach Line, thus avoiding the slower West End. The Sea Beach right-of-way westward from Bath Junction to the steamer landing at the foot of 65th Street on Upper New York Bay continued to be served by trolley cars.[3]

(Yet another railway that became part of the BRT early in the twentieth century should be mentioned. In 1900 the South Brooklyn Railroad and Terminal Company was reorganized as the South Brooklyn Railway and immediately afterward acquired by the BRT. What makes this transaction unusual is that the BRT and various successor entities would retain the South Brooklyn as a formally separate subsidiary for more than a hundred years—a hundred years and counting. The South Brooklyn Railway's status as a separate corporation allows it to haul interchange freight traffic without subjecting the rest of the BRT's rapid transit network to a broad range of federal regulatory requirements. The South Brooklyn Railway of 1900 represents yet another entity featuring the words "South Brooklyn" in its corporate title.)[4]

So the elevated trains were electrified and connected with the excursion railways. The Culver, West End, and Sea Beach Lines used the Fifth Avenue elevated line to gain access to downtown Brooklyn and, ultimately, Manhattan via the Brooklyn Bridge. Thanks to its earlier affiliation with James Jourdan's Kings County Railroad, the Brighton Line made its approach to downtown Brooklyn, and Park Row, over the Fulton Street El. An early problem the BRT experienced on its newly electrified rapid transit system was the lack of standardization of its rolling stock. Because the electrification of both Kings County and Brooklyn Union fleets was done relatively quickly, the BRT found itself with too many cars that were incompatible with one another. In 1904, the *Street Railway Journal* noted, "The mechanical department of the Brooklyn Rapid Transit Company has been greatly hampered for some time past in the operation of its elevated service, owing to the large number of different classes of rolling stock which was bequeathed to it by the former companies, of which the present company is a combination."[5]

A program to achieve greater standardization was quickly developed and prosecuted. Fleets of new elevated cars were ordered from various car-manufacturing firms as quickly as they could be delivered, and between 1903 and 1907 the BRT took delivery of 420 new cars, a major capital investment. These acquisition efforts were complemented by a program of rebuilding older rolling stock—trailer cars from the days of steam power that had been hastily converted to electric traction at the turn of the century, but with no common specifications, the end result being "a conglomerate mass of equipment of a number of different types, requiring unusually heavy maintenance work."[6] Cars did not necessarily emerge from the BRT rebuilding program looking like one another in all external respects, but in vital mechanical areas such as platform equipment, brake apparatus, motors, and wiring, the BRT achieved an important measure of standardization.

To pursue this rebuilding effort, the BRT acquired a facility on Second Avenue adjacent to the 39th Street ferry slips that had been constructed twenty years earlier by the South Brooklyn Railroad and Terminal Company and was intended to be an eight-track passenger depot. The building was never so used, and after the BRT took title to it and installed appropriate tools and machinery, it opened for business in 1904 as a back shop where special projects—like the standardization of older elevated cars—could be handled without interfering with routine maintenance work on the active fleet.[7]

Despite all this effort, the basic design of BRT rapid transit cars would see little major change during the first decade-and-a-half of the twentieth century. The advent of electrification brought with it the comfort and convenience of steady electric heat during winter months. A design feature that recalled John Stephenson's first open streetcar for the Broadway Railroad around 1860 was adopted; many of the BRT's new elevated cars were equipped with window panels that could be removed in summertime, thus giving passengers ample drafts of fresh air on hot summer days. Unlike Stephenson's car of 1860, which lacked sidewalls entirely and could only operate during the summertime, the new BRT elevated cars were called "convertibles" (although "semiconvertibles" is a more accurate term). These cars were built for year-round use. Their side panels were removed in the spring when the weather turned warm, and restored in the fall when the temperature dropped. (Similar flexibility also became a standard feature of many new BRT streetcars.)

The BRT did some experimentation with such designs as an all-steel elevated car with fully enclosed end vestibules, but the basic design of elevated rolling stock remained a fifty-foot car with a wooden body that passengers boarded via open platforms at either end.[8] Underbody framing evolved to make more use of structural steel—a major safety enhancement—and, once it became clear that the extreme crowding that prevailed on the Brooklyn Bridge was about to be mitigated by the construction of under-river subway tunnels as well as additional transit crossings on new East River bridges, elevated cars no longer had to include sliding center doors to facilitate loading and unloading at Park Row. Absence of the center door meant more seats inside the car, which contributed to a more comfortable experience for passengers. Most BRT elevated cars that lacked center doors featured what was generally known as "Manhattan-style" seating. In this arrangement—named after a design that was popular on New York City elevated lines—several sets of cross-seats were located in the center of the car, while closer to each end there was horizontal seating along the sides of the car. This created extra floor space closer to the entrance doors where it was needed most, while the cross-seats at the center provided an inducement for early-boarding passengers to move into this part of the car and leave the entrance ways clear.[9] On BRT elevated trains, the classic slogan attributed to generations of trolley car motormen—"Please move to the rear of the car"—could well have been replaced by a Brooklyn variation— "Please move to the center of the car."

The following table displays relevant information about the elevated cars the BRT acquired between 1902 and 1907.

Numbers	Date Acquired	Builder(s)	Number of Cars
1000–1119	1902	Stephenson	120
1200–1299	1903	Osgood-Bradley; J. G. Brill; Laconia	100
1300–1399	1905	Cincinnati; Jewett; Laconia	100
1400–1499	1907	Jewett; Laconia	100

Source: George Rahilly, "The Wooden Cars of the Brooklyn Elevated Railroads," *Headlights* 56 (July–August 1994): 2–13.

DOUBLE FARES

Although it had nothing to do with the design of rolling stock, BRT elevated trains in the early years of the twentieth century retained a service feature that had long drawn the opposition of Coney Island interests. To travel to the seashore from downtown Brooklyn or lower Manhattan aboard a BRT train required the payment of a double fare. Although in the early years of the twentieth century the standard cost of riding a typical rapid transit train or trolley car in Brooklyn—or New York—was a nickel, passengers traveling to or from Coney Island were required to pay two nickels in each direction.

A ten-cent fare to ride an electric-powered elevated train from downtown Brooklyn all the way to Coney Island could certainly be regarded as a better value than was available some years earlier when a horsecar ride from downtown Brooklyn to the city limits cost five cents, and a steam-powered excursion train from there to the shore an additional ten or fifteen cents, sometimes more. But the allure of a nickel ride was very captivating, and business interests in Coney Island continued to regard the BRT's double-fare policy as discriminatory.

The BRT was not alone in charging a premium fare to take passengers to Coney Island. The Coney Island and Brooklyn Railroad (CI&B) traditionally charged a double fare as well. When Nassau Electric arrived on the scene in the 1890s and lured many Coney Island–bound passengers aboard its cars by charging only a nickel, CI&B was forced to follow suit. But in September 1908 the company returned to its preferred double-fare policy.[10]

The BRT took a firm stand on the issue of Coney Island fares. It retained high-powered consultants to conduct studies that, not surprisingly, reached the conclusion that all precepts of sound business demanded that it levy only premium fares for trips to and from Coney Island. "A city transportation company is a business organization and as such it cannot afford to sell its services at a loss any more than a merchant can afford to sell his stock at a loss," argued J. T. Calderwood, the BRT's general manager.[11] Calderwood pointedly rejected comparisons with elevated lines in Manhattan, where a five-cent fare prevailed on trips comparable in length to his company's Coney Island service. He argued that on a run from the Bronx to South Ferry, Manhattan elevated lines saw a steady turnover of patrons, with heavy traffic in both directions, conditions that were conspicuously absent between downtown Brooklyn and Coney Island.

Members of the Coney Island business community were not the only individuals who opposed the BRT's fare policies. There were also important political factions emerging in Brooklyn—and in New York, as well—that supported the elimination of double fares to Coney Island and that opposed the very idea of private corporations like the BRT operating mass transport facilities. Public transportation was a public service that should be owned and operated by the public sector, they argued. A man by the name of Bird S. Coler was elected borough president of Brooklyn in 1906, after earlier serving as the first comptroller of the newly amalgamated City of New York in 1898 and unsuccessfully seeking the governorship of New York State in 1902. He was a foe of double fares to Coney Island, and among the backers of both Coler and his plat-

form were the always-noisy newspapers owned by William Randolph Hearst.

Petitions were filed with the newly created Public Service Commission of the First District, a state agency that in 1907 took over
many responsibilities previously vested in the state's Board of Railroad Commissions, to force the BRT to eliminate double fares to
and from Coney Island.[12] Although the commission was unwilling
to mandate such a reduction as a general matter, it was able to
negotiate some experimental reductions during certain hours.
This hardly satisfied activists like Coler—much less the Coney
Island business community. On more than one occasion, riots
broke out aboard Coney Island–bound trains and streetcars when
BRT personnel attempted to collect the extra fare.[13]

While the fare issue would remain a source of continuing fric-
tion in Brooklyn, other BRT policies aimed at improving the quality of service the company offered its passengers were widely
applauded. Sometimes they worked, sometimes they did not, but
the company was steady in its efforts to explore better ways of
running its railroad.

BRIGHTON LINE UPGRADE

In 1903, the BRT extended the Brighton Line beyond its original
southern terminal in Brighton Beach along a surface-level right-
of-way to Culver Depot in West Brighton. Culver Depot then became the nerve center for both Culver Line and Brighton Line
operations under the auspices of a unified BRT. The following
year, Culver Depot itself was given an extensive makeover. High-
level platforms were constructed so passengers could board elevated trains more conveniently. To speed service, a system was
established so tickets could be collected by platform personnel in
the depot rather than conductors on board the trains. The *Street
Railway Journal* was impressed with these improvements, claiming that they turned Culver Depot into "the largest and most important pleasure resort terminal in existence."[14]

A major upgrade of the one-time Brooklyn, Flatbush and Coney
Island Railroad began in late 1905. Two years earlier, the state
legislature created a Brooklyn Grade Crossing Commission; five

members were appointed by the mayor of New York, one by the LIRR, and one by the BRT-owned Brooklyn Heights Railroad. This body then went to work and planned a comprehensive program to eliminate grade crossings in Brooklyn, focusing on the BRT's Brighton Line and the Bay Ridge Branch of the LIRR, the cross-Brooklyn line that was once so important an element of Austin Corbin's New York and Manhattan Beach operation. The City of New York provided half the money for the project, the two railroads the other half (although, by law, the city's contribution could not exceed a million dollars).

The project made the Brighton Line the first of the one-time Kings County excursion railways to be given the operational benefit of a right-of-way that was free of grade crossings. The below-grade right-of-way that the Brooklyn, Flatbush and Coney Island Railroad had originally constructed on either side of Prospect Park was extended southward to Foster Avenue. At this point, the Brighton Line ascended a short grade and emerged onto a newly built, earthen embankment that ran from Avenue H all the way to Sheepshead Bay. South of Sheepshead Bay, the line dropped back to surface operation for the final leg into the terminal at Brighton Beach and beyond to Culver Depot.

Street crossings were eliminated on the below-grade section of the route by having intersecting streets cross the railroad on bridges; they were eliminated along the embankment portion by having cross-streets duck under the right-of-way. The BRT replaced the line's trolley wire north of Sheepshead Bay with ground-level third rail for the distribution of electric current, and this meant that streetcars could no longer use the Brighton Beach Line en route to Coney Island. Perhaps the most important change on the line was the expansion of the reconstructed section into a four-track railroad featuring both express and local service. The two outside tracks were for the locals, and they made all station stops. The inside tracks were for express trains, and they stopped only at stations featuring special island platforms positioned between the local and express tracks. Such express stops were established at Sheepshead Bay, Kings Highway, and Newkirk Avenue; all other stops—and there were seven of them on the rebuilt section—were for local trains only.[15]

From the start, the project was an engineering challenge. Open-cut portions were constructed through relatively built-up residential areas where there was little room adjacent to the right-of-way for construction equipment, staging, material storage, and so forth. Regular Brighton service had to be maintained during construction. Furthermore, because so many new homes had been built adjacent to the Brighton right-of-way in the Flatbush area, the Grade Crossing Commission determined that it would be less expensive to build the below-grade portion of the line inside a trench lined with perpendicular concrete walls. The more traditional method for building a below-grade railway called for gently sloped, earthen sides, supplemented by small retaining walls near the bottom. Because the use of such a technique on the Brighton Line would have required substantially more land-taking, the expense of building concrete walls reduced the overall cost of the project since it permitted residential and commercial construction to remain in place right up to the edge of the right-of-way.

It was a little easier building the earthen embankment section. There was more "elbow room" here for crews to work because the embankment traversed less densely settled territory. In addition, Brighton trains were rerouted onto adjacent tracks of the LIRR's New York and Manhattan Beach during the construction project.

The earthen embankment required almost a million cubic yards of fill for its completion. Some of this material—230,000 cubic yards worth—came from excavating the below-grade open cut on the Brighton Line itself north of Foster Avenue, while the remainder was from places where a below-grade right-of-way was built for the Bay Ridge branch of the LIRR as part of the same overall effort to eliminate grade crossings. And if the New York and Manhattan Beach cooperated during the project's construction by allowing Brighton Line trains to use its trackage, the new right-of-way atop the new embankment included room not only for the Brighton's four-track right-of-way, but also for two tracks of the LIRR subsidiary.[16]

In addition to this major upgrade on the Brighton Line south of Prospect Park, portions of the line's interior section between Prospect Park and the connection with the BRT elevated train at Fulton Street were also improved. Grade crossings were eliminated by putting the northern half of the route onto a new elevated structure; the rest of the line remained in its original open cut below the level of surrounding streets.[17]

OTHER IMPROVEMENTS

An important three-way intersection in downtown Brooklyn where Flatbush Avenue, Fulton Street, and Hudson Avenue come together was the only spot in all of Brooklyn where a line of the Brooklyn Union Elevated intersected the rival Kings County Elevated. The Brooklyn Union Line came up Hudson from Myrtle Avenue and turned onto Flatbush en route to Fifth Avenue and South Brooklyn, while James Jourdan's Kings County company was built along Fulton Street from Fulton Ferry to City Line; its elevated structure passed over that of the Brooklyn Union line at this intersection. There was no connection of any sort between the two.

As long as the two companies were independent of each other and, more importantly, while steam locomotives were hauling their trains, the grade-separated intersection at Flatbush and Fulton worked just fine. However, problems developed when, under BRT auspices, plans were made to electrify both lines. Because the vertical clearance underneath the Fulton Street Line was so tight, there was insufficient room for the addition of trolley poles atop newly electrified elevated cars operating on the Fifth Avenue Line—accessories that were necessary not for service along the elevated structure where electric current was distributed by third rail, but for surface operation where a ground-level third rail would constitute a lethal danger and overhead trolley wires had to be strung for safety's sake. To allow Fifth Avenue elevated trains to be so equipped, over the winter of 1902–03, the BRT rebuilt the structure of the former Kings County line with shallower, but stronger, girders, thereby freeing up the few additional inches of clearance that were needed to install trolley poles atop the company's cars and permit through operation over both the Fifth Avenue El and various excursion railways to Coney Island.[18]

The crossing at Flatbush and Fulton also offered the BRT some possibility of congestion relief on its overall elevated system. The Myrtle Avenue Line served as a downtown funnel for three important services—the Lexington Avenue Line, the Fifth Avenue Line, and the Myrtle Avenue Line itself—and it was very heavily trafficked. Fulton Street, on the other hand, was largely a line unto itself; even though starting in 1896 it hosted trains of the Brighton Line, it fed far fewer trains into downtown Brooklyn than did Myrtle Avenue. In peak periods, the Myrtle Avenue El ran on a headway of forty-five seconds, while the shortest headway on the Fulton Street El was three minutes.

In 1901, plans were drawn up to build a junction at Flatbush and Fulton that would allow some trains from the Fifth Avenue Line to join the Fulton Street El at Flatbush and Fulton and then approach the Brooklyn Bridge via Fulton Street, or to use less-congested Brooklyn turn-back facilities of the former Kings County company at Sands Street or Fulton Ferry. However, the only junction that engineers were able to design for Flatbush and Fulton would not have been ideal from an operational perspective. To get to the Fulton Street El, inbound trains off the Fifth Avenue Line would have to cross the outbound tracks of both the Fifth Avenue Line and the Fulton Street Line at grade, a practice that would certainly cause many delays and possibly worsen congestion on the BRT elevated system.[19] Prior to the advent of the BRT, James Jourdan had suggested a more comprehensive rationalization at Flatbush and Fulton as one of the positive results that could be realized by a merger of the two rival companies. Jourdan proposed diverting all Fifth Avenue traffic onto the Fulton Street El and abandoning the Hudson Avenue link entirely.

ELECTRIFYING THE ELEVATED LINES

A factor that facilitated the BRT's electrification of its newly acquired Brooklyn elevated lines was something of an accident. Because of the substantial electric-generating capability of the streetcar system the BRT had acquired from several predecessor companies—Brooklyn City–Brooklyn Heights, Nassau Electric and Brooklyn, and Queens County and Suburban—the BRT could electrify its newly acquired elevated properties without building any new generating plants. There were a few teething problems, though, during the early years. Because of a fire at its Ridgewood powerhouse over the winter of 1900–01, for instance, the BRT had to return many steam locomotives to the elevated lines for several months until repairs could be made.

Meeting the demand for electric current on transit lines that saw heavy travel only at certain times of the year often led to unusual remedies. The Brighton Line, for example, saw much heavier traffic in summer than during the rest of the year. "The cost of furnishing a sufficient feeder system to supply the Brighton Beach cars with current would be very great, and the short duration of the season would hardly warrant such an expenditure," the *Street Railway Journal* noted in 1901.[20] The solution to this short-term problem was a unique "battery train." Leftover open cars from the excursion railways that were not being used on the BRT's newly integrated rapid transit system were converted into a mobile storage battery. Equipped with 248 separate battery units, the seven-car train was set out at an old Brooklyn and Brighton Beach storage yard near the Sheepshead Bay station. During periods of light traffic, electric generators charged the on-board batteries using traction power. Then, when traffic was heavy, the process was reversed and the batteries fed supplementary current to the Brighton Line. With a full charge, the battery train was able to supply 1,000 amps for one hour, 500 amps for three hours, or 250 amps for seven hours.

After the 1900 summer season on the Brighton Line, the BRT battery train was moved to East New York and used to supplement a permanent battery station there. It became such a routine fixture at East New York that it could not be spared for Brighton service the following summer, so steam locomotives were fired up to handle the rush to the seashore that year. The BRT also had a permanent battery facility at the Brooklyn end of the Brooklyn Bridge. It, too, was charged by traction power during off-peak hours and then used to supply additional current during rush hours.

By mid-1901, construction of a permanent rotary substation was under way at Culver Depot in Coney Island. While the BRT generated most of its electricity in company-owed power plants, the new Coney Island substation was fed commercial current from the Kings County Electric Light and Power Company. Thus, the need for battery trains on the Brighton Line was over.

The following table lists the power plants that the BRT owned and operated in 1901.

Generating Station	Location	Former Owner	Generating Capacity
Eastern	Kent Ave. & Division St.	Brooklyn City	9,200 kW
Southern	First Ave. & 52nd St.	Brooklyn City	4,800 kW
Third Avenue	Third Ave. & 1st St.	Atlantic Avenue	4,400 kW
39th Street	39th St. & Second Ave.	Nassau Electric	3,560 kW
Brooklyn Bridge	Prospect St. & Washington St.	Bridge trustees	Supplementary battery station; cable engines
Cable powerhouse	State St. & Willow Pl.	Brooklyn Heights	Cable engines

Source: "The Power Stations and Distribution System of the Brooklyn Rapid Transit Company," *Street Railway Journal* (5 October 1901): 471–480.

To improve operations at Coney Island, the BRT combined the Sea Beach and West End lines into a common terminal. The company considered two options—an expanded facility on the site of West End Depot or a new terminal further to the west and close to Steeplechase Park. The West End site won out—its expansion and improvement was considerably less expensive than laying new track west toward Steeplechase—and Sea Beach trains abandoned their original Coney Island terminal at Sea Beach Palace and moved into West End Depot. The site of Sea Beach Palace then became part of Luna Park.

Neither the dawn of a new century nor the creation of the BRT changed the extraordinarily heavy passenger traffic that crossed the Brooklyn Bridge day after day. Viewing bridge congestion from its offices in the World Building on Park Row at the Manhattan end of the famous span, the *Street Railway Journal* noted in 1901, "The obstacles offered to rapid transit in Brooklyn on account of the congestion at the New York and Brooklyn Bridge and the immense territory covered by the lines which radiate from this terminus present a problem which is probably unparalleled in difficulty on any street railway in the country."[21] The *Street Railway Journal* advanced this assessment in an article telling of the resignation of BRT president Clinton L. Rossiter and his replacement by J. L. Greatsinger, formerly the president of the Duluth and Iron Range Railroad.

During his tenure with the BRT, Greatsinger concentrated on the enormous task of unifying the various railways that had recently been brought under the company's control. Short-term leases had to be converted into long-term ones, and managerial issues had to be addressed. Greatsinger's legacy at the BRT was his sharp focus on consolidating the company's system for generating and distributing the electric current that its streetcars and elevated trains required.

Greatsinger did not remain with the BRT for long, though. In early 1903, he was replaced as president by E. W. Winter, whose previous position was president of the Great Northern Railroad. Although railway presidents might have come and gone, some BRT problems seemed to have an intractable character about them. In an address to the Municipal Club in December 1906, Winter waxed poetic about the continuing matter of Brooklyn Bridge congestion, "If, from the boiling caldron of our transit woes, there could be extracted the essence of the mass, I fancy it would consist of the two following propositions: All Brooklyn roads lead to the bridge, and the very well known but sometimes disregarded axiom in physics, that you can't make two material substances occupy one space at the same time."[22]

The table on page 206 presents the average number of elevated and surface cars that the BRT dispatched from each of its depots on weekdays during the month of June 1909.

While the BRT continued to make improvements in its rapid transit system during the first decade of the twentieth century by combining previously separate and independent elevated and excursion railways into a reasonably cohesive system, a new kind of rapid transit opened for business across the East River in Manhattan that would soon have an impact on the future of mass transport in Brooklyn.

UNDER THE SIDEWALKS OF NEW YORK ... AND BROOKLYN

Something happened in New York in the autumn of 1904 that helped intensify Coney Island's irritation over the BRT's double-fare policy. It also underscored the fact that elevated trains rumbling along at ground level in the middle of Brooklyn thorough-

BRT Depot	Average Number of Cars Operated per Day
Surface cars: Eastern Division	
• Ridgewood	225
• Halsey Street	57
• Maspeth	70
• Crosstown	151
• East New York	210
• Subtotal	713
Surface cars: Southern Division	
• Ninth Avenue	165
• 58th Street	171
• Flatbush	124
• Canarsie	106
• Bergen Street	112
• Subtotal	678
Total number of surface cars	1,391
Elevated cars	
• Eastern Division	419
• Southern Division	332
• Fresh Pond	106
Total number of elevated cars	857

Source: BRT Mechanical Department, William G. Gove, Superintendent of Equipment, Bulletin 1058-A, 1909.

fares at the pace of ordinary street traffic did not represent the last word in up-to-date rapid transit.

On October 27 of that year, the first train on New York's very first subway line carried passengers under the sidewalks of New York. Now passengers could travel from lower Manhattan to the far reaches of the Bronx for a single five-cent fare, and they could do so with great speed aboard modern, all-steel subway trains. Like the rebuilt Brighton Beach Line in Brooklyn, the New York subway of 1904 was a four-track facility that operated both local and express services. Indeed the subway's four-track configuration predated the upgrading of the Brighton Line by several years. Following the opening of the new underground rapid transit system in New York, nothing less than through subway service to and from Coney Island would be satisfactory—through subway service between Manhattan and Coney Island, maybe even the Bronx and Coney Island, for a nickel fare.

The City of New York's decision that the style of rapid transit service provided by its older elevated railways was inadequate, and that more efficient subways would never come to pass unless public funds were used for their construction, is a most interesting story that has been told elsewhere.[23] The city's initial subway line that opened in 1904 served only the boroughs of Manhattan and the Bronx, but municipal officials believed that the citizens of Brooklyn—which since 1898 had been part of an expanded Greater New York—were entitled to comparable mass transit facilities. Subway service reached Brooklyn in 1908, four years after the city's first line opened. (Planning for this extension to Brooklyn had begun before the 1904 route carried its first passengers, though.) Although municipal officials considered alternative arrangements, the initial subway line into Brooklyn was a continuation of the city's 1904 subway and offered through Interborough service from Brooklyn to the Bronx. The southern terminal of the original subway line in 1904 was at City Hall, not far from the Manhattan end of the Brooklyn Bridge. A major express station on the new subway was even closer to the bridge; it was called Brooklyn Bridge. Here subway passengers bound for Brooklyn (and Coney Island) could change to BRT elevated trains or streetcars, although there were no free transfers between the new subway and the BRT. The subway extension that eventually reached Brooklyn continued south beyond Brooklyn Bridge under Broadway with closely spaced stations at Fulton Street, Wall Street, and Bowling Green—the heart of the city's business and financial district. Beyond Bowling Green at the foot of Broadway, a turnaround loop extended to South Ferry—site of a major ferry terminal and of a massive overhead structure that was the principal southern terminal of the Manhattan elevated railway lines.

There was an important junction between Bowling Green and South Ferry on the Interborough subway. From here, a new two-track tunnel crossed under the East River; made its Brooklyn landfall along Joralemon Street; and, after stops at key locations in downtown Brooklyn, terminated at Flatbush and Atlantic Avenues, site of the LIRR's Brooklyn Terminal.

The Interborough Rapid Transit Company, which built and operated the city's initial subway, also built and operated the Brooklyn extension. Once revenue trains reached Brooklyn on January 9, 1908—and were extended to Flatbush and Atlantic Avenues on May 1—through subway service for a single fare was available between Brooklyn, Manhattan, and the Bronx.

The opening of the Interborough's East River tunnel to Brooklyn in 1908 resulted in a measured easing of the overcrowding that had long plagued BRT elevated trains and streetcar service across the Brooklyn Bridge. (As noted earlier, the operation of cable-powered trains across the bridge was discontinued once the Interborough subway reached Brooklyn.) The Brooklyn Bridge continued to carry heavy traffic, though, and it would not be until additional East River rapid transit crossings were completed during the next two decades that traffic conditions on the Brooklyn Bridge appreciably eased. The Interborough's Joralemon Street tunnel of 1908 stands as the first East River rapid transit crossing to supplement the Brooklyn Bridge.[24]

Brooklyn's next subway extended service out Fourth Avenue into residential sections of South Brooklyn and Bay Ridge. The route paralleled the BRT elevated line that ran along Fifth Avenue, which was then providing access to downtown Brooklyn and Manhattan for BRT trains operating over the Culver, West End, and Sea Beach lines (successors, respectively, of the Prospect Park and Coney Island; the Brooklyn, Bath and West End; and the New York and Sea Beach excursion railways).

Construction of the new Fourth Avenue subway got under way in 1909 with a groundbreaking ceremony at Flatbush Avenue Extension and Gold Street. Because long-term municipal bonds would be the sole source of the new subway's funding, the city could not begin construction until it had gone through protracted litigation to establish the formal limits of the city's debt ceiling. When construction did begin, city officials had not yet decided whether the new route would connect with the Interborough subway at Flatbush and Atlantic Avenues and operate in conjunction with it, or if it would remain independent. In addition to the Interborough, other candidates to operate the new Fourth Avenue subway in Brooklyn included the BRT, LIRR, and perhaps a few other intercity railroads. The project that was begun in 1909 extended out Fourth Avenue as far as 43rd Street, although officials anticipated that it would eventually continue further into Bay Ridge and tunnel under the Narrows to provide service to Staten Island.

Regardless of whether the new Fourth Avenue Line connected with the Interborough's Brooklyn extension, it would funnel trains onto the 1909-built Manhattan Bridge, thus providing additional rapid transit between Manhattan and Brooklyn and further easing the congestion on BRT elevated and trolley lines that crossed the East River on the Brooklyn Bridge. When Interborough engineers designed the company's Brooklyn terminal at Flatbush and Atlantic Avenues in the early years of the twentieth century, they incorporated features into the tunnels adjacent to the station that would permit later connections with the planned Fourth Avenue subway, as well as the new Manhattan Bridge crossing. (The Interborough's terminal at Flatbush and Atlantic Avenues was also designed to facilitate connections with the LIRR for joint service, although this plan never came to pass.) Coney Island interests followed these developments closely and began to dream about the day when Interborough subway trains would bring passengers directly to Coney Island from points as far away as the Bronx.

The Dual Subway Contracts

As matters turned out, the Interborough Rapid Transit Company was denied access to the new Brooklyn subway line that was built under Fourth Avenue. Instead, the BRT became the city's partner in the subway's construction. It was a new BRT subway system that in 1915 realized the goal of through subway service between Manhattan (but not the Bronx) and Coney Island—for a five-cent fare.

None of this happened smoothly. All manner of mass transit proposals were debated in New York during the first decade of the twentieth century before city officials formally adopted a comprehensive plan in March 1913. Under this plan, the city built the great majority of subway lines that operate in New York to this very day.

The plan was known as the Dual Subway Systems, or the Dual Contracts.[25] It called for a massive expenditure of both public and private funds—public funds from the city government and private funds from two participating transit companies—to more than double the size of the original Interborough subway, as well as build a separate subway system that would become part of a vastly expanded and upgraded BRT system. The Fourth Avenue subway was planned before the Dual Contracts were executed, and its construction was well along by the time they were signed in 1913. The Fourth Avenue subway line was incorporated into the Dual Contracts scheme and became a principal element of the new subway system.

The three one-time excursion railroads that had been tied into the BRT's Fifth Avenue elevated line, as well as the Brighton Line, were substantially upgraded during the construction of the Dual Subway Systems. The Culver Line saw its street-level right-of-way replaced by a three-track elevated structure, and similar improvements were effected along the right-of-way of the one-time Brooklyn, Bath and West End.[26]

With the Dual Contracts, the Culver and West End lines came together at a new double-deck station close to the site of the Union Depot of 1889, a station called Ninth Avenue. From here subway trains could be routed into the new Fourth Avenue subway, while elevated trains could navigate their way onto the Fifth Avenue El. With respect to the Sea Beach Line, the Dual Contracts called for major change. It was converted into a largely below-grade line whose right-of-way was sharply defined by steep concrete walls—a style of construction the BRT had pioneered when portions of the Brighton Line were upgraded to four-track capacity between 1905 and 1907. Some observers commented that the construction resulted in a rapid transit line that was a subway in all respects, except that it lacked a roof.[27] Although officials originally thought about retaining the Sea Beach as a branch of the West End via Bath Junction, the rebuilt line reclaimed much of the original New York and Sea Beach right-of-way and connected with the Fourth Avenue subway just south of a new express station at 59th Street. In addition, the rebuilt Sea Beach Line featured, like the Brighton Line, a four-track route with tracks for both local and express services. The Sea Beach, though, turned out to be a most unusual four-track line.

Between Coney Island and the point where the Sea Beach Line joins the Fourth Avenue subway near 59th Street, nine separate stations were constructed. All were local-only stops, and the express tracks had no stations along the entire length of the Sea Beach Line between Coney Island and 59th Street.

Exactly why the line was so built remains unclear. An interlocking plant adjacent to the station at Kings Highway allowed trains to switch there from local to express tracks, so it would have been possible for certain trains to run nonstop from 59th Street to Kings Highway, and then make all stops from there to Coney Island. In point of fact, though, the principal service that used the express tracks along the Sea Beach Line operated only on "sunny, summer Sundays" (and a few Saturdays and holidays), providing swift service to the seashore from downtown Brooklyn and lower Manhattan to Coney Island. The extraordinary capital investment required to build a pair of separate express tracks could hardly have been justified if the only service the tracks were intended to handle operated on but eight or ten "sunny, summer Sundays" each year. In any event, summer express service over the Sea Beach Line was discontinued in 1953, and the principal use for these tracks after 1953 was the road testing of rolling stock and dead-head moves by out-of-service trains. In the late 1960s, the New York City Transit Authority tried to develop some revenue use for these otherwise unused Sea Beach tracks; it inaugurated a rush-hour express service designated the NX train, which operated nonstop from 59th Street to Coney Island and then continued beyond Stillwell Avenue to Brighton Beach, where it terminated. The service proved unsuccessful, and it was discontinued soon after it was inaugurated. More recently the express tracks along the Sea Beach Line have been reduced from two to one.

To add to the linguistic imprecision that is so much a part of the Coney Island story, regular service along the BRT's Sea Beach Line—that is, the trains that ran every day and stopped at all the local stations between 59th Street and Coney Island—was referred to as the Sea Beach Express. The usage was legitimate, though, because once Sea Beach trains reached the Fourth Avenue subway, they operated along express tracks and provided express service all the way to the line's northern terminal at Times Square in midtown Manhattan. The Sea Beach Express was even something of a "super express," to anticipate a term from a later era, since during most hours it bypassed two important express stations in downtown Brooklyn, De Kalb Avenue and Myrtle Avenue.

Within the context of the BRT, De Kalb Avenue was more than simply another subway station. Operationally, it was a major junction where the Fourth Avenue subway from South Brooklyn joined a new Dual Contracts subway line that headed southward under Flatbush Avenue, connected with the Brighton Line at Prospect Park, and enabled the Brighton to eliminate its connection with the Fulton Street El and upgrade its service from wooden elevated cars to steel subway equipment. De Kalb Avenue was also where Manhattan-bound trains separated onto two different routes, one crossing the East River over the Manhattan Bridge, the other via a new subaqueous tunnel at the foot of Montague Street.

With respect to terminal facilities in Coney Island, the Dual Contracts called for replacing both Culver Depot and West End Depot with a new elevated terminal that would be built inland from the intersection of Surf and Stillwell Avenues, more or less on the site of West End Depot. Sea Beach and West End services approached the new terminal from the north, Culver and Brighton from the east, although they made a ninety-degree turn to the north just prior to the terminal. Culver and Brighton trains reached Stillwell Avenue along an interesting double-decker elevated structure, while Sea Beach and West End services came together at grade on the mainland side of Coney Island Creek, crossed the waterway on a two-track drawbridge, and then headed up a steep ramp into the eight-track Stillwell Avenue Terminal. Because Brighton and Culver trains approached Stillwell Avenue on separate levels of an elevated structure, the southern end of the eight-track terminal was built on two separate levels. Over the length of the terminal the difference in grade was eliminated; at the point where West End and Sea Beach trains entered the terminal, the northern end, all tracks were at the same level. The new Stillwell Avenue Terminal was commonly referred to as a million-dollar project, since the winning bid for the project submitted by the Lord Construction Company stipulated a construction cost of $1,279,274.00[28] (see map 7).

The Brighton Line, successor of the Brooklyn, Flatbush and Coney Island Railroad of 1878, reached the seashore at Brighton Beach, where the Dual Contracts specified the construction of an

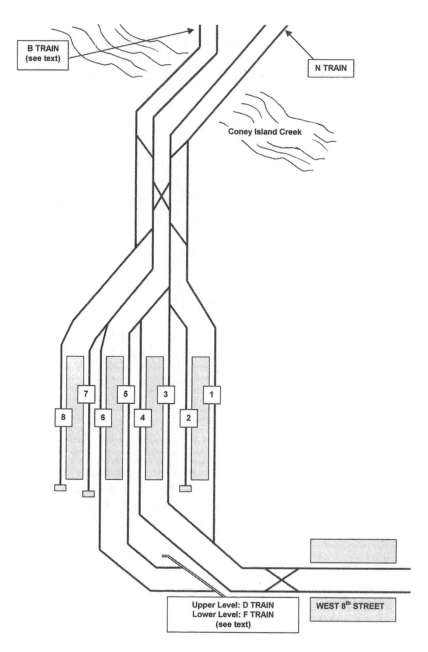

Map 7: Schematic rendition of the track arrangement
at Stillwell Avenue Terminal, circa 1936.

important elevated station over Brighton Beach Avenue. Although the Brighton Line itself continues beyond Brighton Beach to Stillwell Avenue, facilities were incorporated into the station at Brighton Beach so some trains could terminate there. There were—and are—two intermediate stations between Brighton Beach and Stillwell Avenue, one at the point where the line crosses Ocean Parkway, another in Coney Island at West Eighth Street, adjacent to Culver Depot.

The Ocean Parkway station was constructed close to the spot where the Sea View Elevated once crossed Ocean Parkway. As if to compensate for the aesthetic intrusion of the older line onto the grand boulevard, the Brighton Line eschewed conventional steel-girder construction as it crossed Ocean Parkway and was built atop a dramatic concrete structure with sweeping arches. It is one of only two places on the entire Dual Contracts network where such elaborate concrete construction was specified; the other is in Queens where the Corona Line—today's Flushing Line—shares an alignment with Queens Boulevard.[29]

The BRT continued the practice of using a variety of subsidiary companies to handle all manner of specialized tasks. In 1912, the company's various rapid transit lines—the one-time Brooklyn Union elevated system and the connecting excursion railways—were placed under a new operating subsidiary called the New York Consolidated Railway; New York Consolidated would also operate the company's new Dual Contracts subway lines. Another new subsidiary, the New York Municipal Railway, was established to handle the design and construction of the company's new Dual Contracts lines and equipment. Even earlier, another BRT subsidiary called the Transit Development Corporation was set up to attend to such tasks as research into new transit technologies and the construction of new rolling stock for surface and elevated lines.

NORTON'S POINT

In 1879, Andrew Culver had inaugurated a service between West Brighton and the western end of Coney Island so steamboat passengers arriving at Coney Island Point could more easily reach the growing entertainment district of West Brighton. This extension survived the amalgamation of Culver's Prospect Park and Coney Island into the BRT, and it was electrified along with the one-time excursion railway in 1899. By 1920, its clientele were no longer steamboat passengers arriving at Coney Island Point, though. By then the line was serving largely as a feeder line into the BRT elevated system from a section of Coney Island that was becoming a year-round residential district, including an exclusive gated enclave known as Sea Gate that was established on the far western end of Coney Island early in the twentieth century. By this time, the name Coney Island Point had fallen into disuse and the far end of Sea Gate was known as Norton's Point—in memory of Mike "Thunderbolt" Norton, the nineteenth-century character who helped popularize (or some observers might say vulgarize) Coney Island as a seaside resort. Although basic trunk line service over the Culver Line in pre–Dual Contracts days had involved trains (and trolley cars) running in the middle of a conventional thoroughfare (Gravesend Avenue), the line from Culver Depot to Coney Island Point was largely over a private right-of-way. It was hardly high-speed, though, since it was at grade and had to deal with numerous cross-streets.

When the new Stillwell Avenue terminal was constructed, a connection was retained with the feeder line to Norton's Point. A ramp was built from the at-grade right-of-way up into the new terminal, and switch tracks were installed so Culver trains could either terminate at Stillwell Avenue or continue beyond to Norton's Point. Many BRT elevated cars had long been equipped with trolley poles and steps so they could operate along at grade lines, and such equipment was used on the Norton's Point Line. Less than a decade after the Stillwell Avenue Terminal opened in 1919, through service between Culver and Norton's Point lines was phased out, and conventional trolley cars at first supplemented and eventually replaced the elevated trains. However, the ramp up into the Stillwell Avenue Terminal was retained, and trolley cars continued to ply the private right-of-way between the new Dual Contracts subway terminal at Surf and Stillwell and Sea Gate until 1948, when the line was converted to motor bus operation.

Phasing the new Stillwell Avenue Terminal into service created many problems for BRT engineers. Because the terminal was built on the site of the old West End Depot and it was necessary to maintain full rapid transit service during construction, builders had to construct a temporary terminal at ground level and to the east of the new terminal. Coney Island–bound Sea Beach and West End trains terminated here for several months.

A NEW STANDARD IN ROLLING STOCK

Nothing better characterized the corporate upgrade the Dual Contracts represented for the BRT than the revolutionary new subway car the company designed to operate over its new subway routes. Based, in large measure, on an imaginative design that the Boston Elevated Railway had developed for its new Cambridge Subway that opened in 1912, the new BRT cars were thoroughly unlike the subway cars used by the Interborough.

First of all they were bigger. An Interborough car was, in round numbers, fifty-one feet long and nine feet wide, while the new BRT cars were ten feet wide and sixty-seven feet long. But the difference between Interborough and BRT rolling stock involved far more than dimensions. Interborough stock included vestibules at each end of the car, a design feature that reflected the company's dependence on conventional railroad concepts. (Railroad passenger cars of the era included end vestibules.) From the Boston Elevated Railway, the BRT learned that a subway train had no need of end vestibules and that carrying capacity could be substantially increased by their elimination. Like the Cambridge cars, doors on the new BRT cars were strategically spaced at intervals along the sides of the car, and the car had no end vestibules at all. All sixty-seven feet of a car's length was used for carrying passengers, with seating cleverly designed to create alcoves where groups of passengers could sit and pleasantly chat as their train sped along its way. The new BRT car featured a variation of what is today referred to as "three-two" seating—three cross-seats on one side of the car and two on the opposite side. Forcing one's self into a middle seat between two seated passengers was not the last word in comfortable urban travel, but nonetheless the new BRT cars featured a highly imaginative interior design scheme. Because of their narrower width, Interborough cars were equipped with nothing but bench-like longitudinal seating along each side of a car, which underscored their difference with the new BRT cars.

BRT subway cars were smartly designed on the outside, too. A clever use of curves in unexpected places—such as in the corners of certain windows—gave the cars a timeless quality for as long as they remained in service, and they remained in service for a long time. The first of the new cars carried passengers during the presidential administration of Woodrow Wilson. Some of the fleet was still in daily service when President Richard Nixon took the oath of office.[30]

Unfortunately, the new BRT cars never received an appropriate or proper name. Since they were, by default, the standard subway car of the BRT, they were sometimes referred to as "Standards." To distinguish them from the BRT's wooden elevated equipment, company officials sometimes referred to the new subway fleet as "steel cars." In later years, when large numbers were permanently coupled into three-car sets that were identified as B units and single cars were identified as A units, the whole fleet came to be called the ABs. (The final fifty cars in the order were motorless trailers; when they were permanently coupled between two motorized units, the resultant three-car set was called a BX unit.)[31]

The first Standards were ordered from the American Car and Foundry Company (ACF) on February 26, 1914—the BRT placed a firm order for 100 cars, with an option to buy 500 more. The most astounding aspect of the contract between the BRT and ACF was the stipulation that all 100 of those cars would be delivered by December 1, 1914, less than ten months after the contract was signed. The option was exercised, and after ACF turned out the first 600 Standards, the BRT contracted with the Pressed Steel Car Company for an additional 350 units, including the 50 trailers. The cars manufactured by Pressed Steel featured larger and more readable line and destination signs and less streamlined—but more effective—roof ventilators than did the original ACF cars.

An eight-car train of BRT Standards inaugurated service over the first of the company's new Dual Contracts lines on Saturday, June 19, 1915. A ceremonial train carried a group of company officials and other dignitaries from the Chambers Street station on the Centre Street Loop in downtown Manhattan, across the Manhattan Bridge, out the Fourth Avenue Line, and along the Sea

Beach to West End Depot in Coney Island. The city's mayor, John Purroy Mitchel, passed up the BRT gala that day, though. His Honor was piqued with the BRT over some real or imagined slight, and so the mayor headed instead for the Brooklyn Navy Yard that Saturday and there attended the launching of a new Pennsylvania-class battleship for the U.S. Navy. She was BB-39, the U.S.S. *Arizona,* built in Brooklyn and destined to become a monument to infamy on a quiet Hawaiian Sunday in December 1941.

Revenue subway service over the same line from Chambers Street to Coney Island began three days later on June 22, 1915. In following years, as additional elements of the BRT's Dual Contracts network were completed, basic service over the Sea Beach Line would not terminate at Chambers Street on the Centre Street Loop, but at Times Square on the Broadway Line, the BRT's principal Manhattan corridor.[32]

Despite its new fleet of 950 AB units, by the mid-1920s, the BMT needed more new rolling stock to serve its still-expanding subway system. Rather than order additional Standards, the company's engineers developed a new design that carried the basic principles of the AB units to a new level. Thus was created something known as the D unit, or Triplex.

Each D unit featured three forty-five-foot car bodies (hence the name Triplex) that were permanently joined together in a technique known as articulation. What articulation means, in a railway context, is that a single set of trucks serves two separate cars, which are joined together directly over the trucks. A three-section D unit thus has a separate set of trucks at each end, plus an additional truck under the two spots where car bodies are joined together. Because of their articulated design, the three sections of a D unit could not be routinely uncoupled from one another. However, D units could be coupled together, with four three-section D units being the operational equivalent of eight AB units. The overall fleet of 121 D units thus equaled the carrying capacity of 242 AB units.

In the spring of 1925, Pressed Steel delivered the first D units, a full train of four units bearing the numbers 6000 through 6003. The price tag was $300,000. The units were put through a series of grueling preproduction tests before specifications were refined and the full order was formalized. Because a number of modifications were made to the original specifications as a result of the 1925 tests, nos. 6000 through 6003 were also modified to conform with the new design standards.[33]

The 950 AB units and the 121 D units constituted the basic subway rolling stock that provided service over the new subway network that was awarded to the BRT for construction and operation under the terms of the Dual Contracts. The following table provides further information about the two classes of Brooklyn subway cars.

Name or Designation	Number of Cars	Road Numbers	Builder	Year
Standard (motors)	600	2000–2599	American Car and Foundry	1914–1919
Standard (motors)	300	2600–2899	Pressed Steel	1920–1922
Standard (trailers)	50	4000–4049	Pressed Steel	1924
Triplex	121	6000–6120	Pressed Steel	1925–1928

Source: Brian J. Cudahy, *Under the Sidewalks of New York,* 2nd rev. ed. (New York: Fordham University Press, 1995), 175.

STREETCARS DURING THE SUBWAY ERA

Although the early decades of the twentieth century are noted for developments in the rapid transit arena, the era also witnessed substantial change in the operation of Brooklyn streetcars. While subway, elevated, and streetcar services were marketed to passengers as a uniform product of the BRT, streetcar service in Brooklyn retained many of the corporate structures from pre-BRT days. Thus, certain lines continued to operate under legal authorizations that were still held by Nassau Electric, and other BRT lines continued to be owned by the Brooklyn City Railroad, or the Brooklyn, Queens County and Suburban. Such complexity was exacerbated when, in expanding or extending a streetcar line whose core element was part of one underlying company, the BRT built the new segment under the legal authority of a different subsidiary.

A good example of this complexity was an extension of the Nostrand Avenue Line, a one-time Brooklyn City property, into Flatlands. For many years, the line ran from the Manhattan end of the Williamsburg Bridge to Flatbush and Nostrand Avenues—an intersection that, to this day, is referred to in Flatbush as "the Junction." The streetcar line was later extended out Nostrand Avenue to Kings Highway. In exploring the legalities of pushing the Nostrand Avenue Line even further into Flatlands, the BRT found that Nassau Electric owned an old franchise that was originally awarded so the Sea Gate Line could be extended from Sheepshead Bay into Flatbush. Thus, the final element of a line that for many years was called the Nostrand Shuttle—it ran from the Junction to Avenue U—was operated, in part, under legal authority that was vested in the BRT's Nassau Electric subsidiary. The BRT also had to work through its subsidiary companies to conduct business with various state and municipal regulatory agencies.

In late 1904, BRT streetcars such as the Nostrand Avenue Line began to operate into Manhattan across the new Williamsburg Bridge, whose general construction had been completed in December 1903. The city's mayor, George B. McClellan—son of the Civil War general—was annoyed that streetcar service was delayed and not ready for operation when the bridge opened. Like the Brooklyn Bridge, the Williamsburg Bridge had separate tracks for streetcars and elevated trains. In fact, there were two sets of trolley tracks on the Williamsburg Bridge—one so Brooklyn streetcars could cross the river and terminate on the Manhattan side of the bridge, and a second so lines from Manhattan could terminate on the Brooklyn side at a marvelous outdoor trolley terminal called Williamsburg Bridge Plaza.

The delay in the inauguration of streetcar service was attributed to uncertainties associated with how Williamsburg Bridge elevated trains would proceed once they reached Manhattan. It was generally agreed that elevated trains would continue further south to the Manhattan end of the Brooklyn Bridge; what was unsettled was whether this would be as a subway or as an elevated line.

Eventually, BRT trolleys would use an underground Manhattan terminal at Delancey Street. However, because final plans for the El were incomplete in 1904, a temporary street-level terminal was used in early November when every second car of six different BRT streetcar services, including the Nostrand Avenue Line, was dispatched across the new bridge, along with alternate cars on the

Prior to the construction of Stillwell Avenue Terminal, the BRT's West End and Sea Beach services terminated in Coney Island at West End Depot (top), while Brighton and Culver lines used Culver Depot (bottom). The structure beyond the platforms at Culver Depot is the new Dual Contracts elevated line that would soon replace at-grade operations into Culver Depot (*Both photos: Author's collection*).

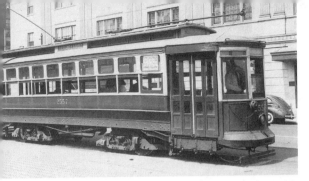

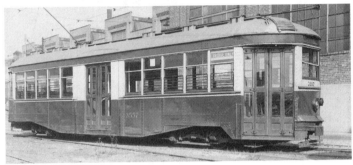

Four classes of Brooklyn trolleys show the evolution of streetcar design during the twentieth century. Top: Car no. 2557, built by Stephenson in 1907, is a classic deck-roof car with entrance and exit via end vestibules. Second from top: The BRT's first experimental center-entrance car was no. 3557, built in 1912, which quickly led to a fleet of similar trolleys. Entrance door at the front of this car was a later addition when conductors were eliminated and streetcars converted to one-man operation. Third from top: The classic Brooklyn streetcar is the 8000-series cars that were delivered between 1923 and 1925. No. 8245 was built by Saint Louis in 1923. Bottom: Car no. 6007 is an Osgood-Bradley product of 1931; it differs from the others shown in that it can operate only in a single direction and requires turning loops at each end of the line *(All photos: Author's collection)*.

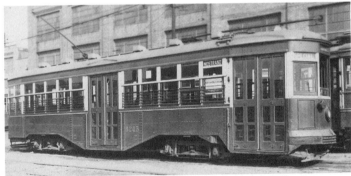

A 1954 scene along the Church Avenue Line. Peter Witt car no. 8361 has been chartered by a group of rail buffs for a pleasant Saturday's outing, while PCC car no. 1016 heads in the opposite direction with revenue passengers on board. The steeple in the background is that of Holy Cross Church—typical in Brooklyn, a community once known as the "city of churches" *(Author's collection)*. Below: Long after deck-roof streetcars carried their final passengers, a small fleet was maintained in Brooklyn for various nonrevenue tasks, such as spreading salt during winter storms. No. 4547 is leaving Coney Island on the McDonald Avenue Line in 1954 on such an assignment. Elevated structure in the background is that of the BMT Culver Line *(Author's collection)*.

A sampling of Brooklyn elevated rolling stock. (Top) No. 745 was built in 1888 by Pullman as a trailer to be hauled by Kings County steam locomotives. The car was converted to electric operation at the turn of the century and the center door added when elevated service was extended across the Brooklyn Bridge and rapid loading and unloading was a necessity at Park Row. (Middle) No. 1086, a Stephenson product of 1902, allows the car's window panels to be removed so passengers received ample drafts of fresh air. Bottom: Car no. 1332 was built by Cincinnati in 1905 and also features removable windows *(All photos: Author's collection)*.

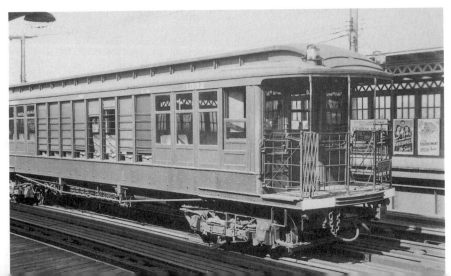

The vast expanse of the New York City Transit Authority's Coney Island Shops. Elevated rapid transit line in the foreground is that of the Culver Line, while the highway it vaults over is the Belt Parkway. Water that edges up to the parkway's foundation is the inner limit of Coney Island Creek. In years gone by, Coney Island Creek continued inland (to the right) and connected with Sheepshead Bay *(Author's collection)*. Below: Electric locomotive no. 5 of the South Brooklyn Railway heads for Coney Island with three boxcars in tow *(Author's collection)*.

Subway rolling stock used by the BRT and BMT to provide service over its Dual Contracts network include 950 cars known as A/B units (top photo) and 121 three-section articulated units such as no. 6046 (bottom photo) *(Both photos: Author's collection)*.

When the Board of Transportation replaced Brooklyn streetcar lines with motor buses after the Second World War, a fleet of 200 electric-powered trolley buses was acquired to test out this technology. No. 3036, operating on the Saint John's Place Route, demonstrates its ability to move around a double-parked truck along Livingston Street in downtown Brooklyn. By the mid-1960s, all such vehicles were retired *(Author's collection)*. Below: A little-known aspect of Brooklyn's transport history is that a small dock railway in Greenpoint continued to operate steam locomotives long after diesels had banished steam from major railroads in the metropolitan area. No. 15 of the Brooklyn Eastern District Terminal is not totally unlike Forney-style steam locomotives that once hauled passenger trains on the Brooklyn elevated lines *(Author's collection)*.

(Top) An IND D train rolls into Stillwell Avenue Terminal in the summer of 1955, mere months after the IND took over operation of the Culver Line from the BMT. (Bottom) The previous summer, 1954, Culver service was provided by typical BMT A/B units *(Both photos: Author's collection).*

Two views of Steeplechase taken a half-century apart. Top: The rides are shut down and the Pavilion of Fun is quiet during the winter of 1964–65. When Steeplechase closed at the end of the 1964 season, it never reopened. Bottom: Steeplechase Pool, shown here in 1912, would see new sun decks built along its sides over the years, but the basic pool remained a steady Coney Island attraction until 1963. Unlike contemporary swimming pools where water is filtered and treated, Steeplechase was filled with ordinary sea water, into which a little chlorine was dumped. *(Both photos: Library of Congress).*

This unlikely looking locomotive was the first engine that ran on the Boynton Bicycle Railway in Coney Island *(Author's collection)*. Below: Trolley companies needed a variety of specialized equipment, in addition to passenger-carrying cars. This "sweeper" was used by the Atlantic Avenue Railroad to brush light accumulations of snow off the rails *(Author's collection)*.

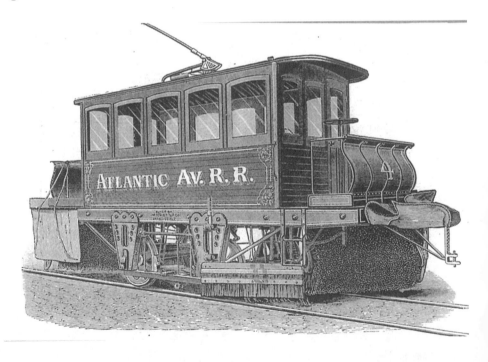

Above: The radically new PCC car. Mayor Fiorello LaGuardia has taken over the motorman's seat aboard car no. 1009 during a ceremony at Park Row in October 1936. (Top right) Brochure issued by the BMT to promote its newly acquired fleet of PCC cars.

Below: Almost twenty years after they entered service with such promise, PCC cars—and street railway service itself—was on its last legs in Brooklyn. Car no. 1067 is leaving Coney Island's West Fifth Street Depot in the summer of 1954 on a run to Prospect Park West and 20th Street, a perfect re-creation of the service pioneered by Andrew Culver's Prospect Park and Coney Island Railroad. Second "headlight" in the 1936 view has been removed. (It was actually a "next car" signal the motorman displayed when the car was full.) *(All photos: Author's collection).*

Top: Coney Island's future rests with new investments like Keyspan Park, a minor league baseball stadium that opened on the site of Steeplechase Park in 2001. The tower in the background is the famous Parachute Jump, brought to Steeplechase following its debut at the 1939–40 New York World's Fair. Bottom: The Coney Island Boardwalk was dedicated in 1923 during the administration of Mayor John Hylan. Today, beach sand has risen almost to the same level as the walkway. Photo looks westward from Brighton Beach. The apartment building to the right occupies roughly the same site as the Brighton Beach Hotel of 1878 *(Both photos: Author's collection)*.

Franklin Avenue Line of the Coney Island and Brooklyn. Cars of the Avenue A and 14th Street Line of New York's Metropolitan Street Railway began crossing the bridge on separate trackage late in the afternoon on New Year's Eve in 1904.

As to elevated service, the municipal government eventually decided that a subway tunnel, not an elevated line, would be built inland from the Manhattan end of the Williamsburg Bridge. Elevated service was begun across the bridge on September 16, 1908, with Mayor McClellan himself handling the controls aboard the inaugural train. The subway was completed between the end of the bridge and a station under the Municipal Building at the Manhattan end of the Brooklyn Bridge, a distance of a little more than a mile, in mid-1913. Planned before the execution of the Dual Contracts, this Centre Street Loop, as it was called, was later absorbed into the BRT's Dual Contracts network.

Streetcar service across the Williamsburg Bridge became very popular, but it never approached the level of intensity that was experienced each day on the Brooklyn Bridge. Almost a decade after trolley cars first crossed the Brooklyn Bridge, the *Street Railway Journal* observed, "The effect . . . was not only to congest the routes leading to the bridge, but on account of the reduction in fare to attract so many new residents to Brooklyn as still further to increase the patronage of the lines reaching New York by the bridge route."[34]

One problem, of course, was the finite capacity of the Brooklyn Bridge, which was partially dictated by the size of the original four-track trolley terminal at Park Row. In 1904, the terminal's original four loop tracks were supplemented by four more, for a total of eight, and sixteen separate Brooklyn streetcar lines now used the bridge. During peak hours, streetcars crossed the bridge on a headway that was measured in distance, not time, with the maximum level of service calling for 102 feet between cars at seven miles per hour. Under such conditions, 300 trolleys per hour could make their way across the Brooklyn Bridge—at least theoretically.

Another problem was how streetcars entered and left the Brooklyn Bridge at the Brooklyn end of the span. Initially, there was but a single point of entry at Sands Street near Washington Street. Trolley cars of the various lines continually backed up at this entrance and induced massive gridlock in an important area of downtown Brooklyn. In 1908, a second entry point for streetcars was constructed to the south of the bridge railway's Sands Street Terminal that allowed seven Brooklyn trolley lines—Fulton Street, Gates Avenue, Putnam Avenue, Myrtle Avenue, Flatbush Avenue, Court Street, and Union Street—to enter the bridge closer to Tillary Street, head up a new ramp, and make a stop at a special streetcar platform inside the Sands Street facility. There was still only a single set of trolley tracks across the bridge, but the second approach in Brooklyn measurably eased congestion around the approaches to the bridge.[35]

As the popularity of streetcar service continued to grow, the BRT had to face the problem of the limited capacity of Fulton Street as a trunk line for funneling trolley service into downtown Brooklyn. Eight important streetcar lines operated along Fulton Street between Flatbush Avenue and Borough Hall, a stretch of trackage commonly referred to as "the gut." The solution to the Fulton Street problem involved a cooperative effort between the BRT and city officials. Because of the unusual street alignment in downtown Brooklyn, there was only one thoroughfare that ran parallel to Fulton Street and offered any possibility of relieving streetcar congestion. This was Livingston Street, one block south of Fulton, but much too narrow to accommodate a double-track streetcar line. The City of New York awarded a franchise to Nassau Electric during a prearranged auction—Nassau Electric was by then a BRT subsidiary—to operate along Livingston Street; for its part, the city undertook a program to widen the street from forty feet to eighty feet between curbs. And so, in 1907, Livingston Street became a secondary trunk line leading into downtown Brooklyn, thus substantially easing congestion on Fulton Street. Three important BRT streetcars lines—Flatbush Avenue, Saint John's Place, and Third Avenue—were rerouted onto the new Livingston Street trackage, thus removing sixty-seven peak-hour streetcars from "the gut." Remaining on the original Fulton Street trackage was Coney Island and Brooklyn's De Kalb Avenue Line, as well as four important BRT services—the Fulton Street Line, the Gates Avenue Line, the Putnam Avenue Line, and the Flatbush–Seventh Avenue Line.[36]

The new Livingston Street option quickly proved its worth for congestion relief during normal operation and as an alternative

route into and out of downtown Brooklyn whenever streetcar service along Fulton Street was disrupted by accidents, fires, and
other emergencies. Previously, a derailed or blocked streetcar
along Fulton Street meant that nothing moved into downtown
Brooklyn at all. With Livingston Street available, cars using Fulton
Street could be shifted to Livingston; while they certainly would
encounter serious congestion, at least they could keep moving.

Under BRT auspices, company architect D. R. Collin designed
a new car barn that the company believed could be replicated
throughout Brooklyn to store out-of-service streetcars and per-
form light maintenance. The prototype of the design was used for
a new facility built in 1903 at Avenue N and Utica Avenue that
was known as Flatbush Depot. Because many BRT car barns were
holdover facilities from predecessor companies that did not require immediate replacement, the new, common design saw relatively little subsequent use, although it did represent an effective
statement of the company's maintenance policies.[37] A one-time
Brooklyn City facility on Second Avenue at 52nd Street and a car
barn built in Ridgewood in 1901 by the Coney Island and Brooklyn
Railroad became the principal heavy maintenance shops for the
BRT's surface car fleet.

New Streetcars

The early years of the twentieth century represented a period of
growth for street railways, and manufacturers found steady markets for larger, faster, and more comfortable streetcars. In the
early days of electrification, a motorman typically worked on an
open platform at the front of the car, protected from the weather
by nothing more substantial than an overhang of the roof and a
waist-high dash—a practice that dated back to the horsecar era.
Soon manufacturers began to enclose these end platforms and fitted them with folding doors for passenger entry and exit. As more
powerful electric motors were developed, trolley cars got larger.

Originally, streetcars featured two axles and four wheels
mounted in a solid frame. But as cars began to exceed twenty and
then twenty-five feet in length, eight wheels became necessary
and something more flexible than a solid frame was needed. Each

pair of axles was fitted into a metal frame called a truck that could swivel independently of the car and independently of the other pair of axles. A car riding on four wheels with two axles was usually referred to as a single-truck car, while the design that came to dominate the industry in the twentieth century was known as a double-truck car. In addition, manufacturers began to use steel for car body construction.[38]

The BRT invested considerable capital in acquiring fleets of new, electric-powered streetcars during the first decade of the twentieth century. More than 750 double-truck cars were purchased from firms such as Laclede Car Company, Kuhlman Car Company, John Stephenson, J. G. Brill, and others. In general appearance, all these early-twentieth-century cars were remarkably similar. True enough, some were convertibles whose sidewalls could be removed during warm-weather months, others were not, and the design and treatment of end vestibules evolved somewhat over the years. But all the company's new cars of this era featured entry and exit via end platforms or vestibules, and all had a raised middle roof section known as a deck roof.

In 1913, the company invested over $1.25 million to rebuild and modernize more than 2,000 of its older cars at the same 39th Street shops where elevated cars had earlier been standardized. The streetcars were equipped with air brakes and new electrical gear.[39] Despite all the BRT's efforts to acquire new cars and rebuild older ones, in the era leading up to the First World War its streetcar fleet could in no sense be characterized as "modern" or up-to-date. The company's cars may have been safe, efficient, and dependable, but they could not be called modern, and they certainly were not exciting.

In 1912, the company more than redeemed itself. A remarkable new streetcar design was developed that called for an all-steel car body, an overall length of forty feet, and the latest in motors and other electrical equipment. Most important, the new car featured a massive set of sliding center doors, not unlike those on a subway car, through which all passengers would enter and exit. In many respects, the new trolley design was the street railway equivalent of the Standard car that the BRT had developed for its new subway lines.

A single experimental car was delivered by the Standard Steel

Car Company in 1912 that was identified as no. 3557.[40] Soon afterward, the BRT placed an order with J. G. Brill for 200 cars of a similar design. Of these, 100 were motor cars—nos. 5000 through 5099—and another 100 were trailer cars to be hauled by other motorized units. The trailers were identified as nos. 6000 through 6099.[41]

The BRT's new center-entrance cars permitted a service called "prepayment." In a typical streetcar of more conventional design, passengers jumped aboard the front or rear platform when the motorman stopped the car, and it was then the task of a second crew member—the conductor—to identify the newcomers, make his way through the car to them between stops, and collect their fares. Assuming perfect honesty on the part of a company's corps of conductors, mere inefficiency often led to passengers' failing to pay the required fare. (Perfect honesty on the part of conductors, though, was an ideal that was imperfectly achieved in the street railway industry. Serious discussion papers, read at formal trade association meetings, continually wrestled with this issue.[42])

With its new center-entrance cars, the BRT was able to adopt a prepayment system, in which the conductor was stationed immediately inside the center doors and passengers paid their fares as they boarded the car. Centralizing the fare collection process in this manner greatly reduced the incidence of nonpayment and eliminated some of the opportunities for conductors to pocket a percentage of fares for themselves.

The BRT's acquisition of this fleet in the second decade of the twentieth century represented a major improvement in the quality of streetcar service for the people of Brooklyn. Eventually, many of the 6000-series trailer units would be converted into motorized cars and renumbered into the 5100 series, and the operation of two-car units would be discontinued in Brooklyn.

MORE RAPID TRANSIT PLANS

After the Dual Contracts were executed, "spheres of influence" developed around the areas served by the two transit systems. The Interborough concentrated on serving Manhattan and the Bronx, with relatively minor incursions into Brooklyn and Queens;

the BRT primarily served Brooklyn, linked it with Manhattan, and operated some service into Queens. In addition, each company continued to explore possibilities for expanding its system to tap new markets, with or without public financing.

A line to Coney Island remained an attractive possibility for the Interborough. This was based less, perhaps, on the prospect of carrying seasonal traffic to Coney Island itself, and more on the prospect of tapping into rapidly growing residential neighborhoods in Flatlands and Gravesend that were likely sources of year-round traffic. At one time in the 1920s, the Interborough proposed to extend its Nostrand Avenue Line to Coney Island. The Nostrand Avenue Line was one of two Interborough routes that were built under the terms of the Dual Contracts and that continued beyond the company's original Brooklyn terminal at Flatbush and Atlantic Avenues. A four-track line continued out Flatbush Avenue to Eastern Parkway where it turned eastward under Eastern Parkway, eventually emerged from underground as a three-track elevated line, and terminated in the New Lots section of Brooklyn. The two-track Nostrand Avenue Line branched off this line at Eastern Parkway and Nostrand Avenue.

It was intended that the Nostrand Avenue Line would eventually probe deeper into residential sections of Flatbush and Flatlands. However, Dual Contracts financing brought the Interborough only as far south as Flatbush and Nostrand Avenues (the Junction), where a temporary terminal was established.

The Coney Island extension envisioned in the 1920s called for the Interborough line to continue a few hundred yards beyond Flatbush and Nostrand Avenues and turn westward along the right-of-way of what was then the Bay Ridge Branch of the LIRR, but had once been the route used by Austin Corbin's New York and Manhattan Beach Railroad. The plan called for Interborough subway trains to then turn southward along the LIRR's little-used Manhattan Beach line and head for the oceanfront, but plans remained vague as to where trains would terminate on Coney Island. A storage yard for subway cars was proposed for the general area that later became the campus of Brooklyn College. Like many post–Dual Contracts subway expansion proposals, this one never got beyond the discussion stage.[43]

The BRT also had some post–Dual Contracts expansion of rapid transit in mind. One proposal would have built a new elevated line across central Brooklyn from the junction of the Fulton Street El and the Brighton Line at Franklin Avenue and Fulton Street to Queens Plaza, serving Williamsburg and Greenpoint along the way. Another expansion of the BRT was discussed at the time the Dual Contracts were negotiated but only partially funded by that agreement. It would have upgraded the Fulton Street El to permit the operation of steel subway cars and feed Fulton Street trains into the new BRT subway just to the south of the De Kalb Avenue station. Under the Dual Contracts, the BRT upgraded portions of the Fulton Street Line to heavier-duty standards, but the critical connection with the subway system—a project known as the Ashland Place connection—never came to pass. Another failed dream was the idea of building a tunnel under the Narrows and extending BRT subway service to Staten Island.

FROM BRT TO BMT

Following the execution of the Dual Contracts in March 1913, the BRT began to transform itself from a rapid transit company whose services were provided by wooden cars along elevated structures into one whose services were provided by all-steel cars operating through newly built subway tunnels. Older elevated lines that were to be retained as feeders for the subway system were rebuilt to bear the weight of the new sixty-seven-foot subway cars. In other cases—including the West End and Culver Lines—totally new elevated lines were built that were intended to serve as feeders to the subway system from the outset. Even though new BRT subway and elevated lines were being built and older routes substantially upgraded, the BRT as a corporate entity would not survive.

It has often been said that the event that eventually pushed the BRT into receivership was a terrible accident on the BRT's Brighton Line on November 1, 1918, which claimed at least ninety-three lives. However, the BRT's overall fiscal condition had deteriorated so badly by late 1918 that the Malbone Street Wreck, as the disaster has been called, was probably not the primary factor in the company's demise.[44]

One significant factor in the BRT's financial downfall was a constraint that it shared with many other U.S. transit systems. Namely, the company was restrained by various contractual and regulatory pressures from increasing income by raising fares, even though inflation was undermining the yield that passenger fares produced. Writing about the decline of the street railway industry many years later, *The New Yorker* summarized the situation, "As long as operating costs stayed somewhere near nineteenth-century levels, the right to charge no less than a nickel guaranteed tremendous profits to trolley-car investors. But the First World War unexpectedly brought sharp inflation to the country—labor costs went up fifty percent between 1916 and 1919— and under these changed circumstances the continuing legal obligation to charge no more than a nickel guaranteed bankruptcy after only a few years."[45]

And that is the crux of the issue. Companies initially welcomed franchise requirements to charge a five-cent fare and felt it represented a bulwark against popular pressure to lower the fare. As matters turned out, though, the five-cent fare became a burdensome obstruction that prevented a transit company's income from keeping pace with inflation.

RECEIVERSHIP AND THE SURFACE LINES

When the BRT entered receivership on the final day of 1918, the company's surface lines were not part of the proceeding. Because of the complex way the BRT was structured with leases, subleases, and underlying companies, it was possible to keep the surface lines separate from rapid transit and, thus, not subject to receivership in December 1918. By mid-1919, however, even the BRT's surface lines were placed under the care of the receiver; intense financial and operational analysis soon followed under the direction of the court.

In the fall of 1919, the transportation engineering firm Stone and Webster delivered a report that outlined the condition and future prospects of BRT surface lines. Stone and Webster found that, although passengers regarded BRT trolley cars as part of a single and unified system, the surface railway system of the BRT, even as late as 1919, actually included six separate companies: the Brooklyn Heights Railroad Company; Nassau Electric Railroad Company; Brooklyn, Queens County and Suburban Railroad Company; the Coney Island and Brooklyn Railroad Company; Coney Island and Gravesend Railway Company; and the South Brooklyn Railway Company. In sorting out the various lines, depots, street-cars, and power-generating equipment owned by each of these subsidiaries, Stone and Webster found that the various companies used one another's assets to such an extent that any simple separation of the BRT into all of its constituent elements would be very difficult.[46]

The BRT was reorganized as the Brooklyn-Manhattan Transit Corporation (BMT) in 1923, although it was primarily the subway and elevated lines that were included in the reorganization. Based on the Stone and Webster report, the court was able to separate out an identifiable component of the BRT's surface lines that seemed capable of standing on its own—the Brooklyn City Railroad. From an operational perspective, there were few changes in day-to-day service patterns, except this latter-day Brooklyn City offered no free transfers to and from other BRT surface lines. However, there were numerous instances where BRT and the new Brooklyn City cars used the same trackage.

The creation of this "Brooklyn City II" as a stand-alone private corporation made fresh capital available for investment in new street railway equipment. Between 1923 and 1925, no fewer than 535 streetcars of a distinctive new design were delivered by three different builders—the Saint Louis Car Company, J. G. Brill, and Osgood-Bradley. Identified as the 8000 series, they were based on the design the BRT had pioneered with its center-entrance cars, but carried it an important step further. Like the earlier cars, the new cars featured a center door, where the conductor was stationed. But passengers boarded the new cars through a front door and did not pay as they entered. They paid either when they left the car via the center doors, or when they continued past the conductor's post to take a seat in the portion of the car to the rear of the center door.

The concept, which was called "pay as you pass," is a service feature that is generally credited to a Cleveland traction executive by the name of Peter Witt; "pay as you pass" cars, like Brooklyn

City's new 8000 series, were often called Peter Witt cars. The new trolleys were forty-four feet long over their end bumpers with an overall width of eight feet four inches, but at 37,500 pounds they were relatively light in weight. Because of Brooklyn's proximity to the Atlantic Ocean, the steel used in the construction of the new cars was actually an alloy of copper and steel that was adopted to reduce corrosion. To advise waiting passengers that an approaching trolley was one of the new pay-as-you-pass cars that must be boarded through the front door, Brooklyn City painted the trolleys' front dash a very different shade of light blue, decorated with an unusual sunburst design around the headlamp. In later years, Brooklyn's 8000-series Peter Witt fleet were converted to a one-man operation—a feature that was anticipated in their design. Conductors were eliminated, and fares were paid to the motorman upon entry. Few would fault the contention that these distinctive cars are the trolley cars that are most identified with street railway service in Brooklyn.[47]

Eventually, the reorganized BMT established a new surface lines subsidiary called the Brooklyn and Queens Transit Corporation (B&QT), and "Brooklyn City II" was folded into this company in 1929.[48] Another series of 200 new streetcars appeared on the property in 1931 and 1932. The cars in this fleet were also known as Peter Witt cars—although they were pay-as-you-enter and one-man operation from the outset. These cars introduced a new feature to Brooklyn street railways, a single-ended car that could only reverse directions by operating around a loop of some sort. (The 8000 series, like virtually all previous Brooklyn streetcars, could operate in either direction.) The B&QT's new cars, identified as the 6000 series, quickly became popular on such important lines as Flatbush Avenue, Fulton Street, Gates Avenue, and Putnam Avenue.[49]

Brooklyn would see the acquisition of only one more fleet of new streetcars, a small order of 100 units that was delivered in 1936. The age of the trolley had reached its apogee in Brooklyn and was about to enter a period of decline. The BMT's new surface subsidiary, the B&QT, included a new modality in urban transport—surface routes that operated gasoline-powered motor buses.

BMT Subway Service

The reorganized BMT gave some early indication that its financing was sound and its future secure. The company posted nominal profits—$4 million in 1924, $5 million the following year—and the BMT was able to establish a stock-ownership program for its employees that 10,000 workers joined. But there were clouds on the horizon, and even stormier weather beyond the horizon.

Six years after the BMT was created, the New York Stock Market crashed and the world was plunged into the Great Depression. The municipal government under Mayor John Hylan continued to delay completion of necessary elements of the Dual Contracts network the BMT took over from the BRT. As a result, the company was unable to realize income from subway lines over which trains could not operate. The legal requirement to charge a nickel fare was yet another constraint on revenue growth. Then, in 1925, came a new development. Hylan and his municipal government undertook the design, construction, and operation of a third subway network in New York. This system would be free from any control by the hated "traction interests" and would represent the boldest example of municipal operation of mass transit yet seen.

The BMT continued to run its trains, and service patterns over the subway network the new corporation inherited from the BRT were adjusted from time to time to achieve better results. One important missing link that affected service on the entire southern division was the fact that a connection between the Montague Street Tunnel under the East River and the lower Manhattan line that was known as the Centre Street Loop remained unbuilt until the early 1930s.

The Centre Street Loop extended from the Williamsburg Bridge to a station under the Municipal Building at Chambers Street near the Manhattan end of the Brooklyn Bridge, a line that was built in advance of the execution of the Dual Contracts. It was originally intended to link the Centre Street Loop with the elevated tracks across the Brooklyn Bridge, but the Dual Contracts modified these plans to extend the Centre Street Loop further southward in Manhattan under Nassau Street and link it with the new BRT/BMT Montague Street Tunnel.

Because the connection between the Centre Street Loop and the Montague Street Tunnel remained unbuilt, the BMT was unable to operate as many subway trains into Manhattan as the Dual Contracts anticipated. As a consequence, while Sea Beach, Brighton, and West End lines provided service into the subway system and operated along the Broadway Line in Manhattan, the Culver Line was forced to remain an elevated operation whose trains reached downtown Brooklyn and Manhattan over the Fifth Avenue El. Culver Line service improved measurably when trains stopped running along the surface on Gravesend Avenue and shifted onto a new Dual Contracts elevated structure directly overhead in 1919. But while the structure was built to accommodate heavyweight, steel subway cars, Culver service continued to be operated with lightweight elevated equipment.

When the Centre Street Loop was eventually extended to a junction with the Montague Street tunnel in 1931, the subway system envisioned for the BRT in the Dual Contracts of 1913 was essentially completed. Adequate subway capacity for BMT trains thus became available in Manhattan, and the Culver Line was able to discontinue much of its elevated service over the Fifth Avenue Line and begin the operation of subway trains into the Fourth Avenue subway. Throughout the 1930s, the Culver Line continued to operate both subway service and elevated service—the latter using the Fifth Avenue El, the former the Fourth Avenue subway. However, it was becoming increasingly clear that the Fifth Avenue El had no long-range role to play in Brooklyn's transportation future. The 1893-built extension of the Fifth Avenue Line to Third Avenue and 65th Street played an even smaller role and was largely served by single-car shuttles that connected with through trains at 36th Street.

With the implementation of subway service over the Culver Line in 1931, a pattern of service developed that would characterize the BMT system for a number of years. The table on page 234 displays the basic outline of this service.

A feature of BMT subway service that deserves more than a passing mention is the rapid-fire way the company was able to dispatch three important express services—Brighton, West End, and Sea Beach—back to Brooklyn from the Times Square station in Manhattan. Trains of the three services were "turned around" just beyond Times Square. The inbound motorman moved his train out of the station; using a pair of crossover tracks that were strategically positioned a full train length beyond the end of the platform, he brought his train to a halt on one of the two tracks beyond the crossover. Meanwhile, a drill motorman who had boarded the train's rear car back at the Times Square station engaged the control station at the opposite end. As soon as the tower man lined up the switches and displayed the proper signals, the drill motorman moved the train back into the Times Square station for its return trip to either Brighton Beach or Coney Island. While this was happening, the inbound motorman walked through the train from one end to the other and took over for the return trip.

It was fascinating to watch this complex operation performed, especially during the height of the rush hour when the headway between express trains on the Broadway Line was less than two minutes. BMT trains featured illuminated indicators in various colors that were called marker lights; these allowed passengers—and BMT personnel—to tell at a glance what service a train was operating and where it was going. Marker lights were located near the top of a car at its end; both marker lights were set on red at the rear of a train, and part of the ritual of turning a train at Times Square called for the drill motorman to change these rear markers from "double red" to whatever code the particular service required once the back of the train became the front for the return trip. As an inbound train was pulling out of Times Square to reverse direction north of the station, the drill motorman unlocked the door of the motorman's cab at the rear end of the train and moved two overhead handles to set the marker lights for the trip back to Brooklyn—red and green for a Brighton Express, green and white for the West End, red and white for the Sea Beach.

Because the Broadway Line operated such heavy service, crowd control on Brooklyn-bound express platforms was a major issue. The BMT developed a system so that each of the three express services stopped at a slightly different spot adjacent to the platform. A series of circular, colored signs were hung from wires along the length of the platform to indicate where the doors of trains operating each of the services were expected to be. These signs were color-coded in a manner that was similar to the marker lights. However, for the system to work properly, motormen had

CMT Coney Island Service circa 1936

	Brighton Local[a]	Brighton Express	West End Express[b]	West End Shuttle	Sea Beach Express[c]	Franklin-Nassau Express[d]	Culver Local[e]	Culver Elevated Service
Southern terminal	Coney Island	Brighton Beach	Coney Island	Coney Island	Coney Island	Franklin Avenue[d]	Coney Island	Coney Island
Northern terminal	57th Street, Manhattan	Times Square	Times Square	Bay Parkway	Times Square	Chambers Street[d]	Chambers Street	Park Row
Crosses East River via	Montague Street Tunnel	Manhattan Bridge	Manhattan Bridge	—	Manhattan Bridge	Manhattan Bridge[d]	Montague Street Tunnel	Brooklyn Bridge
Service	All stops	Express in Brooklyn & Manhattan	Express from 36th Street (Brooklyn) to Times Square	All stops	Express from 59th Street (Brooklyn) to Times Square	Summer express[d]	All stops	All stops
Hours of service	24 hours	Rush hours and midday; Monday through Saturday	24 hours	Rush hours	24 hours	d	Non-rush hours only	Rush hours and midday
Equipment	D units; A/B units	A/B units	A/B units	BU units	D units	A/B units	A/B units	BU units
Marker lights	a	Red-green	Green-white	N/A	Red-white	Green-green	Yellow-green	Yellow-red
Stillwell Avenue track assignment (winter)	C and D	None	A and B	A and B	G and H	None	E and F	E and F
Stillwell Avenue track assignment (summer)	E and F	None	H	H	A and B	C and D	G	G

Sources: Compiled from personal notes taken by the author, plus various editions of *The Complete Guide to Brooklyn*, published annually by The Complete Street Guide, under the direction of Alexander Gross.

ᵃ Brighton Local service operated via Montague Street Tunnel and made all stops between Coney Island and 57th Street, Manhattan, except between 8:00 P.M. and midnight, Monday through Saturday, and 8:00 A.M. and midnight on Sunday. At these hours, Brighton Local service operated via Manhattan Bridge between Coney Island and 57 Street, Manhattan, making local stops in Brooklyn and express stops in Manhattan. During rush hours and midday, Brighton Local service continued beyond 57th Street and terminated at Queens Plaza. Marker lights were displayed as follows: Coney Island to 57th Street or Queens Plaza via tunnel, red-red; 57th Street or Queens Plaza to Coney Island via tunnel, white-white; Coney Island to and from 57th Street via bridge, green-red.

ᵇ During rush hours, the southern terminal became Bay Parkway with shuttle service using elevated equipment operating between Bay Parkway and Coney Island. In addition, a West End Local service, displaying white-orange marker lights, operated from 62nd Street, Brooklyn, to the Nassau Loop via the Montague Street Tunnel to Manhattan and via the Manhattan Bridge to Brooklyn.

ᶜ Certain Sea Beach Express trains at the end of the morning rush hour operated from Times Square to Kings Highway, and then deadhead to Coney Island Yard. Such trains carried red-yellow marker lights.

ᵈ Franklin-Nassau, a summertime-only service, operated as follows: between Franklin Avenue and Coney Island via Brighton Beach Line from 10:00 A.M. through 10:00 P.M. seven days a week, making express stops between Prospect Park and Brighton Beach, except during evening rush hour when Coney Island–bound trains operated as locals. On "sunny, summer Sundays" (and holidays), service from Franklin Avenue continued through Coney Island and operated nonstop via the Sea Beach Line to 59th Street (Brooklyn), then express to Chambers Street via the Manhattan Bridge. In seasons other than summer, a Sunday-only service operated between Franklin Avenue and Brighton Beach making all local stops. In addition to green-green marker lights, all of these special services displayed a round, white metal marker called a "bull's eye" on train's front coupling gate.

ᵉ Culver Local operated steel subway equipment to downtown Brooklyn and Manhattan via Fourth Avenue subway, Montague Street Tunnel, and Nassau Loop, and wooden elevated equipment to downtown Brooklyn and Manhattan via Fifth Avenue El and Brooklyn Bridge. Culver subway service terminated at Coney Island except during rush hours when it became an express and terminated at Kings Highway. During rush hours, the Culver elevated service was available between Coney Island and Kings Highway. Culver Express operated to Manhattan and the Nassau Loop via the Manhattan Bridge, and to Brooklyn via the Montague Street Tunnel, displaying yellow-green marker lights.

to stop their trains very, very precisely. More typically on New York subway lines, motormen merely had to observe stopping marks appropriate for the length of their train. On the BMT Broadway Line, though, there were separate stopping marks for each of the three express services.[50]

THE NEW INDEPENDENT SUBWAY SYSTEM

Even as the BMT was maturing into the rapid transit system originally envisioned when the Dual Contracts were signed in 1913, the BMT and the Interborough Rapid Transit Company (by then commonly referred to as the IRT) were joined in 1932 by a third subway system in New York, the municipally owned and municipally operated Independent Subway System (IND).[51]

The IND was a product of mayor John Francis Hylan, who served in City Hall from 1918 through 1925, and whose principal political passion was a desire to drive the "traction interests" out of their entrenched positions at the two subway systems and convert everything into a unified and publicly operated system. Hylan was unsuccessful in his efforts to eliminate the BMT and the IRT, but he was able to secure funding for the construction of the IND. The IND carried its first passengers in September 1932 and was expanded in increments in the months afterward. It included three important lines that served Brooklyn. One operated across central Brooklyn from Queens and earned the distinction of being the only major New York subway that never operated into Manhattan. The second linked downtown Brooklyn and East New York along Fulton Street; it had to be built while service was maintained above on the BMT's Fulton Street El. The third probed into Flatbush and terminated at Church Avenue and McDonald (nee Gravesend) Avenue. There was a clear intention that the new IND would eventually "recapture" the BMT's Culver Line (that is, acquire the right-of-way using a kind of eminent domain) so municipal service could be extended to Coney Island.[52]

The new IND included two north-south trunk lines in Manhattan, one under Eighth Avenue the other under Sixth Avenue. The IND's Fulton Street Line in Brooklyn was operated as a continuation of the Eighth Avenue Line, and the line that terminated at McDonald and Church Avenues was built to facilitate operation over the Sixth Avenue Line.

The IND adopted a system for train identification that relied on a simple letter code. A single letter indicated express service, a double letter designated local service. The choice of letters was determined by the Manhattan trunk line served and the branch line used by the train on its northern end. For example, any train designed by the letter *A*—a single *A* for an express, a double *A* for a local—operated under Eighth Avenue in mid-Manhattan and used the Washington Heights branch on its northern end.

The following table indicates IND services that were in operation once the system's second Manhattan trunk, the Sixth Avenue Line, opened for business in 1940.

There were plans to supplement the network of original IND lines with an even larger second-phase effort. This project would have seen the construction of new subway lines to virtually every corner of the Borough of Queens and of new Brooklyn lines such as a subway under Utica Avenue. But for a number of reasons— the Great Depression and the Second World War being two of them—the second phase of IND construction never materialized. Many anomalies of the IND were incorporated into its design on the assumption that they would later be linked up with second-phase construction. For example, the IND, as built, included two stub-end terminals in rather curious places—one at Court and Schermerhorn Streets in downtown Brooklyn, the other adjacent to Hudson Terminal in lower Manhattan. The second phase of the IND would have seen these two terminals linked up with each other via a new tunnel under the East River.

Mayor Hylan left office shortly after ground was broken for his new Independent Subway System in 1925 and he was succeeded in City Hall by James J. Walker in 1926. (Walker had defeated Hylan in the Democratic primary in 1925). Under Walker, construction of the IND continued, but a parallel effort was launched that culminated in the unification of the city's three subway systems under public auspices in 1940. This development is covered in more detail in chapter 9.

Train	Service	Northern Terminal	Southern Terminal
A	Eighth Avenue-Washington Heights Express	Washington Heights: 207th Street	Fulton Street & Rockaway Avenue
AA[a]	Eighth Avenue-Washington Heights Local	Washington Heights: 168th Street	Hudson Terminal
BB[b]	Sixth Avenue-Washington Heights Local	Washington Heights: 168th Street	34th Street & Sixth Avenue
C[c]	Eighth Avenue-Concourse Express	Concourse: 205th Street	Brooklyn: Hoyt-Schermerhorn Streets
CC[b]	Eighth Avenue-Concourse Local	Concourse: Bedford Park	Hudson Terminal
D	Sixth Avenue-Concourse Express	Concourse: 205th Street	Hudson Terminal
E[d]	Eighth Avenue-Queens Express	Jamaica: 169th Street	Broadway-Lafayette
F	Sixth Avenue-Queens Express	Jamaica: Parsons Boulevard	Brooklyn: Church Avenue
GG[e]	Brooklyn-Queens Local	Queens: Forest Hills	Brooklyn: Smith-9th Streets
HH[f]	Fulton Street Shuttle	Brooklyn: Court Street	Brooklyn: Hoyt-Schermerhorn Streets

Compiled from various editions of *The Complete Guide to Brooklyn* and *The Complete Guide to New York,* each published annually by The Complete Street Guide, under the direction of Alexander Gross.

[a] AA train operated during non–rush hours only

[b] BB train and CC train operated only during rush hours.

[c] C train provided express service on the Concourse Line before the Sixth Avenue Line was opened in 1940.

[d] Provided Eighth Avenue service to Church Avenue before the Sixth Avenue Line opened in 1940.

[e] Only major New York subway line not to serve Manhattan.

[f] Operated from 1936 until 1946.

IRON STEAMBOATS IN THE AGE OF THE SUBWAY

As newly built subways carried more and more people to Coney Island each season, steamboats carried fewer and fewer. The Iron Steamboat Company, for instance, may have offered a more pleasant trip, but it cost more and the ride took considerably longer. The company's very name, once connoting the latest in transportation technology, now conjured a bygone era, and the subway allowed more hours on the beach or in the amusement parks during a one-day outing. The company's president, Frederick Bishop, found himself in a classic economic tailspin: the company raised prices to compensate for reduced patronage, but then the higher tariff drove more passengers to the less costly subway system. Travel to Coney Island grew by leaps and bounds with the advent of subway service—a million visitors were not unusual on a nice summer Sunday—but it was a growth in which the Iron Steamboat Company never shared. At one time, the longer steamboat ride to Coney Island at least offered passengers the opportunity to relax and imbibe during the trip down the bay—something strictly verboten aboard the subway. The onset of Prohibition in 1919 took away this competitive edge. The subway got people to Coney Island faster, and rumor had it that beverages of various sorts could still be obtained on the island, Volstead Act or no Volstead Act. By 1932, the Iron Steamboat Company's last season, its round-trip fare between Manhattan and Coney Island stood at a dollar (although the company reduced this to 50 cents on Monday and Friday, which were light-traffic days). On the other hand, a round-trip on the faster subway was only a dime, and the free amusement park admissions that steamboat passengers once enjoyed were long gone by 1932.

Other statistics fill in more details about Iron Steamboat's decline. The last year the company turned even a nominal profit was 1929, when it had receipts of $392,000 against expenses of $390,000. In 1931, in the depths of the Great Depression, the company's prudent managers had reduced expenses to $320,000; however, falling patronage had caused revenues to drop to $257,000.46. In the early 1920s, annual patronage on the company's boats averaged over 900,000 cash customers each summer; by 1931, this had fallen to 369,040—a massive drop of 56 percent.[53] As late as 1931, all seven of the original fleet were still under steam, although *Taurus* was chartered to the Meseck Line for service to Rye Beach, New York, for all or part of that summer.[54] During the final season, 1932, with no Rockaway Beach service on the schedule for the first time in decades, at least one boat, *Cetus,* was not brought out of winter quarters and Bishop ran with a reduced fleet. He was even compelled to negotiate a reduction in the docking fees he had earlier agreed to pay the City of New York for the use of by then municipally owned Steeplechase Pier. The Board of Estimate reluctantly agreed and, on May 3, 1932, reduced the annual charge from $15,000 to $12,000.

Still, on the Fourth of July weekend during what proved to be its final season, the Iron Steamboat Company scheduled fourteen daily round-trips between Manhattan and Coney Island, virtually the same level it had operated since the end of the First World War. The Iron Steamboat Company's last day of service to Coney Island was Labor Day, September 5, 1932, when it advertised eleven round-trips.

Once the company closed its books at the end of the season, it had only one option. On November 29, 1932, Bishop petitioned the U.S. District Court, District of New Jersey, to place the company under voluntary receivership, citing liabilities of $750,000 against assets of little more than seven fifty-year-old steamboats. The court appointed a receiver and, on February 1, 1933, the company's assets were auctioned off at Edgewater Basin, New Jersey. The next day George R. Beach, the referee in bankruptcy, confirmed the sale and entered matters in his records at the bankruptcy court, 75 Montgomery Street, Jersey City, New Jersey. Ironically, the court was located just a few minutes' walk from the site where Robert Fulton once assembled a steam engine that he later installed in a boat everyone knows today as *Claremont*. The *New York Times* took note of the Iron Steamboat Company's demise by saying, rather curiously, "Only old people like to sit on a boat and catch the sea breezes—and hardly anybody is old nowadays," but otherwise the paper lamented the end of steamboat service to Coney Island.[55]

Except it was not exactly the end. A postscript was added to the Iron Steamboat story when another firm, Union Navigation Company, bought five of the older firm's vessels; leased a sixth; obtained still another vessel that once steamed between New York and Shelter Island for a maritime subsidiary of the LIRR; and reinstituted service between Manhattan, Coney Island, and Rockaway Beach in the summer of 1933 under the banner of the Rainbow Fleet. Union Navigation certainly gave it the old college try. The ex-Iron Steamboat vessels were renamed, and this time proper steamboat tradition was observed—only a vessel's name, and not that of the company, adorned the paddle boxes. For the inauguration of service in 1933, the company put out a call in the newspapers to find the New Yorker who could remember riding to Coney Island aboard a steamboat earlier than anyone else. The winner of the pseudo-contest was Mrs. Robert Disbrow, aged seventy-seven, of Nostrand Avenue in Brooklyn, who claimed she rode a steamboat to Coney Island Point as a seven-year-old girl in the Civil War year of 1863.

Ex-governor Al Smith was prevailed upon to help the company inaugurate its new service; the day was May 17, 1933, and the ex-LIRR boat—renamed *Empire State,* "the flagship of the Rainbow Fleet"—made the ceremonial first trip to Coney Island. I. H. Gant, a veteran Iron Steamboat captain, was back in uniform and in the wheelhouse. In mid-August of that year, Steeplechase Pier found itself decked out in bunting for a week in a rather contrived celebration of the anniversary of the arrival of the first steamboat at the first iron pier in Coney Island in 1879. In other words, officials of the Rainbow Fleet were mindful of the need to generate what a later generation would call "photo opportunities."

The new service followed the same general schedule as had the Iron Steamboat Company for most of its latter years. Union Navigation offered a dozen or so daily sailings from West 129th Street and North River Pier 1 in Manhattan to Coney Island, with two or three trips each day continuing beyond to Rockaway Beach. Union Navigation cut Iron Steamboat's latter-day round-trip Coney Island fare of a dollar in half. However, even with Prohibition a thing of the past, too few people came to the docks and too many boats steamed down the bay with too little revenue to show for the effort. The Great Depression was not kind to new business ventures of any sort.

As to subway competition, it only became more intense. The excursion season of 1933 was the first summer that the city's new IND was in operation. While it did not itself serve Coney Island, it gave passengers from upper Manhattan who might otherwise have headed for a Coney Island–bound steamboat at the foot of West 129th Street a fast connecting ride to other trains that did.

On Monday, April 29, 1935—following two unsuccessful sea-

sons and just a little more than two years after the original Iron
Steamboat Company was liquidated—another auction was held at
Edgewater, this one under the aegis of a U.S. marshal. Federal
auctioneer J. J. Donnelly handled the proceedings. While the 1897-
built *Empire State* went for an almost respectable $12,000, the five
old iron steamboats brought an average of but $2,270 per vessel
on the block.

Empire State would still see active years. The one-time LIRR
side-wheeler eventually migrated to New England waters. There,
as *Town of Hull,* she ran between Boston and an amusement park
at Nantasket Beach until 1944 when she was fatally damaged in a
hurricane.

None of the seven vessels from 1881 ever carried passengers
again. While one or another of them may have been used on a
charter trip after the close of the regular excursion season in September 1934, it is likely that the very last day any of the original
iron steamboats carried revenue passengers was Sunday, September 9, 1934—the last day of Rainbow Line service to Coney Island.
According to published schedules, the final trip left West 129th
Street and the Hudson River at 6:30 P.M., landed at Pier 1 at 7:15,
and tied up to Steeplechase Pier a little before 8:30. Then, after
boarding whatever passengers were waiting, the steamboat cast
off into the night and steamed away from the bright lights of
Coney Island for one last time—around Norton's Point, up
through the Narrows, across Upper New York Bay, and into the
Hudson River to Manhattan. One can only wonder as to the identity of the steamboat that made that last trip. Was it the newer
Empire State? Or was it one of the original vessels that had been
launched on the Delaware River in 1881?

Seven years later, on January 25, 1941, another link with the
past was broken. Seventy-nine year old Frederick A. Bishop, the
man who guided the Iron Steamboat Company for half of its corporate life, passed away in Brooklyn's Caledonia Hospital. Educated
in the public schools of Brooklyn and associated with the Bridge
Department of the City of New York in the heady years when that
agency was following up the success of the Brooklyn Bridge with
additional East River crossings, Bishop took over the Iron Steamboat Company in 1902 and saw it through the rest of its days.

There would be sporadic efforts to revive steamboat service to

Coney Island in the years between 1934 and the Second World War, but never with the strong corporate identity—or the frequent service from morning through evening—that was the hallmark of the Iron Steamboat Company and, to a lesser extent, Union Navigation's Rainbow Fleet. Steamboats like Sutton Line's *Bear Mountain* tried to find a "market niche" on the Coney Island run, but with no lasting success. In 1935 and 1936 before she was sold to New England interests, *Empire State* ran a one-boat service between Hoboken, New Jersey, Battery Park in lower Manhattan, and Steeplechase Pier under the house flag of the Empire State Excursion Steamship Company of New Jersey.

The years of the Second World War would see a general reduction of excursion boat operations in and around New York Harbor. Fuel was scarce, and some boats were "conscripted" for military use. While services like the Hudson River Day Line remained in operation throughout the war, there was no chance—and no justification—for passenger steamboats to serve Coney Island while war was being waged. Iron Steamboat's *Taurus* may have run to the offshore fishing grounds during the First World War, but there was too much convoy activity originating in New York Harbor during the Second World War to allow excursion boats to pick their way through the Narrows with curious civilians on board taking in all the details. Besides, the military was not about to open and close the harbor's submarine nets several times a day for an excursion boat service whose schedules were published in the newspapers. Crowds continued to travel to Coney Island during the war years. But for the first time since the early 1840s, no steamboats were available to take them there.

MORE AMUSEMENT PARKS

In the early years of the twentieth century, George C. Tilyou's Steeplechase Park, a facility that originally opened in 1897, was joined by two other important Coney Island amusement parks. These three parks would exercise a dominant influence on Coney Island entertainment and recreation for many years.

At the Pan American Exposition in Buffalo in 1901—a world's fair where, unfortunately, President William McKinley was assassinated—George Tilyou became fascinated by a wonderful cyclo-rama-style illusion called A Trip to the Moon. It was the creation of a pair of unusual showmen, Frederic Thompson and Elmer Dundy. Tilyou prevailed upon them to move their attraction to Steeplechase, where it was in place for the 1902 season. At the end of that first season, Tilyou was either unwilling or unable to negotiate an extension with Thompson and Dundy.[56] So the pair dismantled A Trip to the Moon and took an option on the parcel of land where Paul Boyton's Sea Lion Park was on its last legs. On May 16, 1903, they welcomed patrons to Coney Island's newest attraction, a venue they called Luna Park. They retained Boyton's water slide known as Shoot the Chutes in the center of Luna Park, and they built a variety of additional rides and attractions through-out the new park. By early August of that first summer, Thompson and Dundy had recovered 90 percent of their investment, and Luna became a national symbol of a new age with its extraordinary display of decorative electric lights.

The very next summer, 1904, another new amusement park opened in Coney Island, Dreamland Park. Clearly influenced by Luna, Dreamland tried to push its allegorical architectural themes to even grander heights. The vaulted main entrance of Dreamland led to a biblically oriented attraction immediately inside that was called The Creation of the World.

Luna was more strategically located than Steeplechase; it was midway between Culver Depot and West End Depot while Steeple-chase was three blocks beyond the West End Depot. Steeple-chase, though, did extend between Surf Avenue and the beach—as did Dreamland—while Luna was on the inland of Surf Avenue.

On July 28, 1907, Steeplechase was totally destroyed by fire—a perennial Coney Island threat. The blaze began late in the after-noon in a Steeplechase attraction called the Cave of the Winds and quickly spread through most of the park and a number of nearby buildings. It took a four-alarm response from the New York Fire Department to bring the fire under control, and the loss—to Til-you and his neighbors—was estimated at a million dollars.

Tilyou's immediate reaction was that he likely would not re-build. "I don't have one dollar in insurance," he said, and he wanted to take some time to think things over before making any decisions.[57] By the next day, Tilyou had made up his mind, and his reaction to the previous day's devastation has assumed legendary proportions. Before the embers of Steeplechase had fully cooled, he erected a sign in front of his burnt-out park that read, "To Inquiring Friends: I have troubles today that I did not have yesterday. I had troubles yesterday that I do not have today. On this site will be erected shortly a better, bigger, greater Steeplechase Park. Admission to the Burning Ruins—10 Cents."[58]

Tilyou was not exaggerating. In the wake of the fire of 1907, the future of Coney Island was so promising that Tilyou had no difficulty arranging the financing not merely to replace his original park, but to construct a totally different Steeplechase that raised the amusement park to a new level.

A perennial problem at Coney Island—the factor that could turn business success into total failure faster than anything else—was a seeming inevitability, rain. True enough, a stormy day kept many potential customers from ever traveling to Coney Island in the first place; but summer rain often came on unexpectedly, and this is where Tilyou sought to create an advantage for Steeplechase. His new park included a large, enclosed pavilion that measured 450 feet long and 270 feet wide. Under its cavernous roof, a virtually separate amusement park was created. The Pavilion of Fun, as it was soon called, became the defining characteristic of post-1907 Steeplechase. It was not a fully enclosed building in the sense an air-conditioned facility would be today; there were ample openings to allow cool ocean breezes to mitigate summer heat inside the pavilion.

Although Tilyou was able to secure financing to rebuild Steeplechase after it burned to the ground in 1907, rebuilding was never a serious option when Dreamland was destroyed by fire four years later.[59] Dreamland welcomed patrons to its grounds for a mere six seasons. From 1911 onward, the "big three" Coney Island amusement parks were reduced to a mere two, Luna Park and Steeplechase.

THE BOARDWALK

Although it did not involve travel to and from Coney Island, an important transport facility was designed and built in the 1920s that substantially altered the character of the beachfront. During the mayoral administration of John F. Hylan, the city built a municipal boardwalk to define the upper limit of the bathing beach at Coney Island and allow pedestrians to stroll the length of Coney Island in sight of the ocean. In addition, the beach area was expanded by hydraulically pumping almost 2 million cubic yards of beach sand onto the beach from offshore; the beachfront was stabilized with the construction of sixteen rock and timber groins that extended out into the ocean at intervals along the beach. A side benefit of this hydraulic pumping was that the sand retrieved from beneath the sea turned out to be much lighter in color than Coney Island's original sand and so the hue of the beach was altered from light brown to white.

Construction of the Coney Island Boardwalk was accompanied by a fundamental change in patterns of land ownership. Prior to the boardwalk, many individual property owners occupied parcels that extended to the waterline. The legalities were sometimes irregular, since the ownership of much of Coney Island's real estate was shrouded in myth and custom and the legacies of Gravesend from Lady Deborah Moody to Commissioner John Y. McKane (see chapter 1). But the advent of the municipal boardwalk ended all claims of exclusivity with respect to ocean access. Now the City of New York owned the entire beach from Brighton Beach to Sea Gate, no private clubs or amusement parks could claim exclusive use of beach segments, and lifeguards employed by the borough of Brooklyn provided uniform protection for all.

The construction of the boardwalk brought with it some political charges and countercharges that have something of a contemporary ring to them. In the spring of 1923, when a gala opening celebration for the new boardwalk was to be held, Brooklyn Borough President Edward Riegelman—after whom the facility would eventually be named—was forced to alter his intended plan and arrange for the Coney Island business community to donate $15,000 to fund the ceremony. Riegelman had earlier proposed using city resources—special revenue bonds—to pay for the celebration.[60] Even earlier, when the boardwalk was under construction and the municipal government was engaged in extensive land taking under eminent domain procedures, a bit of a flap was touched off when it was learned that one of Riegelman's law partners was representing affected Coney Island property owners.

The boardwalk that was built in 1923 cost $4 million and extended from Ocean Parkway to West 37th Street. The city's Board of Estimate approved the project on July 29, 1921, and the prime contractor was the Phoenix Construction Company. The official dedication of the entire walkway was held on May 15, 1923, although smaller sections had been informally opened for public use the previous fall. (A 1,000-foot segment from Ocean Parkway to West Fifth Street opened on October 28, 1922, and a second section, from West Fifth to Steeplechase, on December 24, 1922.)

The ceremony in May 1923 included all manner of pomp and ceremony. Bands played, marching units marched, and a platform full of local politicians took to the podium and applauded one another many times over. One planned event had to be cancelled when the weather failed to cooperate—a fly-over and aerial exhibition by twenty-five U.S. Army planes from Mitchell Field on Long Island. A scheduled event that seems a trifle insensitive was a baby parade in which two prizes were awarded—one to the healthiest-looking baby on parade, the other to the fattest.

As plans for the boardwalk were advanced and debated during the Hylan administration, many of the city's political leaders made some rather grandiose proposals. In late 1921, Hylan's Dock Commissioner, Murray Hulbert, sought to intrude his department in the overall development by proposing the construction of a massive pier out into the ocean at the foot of Ocean Parkway. Hulbert's pier would have extended a quarter-mile out into the ocean from shore, and among its features would have been a conference hall with seating for 10,000 people.[61] Then, on the day the boardwalk was dedicated, City Controller Charles L. Craig became carried away and suggested, in his formal remarks, that the boardwalk should eventually be extended to twenty miles in length. From Manhattan Beach to Sea Gate, Coney Island itself is a little less than five miles long. Controller Craig delivered his remarks following a luncheon at the Hotel Shelburne in Brighton Beach, and whatever pre-prandials were served there may explain his exaggerated recommendation. (The chairman of the luncheon, incidentally, was George A. Wingate, who had been an associate of

Frederick Uhlmann back in the days of the Brooklyn Union Elevated.)

The 1923 boardwalk project was a walkway that was fifty feet wide and extended slightly less than two miles from Ocean Parkway to West 37th Street. Several years later, on the eve of the Second World War, the boardwalk was extended eastward to Coney Island Avenue in Brighton Beach. A final extension after the war took it a short distance beyond to essentially the western limit of Manhattan Beach, and the boardwalk reached an end-to-end length of two-and-a-half miles.

No More Horse Racing

Thoroughbred horse racing at three Coney Island tracks ensured that at least some visitors to the seaside resort arrived with a little money in their pockets and they spent it on more than a nickel hot dog and a cold drink to wash it down. As noted earlier, two of the three Coney Island racetracks were not located on Coney Island itself, but on the adjacent Kings County mainland. However, after the racing season of 1910 the tracks would not be located anywhere. That was because the State of New York enacted legislation that prohibited betting on horse races. Although there may have been a few individuals who enjoyed thoroughbred racing as a pure sport, the economics of operating a racetrack were such that absent wagering, racing could not survive.

Betting on horse racing would resume in New York State just a few years later when the law was revised. But although New York area tracks such as Jamaica, Belmont Park, and Aqueduct would welcome customers back with open arms, none of the Coney Island establishments reopened.[62]

If it is correct to say that the popularity of Coney Island peaked in the early years of the twentieth century and then entered a long decline, the permanent removal of thoroughbred horse racing from the area's entertainment options clearly stands as a major factor in that reversal, and this matter has been afforded far too little attention by those who have sought to diagnose the resort's decline and fall. It takes very little imagination to conjure a vision of how differently Coney Island might have evolved during the twentieth century had one of the three racetracks been reopened; kept up to date; and, eventually, surrounded by upscale restaurants, new hotels, and other support activities.

But this is just speculation. What is closer to being a matter of fact is that the end of thoroughbred horse racing in 1910 had a negative impact on the subsequent fate of Coney Island.

Coney Island at War
(1940–1945)

IT WAS DURING THE YEARS leading up to the Second World War that a singularly controversial public figure, Robert Moses, began to exert an influence on the subsequent growth and development of New York. While many unhesitatingly blame him for the downfall of Coney Island, a more balanced analysis would suggest that his contributions were at worst benign, perhaps even a bit constructive.

ROBERT MOSES AND CONEY ISLAND

It was in his role as park commissioner of the City of New York that Moses proposed, in 1937, some serious alterations to Coney Island.[1] Because the width of the beach between the boardwalk and high tide had shrunk to virtually nothing in an area between Stillwell Avenue and Ocean Parkway—high tide actually lapped under the boardwalk in certain places—Moses proposed rebuilding the jetties that sustained the beachfront, tearing down the boardwalk along this stretch, and rebuilding it 300 feet inland. In addition, Moses wanted to convert several acres of shabby amusement area directly behind the rebuilt section of the boardwalk into municipal parkland. As reported in the *New York Times,* Moses "wants to broaden beaches, improve traffic arteries and—perhaps most important—to supplant Boardwalk hot dog and apple-on-the-stick shacks with long stretches of playgrounds, landscaping and modern bath houses."[2]

The proposal that Park Commissioner Moses advanced in 1937 was both comprehensive and expensive. The plan, which would have cost $16.1 million had it been implemented fully, called for improvements to the beachfront not merely in Coney Island, but also in Rockaway and at South Beach on Staten Island—facilities that were then under the control of Moses and his Department of Parks.

Reaction to Moses' proposal for Coney Island was very negative, and many jumped to the conclusion that this was merely the first step in turning Coney Island into a resort that more resembled Jones Beach than the Coney Island of old. "Let us confess to a certain pang at the thought of a tidy Coney Island," commented the *New York Times*.[3] Indeed, it was the belief that Moses wanted to replace all of the amusement areas of Coney Island with parks, playgrounds, parkways, and picnic grounds that led to the scaling back of his 1937 proposal two years later.

(The idea of turning Coney Island into natural parklands, and plowing under, so to speak, the island's less-than-natural legacy, was not new. As early as 1890, a bill had been filed in Albany that would have appropriated up to a half-million dollars to create a park adjacent to Norton's Point. This proposal faced prompt opposition from Kings County political leaders— especially John Y. McKane, then the "boss" of Gravesend—and so nothing came of it. A subsequent plan to convert all of Coney Island into a large oceanfront park was proposed in 1899 by Bird S. Coler, the Brooklyn politician who also played a role in opposing the BRT's double-fare policies on its lines to and from Coney Island. Coler's park proposal likewise failed to gain acceptance.[4])

Moses' diagnosis of Coney Island was that, in the past, "public authorities were actuated more by a desire to please the large property owners than to provide proper accommodations for the public." Moses also believed that "any future plan for Coney Island must be based on the supposition that most of the summer patrons will come by rapid transit, that they will have comparatively little money to spend on mechanical amusements, and that more and more they will come for exercise and healthy outdoor activity."[5]

This was not exactly a new or radical appraisal. In the years after the First World War, as Coney Island welcomed larger and larger crowds each summer, the vast majority of visitors were interested in little more than a relaxing day at the beach, perhaps topped off with a frozen custard or a cold glass of root beer on the way home. Amusement parks and all the independent rides and attractions played an important role in Coney Island's overall econ-

omy, but the revenue they took in was always recognized as coming from a small percentage of the island's visitors.[6] In pointing
out this seeming imbalance, Robert Moses said nothing that was
not already part of Coney Island's conventional wisdom. Although
he certainly believed that, in the future, Coney Island would and
should be characterized by "less mechanical noise-making and
amusement devices and side shows, and a more orderly growth of
year-round residents," it is incorrect to suggest that he called for
the complete elimination of Coney Island's mechanical amusements.[7] Had Moses' improvement plan for Coney Island been implemented as proposed, a reasonable argument can be advanced
that it might have helped sustain Coney Island—mechanical
amusements and all—not destroy it. Moses called for an elevated
walkway from the Stillwell Avenue subway terminal to the opposite side of Surf Avenue and conversion of a relatively small portion of the area's ragtag structures into new parkland. But his plan
would have retained a basic commercial amusement infrastruc-
ture that then included two major parks, Luna and Steeplechase,
as principal attractions. Most of the Bowery would also have remained under Moses' proposal, and there is no question that—
whatever else might be said of Robert Moses—his 1937 plan for
Coney Island called for new parklands to supplement and comple-
ment the island's amusement areas, not replace them.

Moses remains a controversial figure in New York politics and
his patrimony is still subject to debate.[8] But the charge that he
intended to convert Coney Island into nothing but beach parkland
in the style of Jones Beach is without basis and does a disservice
to what he actually proposed. Indeed, what may well have been
the most positive and transforming event in all of Coney Island
history was the construction of the municipal boardwalk under
Mayor John F. Hylan in the 1920s, the consequent conversion of
the entire beach from Sea Gate to Brighton Beach into a facility
open to the general public, and the elimination of private enclaves
along the shore. Moses' proposal in the 1930s was very much in
the tradition of what Hylan did in the 1920s. However, it is precisely because of the earlier construction of the boardwalk that
one must disagree with Moses' 1937 assertion that past public officials had paid too much attention to the needs of major landown-

ers on Coney Island, and too little regard to the needs of the general public.

Because Moses gained little popular or political support for his proposal in 1937 and, just as important, because there was no source of funding for its execution, he went back to the drawing board. In 1939, he submitted a new plan for Coney Island—one that addressed the near-crisis issue of surf infringement along the beach between Ocean Parkway and Stillwell Avenue.[9] This plan was enacted; the boardwalk right-of-way was moved inland, but no effort was made to convert any substantial part of Coney Island's amusement areas into parklands. The implementation of Moses' 1939 plan addressed a pressing environmental crisis, ocean destruction of the beach. However, the question of whether Moses' more comprehensive 1937 proposal would have hastened the destruction of Coney Island or, by making targeted new investments, enhanced its future by creating a more diverse recreational experience certainly remains open.

THE BELT PARKWAY

There is more to be said about Robert Moses and Coney Island. An interesting and eminently positive contribution involves his spearheading the construction of the Belt Parkway in the late 1930s. Looking ahead to new urban travel patterns that would see less importance placed on trips into and out of a central city—and less reliance on mass transportation for urban transport—Moses laid out a comprehensive plan for a circumferential highway that would run along the perimeter of Brooklyn and Queens. Most of the Belt Parkway was in place for the opening of the 1939–40 World's Fair in Flushing Meadows, but key links were not finished until some years later.[10]

The route of the new Belt Parkway ran parallel to Coney Island on the Kings County mainland side of Coney Island Creek, and its construction rendered all of Coney Island, from Manhattan Beach to Norton's Point, easily accessible to people traveling by automobile. Indeed, with the opening of the Belt Parkway, Coney Island became far more accessible to automobiles than such important New York recreational and cultural destinations as the Times

Square theater district, the Metropolitan Museum of Art, Central Park, Greenwich Village, or Ebbets Field.

True, parking facilities on Coney Island were expensive and inadequate, and navigating an automobile from the Belt Parkway to Surf Avenue involved travel along congested side streets that would never remind one of the Moses-built parkways that funneled traffic into Jones Beach. But the Cropsey Avenue exit of the Belt Parkway was—and still is—less than a half-mile from the oceanfront, and the construction of the Belt Parkway represented a major new option for people traveling to and from Coney Island.

The oft-heard claim that Robert Moses is the man who sharpened the ax that beheaded Coney Island overlooks a number of important historical facts, not the least of which is that onward from its opening in 1939, the Belt Parkway—a major project of Moses—enhanced Coney Island's accessibility to people who preferred to travel by automobile.

GENERAL PERCEPTIONS

Despite the enormous crowds that headed for Coney Island each summer in the years leading up to the Second World War, the notion continued to gain traction during the 1930s that the resort was not faring well and that its best days were in the past. These were also the years of the Great Depression, of course, and all manner of commercial activities were faring poorly, in Coney Island and throughout the world. But the fact remains that there was a general perception that Coney Island was in decline. Writing in the *New York Times* in 1936, columnist Meyer Berger reflected on the declining fortunes of Coney Island. "The world has moved and Coney Island has not kept pace," Berger maintained, suggesting that the resort "saw its best days between 1903 and 1921."[11]

Coney Island retained a good deal of its appeal, even if Berger's 1936 observations would prove, in the long run, to be more accurate than otherwise. For instance, when Benito Mussolini began to draw up plans for a gala world's fair to be held in Rome in 1942, he instructed his people to ask the Coney Island Chamber of Commerce for a plan and description of the amusement area so he might duplicate Coney Island in marshland between Rome and

Ostia.[12] An editorial in the *New York Times* wondered if "the hot dog will retain its identity in the journey from Coney Island to Rome," and suggested that certain Coney Island amusements might bear tailoring to suit the needs of a totalitarian regime. "Instead of throwing baseballs at dolls, zealous party members could heave dummy hand grenades at effigies of all good enemies of fascism," the newspaper suggested.[13] Any world's fair in 1942, of course—in Rome or elsewhere—became a casualty of the Second World War and so plans to replicate Coney Island in Rome never materialized.

THE BOARD OF TRANSPORTATION

A major change in the governance structure of the New York subways took place in 1940, when Europe was already at war. There had been debate and discussion in New York throughout the 1930s as to how subway service in the city might be unified. Eventually the Interborough Rapid Transit Company and the Brooklyn-Manhattan Transit Corporation (BMT) were purchased by the municipal government and placed under the governance of the city's Board of Transportation, the agency that had been running the Independent Subway System (IND) since its opening in 1932. The notion of a fiscally sound and enduring public-private mass transit partnership that was envisioned by the Dual Contracts of 1913 had foundered on the shoals of unanticipated fiscal conditions that completely undermined all the assumptions on which the contracts were based.[14]

Part and parcel of the city's takeover of the BMT on Saturday, June 1, 1940, was the parallel acquisition of its surface subsidiary, the Brooklyn and Queens Transit Corporation (B&QT). Thus, not only did subway lines to and from Coney Island become municipal responsibilities; so, too, did streetcar lines that carried passengers to Coney Island and its environs along Ocean Avenue, Coney Island Avenue, McDonald Avenue, and 86th Street, as well as special summer services that originated on other lines but continued to Coney Island over one of these four lines.

A major alteration in BMT rapid transit service (see map 8) was implemented prior to that corporation's acquisition by the municipal government, although it was part and parcel of the negotiations that led up to the sale. Namely, major elements of the system's elevated lines that were built in the final decades of the nineteenth century were abandoned and torn down. The mechanism used to effect this abandonment was formal condemnation proceedings of the elevated structures by the city government, a process that had the BMT's full support. Consequently the Fulton Street Line from downtown Brooklyn to Rockaway Avenue was abandoned on May 31, 1940, and subsequently torn down, as was the entire Fifth Avenue elevated line, from its junction with the Myrtle Avenue Line at Myrtle and Hudson all the way to 59th Street and Third Avenue.[15]

Apart from elevated sections of the BMT that were upgraded to heavy-duty standards at the time of the Dual Contracts and operated as part of the subway network, these abandonments left the Myrtle Avenue elevated line and its connecting Lexington Avenue line as the sole remnants of the one-time Brooklyn Union elevated system. The Fulton Street El from Rockaway Avenue to Lefferts Avenue in central Queens was all that remained of the Kings County system. (Under Kings County management, the Fulton Street line was only built as far as Grant Avenue; the extension beyond to Lefferts Avenue was a product of the Dual Contracts.) Because most sections of these lines could only bear the weight of lightweight elevated cars, service continued to be provided by turn-of-the-century wooden equipment.[16]

The Myrtle Avenue Line continued to operate across the Brooklyn Bridge to Park Row. However, in 1944 elevated trains were taken off the bridge and an in-town terminal for both Myrtle Avenue and Lexington Avenue elevated services was established at the Bridge-Jay Street station in downtown Brooklyn.

With respect to Coney Island service, these changes in the BMT's elevated operations meant the elimination of through service over the Fifth Avenue elevated line and the Culver Line. Wooden elevated cars continued to provide supplementary service over the Culver Line, but they only ran between Ninth Avenue and Stillwell Avenue.

A STREETCAR NAMED PCC

Prior to 1940, the BMT's surface subsidiary, the B&QT, was an important participant in an industry-wide effort by U.S. street rail-

Map 8: The BMT subway and elevated system, circa 1936.

ways to develop and design a totally new streetcar, one that would rival the newest motor bus in style and appointment while providing swift and comfortable service that no motorbus could equal.

Design of this new streetcar was entrusted to a group associated with the American Transit Association, successor of the 1892-created American Street Railway Association. Because there would be questions of patent rights associated with technical products developed in the course of the design effort, a subsidiary entity was created and called the Transit Development Corporation—the same name as an earlier BRT subsidiary. The effort got under way in 1929. Basic design work and experimentation was entrusted to a committee composed of presidents from more than two dozen American street railway companies, including the B&QT. And thus did a streetcar design produced by the Electric Railways Presidents' Conference Committee (PCC) come to be called the PCC car.[17]

Much of the experimental work that produced the new PCC car took place in the B&QT's Ninth Avenue Depot, a facility that was built in the first decade of the twentieth century on the site that was once the in-town terminal of Andrew Culver's Prospect Park and Coney Island Railroad. Once the committee developed a final design and a pilot car went through a series of tests in Chicago and Brooklyn, it was the B&QT that first advertised for bids on a fleet of production-model PCC cars. In 1936 the Saint Louis Car Company delivered ninety-nine new PCC cars to the B&QT, and a single car of similar design was delivered by the Clark Railway Equipment Corporation. On October 1, 1936, a ceremony was held at the Manhattan end of the Brooklyn Bridge with New York Mayor Fiorello LaGuardia presiding to mark the introduction of the new fleet into revenue service. Car no. 1009 was dispatched from Park Row that day over the Smith-Coney Island Line and completed its trip an hour or so later at the same West Fifth Street Depot that was built in 1912 by the Coney Island and Brooklyn Railroad (CI&B). The festivities and the excitement of the day would prove illusory, though. The B&QT's 1000-series PCC cars were the last streetcars built for service in Brooklyn.

Things almost turned out differently. The BMT was pleased with its fleet of new PCC cars and quickly decided that more such cars were just what the doctor ordered. While the company was in no position to finance the acquisition of these cars—the company was actively negotiating with the City of New York to sell its entire property to the municipal government—in 1938 the corporation was able to secure preliminary approval for an $8 million line of credit from the Reconstruction Finance Corporation (RFC) to upgrade various elements of its surface system, including the acquisition of 500 more PCC cars.

Mayor LaGuardia was reported to be irritated because he had not been told about the pending loan. Some people in his administration who were involved in the city's acquisition of the BMT believed that allowing the loan to go forward would be in the city's best interest, since the BMT would need all the investment capital it could get once it was acquired by the city. However, on September 27, 1938, Jesse Jones, the RFC chairman, announced that his agency had cancelled the "conditional commitment" it had earlier made to the BMT "because of the city's opposition."[18]

B&QT based its fleet of new PCC cars in the same Ninth Avenue Depot where the cars had been designed. The 100-unit fleet would provide service to Coney Island for two decades, from their introduction in 1936 until the final Brooklyn streetcar line was converted to motorbus operation in 1956. Had the RFC loan gone forward in 1938 and Brooklyn's PCC fleet had grown to 600 cars, it is interesting to speculate how differently the future of Brooklyn streetcars might have played out. Given such a substantial investment in new rolling stock, might Brooklyn have developed reserved rights-of-way for its expanded fleet of PCC cars and become a pioneer in the development of what would later be called light-rail transit? But, of course, the loan was never executed, the 500 cars were never delivered, and Brooklyn's small but pioneer fleet of 100 PCC cars carried passengers for a mere twenty years.[19]

THE NEW YORK WORLD'S FAIR OF 1939–1940

It was during the early years of the Second World War that the Coney Island amusement area saw its final wave of major capital investment, although this investment was more a product of opportunistic bargain hunting than long-range corporate planning. When the New York World's Fair of 1939–40 closed its doors in the fall of 1940, a wide range of rides and other amusements went on the market.[20] The principal World's Fair ride that was transferred to Coney Island was called the Parachute Jump. Steeplechase acquired the ride and installed it at the boardwalk entrance of the famous park, and it began offering rides in the summer of 1941. Regular Steeplechase patrons could ride the Parachute Jump, but only after paying an additional fee. People strolling along the boardwalk could also buy tickets for the ride, even if they did not wish to enter Steeplechase Park itself.

After some complex negotiations involving patent rights were settled, the Parachute Jump was moved to Coney Island over the winter of 1940–41 and construction began in the spring. The foundations were completed on April 5, 1941, steelwork began to rise on April 12, and on Friday, May 30, the Parachute Jump welcomed its first paying customers.[21]

A ride aboard Coney Island's newest amusement was positively frightening. Two patrons were strapped securely in a seat that dangled below a large parachute. The parachute was not free-floating, though. It was securely attached to a number of cables around its perimeter, cables that ran from the ground to the top of the ride. When all was ready, the operator pushed a button and a device called a spider that was attached to the top of the parachute began to haul it upward. The ground receded beneath patrons' feet as the spider continued to lift the parachute and its riders 250 feet into the air.[22]

When the spider reached the top of the tower, the parachute was released with a loud noise and both parachute and rider began to fall. At first, they were unconstrained; but then as the parachute filled with air, the descent slowed and continued to the base of the ride at a lesser speed. The entire downward ride, though, took place without any kind of safety features other than those side cables that ensured a straight descent. The cloth parachute, and the parachute alone, prevented patrons from heading back to earth as freely falling objects.

A factor that prompted Steeplechase Park to acquire the Parachute Jump and make it the major feature of the park's boardwalk entrance was a fire, on July 13, 1939, which took a heavy toll at the boardwalk end of the park. A roller-coaster-like ride called the Flying Turns was totally destroyed, as were elements of the famous Steeplechase Horses ride. The heroism of Steeplechase workers, who quickly manned fire hoses, kept the blaze from spreading to and likely destroying the Pavilion of Fun.[23]

The foundation of the Parachute Jump, as well as ramps and walkways surrounding it, were built of structural steel and concrete. For the remaining days of Steeplechase, this area stood in marked contrast with the less substantial construction that had long been the hallmark of Coney Island. Another Steeplechase acquisition from the World's Fair of 1939–40 was a decoration— four tall columns in the shape of golden stalks of wheat that were installed just inside the Surf Avenue boundary of Steeplechase.

Not nearly as dramatic as the Parachute Jump, another ride from the World's Fair that was transported to Coney Island was called the Bobsled. Like the Flying Turns at Steeplechase that were destroyed in the 1939 fire, the Bobsled was a roller-coaster-like ride; a train of bobsled-like cars was hauled to the top of a grade, and it descended on rubber tires inside a right-of-way built from large circular tubes. The independently owned Bobsled was installed on the Bowery at Stillwell Avenue, just behind Nathan's.

LUNA GOES INTO ECLIPSE

During the Second World War, Luna Park suffered a major fire that would eventually lead to its demise. Even before the fire, Luna had deteriorated into a shadow of its former self. The park's founders, Frederic Thompson and Elmer Dundy, had divested themselves of their interest in Luna many years earlier. The park was taken over by a syndicate headed by Barron G. Collier, a man whose principal business had been the sale and posting of advertising messages on the inside and outside of street railways. Under Collier, Luna fell into bankruptcy in 1934. While new ownership emerged a decade later in 1944 with all kinds of wonderful plans, the plans were never implemented and Luna continued to reflect little more than neglect. In its final days, employees assigned to various rides often worked in their undershirts on warm afternoons. This was a sharp contrast with Steeplechase where, for all of that park's days, the workforce was smartly uniformed in shirts and ties and distinctive red and green hats, with matching red jackets with green trim when the weather was cooler.[24]

On August 12, 1944, the day of the Luna Park fire, New York was in the midst of a summer heat wave and the temperature was well up into the 90s. Consequently, Coney Island was very crowded, with estimates that more than 750,000 visitors had retreated to the shore to escape the summer heat. In midafternoon, a policeman on duty near Luna noticed thick, black smoke coming out of a roller coaster called the Dragon's Gorge. The officer quickly ran and pulled the handle of fire alarm box no. 3564 at Surf Avenue and West 11th Street. The box was pulled at 3:41 P.M. and the Telegraph Bureau of the New York Fire Department (FDNY) on Empire Boulevard quickly transmitted a first alarm that sent two engine companies and two hook-and-ladders to the scene. When Chief David Carberry of the 43rd Battalion arrived several minutes later, the Dragon's Gorge was fully involved and the fire had spread to the Mile Sky Chaser, another Luna coaster, as well as Hellenback, a fun house. The 43rd Battalion was located within sight of Luna Park in a firehouse on West 8th Street just to the north of Surf Avenue.

Because so much of Luna Park was built of highly combustible material, Chief Carberry quickly directed his aide to order a second alarm. But Carberry knew from the outset that this would not suffice for long. The second alarm brought Deputy Chief Charles Marquardt of FDNY's 12th Division to the scene, and under Marquardt the Luna Park fire eventually reached five-alarm status. A special high-pressure fire hydrant system that had been installed in Coney Island for just such eventualities was ordered to increase its pressure to 175 pounds.[25] As the fire spread, flames shot up more than 400 feet into the sky—higher than the new Parachute Jump in nearby Steeplechase—and smoke was visible as far as twenty miles away.[26]

Eventually, FDNY had to exceed the theoretical limit of five alarms to bring the Luna Park fire under control, and equipment was dispatched to Coney Island that represented the equivalent of ten alarms and sixty-two companies. Twenty wooden BMT elevated cars in nearby Stillwell Yard were destroyed when flaming embers from Luna drifted northward and set them afire—the BMT fire alone was treated as two separate two-alarm blazes—but

FDNY was most concerned about nearby gas tanks of the Brooklyn Borough Gas Company. Fortunately, the gas tanks turned out to be little threatened. The great wonder of the day was that, despite the extent of the Luna Park fire, and despite the crowds that were enjoying Coney Island, there were no fatalities or serious injuries from this terrible blaze, although nineteen firemen and several civilian volunteers suffered minor injuries.[27] (Decades after the Luna Park fire, one could still see its evidence in tire tracks in the asphalt pavement along West 12th Street—Luna's western boundary—that were imprinted there by an FDNY pumper because of the heat of the flames.)

On the same day as the Luna Park fire, the New York metropolitan area had to contend with two other major blazes. One was a waterfront fire on Pier Four in Hoboken, New Jersey, and the other was just north of there in Palisades Park, a New Jersey amusement park directly across the Hudson River from upper Manhattan. The *New York Times* editorialized that, while the combined effect of the three fires was "spectacular, destructive and crippling," wartime devastation that had been inflicted on cities such as Nanking, Warsaw, London, and Rotterdam made the three New York fires "seem almost like children's bonfires on vacant lots."[28] (New Jersey was hit by three major fires on August 12—Hoboken; Palisades; and, in the southern part of the state, a block of the boardwalk in Wildwood went up in flames.)

Luna reopened on August 18—a mere six days after the 1944 fire—and 3,000 patrons were on hand to enjoy themselves at the old park. But the fire had destroyed fully half of the place, and Luna would never recapture its old glory. Indeed, most would agree that Luna Park had lost most of its old glory long before the first fire engines arrived on the scene to battle the 1944 fire.

WARTIME

Coney Island prospered, after a fashion, during the travel-restricted years of the Second World War. Servicemen, of course, were welcome in the amusement areas, but there is scant evidence that the patriotic fervor that caused major league baseball parks to waive or substantially reduce admission charges for uniformed military personnel was common in Coney Island. Instead, soldiers and sailors were seen primarily as people with money in their pockets.

Speaking of people spending money, blatant dishonesty often prevailed among those who worked in ticket booths and other money-handling situations at Coney Island. A term used to describe certain transactions was that the patron became a "walk." ("Walk," in this context, was used as a noun.) That is to say, after plunking down a five-dollar bill to buy a pair of dollar tickets to an amusement park, the unwitting patron would walk away from the ticket booth without waiting for his change. The ticket seller employed body language to encourage a patron to become a "walk." But, if challenged, the ever-honest cashier would stoutly deny that any larceny was intended and hand the customer his change.

An even more daring maneuver happened when a ticket seller counted out the proper amount of change—three one-dollar bills in the example noted above. After the customer was convinced he had seen the correct change counted out—and, as a matter of fact, he had—the cashier cleverly flipped a dollar bill onto the floor of his ticket booth from the bottom of the stack he was returning to the customer. The ever-solicitous cashier typically folded the money over before handing it to the patron, often with a whispered piece of advice that the patron should be cautious of pickpockets who were known to be active in Coney Island.

Most patrons simply pocketed the change they were handed and walked away. However, if the cashier noticed that the customer was counting his change, he reached down under his counter and pretended that it had always been his intention to supply the final dollar or two of change in silver. Customers who would never think of leaving a teller's window at a bank without counting their money twice were often the most gullible in believing that Coney Island cashiers would never resort to anything dishonest.

But if Coney Island ticket sellers were out to separate customers from their money as rapidly and completely as they could, subway fares on the now municipal network of lines remained a mere five cents, and travel to and from Coney Island was a bargain throughout the war years. Oddly enough, though, a streetcar practice that dated back to the earliest days of the CI&B was retained on the

B&QT's Coney Island Avenue Line—a former CI&B service. Even after the B&QT became part of the city-owned subway, bus, and trolley network operated by the Board of Transportation in 1940, passengers from downtown Brooklyn had to pay an extra five-cent fare to ride the full length of this line.

A Coney Island tradition that began in 1903—a week-long Mardi Gras celebration at the close of the summer season—continued during the early war years, but was cancelled in 1944 because of rationing and other constraints. The Mardi Gras had been held continuously from 1903 to 1943, save for wartime 1918, when it was cancelled. (An annual Coney Island Mardi Gras would be reinstated after the Second World War, but it only survived for a few seasons before being cancelled permanently.)

The Mardi Gras was a season-ending tradition in Coney Island. In 1936, plans were made to hold a somewhat contrived tercentenary celebration to kick off the summer season. Because there was evidence that 1636 was the year that a man by the name of Wolphert Gerritse van Couwenhoven was awarded a land grant of some sort, a celebration in 1936 seemed to make sense. A parade along Surf Avenue was scheduled for late May, and $50 was set aside in the pageant's budget to rent a team of oxen that would haul a faithful re-creation of a seventeenth-century wagon, complete with solid wooden wheels.

Alas, in 1936 no oxen could be found anywhere on Long Island, and the parade had to go on without the oxen. There were vague reports that such beasts of burden still toiled on small farms in the wilds of New Jersey, but the limited budget was insufficient for finding any, much less bringing them to Coney Island.

After VJ Day (1945–2000)

IN COMPARISON WITH earlier eras, the years between the end of the Second World War and the beginning of the twenty-first century saw rather limited change to the style of transportation that served Coney Island. This is not to say that things were completely static over this interval with respect to Coney Island transportation, and Coney Island itself saw a near total alteration of its nature and identity during these years. Urban transportation in the world at large experienced anything but stability after the Second World War; the private automobile grew in popularity and systems of public transport experienced steady decline between war's end and the mid-1970s, only to see an unexpected renaissance during the final quarter of the twentieth century. But despite such developments, there were far fewer changes in basic Coney Island transportation patterns during this period than there were, for instance, between 1880 and 1890, 1890 and 1900, or 1900 and 1915.

GENERAL DEVELOPMENTS

The Belt Parkway was expanded from two to three lanes in each direction shortly after the war, and traffic levels on this important circumferential roadway grew to levels that even Robert Moses never imagined. Save for this expanded capacity on the Belt Parkway, though, no additional highway access was constructed to serve Coney Island–bound motorists, nor was any proposed. Automobile drivers were able to reach the Belt Parkway more directly from Staten Island, and even from New Jersey and points further west, once the Verrazano-Narrows Bridge opened between Bay Ridge and Staten Island in November 1964. This new bridge, it could perhaps be argued, rendered Coney Island more accessible to a larger population of potential visitors. By the time the Verrazano-Narrows Bridge was built, though, the amusement area of

Coney Island had shrunk to a shadow of its former self, the last of Coney Island's major amusement parks had closed its gates forever, and few would claim that the new bridge had any positive effect on patronage levels at the venerable oceanfront resort.

Another postwar change in transport options between Brooklyn and Coney Island involves Ocean Parkway, although it is something with no statistical significance with respect to the number of people who visited the seashore. A formal bridle path along one side of Ocean Parkway was paved over and the possibility of equestrian travel to and from Coney Island was, for all intents and purposes, eliminated.[1]

During the postwar era, subway service to Coney Island experienced a variety of evolutionary changes, but they were limited to modest alterations in service patterns, the periodic acquisition of new rolling stock, changes in management structure, and minor alterations to stations and other facilities. The Board of Transportation that had been the instrument of subway governance onward from the municipal takeover of the Brooklyn-Manhattan Transit Corporation (BMT) and Interborough Rapid Transit Company (IRT) in 1940—and that had controlled the new Independent Subway System from its inception in 1932—was succeeded by a new, state-created agency, the New York City Transit Authority (commonly referred to as the Transit Authority), that assumed operational control of the system in 1953. Most surface transportation in New York City eventually came under Transit Authority management as well. Because it had been under the control of the Board of Transportation since 1940, bus and trolley car service in Brooklyn was a Transit Authority responsibility from the very first days of the new agency.

MOTORIZATION OF STREETCAR LINES

Brooklyn trolley car lines were converted to motor bus operation in wholesale fashion in the late 1940s, a pattern that had begun before the war but was put on hold for the duration. In most cases, such conversions involved buses operating along the same streets on which the trolleys previously had run. One trolley line in Coney Island, though, was unique in that it operated entirely over its own private right-of-way, and not along city streets. This was the Norton's Point Line, successor to Andrew Culver's New York and Coney Island Railroad that was built in 1879 as an extension of the Prospect Park and Coney Island Railroad (PP&CI) and whose purpose was to link the developing amusement areas adjacent to Culver Depot in West Brighton with the steamboat landing at Coney Island Point.

In its final days, the Norton's Point Line ran from the Stillwell Avenue subway terminal to Sea Gate on a right-of-way that was between, and parallel to, Surf and Mermaid Avenues, although trackage still existed inside Sea Gate that continued all the way to the water's edge where pilings and other remnants of the steamer dock could be seen as late at the 1950s. At one time, a shuttle streetcar operated within Sea Gate as an extension of the Norton's Point Line, but it was motorized before the Second World War. (Today, some vestiges of the right-of-way that Culver's railway used are still evident inside Sea Gate.)

When the Board of Transportation converted the Norton's Point Line itself to bus operation in 1948, the buses operated along Mermaid Avenue and were identified as the B-74, Mermaid Avenue Route. The private right-of-way was abandoned, and the ramp up to the Stillwell Avenue Terminal was dismantled.

One incidental advantage that passengers aboard Mermaid Avenue buses enjoyed that was largely denied passengers making other bus-to-subway transfers in Brooklyn was that the bus route terminated in a new off-street facility located under the Stillwell Avenue subway station. It required two fares to ride both bus and subway—as it previously did to ride the subway and the Norton's Point trolley line—but at least the transfer from bus to subway could be made under shelter from the weather.

A Coney Island trolley car service called the Sea Gate Line operated along Surf Avenue from Sea Gate to Sheepshead Bay, where passengers could transfer to and from the Ocean Avenue Line (a one-time Nassau Electric service). On its way to Sheepshead Bay, the Sea Gate Line turned off Surf Avenue onto West 8th Street and eventually continued eastward along Emmons Avenue. After this line was motorized as the B-36 Surf Avenue Route in 1946, bus service was extended beyond the eastern terminal in Sheepshead Bay to Avenue U and Nostrand Avenue in the Flatlands section of

Brooklyn, thus providing direct bus service to Coney Island from residential communities that had previously not enjoyed such access.[2]

By the late spring of 1951, the Board of Transportation had replaced almost all Brooklyn trolley cars with new diesel-powered buses. An earlier event of more than passing symbolism was the phase-out of trolley car service across the Brooklyn Bridge on March 6, 1950. This ended a tradition that had begun a half-century earlier on December 31, 1897, when tower car no. 1000 of the Nassau Electric Railroad was the first car to operate across the famous span. The final streetcar to carry passengers across the Brooklyn Bridge was PCC no. 1074 operating on the Seventh Avenue Line.

Between 1898 and 1944, trolleys crossing the Brooklyn Bridge operated along trackage that was incorporated into the regular vehicular roadways of the span. The original cable railway and successor electrified elevated trains of the Brooklyn Rapid Transit Company (BRT) and the BMT crossed the bridge on separate trackage in a special reservation between the roadways. After elevated rapid transit service across the bridge was eliminated in March 1944, trolley wires were strung over the former elevated trackage, the third rail was removed, terminal buildings at both Park Row and Sands Street were torn down, trackage was rearranged at the Brooklyn end of the bridge, and streetcar service was shifted to the right-of-way formerly used by the elevated trains. And so, for their final five years of crossing the East River, trolley cars no longer had to compete with motor traffic on the Brooklyn Bridge. But if this was an advantage, removal of the Park Row elevated terminal under which the streetcar loops were located meant that Brooklyn-bound trolley cars had to be boarded in the open air, with passengers exposed to the full fury of foul weather. Previously, the Manhattan station of the cable railway had created a sheltered terminal for trolley cars from Brooklyn.[3]

Following the elimination of streetcar service across the bridge in 1950, the venerable span was thoroughly rebuilt. Tracks that had carried first cable trains, then elevated trains, and finally streetcars were eliminated, and the span was converted into one that now includes three conventional traffic lanes in each direction.

A major push in the way of Brooklyn streetcar motorization that involved no fewer than eleven car lines took place between January and May of 1951. More than 350 streetcars were removed from service and scrapped during this period, several trolley car depots were closed and boarded up, and 120 miles of track were converted to motor bus operation. The famous Flatbush Avenue Line, for example, a one-time Brooklyn City property that ran the length of what is arguably the most famous thoroughfare in all of Kings County, dispatched its final streetcar early on the morning of Sunday, March 4, that year. By the end of spring, such important Brooklyn streetcar lines as Nostrand Avenue, Wilson Avenue, Seventh Avenue, and Smith Street had been converted to motor bus operation and the trolley cars that previously carried passengers along these lines were retired and sent to the scrap heap. (The cars that operated on Seventh Avenue and Smith Street would earn a reprieve—although not on those lines—as will be discussed shortly.)

During the postwar 1940s, the Board of Transportation briefly explored an alternative to the motorization of its Brooklyn streetcar lines, the use of electric-powered trolley coaches. These were rubber-tired vehicles that looked like typical buses, except that instead of being powered by an on-board internal-combustion engine, they were equipped with electric motors and drew current from overhead wires. With streetcars, the rails served as a "return," or "ground," to complete an electric circuit, and only a single overhead wire was required. Vehicles running on rubber tires were insulated, and thus a pair of overhead wires was required to complete an electric circuit for a trolley coach line. Conversion of streetcar lines to trolley coach operation was an effort to make additional use of the extensive electrical generation and distribution systems that had been developed during the days of trolley car operation.

Prior to the Second World War, the Brooklyn and Queens Transit Corporation (B&QT) had acquired a small, experimental fleet of eight electric trolley coaches and deployed them on the B-23 Cortelyou Road Route, linking central Flatbush and, eventually, a point in New Utrecht that was once known as Bath Junction.[4] In the late 1940s, a network of six former streetcar lines that had recently been motorized were equipped with dual trolley coach wires, and a fleet of 200 new trolley coaches built by the Saint Louis Car Company was put to work on them. A new central trolley coach depot was built on the site of an old trolley car barn on Bergen Street to serve these lines, and there is reason to believe that the Board of Transportation had plans to expand trolley coach service beyond these six lines.[5] However, no such expansion ever came to pass. These six lines—along with the Cortelyou Road installation from the early 1930s, which was retained as a noncontiguous element of Brooklyn's postwar trolley coach network—remained the full extent of such service in the borough.

There is one delightful trolley coach story dating from the years of the Second World War that, while undoubtedly untrue, bears repeating, especially since it involves service to and from Coney Island.

Across the Hudson River from New York, the major trolley car operator in the state of New Jersey was Public Service Coordinated Transport, PSNJ. As PSNJ phased out various streetcar lines in the late 1930s, it deployed a fleet of electric-powered trolley coaches in addition to motor buses. PSNJ developed an unusual vehicle—a hybrid trolley coach/motor bus that could run electrically under wires but could also charge up its engine and provide service along any thoroughfare.

PSNJ was a major player in the operation of weekend charter bus service between points in New Jersey and Coney Island, and it frequently used its distinctive "all-service" vehicles on such assignments. One day a number of such PSNJ buses were heading back to New Jersey after a day at the seashore, when the driver of the lead vehicle noticed that he was traveling under the trolley coach wires of the B&QT's route along Cortelyou Road. Ever anxious to conserve fuel during wartime, the drivers of the PSNJ vehicles turned off their engines, raised their trolley poles, and moved along under the wires for several blocks.

Back at BMT headquarters in the Brooklyn Paramount Building, a surface line supervisor was keeping watch on a "clock" that recorded when trolley coaches passed a certain spot on the Cortelyou Road Route. Bearing in mind that the Brooklyn company owned only eight trolley coaches at the time—and not all of these were in service on a Sunday evening—the supervisor was understandably bewildered when ten vehicles passed the "clock" within a few minutes' time (or so the story goes).

Brooklyn's trolley coach network survived into the early 1960s, but under Transit Authority management the vehicles operating out of Bergen Street Depot were regarded as an odd-ball element in an otherwise standardized fleet of diesel-powered motor buses. The final Brooklyn trolley coach carried its last passenger on July 27, 1960.

Returning to the motorization of trolley car lines in the 1950s, a small group of Brooklyn streetcars survived the Board of Transportation's postwar motorization program, at least for a few additional years. This was the fleet of 100 PCC cars that were delivered in 1936 and were still thought to have some years of useful service left in them. They continued to operate for five more years and were based at the Ninth Avenue Depot, a storage and maintenance facility located on the same site adjacent to Green-wood Cemetery where trains of Andrew Culver's PP&CI once terminated and connected with horse-drawn streetcars that operated into and out of the heart of residential Brooklyn.

In the years after 1951, the 100-car PCC fleet served three Brooklyn trolley lines, two of which bear an interesting relationship to the story of how we got to Coney Island. One line ran from Ninth Avenue Depot to Coney Island via McDonald (nee Gravesend) Avenue, an almost perfect recreation of Culver's PP&CI. Another line also ran to Coney Island, but from an intersection called Bartel Pritchard Square on the western end of Prospect Park. It largely operated along Coney Island Avenue and was thus the successor of an important element of the Coney Island and Brooklyn Railroad, a company once so ably managed by General Henry W. Slocum. The third surviving Brooklyn streetcar line did not serve Coney Island at all. It was a one-time Nassau Electric service that ran on an east-west corridor primarily along Brooklyn's Church Avenue from the site of the 39th Street Ferry Terminal on Upper New York Bay across Brooklyn to Rockaway Avenue. (Ferry service between 39th Street in Brooklyn and the foot of Whitehall Street in Manhattan was taken over by the City of New York in 1906, and terminated in 1938. A short-lived municipal service ran between 39th Street and Saint George, Staten Island, from 1924 until 1926.)

These three lines represented the last hurrah of a rich street railway tradition that began when the Brooklyn City Railroad operated its first horse-drawn streetcars in 1854. The two lines that ran to and from Coney Island—McDonald Avenue and Coney Island Avenue—terminated at the shore in the same West Fifth Street terminal that had been built by the Coney Island and Brooklyn Railroad in 1912, just before the company was absorbed by the BRT.

Service on the Coney Island Avenue Line was converted to motor bus operation on November 30, 1955. PCC car no. 1045 made a final run from Bartel Pritchard Square to Coney Island in the early morning hours that day and then deadheaded back to Ninth Avenue Depot over the McDonald Avenue Line. Both the Church Avenue Line and the McDonald Avenue Line ran their final streetcars almost a year later on October 31, 1956. McDonald was abandoned outright, while Church Avenue was converted to motor bus operation. PCC car no. 1039, the last Church Avenue car, was the final streetcar to carry revenue passengers in Brooklyn, a benchmark that came to pass 102 years after the Brooklyn City Railroad placed Brooklyn's first streetcar in service in July 1854.

The nation's initial fleet of PCC streetcars was thus retired after a mere twenty years of service. Two cars were preserved in railway museums; the other ninety-eight were sold, most for scrap, a few to be converted into stationary facilities at a day camp.

IND-BMT Connection

One interesting aspect of streetcar service on the McDonald Avenue Line during its final years relates to a long-delayed improvement in subway service to and from Coney Island. When an important line of the city's new Independent Subway System (IND) was built into Brooklyn in the 1930s, it ended in Flatbush at the intersection of Church and McDonald Avenues. Here E trains from 169th Street-Jamaica terminated, reaching Brooklyn via the Eighth Avenue Line in Manhattan on October 7, 1933. Once the Sixth Avenue Line in Manhattan was opened in late 1940, F trains replaced E trains on this line into Brooklyn.

Shortly after the IND reached Church and McDonald Avenues, a ramp was built south of the Church Avenue station so IND trains could emerge from their below-ground subway tunnel and continue on to Coney Island over a Dual Contracts–built elevated structure that, since 1919, had been used by the BRT/BMT Culver Line.

During early planning, it was proposed that the municipally operated IND would "recapture" the BMT's Culver Line for through service to Coney Island. The transaction was based on the concept of eminent domain and was sanctioned by the terms of the Dual Contracts under which the Culver Line's elevated structure was built in 1919, but it would require payment to the BMT by the city. (The exact terms of the recapture of any rapid transit line varied, depending on how much of a facility was built with private money and how much with public funds.) However, the complexities of recapture became unnecessary; once the entire BMT had been acquired by the city in 1940, the municipal government was the owner of the Culver Line.

Effecting the operational tie-in between the BMT and the IND proved to be protracted. Heavy construction work on the ramp was largely completed in 1941, but the project had to be halted during the war. When work resumed, the BMT elevated structure was strengthened, platforms were extended to accommodate ten-car IND trains, and new electrical substations were constructed and brought on line to provide sufficient current for higher-performance IND equipment.

Pending the completion of this IND-Culver connection, extra trolley cars were operated along McDonald Avenue for passengers getting off subway trains at Church Avenue and heading for residential points south of there. Because the 100-unit fleet of PCC cars was insufficient to handle all this traffic, twenty 8000-series Peter Witt cars were retained for supplementary service along McDonald Avenue. By thus surviving the Board of Transportation's massive motorization programs and carrying passengers for a few extra years, these twenty cars became the last of the distinctive 8000-series fleet—cars that had long been identified with Brooklyn. Because they were "double-ended" and could operate equally well in either direction, the 8000-series cars that supplemented McDonald Avenue PCCs in carrying subway passengers south from the subway station at Church Avenue generally operated only as far as Avenue I—a section of Kings County often referred to as Parkville—where they reversed direction and headed back to Ninth Avenue Depot for another trip. The crossover track these cars used for this maneuver was part of a junction between the McDonald Avenue Line and the Long Island Railroad, a link that dated back to the nineteenth century when Andrew Culver and Austin Corbin established cooperative services over their respective railroads via an earlier version of this same junction.

Another oddity of the McDonald Avenue Line bears mentioning. Recall from chapter 4 that, in 1889, Andrew Culver rerouted the bulk of his Coney Island service into a new Union Depot at Fifth Avenue and 36th Street, the better to tap patronage traveling out from central Brooklyn aboard the new Fifth Avenue elevated line.

To reach Union Depot, Culver's PP&CI built a short, eight-block connecting link that left the PP&CI's Gravesend Avenue right-of-way at Kensington Junction and headed west parallel to 37th Street and, eventually, along the southern rim of Green-wood Cemetery. After the BRT takeover of the PP&CI—but prior to the implementation of the Dual Contracts—surface-running Culver Line trains used this same route to reach the Fifth Avenue El, where they continued on to downtown Brooklyn and Manhattan via the El. The Culver Line's Dual Contracts elevated structure was built along this same right-of-way.

When the elevated structure was placed in service in 1919, surface trackage along Gravesend Avenue was converted into a conventional streetcar line, with trolleys following the original PP&CI route to Ninth Avenue and 20th Street, not the later spur to 36th Street. Surface trackage that formerly led to Union Depot was retained, though, and became the province of the BRT/BMT subsidiary that was called the South Brooklyn Railway.

The South Brooklyn Railway was a freight railway whose principal customer was the BRT/BMT itself, with the sprawling complex known as Coney Island Yards requiring frequent shipments of car-load freight, as well as the delivery of new subway cars. There were other freight customers along Gravesend/McDonald that the South Brooklyn Railway also served. The freight line linked the waterfront near the 39th Street Ferry with Coney Island Yards over a combination of its own trackage, elements of the

BRT/BMT subway system, plus the McDonald Avenue Line. During midday hours when streetcar service on McDonald Avenue was not terribly heavy, one would often encounter a four- or five-car freight train hauled by an electric locomotive rumbling along between scheduled streetcars.

The South Brooklyn Railway was conveyed to the City of New York when the BMT itself was acquired by the municipal government in 1940, became a subsidiary of the Transit Authority in 1953, and survived as a street-running railway in Brooklyn for many decades after trolley service on the McDonald Avenue Line was abandoned.

The South Brooklyn Railway retained its independent identity for a variety of regulatory reasons. However, in the tangled web of BRT/BMT corporate subsidiaries and their various accounting procedures, a portion of the fares paid by passengers riding streetcars along McDonald Avenue and on the Norton's Point Line between Stillwell Avenue and Sea Gate was conveyed to the South Brooklyn Railway as rental payment for the use of its trackage.

The South Brooklyn Railway was an electric line, but in 1961—five years after the last streetcar carried passengers along McDonald Avenue—the trolley wires were deenergized and the South Brooklyn Railway then relied entirely on a fleet of small diesel locomotives. The South Brooklyn Railway remains a wholly owned subsidiary of the Transit Authority in the early years of the twenty-first century. However, since the late 1980s it has not run trains along McDonald Avenue and it has restricted its operations to Transit Authority trackage, as well as short stretches of its own right-of-way adjacent to the South Brooklyn waterfront.[6]

Returning to the subway link between the IND Brooklyn Line and the BMT Culver Line, on Saturday, November 1, 1954, IND D trains from the Bronx began running through to Coney Island over the one-time BMT elevated structure. (F trains that previously terminated at Church Avenue were rerouted, but would return to Brooklyn, and the Culver Line, in 1967.) In 1954 when this change was implemented, the BMT and the IND were still separate divisions within the overall structure of the New York City Transit Authority, and service over the Culver Line was formally transferred from BMT to IND jurisdiction. During the early days of through service, when IND trains reached Ditmas Avenue (the first station on the Culver Line) a BMT motorman came aboard to help familiarize the IND motorman with the new route—much as an inbound ocean liner pauses outside a port to take aboard a local harbor pilot. Some effort was made to refer to the IND trains that began using the Culver Line in 1954 as the "Concourse-Culver" service, but the name never caught on; once F trains replaced D trains in 1967, the usage was no longer accurate.

A BMT Culver Line continued to operate into the Fourth Avenue subway from a new single-track stub terminal that was built adjacent to the elevated station at Ditmas Avenue. This was later downgraded into a shuttle service between Ninth Avenue and Ditmas, and eventually it was abandoned outright.

STILLWELL AVENUE TERMINAL

Before the IND arrived at Coney Island in the fall of 1954, important track and structure changes were made. The "lower-level" elevated structure between West Eight Street and Stillwell Avenue became exclusive IND territory, and a ramp that once linked this lower level with the Brighton Beach Line at Ocean Parkway was deactivated. As a result, summer express service to Coney Island from Franklin Avenue was eliminated. Likewise eliminated in advance of the IND's arrival at Coney Island were summer express trains to and from Coney Island that had operated over the otherwise unused express tracks along the BMT's Sea Beach Line.

Another colorful, albeit inefficient, aspect of subway service to Coney Island that was phased out at roughly this same time was a practice that had been adopted because the BMT was chronically short of steel subway cars—but had an abundance of wooden elevated equipment left from the days when its elevated network was much larger. During peak rush hours when passenger travel was heaviest, both the Culver Line and the West End Line terminated their service from Manhattan at stations that were not as far from the city's business district as was Coney Island, and thus fewer steel subway cars were required to meet schedules. Culver subway trains terminated at Kings Highway during rush hours, West End subway trains terminated at Bay Parkway, and each line then operated shuttle service beyond to Coney Island with wooden equipment left over from the days of the Fulton Street El and the Fifth Avenue El.

Shortly after the extension of IND service to Coney Island in 1954, the Transit Authority began to replace the oldest of the system's subway rolling stock. Subway cars that several generations of Brooklynites will always identify with summer trips to Coney Island were replaced by newer equipment. The last of the BMT 6000-series D units that operated on the Brighton and Sea Beach lines were retired in the late 1960s, while some of the older BRT/BMT Standard units survived until early in the 1970s. Even the fleet of cars that inaugurated service on the IND in the 1930s came due for replacement. Newer rolling stock tended to feature shiny exteriors of stainless steel, more robust motors for faster acceleration, and full air conditioning to ease the impact of hot summer days.

Eventually, under Transit Authority management, the IND and BMT divisions were merged into a single operational entity known as the B Division. (The IRT, which operates rolling stock of slightly smaller dimensions, was designated the A Division.) A new color-coded letter system was developed to designate various services on the newly combined network of the B Division, a system that was essentially an expansion of an earlier letter-code system developed for the IND in the 1930s. The IND system originally used single letters to designate express service and double letters for local service, and the Transit Authority retained this distinction for a few years. More recently, in the interests of clarity, a new single-letter code has been adopted that is indifferent to whether a train is an express or a local.

Today, at the turn of the twenty-first century, four color-coded subway lines—successors of the one-time excursion railways—normally serve Coney Island. The precise identity of the lines varies, as both permanent and temporary service adjustments are made in the overall subway system. The following table identifies the services in operation in early 2002.

The arrival of IND trains at Stillwell Avenue in 1954, and prior to this the elimination of special summer express services to and from Coney Island, resulted in a phasing out of what had become a BMT summer tradition, a seasonal change in platform assignments at the terminal.

During winter months, the pattern typically called for West End

Subway Service at Stillwell Avenue Terminal, 2000

Identity	N Train[a]	Q Train[b]	F Train	W Train[c]
Current northern terminal	Astoria	57th Street, Manhattan	Jamaica-179th Street	Astoria
Current service	Broadway Local	Broadway Express	Sixth Avenue-Queens Express	Broadway Express
Current Manhattan trunk	Broadway	Broadway	Sixth Avenue	Broadway
Previous BMT identity	Sea Beach Express	Brighton Local	Culver Line	West End Express
Previous BMT Manhattan trunk	Broadway	Broadway	Nassau Loop	Broadway
Previous BMT northern terminal	Times Square	Queens Plaza	Chambers Street	Times Square
Excursion railroad identity	New York & Sea Beach Railroad	Brooklyn, Flatbush & Coney Island Railroad	Prospect Park & Coney Island Railroad	Brooklyn, Bath & West End Railroad

Source: The Map (New York: Metropolitan Transportation Authority, 2001).

[a] N train temporarily cut back to 86th Street to permit reconstruction work at Stillwell Avenue.

[b] D train to 205th Street-Grand Concourse via Sixth Avenue will likely replace Q train via Broadway once repair work on Manhattan Bridge is completed circa 2004.

[c] B train via Sixth Avenue will likely replace W train via Broadway once repair work on Manhattan Bridge is completed circa 2004.

Express (and shuttle) trains to use Tracks 1 and 2, the Brighton Local was assigned to Tracks 3 and 4, the Culver Line operated out of Tracks 5 and 6, while the Sea Beach Express terminated on Tracks 7 and 8. (Actually, during BMT days the tracks at Stillwell Avenue were designated by letters—A through H. The current numbering system is of more recent vintage.)

During the summer, ordinary Sea Beach service was moved to Tracks 1 and 2. Special summer express operations—Franklin Avenue service every day, express service over the Sea Beach Line on "sunny, summer Sundays"—used Tracks 3 and 4. (As a practical matter, Sea Beach and Franklin Avenue summer express services were typically operated as a single service, with Stillwell

Avenue serving as a way station for trains that made their way along the Brighton Line from Franklin Avenue and then over the Sea Beach Line to Chambers Street.) The Brighton Local was rerouted into Tracks 5 and 6, making use of a ramp between Ocean Parkway and West Eighth Street that led to the lower level of the elevated approach to Stillwell Avenue and was only activated during the summer. Culver Line service was restricted to Track 7, and the West End used Track 8.

When the Stillwell Avenue terminal was built in 1920, both the West End and the Sea Beach crossed Coney Island Creek on a two-track drawbridge before heading up a ramp into the elevated terminal at Stillwell Avenue. This bridge became a bottleneck, obviously, if it had to be raised to permit the passage of marine traffic. But it was also a bottleneck because Sea Beach and West End trains had to be accommodated on a single pair of tracks, tracks that were also used by trains heading into and out of nearby storage yards.

The 1960s saw major improvements here. The original drawbridge was deactivated as a movable span, since Coney Island Creek was no longer an active commercial waterway. In addition, a new two-track fixed bridge was constructed immediately to the east of the original span so Sea Beach and West End services no longer have to share trackage (see map 9).

As this book is written, the biggest change to the Stillwell Avenue Terminal is yet to come. Transit officials, concerned that salty sea air may be having a deteriorating effect on steel that reinforces the facility's concrete pillars, have initiated a major rebuilding effort. The exact shape of the rebuilt terminal remains to be seen, and the terrorist attack on the World Trade Center on September 11, 2001, forced the reallocation of capital resources so damage in lower Manhattan can be repaired. In late 2001, N train service (the old Sea Beach Line) was cut back to the 86th Street station to permit reconstruction of Tracks 1 and 2 at Stillwell Avenue. Additional service disruptions can be expected until the project is completed.

LAST OF THE EXCURSION BOATS

Following the end of the Second World War, there were some efforts to revive excursion boat service to Coney Island. This ser-

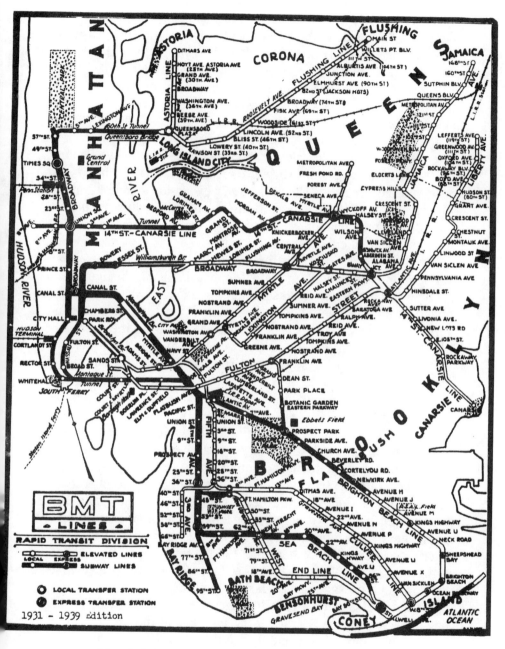

Map 9: Schematic rendition of the track arrangement
at Stillwell Avenue Terminal, circa 2000.

vice was not via the ocean and Steeplechase Pier, but rather to the Gravesend Bay side of the island—not unlike service patterns that were operated before the first iron pier was built in 1879 and steamboats landed inside what is now known as Norton's Point. But where Coney Island–bound excursionists of the mid-nineteenth century could find a day's relaxation adjacent to the steamer dock, or in later years ride one of Andrew Culver's shuttle trains to the amusement areas of West Brighton, passengers getting off excursion boats along Neptune Avenue in the 1940s and 1950s faced a long walk through residential neighborhoods to reach the beach. An ex-Delaware River excursion steamer named *Bojangles* is most associated with these postwar ventures, but the bayside docking location was simply too removed from the amusement area to make the efforts successful.

In mid-July of 1956 what is thought to be the last scheduled boat service between Manhattan and Coney Island was inaugurated. After five completely unsuccessfully weeks, it was mercifully ended. A man by the name of Jeremiah Driscoll acquired a converted U.S. Navy LCI(L)-class landing craft bearing the improbable name *San Jacinto*—she had previously sailed Texas waters to the San Jacinto battlefield outside Houston for an excursion boat impresario by the name of B. B. Wills—and inaugurated a route between the Battery and Gravesend Bay/West 23rd Street/Coney Island on July 18, 1956.[7] She was decked out in dress flags with the words "Coney Island Boat" painted amidships on her port side in red letters that were much larger than her name. The style of decoration was probably just a coincidence. Or perhaps someone associated with Captain Driscoll's Panorama Line remembered an earlier fleet of Coney Island boats whose service was rendered across their paddle boxes in larger letters than their names. Few passengers rode *San Jacinto* to Coney Island in 1956 and, soon afterward, Driscoll put her into the around–Manhattan Island sightseeing trade after having her rebuilt with a lower wheelhouse to allow clear passage under Harlem River bridges.

During the summer of 1957, Driscoll ran a one-round-trip-per-day service between Newark, New Jersey, and the same Gravesend Bay side of Coney Island that *San Jacinto* had used the previous summer, with a vessel called *Manhattan*. In the heyday of the Iron Steamboat Company, service between Newark and Coney

Island via the ocean piers had been commonplace. When Panorama Sightseeing Company's wooden-hull and by then diesel-powered *Manhattan* pulled away from West 23rd Street in Coney Island during the early evening hours of Labor Day, September 2, 1957, the long and interesting history of scheduled excursion boat service to Coney Island came to a seemingly permanent end. Who could possibly have known that forty-four summers later a passenger vessel would return to Coney Island and dock not on the bay side of the resort, but at Steeplechase Pier?

CHANGES IN CONEY ISLAND

Although the principal transportation developments associated with Coney Island in the years following the Second World War can be described as modest and evolutionary, what happened to the Coney Island amusement industry along Surf Avenue, the Bowery, and the Coney Island Boardwalk during the same period was totally transformational in nature.

Luna Park struggled after the 1944 fire and remained in partial operation. But it was fighting long odds and had little to fight with. There was no investment capital for its rebuilding, and in 1946 Luna closed its doors for good.

Steeplechase remained in reasonably good health after the Second World War and survived for another two decades. Many would later argue that Steeplechase, at the west end of the Coney Island amusement zone, had served to "anchor" all of Coney Island, much in the way that a major department store is said to anchor a contemporary shopping mall.[8] When Steeplechase closed its doors for good at the end of the 1964 season, this event—as much as any single event can—signaled the final death spiral for a large portion of the Coney Island amusement zone.

There has been some interesting scholarship in recent years—aided in substantial measure by the publication of diaries kept by the long-time manager of Steeplechase, James Onorato—suggesting that the Tilyou family, who continued to run Steeplechase until its final day, were so beset by internal rivalries that keeping their amusement park going was never a real option.[9] The property was sold to New York developer Fred Trump, whose son

Donald was present when the deal was consummated. While the elder Trump had grandiose plans for turning his newly acquired Steeplechase property into pricey seaside condominiums, for one reason or another the plans were never realized. The site, once leveled, would sit idle for more than three decades.[10]

The demise of Coney Island during the 1960s and the 1970s involved a good deal more than the elimination of Steeplechase or any of the rides along the Bowery. Appealing to a totally different clientele than an amusement park, Coney Island was long the home of a variety of what would today be called swim clubs. These clubs were not marketed to people who made only one or two visits to Coney Island each summer; their specialty was season-long memberships to people who might visit once or twice a week, possibly more, between May and September. Coney Island's beach and swim clubs represented a very important element of the resort's latter-day economy. These clubs typically featured changing lockers, steam rooms and showers, eating facilities, sports activities like handball, and—of course—access to the ocean beach. (Such access was typically via a passageway under the boardwalk, since persons wearing bathing attire were nominally prohibited from using the boardwalk.)

Some clubs such as Ravenhall, Washington Baths, Washington Baths Annex, and Ocean Tide also included salt water swimming pools for their members. Tilyou's Steeplechase even had its own outdoor pool.[11] After the Second World War, though, Steeplechase Pool began to restricted its membership to "season bathers only." Some have commented that, by prohibiting ordinary day patrons of Steeplechase Park from taking a swim in the pool, the policy kept nonwhite customers out of the water—a form of discrimination that the owners believed was necessary to preserve the customer base of season bathers and the important cash flow they represented for the Steeplechase enterprise.[12] Steeplechase Pool closed following the 1963 season, the year before Steeplechase Park shut its gates for good, and the other swim clubs soon followed suit.

In the years following the demise of Steeplechase, the amusement zone of Coney Island shrank in size and intensity to a small fraction of its former self. Among the rides that closed once Steeplechase was no longer in business were two important roller coasters—the Tornado and the Thunderbolt—the Bobsled that came to Coney Island after the 1939–40 World's Fair, plus any number of smaller, independent rides.

By the end of the twentieth century, all that remained of Coney Island's once extensive amusement zone was a cluster of rides just off the boardwalk between West 10th and West 12th Streets known as Astroland. Astroland, established in 1963, occupies much of the same site where Feltman's Restaurant and Beer Garden once stood. It features a fascinating collection of newer rides, plus some classics from Coney Island's golden age including the 1920-built Wonder Wheel and the Cyclone roller coaster that has been in steady operation since 1927. The Cyclone receives steady attention from roller coaster enthusiasts the world over, and it is a frequent subject of documentary specials on various broadcast and cable television networks.

And then there is the beach—steady and unchanging, although in some ways always changing. One dramatic difference, for instance, that distinguishes the beach at Coney Island in 2002 from earlier eras is that the level of sand has substantially increased. In fact it has increased to such a degree that the boardwalk is virtually at the same level as the beach.

It's funny the way Coney Island manages to intrude itself on popular culture. Because of all this additional sand on the beach, the catchy song "Under the Boardwalk" will soon lose its point with respect to Coney Island, because you can't go under the boardwalk any more. Speaking of popular songs, many people think "Meet Me Tonight in Dreamland" is about a nocturnal state of unconsciousness. It isn't. It's about an amusement park called Dreamland. You can't go there any more, either.

EPILOGUE: KEYSPAN PARK

After decades of decay and countless unfulfilled promises, the year 2001 saw Coney Island take a few tentative steps in the direction of a new and promising future. Because none of the plans over the years for using the Steeplechase property had ever advanced, and more importantly because the entire twelve-acre parcel had not been subdivided, it remained available for large-scale development. In 2001 a brand new minor league baseball stadium called Keyspan Park, the home of a new minor league team called the Brooklyn Cyclones, opened on the site. In keeping with a common practice in the sporting world, the name Keyspan was not randomly selected. Keyspan, formerly known as the Brooklyn Union Gas Company, purchased the "naming rights" for the new stadium, a facility that was built with $39 million in municipal funds and that welcomed its first crowds in July 2001.

Wonder of wonders, when the Brooklyn Cyclones played a home-and-home weekend series with another new minor league baseball team, the Staten Island Yankees whose new field was built on an old railroad yard adjacent to the ferry terminal at Saint George, municipal officials felt that there was an appropriate way for fans of either team to reach the opponent's ballpark. The 1986-built municipal ferryboat *John A. Noble* made several trips between Steeplechase Pier in Coney Island, a short walk from Keyspan Park, and the Staten Island ferry terminal at St. George, a short walk to Richmond County Bank Ballpark. This marked the first waterborne passenger service to Steeplechase Pier since before the Second World War, and it is an appropriately optimistic note on which to bring the story of how we got to Coney Island to an end—at least for now.

Appendix A

BRT and BMT Rail Passenger Cars, 1900–1940

RAPID TRANSIT

Series	No. of Units[a]	Year Built	Builder	Description[b,c]	Type
436–440[d]	5	1900	J. G. Brill	48-foot, open platform	Elevated rolling stock
628–632[e]	5	1900	J. G. Brill	48-foot, open platform	Elevated rolling stock
450–499[f]	50	1901	Jewett	48-foot, open platform	Elevated rolling stock
1000–1119[g]	120	1902	Stephenson	48-foot, open-platform convertible	Elevated rolling stock
1200–1234[h]	35	1903	Osgood-Bradley	48-foot, open platform	Elevated rolling stock
1235–1259	25	1903	Brill	48-foot, open platform	Elevated rolling stock
1260–1299	40	1903	Laconia	48-foot, open platform	Elevated rolling stock
999[i]	1	1905	Company shops	48-foot, closed-vestibule instruction car	Elevated rolling stock
1300–1349[j]	50	1905	Cincinnati	48-foot, open-platform convertible	Elevated rolling stock
1350–1374[j]	25	1905	Jewett	48-foot, open-platform convertible	Elevated rolling stock
1375–1399	25	1905	Laconia	48-foot, open-platform convertible	Elevated rolling stock
1400–1449	50	1907	Jewett	48-foot, open platform	Elevated rolling stock
1450–1499	50	1907	Laconia	48-foot, open platform	Elevated rolling stock
998	1	1908	Pressed Steel	48-foot, closed-vestibule steel experimental	Multipurpose rolling stock

2000–2599[k]	600	1914–1919	American Car & Foundry	67-foot, steel motors	Subway rolling stock
2600–2899[k]	300	1920–1922	Pressed Steel	67-foot, steel motors	Subway rolling stock
1500–1501[i]	2	1923	Company shops	3-car units	Elevated rolling stock
4000–4050[k]	50	1924	Pressed Steel	67-foot, steel trailers	Subway rolling stock
1502–1526[j]	24	1925	Company shops	3-car units	Elevated rolling stock
6000–6120[m]	121	1925–1928	Pressed Steel	137-foot, 3-section articulated	Subway rolling stock
7003	1	1934	Pullman	170-foot, 5-section articulated	Multipurpose rolling stock
7029	1	1934	Budd	168.5-foot, 5-section articulated	Multipurpose rolling stock
7004–7013	10	1936	St. Louis	179-foot, 5-section articulated	Multipurpose rolling stock
7014–7028	15	1936	Pullman	179-foot, 5-section articulated	Multipurpose rolling stock
1600–1629[n]	30	1938–1939	Company shops	3-car units	Elevated rolling stock
1630–1642[o]	13	1939	Company shops	2-car units	Elevated rolling stock
8000–8005	6	1938, 1940	Clark	3-section articulated	Multipurpose rolling stock

[a] With the exception of cars and units preserved at various railway museums, all rolling stock displayed in these rosters are out of service and retired.

[b] All 48-foot equipment listed, except no. 998, featured wooden car bodies. In later years, when designations such as A/B units, D units, and C units became company notation, remaining open-platform elevated cars on the roster were commonly referred to as BU units.

[c] Unless noted otherwise, all rolling stock listed are motorized units.

[d] Later renumbered in 600 series, still later in 900 series.

[e] Later renumbered in 900 series.

[f] Later renumbered in 600 series. Car no. 659 preserved at Shore Line Trolley Museum, East Haven, Connecticut.

[g] Only BRT elevated cars with arched roofs.

[h] Car no. 1227 preserved at Shore Line Trolley Museum, East Haven, Connecticut.

[i] This car preserved at Shore Line Trolley Museum, East Haven, Connecticut.

[j] Car nos. 1349 and 1362 preserved at Shore Line Trolley Museum, East Haven, Connecticut; car no. 1365 preserved at the National Museum of Transport, St. Louis, Missouri.

[k] Many 2000-series cars were semipermanently coupled into three-car sets known as B units, while single cars were called A units. Three-car units with a 4000-series trailer in the middle were identified as BX units. Car no. 2204 preserved at New York Transit Museum, Brooklyn, New York; car nos. 2390, 2391, and 2392 preserved in Brooklyn, New York; car no. 2775 preserved at Shore Line Trolley Museum, East Haven, Connecticut.

[l] Three-car units rebuilt from older elevated equipment as follows: two end cars were motor units rebuilt from 1200- and 1400-series, open-platform elevated cars, while unpowered center car was rebuilt from even older trailer elevated cars. All rebuilt cars fully enclosed with sliding doors for passenger entry and exit. Identified in BRT/BMT notation as C units.

[m] Units 6019, 6095, and 6112 preserved under auspices of New York Transit Museum, Brooklyn, New York.

[n] Three-car units rebuilt from 1200- and 1400-series elevated equipment for service to the 1939–40 New York World's Fair. All cars powered and fully enclosed with sliding doors for passenger entry and exit; identified in BMT notation as Q units. Transferred to IRT Division in 1950 for service on the Third Avenue El; later returned to BMT to replace 1300-series open-platform elevated cars on the Myrtle Avenue Line. Car no. 1622A (ex-1407), no. 1622B (ex-1273), and no. 1603C (ex-1404) rebuilt back to open-platform configuration and preserved at the New York Transit Museum, Brooklyn, New York. Car no. 1612C preserved at same location in Q unit configuration.

[o] Two-car units rebuilt from 1200- and 1400-series elevated equipment for service to the 1939–40 New York's World's Fair. All cars powered and fully enclosed with sliding doors for passenger entry and exit. Identified in BMT notation as QX units.

STREETCARS

Series	No. of Units	Year Built	Builder	Description[a]
800–849[b]	50	1900	American	13-bench, open
850–899	50	1900	Briggs	13-bench, open
1000–1099	100	1900	American	13-bench, open
1100–1153[c]	54	1899–1903	J. G. Brill	10-window, closed
1200–1299	100	1900	Laconia	13-bench, open
2700–2704	5	1900–1901	Company shops	10-window, semiconvertible
1400–1499	100	1901–1902	Stephenson	13-bench, open
1600–1649	50	1902	Stephenson	13-bench, open
2000–2099[c]	100	1899–1900, 1904	J. G. Brill	13-bench, open
2200–2208[c]	9	1904	J. G. Brill	13-bench, open
2380–2399[c]	20	1905, 1907	J. G. Brill	8-window, semiconvertible
2705–2799	95	1901–1902	Laclede	10-window, semiconvertible
2905–2954	50	1902	Stephenson	10-window, semiconvertible
2900–2904; 2955–2999; 3100–3154	105	1902	Laclede	10-window, semiconvertible
3155–3199; 3300–3304; 3355–3399[d]	100	1903–1904	Stephenson	10-window, semiconvertible

3305–3354	50	1904	Kuhlman	10-window, semiconvertible
1154–1178[c]	25	1904	Kuhlman	10-window, semiconvertible
3500–3554	55	1904–1905	Stephenson	10-window, semiconvertible
3555	1	1905	Stephenson	12-window, semiconvertible
3556	1	1906	Pressed Steel	12-window, semiconvertible
3700–3799; 3900–3924	125	1905	J. G. Brill	12-window, convertible
3925–3974	50	1905	Stephenson	12-window, convertible
4100–4199[e]	100	1906	Stephenson	12-window, convertible
4300–4349; 4500–4549[f]	100	1906	Laconia	12-window, convertible
4550–4599[g]	50	1906	Jewett	12-window, convertible
2500–2599	100	1907	Stephenson	10-window, convertible
3557	1	1912	Standard Steel	Center entrance
5000–5099[h]	100	1912	J. G. Brill	Center entrance
4900[i]	1	1915	Company shops	Experimental articulated
6000–6099	100	1919	J. G. Brill	Center-entrance trailers
7000–7199[j]	200	1919	J. G. Brill	Single-truck Birney
4600[k]	1	1923	Company shops	Experimental articulated
8000–8099	100	1923	J. G. Brill	Double-ended Peter Witt
8100–8299[l]	200	1923	St. Louis	Double-ended Peter Witt
5100–5153[m]	54	1923–1924	Company shops	Center entrance
8300–8449[n]	150	1925	J. G. Brill	Double-ended Peter Witt
8450–8534[l]	85	1925	J. G. Brill	Double-ended Peter Witt
4700–4707[o]	8	1927	Company shops	Rebuilt older cars
4800[p]	1	1929	Company shops	Experimental
6000–6049[q]	50	1931–1932	Osgood-Bradley	Single-ended Peter Witt
6050–6199[q]	150	1931–1932	J. G. Brill	Single-ended Peter Witt
1001–1099[r]	99	1936	St. Louis	Single-ended PCC
1000[s]	1	1936	Clark	Single-ended PCC

[a] Unless noted otherwise, all streetcars shown above are of double-truck design.

[b] Open streetcars were commonly (and easily) identified by the number of cross-car benches they contained, while closed cars were identified by the number of windows along either side of the car.

[c] Purchased by Coney Island and Brooklyn Railroad prior to its acquisition by the BRT in 1914.

[d] In 1945, car no. 3740 was towed to the Manhattan side of Brooklyn Bridge to serve there as a waiting room for streetcar passengers.

[e] 4100-series cars used to haul unpowered 6000-series trailer cars.

[f] Car no. 4547 preserved at Seashore Trolley Museum, Kennebunkport, Maine.

[g] Car no. 4550 preserved in Pittsburgh, Pennsylvania; car no. 4573 preserved at Shore Line Trolley Museum, East Haven, Connecticut.

[h] All or most of this series converted to multiple-unit operation around 1918.

ⁱ Experimental articulated car built from two older, single-truck cars of the 1890s, nos. 167 and 168.

ʲ Birney Safety Cars, so called, proved unsuccessful in Brooklyn. Contrary to some published accounts, they were not intended for lightly traveled routes. Because most conventional city streetcars of the era required both a conductor and a motorman for their operation, the design philosophy behind the smaller Birney car was that the substitution of single-operator cars would allow street railways to operate more frequent service at little or no additional cost. The onset of one-man operation of conventional streetcars was instrumental in the downfall of the Birney car.

ᵏ Experimental articulated car built from two older, double-truck cars, nos. 4528 and 4529.

ˡ Car no. 8111 preserved at Shore Line Trolley Museum, East Haven, Connecticut. Cars 8100 through 8156, 8186, and all 8500s, were rewired for high-speed operation. In addition, 8500-series cars, while retaining controls at both ends, were operated in passenger service as single-ended cars.

ᵐ Date shown refers to date of conversion into motorized units from 1919-built 6000-series trailers.

ⁿ Car no. 8361 preserved at Transit Museum of New York, Kingston, New York.

ᵒ Date shown references rebuilding of older cars from the 3700, 3900, and 4100 series.

ᵖ Reconstruction of car no. 3900 to permit and test one-man operation.

ᑫ All 6000-series cars equipped with leather seats; 6100-series cars featured wooden seats.

ʳ Car no. 1001 preserved at Shore Line Trolley Museum, East Haven, Connecticut.

ˢ Car no. 1000 preserved at Transit Museum of New York, Kingston, New York.

TRACKLESS TROLLEYS, 1930–1948

Series	No. of Units	Year Built	Builder
1000ᵃ	1	1930	American Car and Foundry
1001ᵃ	1	1930	Twin Coach
1002–1007ᵃ	6	1932	Pullman-Standard
3000–3199	200	1948	St. Louis

ᵃ Operated on Cortelyou Road Route (see chapter 9).

SOURCES AND FURTHER READING

For additional data and information about Brooklyn Rapid Transit and streetcar rolling stock, including equipment acquired prior to 1900, see:

Greller, James C., and Edward B. Watson. *The Brooklyn Elevated.*
Hicksville, N.Y.: N.J. International, 1988, 118–119.

———. *Brooklyn Trolleys.* Hicksville, N.Y.: N.J. International, 1986,
114–118.

Rahilly, George. "The Time of the Trolley in Brooklyn." *Headlights*
55 (January–February 1993): 2–11.

———. "The Wooden Cars of the Brooklyn Elevated Railroads."
Headlights 56 (July–August 1994): 2–13.

For roster information about the Interborough Rapid Transit Company, the Independent Subway System, as well as equipment acquired for use over former BMT lines in the years after subway unification in 1940, see:

Cudahy, Brian J. *Under the Sidewalks of New York.* New York: Fordham University Press, 1995, 173–176.

Rail and Steamboat Schedules, Summer 1880

BROOKLYN, FLATBUSH, AND CONEY ISLAND RAILROAD

Southbound
Trains leave Flatbush & Atlantic Avenues (LIRR Depot) for
Brighton Beach as follows:
6:30 A.M.; 7:30 A.M.; 8:30 A.M.; 9:15 A.M.;
then half-hourly until 9:45 P.M.
Additional trains leave Bedford Terminal for Brighton Beach
half-hourly from 11:34 A.M. until 9:34 P.M.

Northbound
Trains leave Brighton Beach for Flatbush & Atlantic Avenues
(LIRR Depot) as follows:
6:40 A.M.; 7:40 A.M.; 8:40 A.M.; 9:10 A.M.; 9:40 A.M.; 10:10 A.M.;
10:40 A.M.; 11:10 A.M.; 12:10 P.M.; then half-hourly until 9:40 P.M.
Trains leave Brighton Beach for Prospect Park and
Bedford Terminal as follows:
6:40 A.M.; 7:40 A.M.; 8:40 A.M.; 9:10 A.M.; 9:40 A.M.; 10:10 A.M.;
10:40 A.M.; 11:25 A.M.; 12: 55 A.M.; then
half-hourly until 9:25 P.M.; 9:40 P.M.

NEW YORK AND MANHATTAN BEACH RAILROAD

Southbound
Via Bay Ridge
Steamer *D.R. Martin* leaves East River Pier 1 (foot of Whitehall
Street) at 9:25 A.M. and hourly until 7:25 P.M., connecting at Bay
Ridge with trains for Manhattan Beach.

Northbound
Via Bay Ridge
Trains leave Manhattan Beach at 8:20 A.M., 10:20 A.M.; then hourly until 8:20 P.M., connecting at Bay Ridge with steamer *D.R. Martin* for connecting service to East River Pier 1 (foot of Whitehall Street).

Southbound
Via Greenpoint
Steamer *Sylvan Grove* leaves foot of East 23rd Street (East River) at 9:45 A.M., then hourly until 6:45 P.M., connecting in Greenpoint with trains for Manhattan Beach.

Northbound
Via Greenpoint
Trains leave Manhattan Beach at 7:35 A.M.; 11:05 A.M.; then hourly until 8:05 P.M., connecting in Greenpoint with steamer *Sylvan Grove* for connecting service to the foot of East 23rd Street (East River).

Trains operating between Greenpoint and Manhattan Beach connect in East New York with Long Island Railroad trains to and from Flatbush & Atlantic Avenues.

PROSPECT PARK AND CONEY ISLAND RAILROAD

Southbound
Trains leave Brooklyn Depot (Ninth Avenue & 20th Street) for West Brighton at 6:30 A.M.; 7:40 A.M.; 9:00 A.M.; 10:00 A.M.; then half-hourly until 1:30 P.M.; then every quarter-hour until 9:00 P.M.

Northbound
Trains leave West Brighton for Brooklyn Depot (Ninth Avenue & 20th Street) at 7:05 A.M.; 8:10 A.M.; 9:30 A.M.; 10:30 A.M.; then half-hourly until 2:00 P.M.; then every quarter-hour until 9:30 P.M.
(On rainy days, trains will only operate half-hourly.)

BROOKLYN, BATH, AND CONEY ISLAND RAILROAD

Southbound
Trains leave Greenwood Depot (Fifth Avenue & 27th Street) for Coney Island at 6:20A.M.; 7:20 A.M.; 8:10 A.M.; 9:00 A.M.; 9:50 A.M.;

10:40 A.M.; 11:30 A.M.; 12:30 P.M.; 1:30 P.M.; 2:15 P.M.; 3:00 P.M.;
3:45 P.M.; 4:30 P.M.; 5:15 P.M.; 6:00 P.M.; 6:50 P.M.; 7:40 P.M.; 8:30 P.M.
(On Sunday, first southbound departure is 8:10 A.M.)

Northbound
Trains leave Coney Island for Greenwood Depot (Fifth Avenue &
27th Street) at 7:30 A.M.; 8:20 A.M.; 9:10 A.M.; 10:00 A.M.; 10:50 A.M.;
11:40 A.M.; 12:35 P.M.; 1:35 P.M.; 2:30 P.M.; 3:05 P.M.; 3:50 P.M.;
4:35 P.M.; 5:20 P.M.; 6:05 P.M.; 6:55 P.M.; 7:45 P.M.

Round trip fare: 25 cents.

NEW YORK AND SEA BEACH RAILROAD

Southbound
Via Brooklyn
Trains leave depot at Third Avenue & 65th Street for Sea Beach
Palace at 9:00 A.M.; then hourly until 2:00 P.M.;
then half-hourly until 6:30 P.M.

Northbound
Via Brooklyn
Last train leaves Sea Beach Palace for depot at Third Avenue &
65th Street at 7:00 P.M.

Southbound
Via Bay Ridge
Steamer *Idlewild* leaves foot of West 24th Street (North River) at
9:00 A.M.; 11:00 A.M.; 1:00 P.M.; 3:00 P.M.; and 5:00 P.M., connecting
in Bay Ridge with trains for Sea Beach Palace.

Northbound
Via Bay Ridge
Trains leave Sea Beach Palace for Bay Ridge at 9:30 A.M.;
11:30 A.M.; 1:30 P.M.; 3:30 P.M.; and 6:00 P.M., connecting in Bay
Ridge with the steamer *Idlewild* for continuing service to
West 24th Street (North River).

Excursion tickets from New York to Sea Beach Palace: 40 cents

Steamers *Idlewild* and *Josephine* connect with this company's trains at Bay Ridge.

CONEY ISLAND AND BROOKLYN RAILROAD

Southbound
Cars leave City Line Depot (Park Circle) for West Brighton at 7:00 A.M.; 8:00 A.M.; 9:00 A.M.; 9:40 A.M.; then half-hourly until 12:40 P.M.; 1:20 P.M.; 2:00 P.M.; then half-hourly until 5:00 P.M.; 5:40 P.M.; 6:10 P.M.; 6:50 P.M.; 7:20 P.M.; 7:50 P.M.; 8:30 P.M.; 9:00 P.M.; 9:40 P.M.

Northbound
Cars leave West Brighton for City Line Depot (Park Circle) at 6:00 A.M.; then hourly until 9:00 A.M.; 9:30 A.M.; 10:00 A.M.; 10:40 A.M.; 11:10 A.M.; 11:40 A.M.; 12:20 P.M.; then half-hourly until 2:20 P.M.; 3:00 P.M.; 3:30 P.M.; 4:00 P.M.; 4:40 P.M.; 5:10 P.M.; 5:40 P.M.; 6:10 P.M.; 6:50 P.M.; 7:30 P.M.; 8:00 P.M.; 8:40 P.M.; 9:40 P.M.

Round trip excursion tickets between City Line and Coney Island: 15 cents.

STEAMBOAT SERVICE TO IRON PIER

Steamers *John Sylvester* and *Eliza Hancox* will operate the following schedule:

Leave W. 23rd Street (North River)	9:00 A.M.	10:00 A.M.	12:15 P.M.	1:30 P.M.	3:30 P.M.	4:30 P.M.
Leave Leroy Street (North River)	9:15 A.M.	10:15 A.M.	12:30 P.M.	1:45 P.M.	3:45 P.M.	4:45 P.M.
Leave Pier 8 (North River)	9:30 A.M.	10:30 A.M.	12:45 P.M.	2:00 P.M.	4:00 P.M.	5:00 P.M.
Leave Iron Pier (Coney Island)	10:30 A.M.	11:30 A.M.	2:00 P.M.	3:00 P.M.	5:30 P.M.	6:30 P.M.

One-way tickets: 35 cents; round-trip excursion tickets: 50 cents.

Steamers *Nelly White, Stockton,* and *Kill Von Kull* may also operate this schedule.

Source: Townsend Percy, *Percy's Pocket Dictionary of Coney Island* (New York: Leypoldt, 1880), 111–113.

ENDNOTES

Preface

1. Brian J. Cudahy, *Around Manhattan and Other Maritime Tales of New York* (New York: Fordham University Press, 1997); Brian J. Cudahy, *The Malbone Street Wreck* (New York, Fordham University Press, 1999).

Chapter 1

1. At this writing in early 2002, extended repairs on the Manhattan Bridge have resulted in the presumably temporary suspension of D train service on the Brighton Line, and its replacement by additional Q train service.

2. In New York, the term *El* generally refers to an older elevated line that was built in the nineteenth century and was never upgraded to operate in conjunction with newer subway lines. These lines could not handle the weight of heavier, all-steel subway cars and continued to be served by lightweight elevated equipment; all such Els have been abandoned in New York. Transit lines that run along elevated structures, but are extensions of the subway system, are often called subways. They are frequently called Els, as well.

3. Streets of the west series continue inland on the Kings County mainland and are not located solely on Coney Island. Certain lower-numbered streets that cannot be found on Coney Island—such as West 7th Street and West 9th Street—are found inland. West 17th, West 26th, and West 34th streets have no mainland equivalents, though, and their absence can be regarded as a purely Coney Island phenomenon.

4. For additional information on such contemporary Brooklyn neighborhoods as Sea Gate, Manhattan Breach, Brighton Beach, and Coney Island, see John B. Manbeck, ed., *The Neighborhoods of Brooklyn* (New Haven, Conn.: Yale University Press, 1998).

5. The land that Coleman explored when he went ashore was described as "pleasant with grass and flowers and handsome trees as they have seen, and that very sweet smells came from them. They went in six

miles, saw an open sea, and returned." These words, written on board
the *Half Moon* by Robert Juet, describe "The Third Voyage of Master
Henry Hudson." See Donald S. Johnson, *Charting the Sea of Darkness:
The Four Voyages of Henry Hudson* (Camden, Maine: International Marine, 1993), 117. The description hardly characterizes Coney Island,
though, and suggests an incursion across Kings County. On the other
hand, Juet places the ship's anchorage at 40 degrees, 30 minutes north,
which, if accurate, would be in the ocean just off Coney Island, and not
in Gravesend Bay.

6. For information about the original towns of Kings County, see
Ellen M. Snyder-Grenier, *Brooklyn: An Illustrated History* (Philadelphia:
Temple University Press, 1996), 2–13.

7. The land inside the stockade was also divided among the original
settlers. See Edo McCullough, *Good Old Coney Island: A Sentimental
Journey into the Past* (New York: Fordham University Press, 2000), 17–25.
McCullough's work was originally published in 1957; the cited edition is
a reprint.

8. For additional details on the Coney Island House, its guests, and
successor hotels, see McCullough, *Good Old Coney Island,* 22–26.

9. See Oliver Pilat and Jo Ranson, *Sodom by the Sea: An Affectionate
History of Coney Island* (New York: Doubleday/Doran, 1941), 1–5.

10. For an interesting collection of old photographs that depict various aspects of the town of Gravesend, including Coney Island, see Eric
J. Ierardi, *Gravesend Brooklyn: Coney Island and Sheepshead Bay*, Images
of America Series (Dover, N.H.: Arcadia, 1996).

11. "Alderman Sandy Ehrmann of Coney Island introduced an
amendment to the Code of Ordinances in the Board of Aldermen yesterday permitting the wearing of topless bathing suits by men on city
beaches this summer." *New York Times,* 3 June 1936, 23.

12. McCullough, *Good Old Coney Island,* 320–321.

13. For an interesting account of how Coney Island represented a
free-form antithesis to the structured and uplifting entertainment characterized by the World's Columbian Exposition of 1893 in Chicago and permanent venues such as New York's Central Park, see John F. Kasson,
Amusing the Millions: Coney Island at the Turn of the Century (New York:
Hill and Wang, 1978).

14. McCullough, *Good Old Coney Island,* 154–182.

Chapter 2

1. Ironically, the Dodgers abandoned their old home in 1957, the
year after the last trolley car carried passengers in Brooklyn. Today, Los

Angeles can boast a new "light rail" transit system—the contemporary name for a trolley car—so perhaps there are residents there who now merit the designation "trolley dodgers."

2. For additional details on the early development of street railways, see Brian J. Cudahy, *Cash, Tokens, and Transfers* (New York: Fordham University Press, 1990), 7–21; William D. Middleton, *The Time of the Trolley: The Street Railway from Horsecar to Light Rail* (San Marino, Calif.: Golden West, 1987), 11–51.

3. *Brooklyn Daily Eagle*, 3 July 1854, 2.

4. *Brooklyn Daily Eagle*, 5 July 1854, 2.

5. *New York Times*, 3 July1854, 3

6. *Annual Report of the Board of Railroad Commissioners of the State of New York* (Albany, N.Y., 1886), 296–297.

7. For additional details about the Stephenson Company, see John W. White Jr., *Horsecars, Cable Cars and Omnibuses* (New York: Dover, 1974).

8. The Gowanus was a creek, not a canal. It was formally designated a canal by an act of the state legislature in 1837 so work could be done to stabilize its banks and ensure its future as an industrial waterway.

9. *New York Times*, 21 August 1863, 5.

10. An early president of the Brooklyn City Railroad was a distinguished Brooklynite by the name of Cyrus Porter Smith. Born in Hanover, New Hampshire, and a graduate of Dartmouth College, he was elected the fourth mayor of Brooklyn in 1839 and held that office until 1842. While serving in the state senate in the 1850s, Smith was instrumental in the passage of important transportation legislation, and onward from 1855 he was the managing director of the Union Ferry Company. He assumed the presidency of Brooklyn City Railroad in January 1869. See Henry R. Stiles, *A History of the City of Brooklyn* (Brooklyn, N.Y., 1869), 2:263–264.

11. *Annual Report of the Board of Railroad Commissioners of the State of New York* (Albany, N.Y., 1882), 1196.

12. Ibid., 1197.

13. *Brooklyn Daily Eagle*, 17 July 1877, 2. For additional information on the problems American street railways faced when they attempted to supplement horse-drawn streetcars with steam-powered rail vehicles, see John H. White Jr., "Grice and Long: Steam-Car Builders," *Prospects: An Annual of American Cultural Studies* (1976): 25–39.

14. *Brooklyn Daily Eagle*, 19 July 1878, 4.

15. For further details on Brooklyn and streetcar companies whose operations continued into Queens County, see Vincent F. Seyfried, *Brooklyn Rapid Transit Trolley Lines in Queens* (East Norwich, N.Y.: N.J. International, 1998).

16. For further details on Sprague's work in Richmond, see Cudahy, *Cash, Tokens and Transfers,* 35–50; Middleton, *The Time of the Trolley,* 5, 52–73.

17. Frank Sprague, "The Story of the Trolley Car," reprinted in *Headlights* 23 (March 1961): 6.

18. *Street Railway Journal* (September 1890): 440.

19. The words "South Brooklyn" appear in the corporate titles of several Kings County railways of the nineteenth century, and the various companies are often, and understandably, confused. The company from which Brooklyn City acquired the Second Avenue franchise to test electric-powered trolley cars was called the South Brooklyn Street Railroad Company.

20. *New York Times,* 4 July 1862, 3.

21. Ibid., 7

22. For further treatment of ferryboat lines that operated in New York Harbor, including tabular information on all routes and vessels that operated between 1812 and 1990, see Brian J. Cudahy, *Over and Back* (New York: Fordham University Press, 1990).

23. *Brooklyn Daily Eagle,* 3 July 1862, 2.

24. *New York Times,* 25 May 1890, 20.

25. For details about this disaster, see Irving Werstein, *The General Slocum Incident* (New York: John Day, 1965); James M. Merrill, "The Day New York Shocked the World," *Steamboat Bill* 79 (fall 1961): 67–73; *New York Times,* 16 June 1904, 1.

26. E. M. Bentley, "The First Electric Street Car in America—1884," *Electrical World and Engineering* 42 (5 March 1904): 439.

27. *Street Railway Journal* (25 May 1890): 20.

28. *Street Railway Journal* (December 1891): 675.

29. *New York Times,* 23 April 1891, 8.

30. For further details on the early history of the Long Island Railroad, see Vincent F. Seyfried, *The Long Island Railroad: A Comprehensive History,* 7 vols. (Garden City, N.Y.: Author, 1961–1975); Elizabeth B. Hinsdale, *History of the Long Island Railroad Company, 1834–1898* (New York: Evening Post Job Printing House, 1898); Mildred H. Smith, *Early History of the Long Island Railroad: 1834–1900* (Uniondale, N.Y.: Salisbury, 1958).

31. Hinsdale, *History of the Long Island Railroad Company,* 6.

32. *Annual Report of the Board of Railroad Commissioners of the State of New York* (Albany, N.Y., 1883), 1181.

33. By convention, Williamsburgh was spelled with a terminal "h" until the end of the nineteenth century, without it afterward. Today, a large bank building in Williamsburg proudly proclaims itself to be the Williamsburgh Savings Bank, since its charter was issued before 1900.

CHAPTER 3

1. The lithograph is reproduced in Ellen M. Snyder-Grenier, *Brooklyn: An Illustrated History* (Philadelphia: Temple University Press, 1996), 171.

2. There are several important sources about early steamboats. One of these is a venerable publication of the U.S. government that is based on official vessel documentation records and is entitled *Merchant Vessels of the United States. MVUS* was issued annually starting in 1867. In an important work of historical scholarship, the Steamship Historical Society of America has attempted to provide vessel information for the period prior to the publication of *MVUS*. See *Merchant Vessels of the United States, 1790–1868* (Staten Island, N.Y.: Steamship Historical Society of America, 1975). Popularly known as "The Lytle-Holdcamper List," supplements to the 1975 work have been issued by the same organization in 1978, 1982, and 1984. Another work of scholarship about early steamboats was produced by Samuel Ward Stanton, a man who tragically lost his life aboard the *Titanic* in 1912. See Samuel Ward Stanton, *American Steam Vessels* (New York: Smith and Stanton, 1895). Stanton's work has been republished in a series of regionally oriented paperback volumes. With respect to Coney Island service, the relevant document is *New York Bay* (New York: Elizabeth S. Anderson, 1968). For more detailed information about vessel documentation resources, see Brian J. Cudahy, *Over and Back* (New York: Fordham University Press, 1990), 355–356.

3. Fred Erving Dayton, *Steamboat Days* (New York: Tudor, 1925), 434–435.

4. Snyder-Grenier, *Brooklyn,* 171.

5. See "Hints on Bathing," in Townsend Percy, *Percy's Pocket Dictionary of Coney Island* (New York: Leypoldt, 1880), 77–94.

6. For details on how John Y. McKane came to be a controlling force in Gravesend politics and how he used that force to shape and form Coney Island, see Edo McCullough, *Good Old Coney Island: A Sentimental Journey into the Past,* 45–49; see also Pilat and Ranson, *Sodom by the Sea,* 25–41.

7. Dayton, *Steamboat Days,* 435.

8. For more details, see "The Sylvan Steamboats on the East River: New York to Harlem," *The New-York Historical Society Quarterly Bulletin* 8 (October 1924): 59–71.

9. *New York Times,* 28 May 1880, 8.

10. *New York Times,* 28 September 1880, 8.

11. *New York Times,* 24 May 1881, 8.

12. *New York Times,* 5 July 1885, 7.

13. *New York Times,* 30 May 1881, 8.

14. *New York Times,* 7 July 1883, 7.

15. *New York Herald,* 1 July 1901, 4.

16. *New York Times,* 4 July 1913, 8.

17. *New York Times,* 18 November 1917, 29.

18. For information about the migration of northern steamboats to southern waters during the northern off-season, see Edward A. Mueller, *St. John's River Steamboats* (Jacksonville, Fla.: Author, 1986), 196–199.

19. *New York Times,* 20 September 1915, 5.

20. For a perspective on the Iron Steamboat Company's following season, 1916, see Roger W. Mabie, "A Year in the Life of *Perseus,*" *Steamboat Bill* 135 (fall 1975): 151–153. Mabie obtained original log books from *Perseus* at the time the vessel was scrapped, and this article contains material from the 1916 operating season. See also Roger W. Mabie, "The *Perseus* at Twilight," *Steamboat Bill* 137 (spring 1976): 21–23, for a similar account from the years 1929, 1930, and 1931.

CHAPTER 4

1. Gunther was born in New York in 1822 and, after an early career as a merchant, he entered politics; his allegiance was to the Democratic Party. Defeated in his first run for mayor in 1861, he was eventually elected in 1863. For general information about the state of the railway at the time of Gunther's acquisition, see *New York Times,* 18 November 1878, 2.

2. *Annual Report of the Board of Railroad Commissioners of the State of New York* (Albany, N.Y., 1882), 326.

3. *Brooklyn Daily Eagle,* 12 July 1892, 2.

4. *New York Times,* 16 July 1892, 2.

5. The terminal was located on a site bounded by Second and Third Avenues and 37th and 39th Streets.

6. *Brooklyn Daily Eagle,* 23 February 1896, 1.

7. *Poor's Manual of the Railroads of the United States* (New York, 1891), 76.

8. *Brooklyn Daily Eagle,* 19 June 1875, 3.

9. *Brooklyn Daily Eagle,* 18 June 1878, 8.

10. *Annual Report of the Board of Railroad Commissioners of the State of New York* (Albany, N.Y., 1882), 1313.

11. *Proceedings of the Street-Railway Association of the State of New York* (Brooklyn, N.Y.: 1886), 10.

12. *Poor's Manual of the Railroads of the United States* (New York, 1891), 450.

13. *Brooklyn Daily Eagle,* 17 July 1877, 2. In delivering one of the many toasts offered at the banquet, General Henry W. Slocum proposed this: "In the ferry, the railway and hotel improvements, whose completion we this day celebrate, we have renewed evidence that Peace hath her victories no less than war."

14. In describing the various reporters who gathered on a New York pier for the inaugural trip to the Manhattan Beach Hotel in 1878, a scribe for the *New York Times* reveals something of the relationships and rivalries that existed within the New York newspaper business in the 1870s. "About a dozen of them were men who earn their baked beans by the sweat of their lead-pencils, and the remainder were the peculiar and exclusive kind of press representatives who never show their faces in public unless there is a fine dinner in prospect," the man reported. *New York Times,* 16 May 1878, 2.

15. Three-foot gauge was by far the most common specification for common carrier railroads in the United States that were less than standard gauge in width, although some featured three-and-a-half feet between the rails. Popular primarily in the state of Maine were narrow-gauge lines whose rails were two feet apart. For a thorough study of narrow-gauge railroads in America, see George W. Hilton, *American Narrow Gauge Railroads* (Stanford, Calif.: Stanford University Press, 1990).

16. Corbin had earlier railway experience in the Middle West. In 1875 he was associated with the Indiana, Bloomington and Western Railroad.

17. Hilton, *American Narrow Gauge Railroads,* 457.

18. Kings County Hospital and Holy Cross Cemetery are still active institutions in Brooklyn. The site of Kings County Penitentiary later became Jesuit-run Brooklyn Preparatory School, and it is now a campus of Medgar Evers College of the City of New York.

19. Hilton, *American Narrow Gauge Railroads.*

20. *New York Times,* 23 July 1879, 1.

21. Ibid.

22. *New York Times,* 25 July 1879, 8. An anthology published in 1977 provides additional treatment of this matter. See Gerald N. Grob, ed., *Anti-Semitism in America, 1878–1939* (New York: Arno, 1977). The piece in this anthology that deals with Corbin is a reprint of a pamphlet that was originally published in 1879, *Coney Island and the Jews* (New York: G.W. Carleton & Company, 1879).

23. For an account of the early development of Manhattan Beach, see Edward W. Denny, *The Story of Manhattan Beach* (New York: Francis Hart & Co., 1879). Denny's book is silent, however, on the matter of Corbin's anti-Semitism.

24. *Brooklyn Daily Eagle,* 2 July 1878, 2.

25. Ibid.

26. Ibid.

27. *Brooklyn Daily Eagle,* 20 August 1878, 2.

28. *Poor's Manual of the Railroads of the United States* (New York, 1880), 142.

29. *Brooklyn Daily Eagle,* 28 August 1887, 2.

30. *Poor's Manual of the Railroads of the United States* (New York, 1891), 75.

31. *Brooklyn Daily Eagle,* 11 November 1896, 12.

32. Another structure from the Philadelphia exposition was moved to Coney Island by Andrew Culver. It was a 300-foot iron tower, with two steam elevators, that was set up outside Culver Depot and for many years was the tallest structure in the state of New York. It was destroyed in a terrible Coney Island fire in 1911.

33. *Brooklyn Daily Eagle,* 11 January 1896, 12.

34. For an extended treatment of the New York and Sea Beach Railroad, see William W. Fausser, *The Sea Beach to Coney Island* (Mineola, N.Y.: Author, 1979).

35. First-class service on the PP&CI was provided by the Woodruff Sleeping and Parlor Coach Company. To ride to the track in a parlor car, a patron had to pay an extra 25 cents.

36. *New York Times,* 27 May 1896, 9.

37. *New York Times,* 2 June 1896, 5.

38. *Brooklyn Daily Eagle,* 4 August 1880, 2.

39. *New York Times,* 27 November 1880, 8.

40. For information on the Boynton project, see Fausser, *The Sea Beach to Coney Island,* 36–38; *Boynton Bicycle Railway System, 1891* (New York: Boynton Bicycle Railroad Company, 1891; reprint, Americana Foundation, Inc., 1953).

41. *Annual Report of the Board of Railroad Commissioners of the State of New York* (Albany, N.Y., 1882), 1230.

42. As mayor, Gaynor was wounded in an assassination attempt in 1910. Many believe that his death three years later can be attributed to the 1910 attack.

CHAPTER 5

1. *Street Railway Journal* (October 1896): 605.

2. For details of proposals that were submitted to Mayor Howell by a specially appointed Board of Rapid Transit Commissioners, see *Brook-*

lyn Daily Eagle, 4 June 1878, 4. Several weeks later, the *New York Times* reported, "Mayor Howell has announced his intention of vetoing any resolution passed by the Common Council authorizing the construction of an elevated railroad over either Fulton or Myrtle avenues." *New York Times,* 1 August 1878, 8.

    3. *Brooklyn Daily Eagle,* 19 July 1878, 2.

    4. Husted was also an active investor in several Kings County street railways.

    5. *Brooklyn Daily Eagle,* 5 August 1880, 2. Several days earlier, Mayor Howell had put matters this way: "The interest manifested in the subject of securing an elevated steam railway over some feasible route, taken in conjunction with the reluctance of owners of property on the main thoroughfares of the city to submit their property to the peril of depreciation, and the opposition to those whose business on the popular streets of travel, renders the subject of great complication." *Brooklyn Daily Eagle,* 1 August 1880, 2.

    6. *Brooklyn Daily Eagle,* 10 November 1872, 3.

    7. *New York Times,* 11 January 1879, 3.

    8. See James Blaine Walker, *Fifty Years of Rapid Transit* (New York: Law Printing, 1918), 274–277.

    9. *Brooklyn Daily Eagle,* 13 May 1885, 1.

    10. *Brooklyn Daily Eagle,* 13 May 1879, 5.

    11. *New York Times,* 17 May 1879, 5.

    12. *New York Times,* 20 July 1879, 2.

    13. The *Eagle* welcomed the city's first elevated railway with extensive coverage, including a lengthy article on the earlier history of elevated railway development in Brooklyn. See "Done At Last; The Brooklyn Elevated Road Ready for the Public; Its Record for Eleven Years," *Brooklyn Daily Eagle,* 13 May 1885, 1.

    14. *Brooklyn Daily Eagle,* 13 May 1885, 6.

    15. Ibid.

    16. *New York Times,* 5 August 1881, 8.

    17. *New York Times,* 29 November 1881, 3.

    18. *New York Times,* 28 December 1881, 3.

    19. *New York Times,* 18 December 1882, 8.

    20. For a technical treatment of elevated railway steam locomotives, albeit with an emphasis on New York rather than Brooklyn, see John H. White Jr., "Spunky Little Devils: Locomotives of the New York Elevated," *Railroad History* 162 (spring 1990): 20–79.

    21. John H. White Jr., *American Locomotives: An Engineering History, 1830–1880* (Baltimore: Johns Hopkins University Press, 1968, 1997), 603–606.

22. *Brooklyn Daily Eagle,* 13 May 1885, 1.

23. When it opened in early 1889, the Myrtle Avenue Line did not feature through service. Trains to and from the line's western terminal had to turn onto the original line at Grand Avenue en route to downtown Brooklyn, while trains that reached downtown via the new Myrtle Avenue Line turned at Grand Avenue and operated to and from East New York via the Lexington Avenue Line. Through Myrtle service was instituted in December 1889, and service over the original line between Myrtle/Grand and Hudson/Park was abandoned.

24. *Brooklyn Daily Eagle,* 7 November 1888, 6.

25. Ibid.

26. There is an interesting Coney Island twist to the 1888 presidential election. Four years earlier in 1884, by means fair and foul, Gravesend's John Y. McKane successfully delivered a number of popular votes for Cleveland that exceeded the candidate's plurality in New York State. Since Cleveland would have been defeated by Republican James K. Blaine without New York, McKane felt proud of his role. According to McCullough, "he became a man of self-importance, exacting subservience, intolerant of opposition." See McCullough, *Good Old Coney Island,* 59. McKane was never constrained by party loyalty, though, and in 1888 he threw his support—and his organization—behind Harrison. "Gravesend handed a tremendous vote to Harrison, who carried New York State by a narrow margin over Grover Cleveland, and once again New York's thirty-six electoral votes turned the balance in the electoral college." See Pilat and Ranson, *Sodom by the Sea,* 39–41.

27. When Fifth Avenue service was routed over the Myrtle Avenue Line in late 1889, the crossing at Myrtle and Hudson was eliminated and the original Brooklyn Elevated Line down to Fulton Ferry was made a branch of the Myrtle Avenue Line.

28. A meeting to elect the new board was held on January 2, 1879. See *New York Times,* 3 January 1879, 3.

29. *New York Times,* 29 April 1879, 10; 13 May 1879, 5. In addition, Brooklyn Union came close to being awarded franchise rights to build an elevated line along Fulton Street.

30. *New York Times,* 19 December 1886, 6.

31. *Brooklyn Daily Eagle,* 24 April 1888, 6.

32. The extension was built under the formality of a separate company, the Fulton Elevated Railway.

33. *Street Railway Journal* (October 1896): 605.

CHAPTER 6

1. For a detailed study of cable-powered street railways, including treatments of all individual U.S. cable companies, see George W. Hilton,

The Cable Car in America, rev. ed. (Stanford, Calif.: Stanford University Press, 1997). For Hilton's treatment of the two Brooklyn operations, see pp. 361–365.

2. *Brooklyn Daily Eagle,* 9 July 1891, 4.

3. *Street Railway Journal* (April 1891): 208.

4. The name of the gripman assigned to the inaugural car, Thomas Halliday, was ironic. Nineteen years earlier, in San Francisco, a man by the name of Andrew S. Hallidie designed and built the world's first street-running cable railway. See Hilton, *The Cable Car in America,* 13–28.

5. Daniel Lewis's father, William D. Lewis, worked for Brooklyn City in a variety of positions from 1866 until his death in 1884. Daniel Lewis joined the company as a ticket agent and was elected president of the company in 1886, succeeding William Hazzard.

6. "Mr. Lewis has, as is well known, gone into another railroad scheme—the Montague street cable road—in which the Brooklyn City company has no interest." *Brooklyn Daily Eagle,* 16 February 1892, 6.

7. *Brooklyn Daily Eagle,* 4 January 1893, 12.

8. For additional treatment of the Coney Island racetracks, see McCullough, *Good Old Coney Island,* 130–153. See also Pilat and Ranson, *Sodom by the Sea,* 66–79.

9. For background on Flynn and Nassau Electric, see "The Nassau Electric Railroad Company," *Street Railway Journal* (September 1895): 567; see also *Brooklyn Daily Eagle,* 14 July 1898, 3.

10. By an interesting turn of fate, in 1956 Patrick Flynn's Church Avenue Line would become the last operating trolley car line in Brooklyn.

11. *Street Railway Journal* (September 1895): 567.

12. *New York Times,* 20 November 1894, 2.

13. *Street Railway Journal* (January 1899): 345.

14. *New York Times,* 20 March 1894, 2.

15. *New York Times,* 18 November 1892, 5.

16. *Brooklyn Daily Eagle,* 18 November 1892, 1.

17. *Brooklyn Daily Eagle,* 17 November 1892, 1.

18. Early discussion of LIRR's building an Atlantic Avenue elevated line apparently assumed that such a line would feature closely spaced stations and cater to short-haul markets.

19. *Brooklyn Daily Eagle,* 14 March 1893, 10. Brooklyn City streetcars that inaugurated electrified service along Court Street in December 1892 were painted dark green, while Brooklyn City and Newton's De Kalb Avenue cars featured an exterior color that the *Brooklyn Daily Eagle* described as a "peculiar yellow."

20. *New York Times,* 18 January 1893, 2.

21. *Street Railway Journal* (September 1894): 580.

22. *Brooklyn Daily Eagle,* 17 November 1893, 1.

23. *Street Railway Journal* (April 1892): 255.

24. *Street Railway Journal* (May 1893): 275–276.

25. *Brooklyn Daily Eagle,* 11 November 1892, 3.

26. *Brooklyn Daily Eagle,* 14 March 1893, 10.

27. For an obituary of Richardson, see *Street Railway Journal* (January 1894): 57.

28. *Report of the Thirteenth Annual Meeting of the Street-Railway Association of the State of New York* (New York, 1895), 22.

29. Littell was one of the forces behind the organization of the American Street Railway Association in 1883 and served as its first president. For his reflections on this matter, see Hardin H. Littell, "The Founding of the American Street Railway Association," *Street Railway Journal* (8 October 1904): 517.

30. Johnson has described his unusual career in an autobiography. See Tom L. Johnson, *My Story,* ed. Elizabeth J. Hauser (Kent, Ohio: Kent State University Press, 1993).

31. *Brooklyn Daily Eagle,* 13 January 1899, 1,

32. *Brooklyn Daily Eagle,* 22 May 1899, 5.

33. For more details on the corporate predecessors of the Brooklyn, Queens County and Suburban Railroad, see Vincent F. Seyfried, *Brooklyn Rapid Transit Trolley Lines in Queens* (East Norwich, N.Y.: N.J. International, 1998).

34. *Brooklyn Daily Eagle,* 29 July 1890, 8.

35. Ibid.

36. *Brooklyn Daily Eagle,* 9 September 1890, 16.

37. Ibid.

38. *New York Times,* 7 May 1891, 9.

39. Ibid.

40. *Street Railway Journal* (December 1891): 675–676.

41. *New York Times,* 22 December 1891, 5.

42. Ibid.

43. *Brooklyn Daily Eagle,* 18 November 1892, 1.

44. For a technical description of Brooklyn City's electrical-generating capability, both the 52nd Street powerhouse and a second one that was built later on Kent Avenue, see "The Power Stations of the Brooklyn City Railway," *Street Railway Journal* (October 1892): 598–613.

45. *New York Times,* 18 February 1892, 16.

46. *New York Times,* 6 March 1892, 16.

47. *New York Times,* 31 December 1892, 8.

48. See O. F. Nichols, "The Myrtle Avenue Improvement on the Brooklyn Elevated Railroad," *Transactions of the American Society of Civil*

Engineers 32 (October 1894): 363–388; "Grade Lowering on the Brooklyn Elevated," *Street Railway Journal* (September 1893): 573–574.

49. *New York Times,* 11 July 1892, 8.

50. *New York Times,* 15 August 1896, 8.

51. *Brooklyn Daily Eagle,* 15 November 1892, 1. The paper signaled its displeasure with this apparent turn of events by headlining the story "We're Being Driven Out."

52. *Brooklyn Daily Eagle,* 9 December 1892, 1.

53. *Brooklyn Daily Eagle,* 24 December 1892, 1.

54. "Not only was it the first strike since the trolley was introduced in Brooklyn, but it was the first general electric strike in the United States, and in magnitude it has never been surpassed by any street-car strike in any of the great cities, East or West." *Brooklyn Daily Eagle,* 15 January 1895, 1.

55. *New York Times,* 15 January 1895, 1.

56. *Brooklyn Daily Eagle,* 14 January 1895, 1.

57. In 1895, Brooklyn City purchased five double-truck electric streetcars from the J. G. Brill Company of Philadelphia. One-half of each car was equipped with seats for carrying passengers, while the other half was a closed-off section that was used for carrying U.S. mail. See Debra Brill, *History of the J. G. Brill Company* (Bloomington, Ind.: Indiana University Press, 2001), 66. Published rosters of Brooklyn streetcars note that the BRT later operated seven such railway post office cars, all built by Brill in 1895. See James G. Grolier and Edward B. Watson, *Brooklyn Trolleys* (East Norwich, N.Y.: N.J. International, 1986), 114–118; George T. F. Rahilly, "The Time of the Trolley in Brooklyn," *Headlights* 55 (January–February 1993): 2–15.

58. *New York Times,* 16 January 1895, 1, 2.

59. *Street Railway Journal* (February 1895): 104.

60. *New York Times,* 16 January 1895, 2.

61. The federal installation that was popularly called the Brooklyn Navy Yard was formally designated the New York Naval Shipyard. The U.S.S. *Castine* was 204 feet long and displaced 1,177 tons. She was launched at Bath Iron Works on May 11, 1892, and commissioned on October 22, 1894. She served through the First World War and was decommissioned in August 1919.

62. *Street Railway Journal* (March 1895): 163.

63. Ibid.

64. For an in-depth review of the construction of the Brooklyn Bridge, see David McCullough, *The Great Bridge* (New York: Simon & Schuster, 1972).

65. It is known that some of the original cars were thirty-six feet long

and subsequent orders were for fifty-foot cars. What is unclear is whether some, or all, of the thirty-six-footers were later rebuilt as fifty-foot cars, or if some of the original cars were fifty feet long from the outset. See Charles S. Small, "The Railway of the New York and Brooklyn Bridge," *Bulletin of the Railway and Locomotive Historical Society* 97 (October 1957): 7–20.

66. The bridge railway owned twelve different steam locomotives over the years, although not all at the same time. See Small, "The Railway of the New York and Brooklyn Bridge," 13.

67. According to figures released by the bridge trustees, the steam locomotives did 13 percent of the work and yet accounted for 56 percent of overall costs. See "The Reasons Why Electric Motors Will Be Used on the Bridge," *Street Railway Journal* (March 1896): 164–166.

68. *New York Times,* 3 November 1896, 8.

69. *Street Railway Journal* (February 1897): 73.

70. *New York Times,* 15 April 1890, 1.

71. *Street Railway Journal* (May 1892): 276.

72. *New York Times,* 16 February 1897, 12.

73. Manhattan Railways built a short spur down Park Row from Chatham Square to the Manhattan end of the Brooklyn Bridge for its Third Avenue El, and later added a second level to the spur for its Second Avenue El. On the Brooklyn end, the Kings County El had a transfer station to the south of the bridge railway's Sands Street station. It was a stop for trains bound to and from Fulton Ferry and also included a small stub-end terminal so other trains could begin and end their runs at the bridge. Brooklyn Union initially used a two-track, stub-end terminal that was built along Sands Street over and perpendicular to the bridge railway. Eventually a similar terminal along nearby High Street that had been intended for Kings County trains but never used by that company was joined with the Sands Street facility to create a loop terminal for Brooklyn Union.

74. *New York Times,* 14 September 1897. One of the people who advocated extending the Brooklyn Bridge railway to various lower Manhattan locations was William Barclay Parsons, the engineer who headed the team that designed and built New York's first subway. See "Parsons' Solution of Brooklyn Bridge Problem," *Street Railway Journal* (12 July 1902): 73–74.

75. Frank Sprague was a Naval Academy graduate who did more to foster the electrification of street and elevated railways than any other individual. He designed and implemented what is regarded as the world's first successful street railway electrification in Richmond, Virginia, in 1888. His later development of multiple-unit controls enabled

electric-powered elevated, subway, and railroad cars to be operated in tandem by one person from the lead car. For additional details, see Frank J. Sprague, "Some Personal Experiences," *Street Railway Journal* (8 October 1904): 566.

76. Bridge railway motor cars had third-rail shoes that were ten inches wide, while the shoes on BRT elevated cars could not be greater than eight inches in width. See *Street Railway Journal* (30 July 1905): 148–150.

77. I received this piece of intelligence in a handwritten note from the late George Krambles, the long-time general manager of the Chicago Transit Authority.

78. This was the second time Flower had to stand aside for Cleveland. In 1882, Flower and Henry Slocum were deadlocked in their pursuit of the Democratic nomination for governor and a state convention turned to Cleveland as a compromise candidate.

79. *New York Times,* 19 January 1896, 7.

80. *Street Railway Journal* (March 1895): 162–163.

81. *New York Times,* 19 March 1899, 12.

82. Ibid.

83. *New York Times,* 22 March 1899, 9.

84. *New York Times,* 14 April 1899, 10.

85. Ibid. There were actually two Brooklyn traction companies that remained outside the BRT fold in 1899, the Coney Island and Brooklyn and the Van Brunt Street and Erie Basin. The latter was a very small operation, though, and the accuracy of Flower's characterization need not be challenged.

86. Quoted in *Electric Railway Journal* (20 December 1915): 1053.

87. *New York Times,* 25 January 1893, 3.

88. *Brooklyn Daily Eagle,* 20 July 1891, 6.

89. Corbin hoped to build a four-track elevated line between East New York and Flatbush Avenue, with a two-track structure from there to South Ferry.

90. *New York Times,* 24 April 1891, 8. George Wingate was also associated with Frederick Uhlmann and Brooklyn Union.

91. For construction details about the project, see "Improvements on Atlantic Avenue, Brooklyn," *Street Railway Journal* (24 May 1902): 628–629; Vincent F. Seyfried, *The Long Island Rail Road: A Comprehensive History* (Garden City, N.Y.: Author, 1975), 7:24–42.

92. *Brooklyn Daily Eagle,* 8 March 1893, 7.

93. "The negotiations for a traffic agreement between the Brooklyn Rapid Transit Company and the Long Island Railroad have been successfully ended, and as has been previously predicted in these columns, the

formal contract has been executed by the officials of the two systems named." See *Brooklyn Daily Eagle,* 3 April 1899, 1. This news account contains full details of the agreement.

94. For an extremely clear and accurate description of these joint services, see Hugh A. Dunne, "In Traction There Is Always a Prototype," *Headlights* 28 (March 1966): 5–7.

95. For an account of Corbin's plan in his own words, see Austin Corbin, "Quick Transit between New York and London," *North American Review* 161 (November 1895): 513–527.

96. *Brooklyn Daily Eagle,* 8 October 1892, 4. The paper even wrote an editorial about the letter, saying that it "unites the strength of logic with the fervor of strong appeal on behalf of the view which it adopts."

97. In the early years of the twenty-first century, a new proposal has surfaced to build a rail tunnel to Brooklyn—perhaps from Staten Island, perhaps from New Jersey. Its purpose would be to ease congestion on the area's bridges and tunnels by shifting a measure of freight traffic from highways to rail.

98. For a detailed description of the West Fifth Street Depot when it was new, see "Coney Island Terminal of the Coney Island & Brooklyn Railroad," *Electric Railway Journal* (11 May 1912): 790–793.

99. For a short account of Huff's background at the time he joined CI&B, see *Street Railway Journal* (22 February 1908): 305.

100. *New York Times,* 1 January 1898, 2.

101. See McCullough, *Good Old Coney Island,* 296–300.

102. The Elephant Hotel included 34 rooms. Because guests of the establishment were often individuals in quest of illicit pleasures, "doing the elephant" emerged as a distinctive Coney Island expression. For a serious treatment of technical construction details, see "The Colossal Elephant of Coney Island," *Scientific American* (11 July 1885): 1, 21. The elephant was destroyed by fire in 1896.

103. In describing McKane's release from prison in April 1898 and his return to Coney Island, McCullough says: "Changed, he came back to a changed Coney Island. As for him, he was old and tired and embittered. As for his island, the fix was no longer in and his old gang had departed." McCullough, *Good Old Coney Island,* 112. McKane made an effort to enter the insurance business, but his health was failing. He passed away quietly in his sleep in September 1899.

104. The Saint Louis World's Fair of 1904 achieved immortality of its own when a fictional character played by movie actress Judy Garland urged a gentleman friend by the name of Louie to "Meet me in Saint Louis, Louie; Meet me at the fair."

105. For additional information on George Tilyou and the creation of

Steeplechase Park, see McCullough, *Good Old Coney Island,* 285–319;
Pilat and Ranson, *Sodom by the Sea,* 130–135.

CHAPTER 7

1. After the Second World War, the same facility was converted into
a bus depot. More recently, an essentially new bus depot has been built
on the site. It is named in honor of television personality Jackie Gleason,
to commemorate Gleason's role as bus driver Ralph Cramden in *The
Honeymooners.* For information on the initial conversion from Union
Depot to rail car repair facility, see "The Elevated Shops and Terminals
of the Brooklyn Rapid Transit Company—the Thirty Sixth Street Inspection Plant," *Street Railway Journal* (9 March 1907): 407–414
2. For additional details, see Fausser, *The Sea Beach to Coney Island,* 50–56.
3. Under the BRT, Sea Beach trolley service also connected with
the Fifth Avenue El at Third Avenue and 59th Street.
4. For additional details about the last Kings County railway enterprise to include the words South Brooklyn in its title, see Karl F. Groh,
"The South Brooklyn Railway," *Headlights* 55 (May–June 1993): 3–12.
5. *Street Railway Journal* (13 August 1904): 22.
6. Ibid.
7. For details on the conversion of this facility, see "New Repair
Shops of the Brooklyn Rapid Transit Company," *Street Railway Journal*
(13 December 1902): 954–957.
8. One of the experimental cars, no. 999, was long used as an in-
struction car for the training of BRT personnel. Another, no. 998, was
later converted into a trash-collection car. See *Street Railway Journal*
(1906): 162–165. See also James C. Greller and Edward B. Watson, *The
Brooklyn Elevated* (Hicksville, N.Y.: N.J. International, 1988), 118–119.
9. For additional details about the 1905-built 1300-series elevated
cars, see "New Semi-Convertible Cars with Steel Underframes, for the
Brooklyn Rapid Transit Company," *Street Railway Journal* (6 May 1905):
804–811. For information on the BRT's program of rebuilding and stand-
ardizing older elevated equipment, see "Extensive Improvement in Elevated Car Equipments [sic]—Brooklyn Rapid Transit Company," *Street
Railway Journal* (13 August 1904): 221–223. The BRT also adopted a standard truck, built by the Peckham Manufacturing Company of Kingston,
New York, for its elevated equipment. See "M.C.B. Trucks for Brooklyn
Elevated Railway," *Street Railway Journal* (20 June 1903): 911–912.
10. *New York Times,* 12 August 1909, 16.

11. *Electric Railway Journal* (19 March 1910): 490. For additional details, see "Cost of Carrying Passengers to Coney Island," *Street Railway Journal* (30 May 1908): 888–889.

12. For details about the creation of the Public Service Commission for the First District and its unique jurisdiction, see James Blaine Walker, *State Regulation of Public Service Corporations in the City of New York* (New York: Public Service Commission for the First District, 1911).

13. "Street Railway Riots in Brooklyn," *Street Railway Journal* (18 August 1906): 277.

14. "An Improved Terminal for Handling the Heavy Coney Island Crowds—Brooklyn Rapid Transit Company," *Street Railway Journal* (11 June 1904): 884–889.

15. For details of this project, see "The Brighton Beach Improvement of the Brooklyn Heights Railroad," *Street Railway Journal* (11 May 1907): 830–833. Kings Highway—in the twenty-first century an important station on three of the four transit lines that serve Coney Island—is an old and venerable Kings County thoroughfare that was laid out in 1704 and was long the only road people from points in Brooklyn's Eastern District could travel if their final destination was Coney Island. For an interesting reflection on this roadway's history, see "To Close a Portion of an Historic Road," *Brooklyn Daily Eagle*, 1 April 1900, 6.

16. Following its reconstruction, the right-of-way of the NY&MB was located immediately adjacent to the Brighton Line all the way from Manhattan Beach Junction to Sheepshead Bay. Prior to this project, portions of the NY&MB right-of-way were several blocks to the east of the Brighton Line.

17. For details, see "The Franklin Avenue Improvement of the Brighton Beach Line of the Brooklyn Rapid Transit Company," *Street Railway Journal* (22 June 1907): 1104–1107.

18. *Street Railway Journal* (21 March 1903): 451.

19. For details, see "A Plan to Reduce Congestion on the Brooklyn Elevated," *Street Railway Journal* (1 June 1901): 665.

20. *Street Railway Journal* (1 June 1901): 665–666.

21. *Street Railway Journal* (30 March 1901): 376

22. *Street Railway Journal* (8 December 1906): 1103.

23. For general information on the advent of the Interborough subway, see Brian J. Cudahy, *Under the Sidewalks of New York*, 2nd rev. ed. (New York: Fordham University Press, 1995). More complete details may be found in Clifton Hood, *722 Miles* (New York: Simon & Schuster, 1993). For a reprint of a book published by the Interborough in 1904 to commemorate the opening of New York's first subway, see Interborough Rapid Transit Company, *The New York Subway: Its Construction and Equipment* (New York: Fordham University Press, 1991).

24. The name Joralemon Street Tunnel has become the common designation for this first rapid transit crossing of the East River. When it was new, however, it was often called the Brooklyn-Battery Tunnel, a name that would later be appropriated by an automobile tunnel linking Brooklyn and lower Manhattan,

25. For in-depth information about the Dual Contracts, including an extensive bibliography, see Peter Derrick, *Tunneling to the Future: The Story of the Great Subway Expansion that Saved New York* (New York: New York University Press, 2001).

26. Placing the West End Line on an elevated structure brought an end to multiple routings that the line had previously enjoyed in the Bath Beach area. The new elevated structure was built over New Utrecht Avenue, 86th Street, and Stillwell Avenue. Prior to the Dual Contracts, surface-running trains were able to use Bath Avenue as an alternate to 86th Street.

27. When the company developed a distinctive route map of its new rapid transit system, the graphics included a visual distinction between "subway" and "elevated" service. Below-grade portions of the Brighton and Sea Beach lines—out of doors and open air—were shown as if they were bona fide subway services.

28. *Electric Railway Journal* (25 April 1916): 514.

29. Somewhat similar concrete construction may also be found at various stations on Interborough elevated lines that were built under the terms of the Dual Contracts.

30. The new BRT cars were described in a series of articles in the *Electric Railway Journal*. See "Public Inspection of Proposed Brooklyn Subway Car," *Electric Railway Journal* (27 September 1913): 503; "The New York Municipal Car—Design," *Electric Railway Journal* (6 June 1914): 1261–1267; "The New York Municipal Car—Body," *Electric Railway Journal* (13 June 1914): 1327–1333; "The New York Municipal Car—Trucks, Brake Rigging and Draft Gear," *Electric Railway Journal* (26 December 1914): 1376–1381.

31. Operating rules prohibited BX units from crossing the Manhattan Bridge in passenger service since they featured fewer motors than conventional rolling stock and were likely to disrupt schedules. Because Manhattan Bridge service was such an important part of Southern Division operations, BX units spent most of their days assigned to the company's Eastern Division.

32. The Centre Street Loop began at the Manhattan end of the Williamsburg Bridge and proceeded south to a major terminal station at Chambers Street under the Municipal Building. Original plans called for the line to achieve "loop" characteristics by returning to Brooklyn over

the Brooklyn Bridge from this point. The Dual Contracts changed these plans, and the Centre Street Loop would continue south through the downtown financial district under Nassau and Broad streets and connect with a new BRT East River crossing called the Montague Street Tunnel. The BRT's principal Manhattan trunk line was not this Centre Street Loop, but a north-south subway under Broadway that eventually tunneled back under the East River to Queens.

33. Some of the modifications included the installation of then-novel illuminated line and destination signs, as well as color codes to indicate whether a given train was operating over the Manhattan Bridge (green) or through the Montague Street Tunnel (white). The D units were used exclusively on the company's Southern Division, where for many years they were the exclusive rolling stock used for Sea Beach Express service, while the rest of the D units shared Brighton Line assignments with conventional A/B units. The *Electric Railway Journal* devoted five special articles to describing these novel new subway cars. See "Articulated Cars in Subway Service" (19 September 1925): 425–428; "Four 200-Hp. Motors on Articulated Cars" (31 October 1925): 773–778; "Novel Devices Give Uniform Braking on B.-M.T. Articulated Cars" (28 November 1925): 951–954; "Flexible Door Control Is Provided on the B.-M.T. Articulated Cars" (19 December 1925): 1069–1072; "Improved Auxiliary Devices Installed on B.-M.T. Articulated Cars" (26 December 1925): 1107–1110. For an analysis by William G. Gove, the BMT's Superintendent of Equipment and the man most responsible for the development of the D unit, see "Cars for Rapid Transit Mass Transportation," *Electric Railway Journal* (4 July 1925): 16–19.

34. *Street Railway Journal* (October 1901): 639.

35. *New York Times,* 29 September 1908, sec. II, p. 10.

36. *Street Railway Journal* (16 November 1907): 984–985.

37. See "A New Car House for Brooklyn of Novel Design," *Street Railway Journal* (3 August 1901): 120–122.

38. For additional technical details about the design and construction of streetcars, including the adoption of such betterments as air brakes, see William D. Middleton, *The Time of the Trolley: The Street Railway from Horsecar to Light Rail* (San Marino, Calif.: Golden West, 1987), 216–224.

39. See "Modernizing 2,411 Cars," *Electric Railway Journal* (31 October 1914): 995–998.

40. For technical information about experimental car no. 3557, see "All-Steel Center-Entrance Car for Brooklyn," *Electric Railway Journal* (30 March 1912): 502–503; "The Brooklyn Center-Entrance Car," *Electric Railway Journal* (22 June 1912): 1066–1071.

41. For technical information about production model center-entrance streetcars, see "Center-Entrance Cars for Brooklyn," *Electric Railway Journal* (17 April 1913): 708–709.

42. For further discussion of the question of the honesty of street railway conductors, see Brian J. Cudahy, *Cash, Tokens and Transfers* (New York: Fordham University Press, 1990), 15–21.

43. Had this Interborough extension to Coney Island been constructed, it would have represented a reasonable re-creation of the Kings County Central Railroad of 1878 (see chapter 4).

44. For additional details about the relationship between the Malbone Street Wreck and the BRT bankruptcy, see Brian J. Cudahy, *The Malbone Street Wreck* (New York: Fordham University Press, 1999).

45. Tony Hiss, "Annals of Transportation; Light Rail," *The New Yorker* (6 March 1989): 70–90.

46. *Report on the Surface Railway System of the Brooklyn Rapid Transit System* (New York: Stone & Webster, 1919).

47. For technical information about Brooklyn City's 8000-series cars, see *Electric Railway Journal* (27 June 1925), 1003–1007. For a wonderfully personal retrospective about the same cars—and the Brooklyn neighborhoods they served—see Stan Fischler, *Confessions of a Trolley Dodger from Brooklyn* (Flushing, N.Y.: H&M Productions, 1995). See also James C. Greller and Edward B. Watson, *Brooklyn Trolleys* (Hicksville, N.Y.: N.J. International, 1986), 56–65.

48. For a sequence of newspaper articles describing developments leading up to the BMT's acquisition of "Brooklyn City II," see *New York Times,* 8 January 1929, 25; 14 February 1929, 20; 5 June 1929, 60; 8 June 1929, 19.

49. Before the acquisition of the 8000-series cars, a fleet of 200 7000-series cars joined the BRT fleet in 1918. These were smaller, single-truck cars of a new design called the Birney Safety Car. Birney cars did not prove very successful in Brooklyn service and all were off the property before the Second World War.

50. Stopping marks for Sea Beach and West End services used the same colors as the marker lights for these services, white-red and white-green, respectively. The Brighton Express used red-green marker lights, but its stopping marks were black letters on a white background.

51. For details on the design and construction of the IND, see Frederick A. Kramer, *Building the Independent Subway* (New York: Quadrant, 1990).

52. For a discussion of the IND's relationship with the older transit companies, see Hood, *722 Miles,* 214–239; Derrick, *Tunneling to the Future,* 237–244.

53. *New York Times,* 20 April 1932, 46.

54. Meseck Line's principal excursion service was between New York and a Westchester County amusement park on the shore of Long Island Sound called Playland, in Rye Beach. "Cruise to Playland, Rye" was long Meseck's advertising slogan. Unlike Coney Island, whose amusement area underwent substantial change during the final half of the twentieth century, Playland has retained a timeless character, save for the absence of excursion boats that once brought patrons there from New York.

55. *New York Times,* 3 February 1933, 16.

56. McCullough suggests that Tilyou deliberately proposed a less-than-satisfactory contract extension to Thompson and Dundy so they would venture out on their own, take over Boyton's property, and expand entertainment options on Coney Island. See McCullough, *Good Old Coney Island,* 303–304.

57. *New York Times,* 29 July 1907, 1, 3.

58. Quoted in Richard Snow, *Coney Island: A Postcard Journey to the City of Fire* (New York: Brightwaters, 1984), 67.

59. For news reports of the Dreamland fire, see *New York Times,* 27 May 1911, 1; 28 May 1911, 1. McCullough provides a unique, first-person account, as he was a youngster living in Coney Island on the night Dreamland burned down. See McCullough, *Good Old Coney Island,* 204–233. For a later analysis from the perspective of a professional FDNY firefighter, see John P. Cunningham, "Dreamland Park Fire," *WNYF* (April 1946): 24–27.

60. *New York Times,* 9 May 1923, 6.

61. *New York Times,* 23 October 1921, sec. XII, p. 1. Hulbert's proposal may have been prescient in that it called for the first level of the huge dock to be used as a public parking garage.

62. For additional information about thoroughbred horse racing in Coney Island, see McCullough, *Good Old Coney Island,* 127–153; Pilat and Ranson, *Sodom by the Sea,* 66–79.

CHAPTER 8

1. The City of New York's Corporation Counsel issued a ruling in 1937 that, under the provisions of a new city charter, jurisdiction over beaches and boardwalks must be transferred to the Department of Parks. Previously administered by the various borough presidents, the change in status was effective January 1, 1938.

2. *New York Times,* 8 December 1937, 24.

3. Ibid.

4. *New York Times,* 13 July 1899, 14.

5. Transmittal letter from Robert Moses to Mayor Fiorello H. La-Guardia, published in *The Improvement of Coney Island, Rockaway and South Beaches* (New York: Department of Parks, 1937), 3–8.

6. The largest single-day's crowd in the history of Steeplechase Park was slightly more than 18,000 people on Saturday, September 16, 1961. On this same day, there were several hundred thousand visitors elsewhere on Coney Island, most of whom were there simply to spend the day on the beach. See James J. Onorato, *Steeplechase Park, Coney Island, 1928–1964: The Diary of James J. Onorato* (Bellingham, Wash.: Pacific Rim Books, 1997), 4: 241, 420.

7. Letter from Moses, in *The Improvement of Coney Island, Rockaway and South Beaches,* 3–8.

8. The definitive treatment of Moses is that of Robert A. Caro, *The Power Broker* (New York: Random House, 1975). Caro's thesis with respect to Moses is evident in his subtitle, "Robert Moses and the Fall of New York."

9. For an account of this revised plan, see *New York Times,* 21 August 1939, 15.

10. For basic details about this new roadway, see *The Belt Parkway* (New York: Department of Parks, 1940). Building a 34.9-mile parkway from the Bronx-Whitestone Bridge to Owl's Head in Bay Ridge cost $29.9 million, $12 million of which was a grant from the federal government. Initially, the Department of Parks believed that sections of the Belt Parkway would be separately named and identified with graphics in a distinctive color. Thus, the segment from Owl's Head to Woodhaven Boulevard was known as the Shore Parkway (red), from Woodhaven Boulevard to Sunrise Highway was called the Southern Parkway (blue), and the final leg from there to the Bronx-Whitestone Bridge was the Cross Island Parkway (green). A section that was not ready in 1940, from Owl's Head to the also incomplete Brooklyn-Battery Tunnel, would be called the Gowanus Parkway.

11. *New York Times,* 30 August 1936, sec. VII, p. 8.

12. *New York Times,* 18 July 1939, 21.

13. *New York Times,* 25 July 1939, 18.

14. For information on the municipal takeover of both the Interborough and the BMT, see Cudahy, *Under the Sidewalks of New York,* 115–122; Hood, *722 Miles,* 224–239.

15. The precise sections of BMT elevated lines subject to condemna-

tion proceedings included the Fulton Street Line from Brooklyn Bridge to Rockaway Avenue; the Fifth Avenue Line from Myrtle and Hudson to Third Avenue and 38th Street; and the Broadway Ferry spur from Marcy Avenue to Broadway Ferry. The condemnation order was signed on April 30, 1940, by Justice Charles C. Lockwood. See *New York Herald Tribune,* 1 May 1940, 8. The 65th Street extension of the Fifth Avenue El was not part of the formal condemnation proceedings. Although it would no longer be used for rapid transit purposes, its support pillars would be incorporated into the Gowanus Parkway.

16. The BMT did design and purchase a small fleet of new, lightweight rapid transit cars that could operate over sections of its older, elevated lines where conventional, heavyweight subway equipment was prohibited. Using the same principal of articulation that was pioneered in the D units, it acquired twenty-five five-section units in 1936. Because they were built of metal, they could also operate in subway tunnels, where wooden equipment was banned. Primarily assigned to the 14th Street-Canarsie Line in the BMT's Eastern Division, they were also used in a joint rush-hour service that linked the 14th Street subway and the outer end of the Fulton Street El. For more details, see Cudahy, *Under the Sidewalks of New York,* 108–111.

17. For complete details on the development of the PCC car, see Stephen P. Carlson and Fred W. Schneider, *PCC: The Car That Fought Back* (Glendale, Calif.: Interurban Press, 1980).

18. *New York Times,* 28 September 1938, 29. Mayor LaGuardia was not enamoured of trolley cars, whatever their vintage. When legal proceedings were under way to condemn the Brooklyn Els, the mayor was quoted as saying; "There's another thing I want to see removed in Brooklyn when these 'Els' come down. That's the trolley lines." *New York Herald Tribune,* 1 May 1940, 8.

19. I offer a factual parallel here as pure speculation. The Chicago Surface Lines acquired a fleet of 683 new PCC cars in the 1930s and 1940s. Despite the investment it represented, when the system became part of the publicly operated Chicago Transit Authority in 1945, the still-new streetcars were "traded in" toward the purchase of new rapid transit cars, with substantial portions of their components used to build the new transit cars. For details, see Brian J. Cudahy, *Destination: Loop* (Brattleboro, Vt.: The Stephen Greene Press, 1982), 70–73.

20. For a pictorial treatment of the New York World's Fair of 1939–40, see Larry Zim, Mel Lerner, and Herbert Rolfes, *The World of Tomorrow* (New York: Harper & Row, 1988).

21. James J. Onorato, *Steeplechase Park, Coney Island, 1928–1964;*

The Diary of James J. Onorato, ed. Michael P. Onorato (Bellingham, Wash.: Pacific Rim Books, 1997), 39.

22. The Parachute was always promoted as a ride that was 250 feet high. Various navigational charts for the waters off Coney Island, and the air space above it, use the figure 305 feet in describing the tower.

23. For details on the 1939 fire, see James J. Onorato, *Steeplechase Park, Coney Island, 1928–1964,* 1: 346, note 140. Notes were prepared by the editor of this series, Michael P. Onorato.

24. Because of these uniforms, workers on the rides at Steeplechase were commonly referred to as "red coats." James J. Onorato, the long-time general manager of Steeplechase would typically say things like, "I better send a few extra red coats over to work on the Bowery gate."

25. Because of the extraordinary fire threat that the amusement area represented, Coney Island was the only place in the city outside of Manhattan and downtown Brooklyn where FDNY installed a high-pressure hydrant system. The Coney Island system was originally installed in 1905 and was connected to a pumping station on the shore of Gravesend Bay. While high-pressure systems in Manhattan and downtown Brooklyn used city water, the Coney Island network relied on salt water pumped from the bay. In the event that the pumping station became disabled, the station included provisions so fire boats could tie up and use their pumps to energize the high-pressure system. For additional details, see Robert A. McDermott, "High Pressure," *WNYF* (January 1945): 24–27. The Coney Island high-pressure system was substantially rebuilt in 1937, including a completely new pumping station. During a devastating blaze along the boardwalk in July 1932, the high-pressure system essentially failed. The Coney Island high-pressure system also failed at the time of the Dreamland fire in 1911.

26. The aide to Batallion Chief Carberry mentioned in the text was my father, John J. Cudahy. I myself vividly recall seeing smoke from the Luna Park fire swirling skyward. I was getting a haircut at the time in a bungalow colony called Roxbury across Jamaica Bay from Coney Island. My father always regarded the Luna Park fire as the most severe blaze he ever worked. On the other hand, an FDNY deputy chief by the name of Tom Lyons, whom my father later served, felt that the 1911 Dreamland fire was the most severe fire he ever worked.

27. For further information about the Luna Park fire, see Martin Carrig and John P. Cunningham, "Flames Strike Luna Park," *WNYF* (October 1944): 4–6; for a news account, see *New York Times,* 13 August 1944, 1, 34.

28. *New York Times,* 14 August 1944, 16.

CHAPTER 9

1. The bridle path along Ocean Parkway connected with a network of similar paths inside Prospect Park, making it possible to travel by horseback from Grand Army Plaza to Coney Island.

2. Nassau Electric once held a franchise under which its Sea Gate Line might well have been extended into Flatlands in much the same fashion as the Surf Avenue Route later was.

3. With the new arrangement, the Board of Transportation placed an old, out-of-service Brooklyn streetcar, no. 3740, at Park Row to serve as a waiting room for trolley passengers.

4. Trolley coach service was instituted on the Cortelyou Road Route in two phases. Two trolley coaches were purchased in 1930 and service was inaugurated between Flatbush Avenue and Coney Island Avenue. In 1932, six additional vehicles were acquired and service was extended to 62nd Street and New Utrecht Avenue.

5. Evidence for this suggestion is the fact that when the 200 new Saint Louis Car Company trolley coaches were delivered, their line and destination signs included readings for a variety of routes such as Ocean Avenue that were not then part of the trolley coach network—and, as matters turned out, never would be.

6. For additional information about the South Brooklyn Railway, see Karl F. Groh, "The South Brooklyn Railway," *Headlights* 55 (May–June 1993): 3–12.

7. The design of the Navy's LCI(L) class landing craft lent itself to a variety of civilian conversions after the war. It was very simply built and relied on a wide range of routine components. The LCI(L) was powered, for instance, by eight diesel engines of the kind typically used in mass transit buses. New York's Circle Line was still operating three ex-LCI(L)s in its Manhattan Island sightseeing service in the early years of the twenty-first century. For more details, see Brian J. Cudahy, *Around Manhattan Island and Other Maritime Tales of New York* (New York: Fordham University Press, 1997), 1–46, 225–240.

8. For a discussion of Steeplechase's role as an "anchor," see Michael P. Onorato, "Epilogue," in McCullough, *Good Old Coney Island*, 339–352.

9. See Michael P. Onorato's preface to a volume of his father's diaries for the years after Steeplechase closed. *Life without Steeplechase Park: The Diaries and Papers of James J. Onorato: 1967–1971* (Bellingham, Wash.: Pacific Rim Books, 2000), vii–xvii.

10. For the sad story of the destruction of the Pavilion of Fun, see

Michael P. Onorato, *Steeplechase Park: Destruction of the Pavilion of Fun, 1966* (Bellingham, Wash.: Pacific Rim Books, 1998).

11. There was also an indoor pool at Steeplechase, inside the Pavilion of Fun at the ocean end of the building. It was closed at the end of the 1928 season, and various rides were built over it.

12. For a discussion of this Steeplechase policy, see Michael P. Onorato, "A Conversation with My Father," in *Another Time, Another World: Coney Island Memories* (Fullerton, Calif.: The Oral History Program, 2000), 79.

BIBLIOGRAPHY

"An Improved Terminal for Handling the Heavy Coney Island Crowds—Brooklyn Rapid Transit Company." *Street Railway Journal* 23 (June 11, 1904): 884–888.

Armbruster, Eugene L. *Brooklyn's Eastern District* (Brooklyn, N.Y.: Author, 1942).

Arnoux, George V. "Manhattan Bridge Three-Cent Line." *Electric Railroads* 32 (December 1962): 1–8.

"Boynton Bicycle Railway System; 1891." Brochure issued by the company in 1891. Reprint, Americana Foundation, Inc., 1953.

"The Bridge Transportation System between Brooklyn and New York." *Street Railway Journal* 13 (February 1897): 69–80.

Brill, Debra. *History of the J. G. Brill Company.* Bloomington, Ind.: Indiana University Press, 2001.

Brooklyn Daily Eagle.

Brooklyn Rapid Transit Company. *President's First Annual Report to Stockholders.* Brooklyn, N.Y.: 1899.

"Brooklyn Street Railways." *Street Railway Journal* (May 1892): 272–276.

"Brooklyn's Urgent Need: An Outline of the Rapid Transit Situation." *New York Times,* 19 December 1886, 6.

Condit, Carl W. *The Port of New York: A History of the Rail and Terminal System from the Grand Central Electrification to the Present.* Chicago: University of Chicago Press, 1981.

"Cost of Carrying Passengers to Coney Island." *Street Railway Journal* 31 (30 May 1908): 889–891.

Cudahy, Brian J. *Around Manhattan Island and Other Maritime Tales of New York.* New York: Fordham University Press, 1997.

———. *The Malbone Street Wreck.* New York: Fordham University Press, 1999.

———. *Under the Sidewalks of New York.* 2nd rev. ed. New York: Fordham University Press, 1995).

Cunningham, Joseph, and Leonard De Hart. *Rapid Transit in Brooklyn.* New York: Authors, 1977.

Dayton, Fred Erving. *Steamboat Days.* New York: Tudor, 1925.

Denson, Charles. *Coney Island Walking Tour: Map and Guide.* Berkeley, Calif.: Dreamland Press, 1998.

Derrick, Peter. "Catalyst for Development: Rapid Transit in New York." *New York Affairs* 9 (Fall 1986): 29–59.

———. *Tunneling to the Future: The Story of the Great Subway Expansion That Saved New York.* New York: New York University Press, 2001.

"Done At Last; The Brooklyn Elevated Road Ready for the Public." *Brooklyn Daily Eagle,* 13 May 1885, 1.

"Elevated Railway Cars for Brooklyn." *Street Railway Journal* (1 December 1900): 1189–1190.

"The Elevated Shops and Terminals of the Brooklyn Rapid Transit Company—The Thirty-Sixth Street Inspection Plant." *Street Railway Journal* (9 March 1907): 407–414.

"Extensive Improvements in Elevated Car Equipments [sic] —Brooklyn Rapid Transit Company." *Street Railway Journal* 24 (13 August 1904): 222–228.

Fausser, William W. *The Sea Beach to Coney Island.* Mineola, N.Y.: Author, 1979.

Fischler, Stan. *Confessions of a Trolley Dodger from Brooklyn.* Flushing, N.Y.: H&M Productions, 1995.

Greller, James C., and Edward B. Watson. *The Brooklyn Elevated.* Hicksville, N.Y.: N.J. International, 1988.

———. *Brooklyn Trolleys.* Hicksville, N.Y.: N.J. International, 1986.

Groh, Karl. "Above the Streets of Brooklyn." *Headlights* 37 (September–November 1975): 2–20.

Harold, Donald W., Arthur J. Lonto, Robert L. Presbrey, and Edward B. Watson. "20 Years Ago in Brooklyn." *Headlights* 22 (June 1960): 1–3.

Heyl, Erik. *Early American Steamers.* 7 vols. Buffalo, N.Y.: Author, 1956–1969.

Hilton, George W. *American Narrow Gauge Railroads.* Stanford, Calif.: Stanford University Press, 1990.

———. *The Cable Car in America.* Stanford, Calif.: Stanford University Press, 1982, 1997.

Hinsdale, E. B. *History of the Long Island Railroad Company: 1834–1898*. New York: Evening Post Job Printing House, 1898.

The History of Coney Island from Its First Discovery Down to Last Night. New York: Morrison, Richardson, 1878.

Hood, Clifton. *722 Miles*. New York: Simon & Schuster, 1993.

Ieradi, Eric J. *Gravesend Brooklyn: Coney Island and Sheepshead Bay*. Dover, N.H.: Arcadia, 1996.

Interborough Rapid Transit Company. *The New York Subway: Its Construction and Equipment*. 1904. Reprint, New York: Fordham University Press, 1991.

Johnson, Donald S. *Charting the Sea of Darkness: The Four Voyages of Henry Hudson*. Camden, Maine: International Marine, 1993.

Kahn, Alan Paul, and Jack May. *The Tracks of New York*. No. 2: *Brooklyn Elevated Railroads*. New York: Electric Railroaders' Association, 1977.

Latimer, Margaret, ed. *Brooklyn Almanac*. Brooklyn, N.Y.: Brooklyn Educational and Cultural Alliance, 1984.

Manbeck, John B., ed. *The Neighborhoods of Brooklyn*. New Haven, Conn.: Yale University Press, 1998.

McCullough, Edo. *Good Old Coney Island: A Sentimental Journey into the Past*. New York: Fordham University Press, 2000.

"New Semi-Convertible Cars with Steel Underframes for the Brooklyn Rapid Transit Company." *Street Railway Journal* 25 (6 May 1905): 804–811.

"The New York Municipal Car—Body." *Electric Railway Journal* 43 (13 June 1914): 1327–1333.

"The New York Municipal Car—Design." *Electric Railway Journal* 43 (6 June 1914): 1261–1267.

"The New York Municipal Car—Trucks, Brake Rigging and Draft Gear." *Electric Railway Journal* 44 (26 December 1914): 1376–1381.

New York Times.

Onorato, James J. *Life without Steeplechase Park; The Diary and Papers of James J. Onorato, 1967–1971*. Edited by Michael P. Onorato. Bellingham, Wash.: Pacific Rim Books, 2000.

———. *Steeplechase Park, Coney Island, 1928–1964; The Diary of James J. Onorato*. 4 vols. Edited by Michael P. Onorato. Bellingham, Wash.: Pacific Rim Books, 1997.

———. *Steeplechase Park, Sale and Closure, 1965–66; The Diary and Papers of James J. Onorato.* Edited by Michael P. Onorato. Bellingham, Wash.: Pacific Rim Books, 1998.

Onorato, Michael P. *Another Time, Another World: Coney Island Memories.* Fullerton, Calif.: Oral History Program, California State University, 2000.

———. *Steeplechase Park, Demolition of the Pavilion of Fun, 1966.* Bellingham, Wash.: Pacific Rim Books, 1998.

Percy, Townsend. *Percy's Pocket Dictionary of Coney Island.* New York: Leypoldt, 1880.

Pilat, Oliver, and Jo Ranson. *Sodom by the Sea: An Affectionate History of Coney Island.* New York: Doubleday, Doran, 1941.

Public Service Commission for the First District. *New Subways for New York; The Dual System of Rapid Transit.* New York: Public Service Commission, 1913.

Rahilly, George. "The Time of the Trolley in Brooklyn." *Headlights* 55 (January–February 1993): 2–15.

———. "The Wooden Cars of the Brooklyn Elevated Railroads." *Headlights* 56 (July–August 1994): 2–13.

Redding, George C. P. "1951—Year of Disaster." *Trolley Talk* 252 (2001): 2–8; 253 (2001): 2–7.

Report of the Annual Meeting of the Street-Railway Association of the State of New York. Brooklyn, N.Y.: Annually, from 1884.

Seyfried, Vincent F. *Brooklyn Rapid Transit Trolley Lines in Queens.* East Norwich, N.Y.: N.J. International, 1998.

———. *The Long Island Rail Road: A Comprehensive History.* 7 vols. Garden City, N.Y.: Author, 1961–1975).

Seyfried, Vincent, and William Asadorian. *Old Rockaway, New York in Early Photographs.* Mineola, N.Y.: Dover, 2000.

Small, Charles S. "The Railway of the New York and Brooklyn Bridge." *Bulletin of the Railway and Locomotive Historical Society* 97 (October 1957): 7–20.

Smith, Mildred H. *Early History of the Long Island Railroad: 1834–1900.* Uniondale, N.Y.: Salisbury, 1958.

Snyder-Grenier, Ellen M. *Brooklyn: An Illustrated History.* Philadelphia: Temple University Press, 1996.

Stanton, Samuel Ward. *American Steam Vessels.* New York: Smith and Stanton, 1895.

———. *New York Bay Steam Vessels.* American Steam Vessels Series. Meriden, Conn.: Meriden Graveur, 1968.

Stiles, Henry R. *History of the City of Brooklyn.* 3 vols. Albany and Brooklyn, N.Y.: 1869–1870.

Stone and Webster, "Report on the Surface Railway System of the Brooklyn Rapid Transit Company." New York, 1919.

"Test of a 5-Cent Coney Island Fare." *Street Railway Journal* 38 (29 July 1911): 181–182.

Wall, A. J. "The Sylvan Steamboats on the East River: New York to Harlem." *The New-York Historical Society Quarterly Bulletin* 7 (October 1924): 59–72.

Watson, Edward B. "One Hundred Years of Street Railways in Brooklyn, 1854–1964." *Headlights* 16 (July 1954): 1–5.

White, John H. Jr. "Spunky Little Devils: Locomotives of the New York Elevated." *Railroad History* 162 (Spring 1990): 20–79.

Younger, William Lee. *Old Brooklyn in Early Photographs, 1865–1929.* New York: Dover, 1978.

INDEX

Unless noted otherwise, street, section and neighborhood designations refer to Brooklyn and/or Kings County locations, while citations rendered in italics, unless specified otherwise, are the names of vessels.

AB units, 217, 288
accidents: collision at Myrtle and Hudson (1888), 116, 118; *General Slocum* disaster (1904), 40; horsecar into Gowanus Canal (1863), 29; Malbone Street wreck (1918), 227
Adams Street, 116, 165
Albany, N.Y., 13–14, 27, 169, 170, 251
all-service vehicles, 271–72. *See also* trolley coaches
Amalgamated Association of Street Railway Employees of America, 153
amalgamation of Greater New York, 14, 124, 183–86
Ambrose Channel, 3, 180
America Car and Foundry Company (ACF), 217, 218–19, 288, 291
American Street Railway Association (ASRA), 46, 258, 310
American Transit Association (ATA), 258
Americus, 55, 59
amusement parks, 21, 124, 186–189, 243–245; early development, 21, 186–189; world's first, 187. *See also* Astroland, Dreamland Park, Luna Park, Sea Lion Park, Steeplechase Park
articulation/articulated railway equipment, 218–19, 288, 290–91
Ashland Place connection, 227
Astroland, 9, 285
at-grade railway construction, 120, 176, 192, 199–200
Atlantic Avenue, 37, 43–44, 45–46, 89, 105, 106, 134, 135, 148, 176, 177

Atlantic Avenue elevated line, 105, 134, 177
Atlantic Avenue ferryslip, 45. *See also* South Ferry
Atlantic Avenue Rapid Transit Commission, 177
Atlantic Avenue R.R., 35, 43–47, 75, 76, 125, 129, 131, 133–34, 136–37, 140–41, 145, 152–55, 157, 175
Atlantic Ocean, 3, 13, 36, 57, 75, 230
A units, 217, 288
Avenue A and 14th Street Line (Manhattan), 220
Avenue H, 82, 199
Avenue U, 220, 268

Babcock and Wilcox, 136
Baldwin, William H., 180
Baldwin Locomotive Works, 31
Baltimore and Ohio R.R., 62, 181
B&QT. *See* Brooklyn and Queens Transit Corp.
Barnaby, Frank, 143
Bartel Pritchard Square, 272
Bath Beach, 68, 73, 131
Bath Junction, 82, 93, 94, 193, 170
Battery Park/the Battery (Manhattan), 12, 243, 283
battery-powered trains/battery power, 203–4
Bay Ridge, 26, 55, 77, 81, 83, 93, 94, 96, 105, 116, 177–78, 266–67
Bay Ridge Branch (of LIRR), 199–200, 206
Beach, George R., 240
beaches, development at Coney Island, 4, 19–20, 285

Gravesend Bay, 9, 12, 13, 50, 68, 99, 282
Great Depression, 237
Greater New York, 15, 173, 177, 183–86, 207
Greatsinger, J. L., 204–5
Greenpoint, 26, 32, 83, 85, 226
Greenpoint and Lorimer R.R., 34, 175
Greenport, N.Y., 43, 44
Greenwood, 29, 76, 112
Green-wood Cemetery, 68, 73, 77, 137, 272, 275
Gunther, C. Godfrey, 70, 81, 93, 94
gut, the, 222

Half Moon Hotel, 21
Halliday, Thomas, 128, 309
Hallidie, Andrew S., 309
Halsey Street Depot, 206
Hamburg Avenue Line, 132
Hamilton Avenue, 29, 30, 36, 37
Hamilton Ferry, 37
Harlan and Hollingsworth, 120
Harlem River, 282
Harrison, President Benjamin, 118
Hazzard, William H., 30
Hearst, William Randolph, 198
Hicks Street, 126, 155
Highlands Navigation Company, 63
Hilton, George W., 84–85, 305, 308–9
Hinsdale, Elizabeth, 44
Hooker, General Joseph, 39
horsecars/horse-drawn streetcars, 24–48, 35, 131; first in the United States, 24; first in Brooklyn, 25–26
Howell, Mayor James, 105–6, 113, 161–62
Hudson Avenue, 78, 116, 201, 256
Hudson River, 14, 56, 66, 242, 263
Hudson River Day Line, 65, 243
Hudson Terminal (Manhattan), 237
Huff, Slaughter W., 183
Hulbert, Murray, 247
Hunt, Francis, 29
Hunter's Point, N.Y., 45
Husted, Seymour L., 26, 105
Hylan, Mayor John F., 231, 246, 252

Idlewild, 55, 295, 296
IND. See Independent Subway System

IND-BMT connections, 273–77
IND Division, 236–38, 273–77. See also City of New York: Board of Transportation
Independent Subway System, 236–38, 241, 255–56, 273–78. See also City of New York: Board of Transportation
Indiana, Bloomington and Western R.R., 305
Interborough Rapid Transit Company, 205–9, 216, 226–27, 236, 267, 289, 292
Intramural R.R., 135
Iron Pier, 54, 57, 61, 63, 65
Iron Steamboat Company, xvii, 53, 55–66, 77, 238–43, 283–84
Iron Steamboat Company of Long Branch, 63
Iron Steamboat Company of New Jersey, 63
IRT. See Interborough Rapid Transit Company

Jamaica, N.Y., 32, 33, 45, 72, 139
Jamaica Bay, 3, 101, 192
Jewett Car Company, 196, 287, 290
J. G. Brill and Company, 28, 223, 225, 229, 287, 289, 290, 311
John Roache and Sons, 56, 57
Johnson, Tom L., 138, 150
John Stephenson and Company, 28, 31, 90, 195, 196, 223, 287, 289, 290
John Sylvester, 55, 296
Jones Beach, N.Y., 251, 253
Joralemon Street, 15, 208
Joralemon Street Tunnel, 208
Jourdan, James, 39–40, 41, 92, 119–22, 123, 146–48, 194, 201–2
Juet, Robert, 300
Junction, the, 220, 226
J. W. Fowler Car Company, 143

Kensington Junction, 78, 275
Kent Avenue, 145, 161
Keyspan, 286
Keyspan Park, 10, 286
Kill von Kull, 55, 100, 297
Kings County, 6–8, 22, 32, 49, 67, 68, 72, 81, 84, 87, 95, 106, 112, 114, 124, 129, 169, 172, 251, 253, 270

William Cramp and Sons, 56–58
Williams, Timothy S., 170, 172
Williams, William, 118
Williamsburg Bridge, 132, 179, 220
Williamsburg Bridge Plaza, 220
Williamsburgh, 15–16, 47, 105, 302
Willink entrance (to Prospect Park)/
  Willink family, 88–89
Wills, Benjamin Bowling, 282
Wilson, President Woodrow, 217
Wilson Avenue Line, 270
Wiman, Erastus, 181
Wingate, George, 177, 247–48
Winter, E. M., 205
Witt, Peter, 229
WNYF (journal), 323

world's fairs: Buffalo (1901), 243–44;
  Centennial Exposition (1876), 84,
  94, 187, 306; Chicago (1893), 135,
  188, 300; New York (planned for
  1883), 56; New York (1939–40), 21,
  253, 259–61, 289, 322; Pan American
  Exposition (1901), 243–44; Philadelphia (1876), 84, 94, 187, 306; Rome
  (planned for 1942), 254–55; St. Louis
  (1904), 188; World's Columbian Exposition, 135, 188, 300
World Trade Center, 40, 280
World War I, 50, 79, 224, 240, 243, 251
World War II, 4, 50, 237, 243, 248, 250,
  259, 263–65, 268, 284, 286

Yonkers, N.Y., 61